FRONTIERS OF ECONOMICS

FRONTIERS OF ECONOMICS

Nobel Laureates of the Twentieth Century

Edited by Abu N.M. Wahid

GREENWOOD PRESS
Westport, Connecticut • London

#47625342

Library of Congress Cataloging-in-Publication Data

Frontiers of economics : Nobel laureates of the twentieth century / edited by Abu
N.M. Wahid.
     p. cm.
  Includes bibliographical references and index.
  ISBN 0–313–32073–X (alk. paper)
   1. Economists—History—20th century. 2. Economics—Awards—History—20th century.
  3. Nobel Prizes—History—20th century. I. Wahid, Abu N.M.
  HB87.F76 2002
  330′.92′2—dc21   2001040555

British Library Cataloguing in Publication Data is available.

Library of Congress Catalog Card Number: 2001040555
ISBN: 0–313–32073–X

First published in 2002

Greenwood Press, 88 Post Road West, Westport, CT 06881
An imprint of Greenwood Publishing Group, Inc.
www.greenwood.com

Printed in the United States of America

The paper used in this book complies with the
Permanent Paper Standard issued by the National
Information Standards Organization (Z39.48–1984).

10 9 8 7 6 5 4 3 2 1

To my loving wife – Bithi – who persistently
encouraged me to complete this project.

Contents

Preface

The idea to produce this volume came to my mind in 1992, when I first read Stephen Hawking's *A Brief History of Time: From the Big Bang to Black Holes*. When it appeared in the market, Hawking's book became a best seller–as it was a successful and celebrated work on the frontiers of physics–written for a lay audience. I thought a similar book on economics could be as useful and successful as Hawking's book. Thus, I decided to author this book. My goal initially was to survey the major contributions of the economics Nobel laureates in such a way that it would be equally easily understandable to economists and noneconomists alike. Accordingly, I collected most of the background materials and prepared to begin writing the manuscript. Meanwhile, I relocated from Eastern Illinois University and accepted a more challenging job here in the College of Business at Tennessee State University.

My new job warranted me to solicit funds for research and make journal publications in addition to teaching new courses. Thus, I became busy otherwise and was about to lose interest on this project. However, by the persistent encouragement of my department head, college dean and above all, the president of Tennessee State University, I renewed my resolve to complete the project at any cost. At that point, however, I changed my mind to make it an anthology instead of writing the whole book myself.

Then I started contacting people, seeking their contributions to the book. The initial response was very disappointing, but I did not give up. I kept trying to convince my friends, colleagues, and mentors at home and abroad that it would be a fruitful and meaningful endeavor. Every year passed by, more laureates were added to the list, and it was getting harder for me to find authors to write on them. Finally, after so many years of painstaking efforts and repeated requests to the contributors, I have succeeded in putting together the whole manuscript.

I give thanks to all the authors who contributed to this volume. I sincerely apologize to those who submitted their works long before and had to wait several years to see the book in print. I must express my gratitude to some of my friends and mentors who helped me complete this project in various capacities. They are professors Saud Choudhry of Trent University, Anis Chowdhury of the University of Western Sydney, James Dean of Simon Fraser University, A.K. Enamul Haque of North South University, Salim Rashid of the University of Illinois at Urbana-Champaign, and Baker Siddiquee of the University of Illinois at Springfield Bernard Tucker of Tennessee State University, Nashville. I would also like to thank Kimberly Branch, Kenya Jones, Mosharrof Hossain, Yolanda Gist, Mehdi Saidi, and Sangeeta Rao, graduate students in the College of Business at Tennessee State University for their help in typing and reading earlier versions of some of the chapters of the book. I also express my gratitude to Asrarul Islam Chowdhury, who helped me establish contact with James Mirrlees at Cambridge University. If I have missed any relevant name(s) in this context, I apologize for that and remain thankful to him (them) as well.

During the course of editing this book, on many occasions, I deprived my children–Asaad, Najla and Naila, of the use of our only home computer. I also disturbed my wife, Bithi many times in various ways. I am grateful to them all. I would consider this effort to be a success if it can arouse any of our readers' interest in the science of economics.

Abu N.M. Wahid
Nashville, TN
April, 2002

About the Editor
and Contributors

Abu N. M. Wahid is a professor of economics at Tennessee State University and the editor of the *Journal of Developing Areas*. He received his Ph.D. from the University of Manitoba, Canada, in 1989. Prior to joining Tennessee State University, he taught at various colleges and universities of the U. S., Canada, and Bangladesh. Dr. Wahid specializes in money and banking, macroeconomics, and international trade. Besides the present book, he has published four books as author and editor. They are on the Grameen Bank, the economy of Bangladesh, the ASEAN region, and the New Cambridge model. In addition, he has made about forty publications in the form of refereed journal articles and book chapters. He also wrote several papers for non-refereed journals and conference proceedings. He published quite a few book reviews in refereed journals as well. Dr. Wahid spent the summer of 1997 in Bangladesh as a Fulbright scholar. He received research grants from the Japan Foundation, American Institute of Bangladesh Studies, University of Michigan-Ann Arbor, Eastern Illinois University and Tennessee State University. He is the recipient of faculty excellence awards for research from Tennessee State University, Eastern Illinois University, and the College of Business at Tennessee State University.

Salah Uddin Ahmed is a Deputy Team Leader, Protection Analysis and Trade Cooperation Component, Bangladesh Export Diversification Project, World Bank (until August 2002). He received his M.S., M.Phil. and Ph.D. in Economics from Yale University in the late 1970s. He has taught in Pakistan, USA and Bangladesh for over 20 years. He worked for the United Nations Department for Technical Cooperation for Development as Chief Technical Adviser in Nigeria. He has been adviser to the Bangladesh Planning Commission since 1984. He has been on several Government Committees. Dr. Ahmad has several publications to his credit and presented papers in various international conferences.

B. Mak Arvin is a professor of economics at Trent University in Canada. He holds a Ph.D. from Queen's University. He has held appointments at Queen's University and Boston College, and has been teaching at Trent for the past fourteen years. Arvin's research has resulted in over fifty publications in various journals and monographs. He is on the editorial board of two journals and has been a guest editor of one. Arvin was a recipient of Trent University's merit award for excellence in research in 1992, 1996, 1998, and 2000. He has also acted as a consultant to the Government of Germany. His main research interest is in the economics of foreign aid.

Linda L. Carr is an associate professor of business administration at Tennessee State University. She received her Ph.D. in Business Administration from Georgia State University. Dr. Carr's articles have appeared in *The Journal of Business Ethics, The Journal of Small Business Management,* and other scholarly publications. Her research interests include strategic human resource management, business policy, and firm performance. Dr. Carr is a CPA and has many years of business experience.

Bruce Cater is an assistant professor of economics at Trent University. He received his Ph.D. from York University in 1996. Professor Cater's research interests include contract theory, applied econometrics, and the economics of impairment and disability.

Saud A. Choudhry is an associate professor and chair of economics at Trent University, Canada. He received his Ph.D from the University of Manitoba in 1989. Dr. Choudhry specializes primarily in economic development, public finance and applied microeconomics. He has over thirty publications in these areas and they were published in the form of both refereed journal articles and as chapters in edited books. Professor Choudhry was awarded the Trent Merit Award for Excellence in Research in 1998 and again in 2000. He is a dedicated teacher as well, and was nominated for the Symon's Award for Excellence in Teaching (at Trent) in 1991.

Khashruzzaman Choudhury is a professor of economics and public policy at Southern University, Baton Rouge, Louisiana. He received a Master in Public Administration (MPA) degree from Harvard University and a Ph.D. in economics from the Maxwell School of Syracuse University. Prior to joining Southern University, Dr. Choudhury taught at various universities, including Syracuse University and New School for Social Research. He specializes in public sector, international, and health care economics. Dr. Choudhury is the author of six books on economics and education, and was published widely in refereed journals. He also writes fiction, and has authored many books, short stories, poems, and essays.

Masudul A. Choudhury is a professor of finance and economics at the School of Business, University College of Cape Breton. Professor Choudhury earned his Ph.D. in political economy with specialization in human resource development and economic growth from the University of Toronto in 1979. He teaches economic theory, development studies, economic policy, and political economy of social issues. His research focus is on the epistemology of Islamic political economy and world systems. Professor Choudhury has published many academic books and refereed articles in these areas. His major work comprises six volumes entitled, *The Epistemological Foundations of Islamic Economic, Social and Scientific Order* (1995). His most recent book is *The Islamic Worldview, Socio-Scientific Perspectives* (2000).

Abdur R. Chowdhury teaches economics at Marquette University, Wisconsin. Prior to joining Marquette in 1989, he taught at Bentley College. His current research interest includes open economy macroeconomics, monetary economics, and financial reform in the Asian and Pacific Basin countries. He has published extensively in these areas in various refereed journals, including *The Review of Economics and Statistics, Southern Economic Journal, The Journal of Macroeconomics, The American Journal of Political Science, Applied Economics, Open Economies Review.* He has also served as a senior Fulbright scholar in Thailand, as a visiting research scholar at the World Institute for Development Economics Research (WIDER), and as a visiting professor in the China program of the School for Advanced International Studies, Johns Hopkins University.

Mussaddeq Chowdhury is an associate professor of economics at the University of Redlands (UOR). He received a bachelor's degree with honors and masters degree in economics from Dhaka University. He completed his Ph.D. from the University of Southern California (USC) in 1993. His research and intellectual interests include applied microeconomics, econometrics, economic development, and public choice theory. Prior to joining the UOR, he taught a wide variety of courses at USC, California State University at Northridge, and Humboldt State University. He has received research grants and fellowships from several organizations, including the Haynes Foundation.

Minh Q. Dao is a professor of economics at Eastern Illinois University. He received his Ph.D. from the University of Illinois at Urbana-Champaign in 1987. Professor Dao specializes in public finance, economic development and econometrics. He has published several articles in the *Oxford Bulletin of Economics and Statistics*, the *Journal of Economic Studies, Applied Economics Letters*, and *Studi Economici*. He obtained research grants and fellowships from both Eastern Illinois University and the University of Illinois. He received a faculty excellence award in the area of research/creative activity in 1996. He was named Teacher-Scholar in the College of Arts and Sciences in 1999 and 2000.

James W. Dean holds B.S., M.A., and Ph.D. degrees from Carleton and Harvard universities, where he studied mathematics and then economics. He has taught at Simon Fraser University since 1969, and has held visiting appointments at about twenty universities and research institutions world wide. Professor Dean specializes in international macroeconomics and finance. For the past ten years his research has focused on debt, currency and banking crises and their resolution. Some of this work is summarized in his recent monograph, *Has the Market Solved the Sovereign Debt Crisis? (Princeton Studies in International Finance, No. 83.)* He frequently consults and lectures internationally, and has published about 100 books and articles. He also plays very mediocre jazz saxophone.

Abul Hasnat Dewan teaches economics at University College of the Cariboo (UCC) in Canada. He received his M.A. from Yale University and Ph.D. from the University of Texas (UT) at Austin, USA. Before joining UCC, he taught at

UT-Austin, USA, Jahangirnagar University, Bangladesh, and Malaspina University College, Canada. Being a Fulbright scholar, Dr. Dewan specializes in environmental and resource economics, urban and regional economics, and sustainable development. His past research work and publications include, but are not limited to, the development of a sustainability index, training of people in the high technology industry, energy modeling, and rural unemployment.

Akhter Faroque is an associate professor of economics at Laurentian University in Ontario, Canada. Prior to joining Laurentian University in 1987, he taught at several other universities in Canada and Bangladesh, including, the University of Toronto, Guelph University, Brock University, and Jahangirnagar University. Dr. Faroque received his Ph.D. from McMaster University in Ontario, Canada. He specializes in applied macroeconomic forecasting, credit rationing problems and development economics. His publications appear in several scholarly economics journals in the United States, Canada, and the U.K. While teaching at the University of Toronto, professor Faroque received recognition as one of the top ten economics teachers, and he has also received faculty excellence awards for research and teaching from Laurentian University.

Lorenzo Garbo is an associate professor of economics at the University of Redlands. He received a degree with honors in economics from the University of Venice (Italy) and completed a Ph.D. in economics at Columbia University in 1985. He specializes in international trade and economic development. Prior to joining the University of Redlands, Dr. Garbo taught a variety of courses at the School of International and Public Affairs of Columbia University, and held positions as research associate at the Commission on Global Governance (Geneva) and at the Center on International Cooperation at New York University. He received the Outstanding Teaching Award from the University of Redlands in 1998 and research grants and fellowships from several organizations.

Norman D. Gardner is an associate professor of finance, economics, and enterprise strategy at Utah Valley State College. He earned an MBA at Brigham Young University in 1968 and a Ph.D. in business administration at the University of Utah in 1974. After teaching for fourteen years at Boise State University, he spent seven years in full-time consulting before assuming his current position at Utah Valley State College. Dr. Gardner spent several years working in the securities industry with regional and New York Stock Exchange (NYSE) member firms. He held positions as registered representative, registered principal, broker-dealer, and as vice president of operations of a regional securities firm. Dr. Gardner's research interests are in the area of portfolio theory and efficient markets.

A. K. Enamul Haque is an associate professor of economics at North South University, Dhaka, Bangladesh. He received his Ph.D. from the University of Guelph, Canada in 1991. Prior to joining North South University, he taught at Bangladesh Open University and Chittagong University. Dr. Haque specializes in environmental and resource economics. He has published several journal articles, a lexicon of environmental terms. He has edited two books: one on Japanese style management and the other on the state of Bangladesh environment. Dr. Haque is a member of World Commission on Environmental Economics and

Social Policy. He is also the Life Member of Bangladesh Economic Association. Dr. Haque is a recipient of Canadian Commonwealth scholarship. He is now working on mangrove economy-ecology modeling in Bangladesh with a grant from South Asian Economic Research Institute (SANEI).

Syed M. Harun is a visiting assistant professor of Finance at the Department of Economics and Finance at Texas A&M University–Kingsville. He is currently working on his Ph.D. dissertation at the University of New Orleans. Prior to joining Texas A&M University–Kingsville, he taught at University of New Orleans and several universities in Bangladesh. His research interest includes stock return predictability, stock market anomalies, monetary policy and the stock markets. He has published several articles and book chapters and presented papers in several national conferences.

M. Kabir Hassan is LREC professor of economic development and finance and associate chair of the department of economics and finance at the University of New Orleans. He received his Ph.D. in finance from the University of Nebraska, Lincoln, in 1990. Since then he has been with the University of New Orleans. He is a financial economist with consulting, research, and teaching experience in development finance, money and capital markets, corporate finance, investments, monetary economics, macroeconomics, and international trade and finance. He has published one book and over fifty articles in refereed academic journals. He has presented over 100 research papers in professional conferences. Dr. Hassan has worked as a consultant with USAID, the World Bank, the International Monetary Fund, IDB, ICDT, government of Bangladesh, USIA and the Nathan Associates. Dr. Hassan has received many awards and recognition for his outstanding teaching and research.

John M. Hasty is a professor of finance on the faculty of the College of Business, Tennessee State University (TSU), Nashville. He received his Ph.D. in finance in 1973. His professional career since has included teaching, research, and consulting with small businesses. His primary area of research has been related to the assessment of investment risk. His teaching has been at the University of Tennessee at Nashville and Tennessee State University. His teaching experience has included serving as faculty advisor to the Finance and Investment Club, a TSU student organization. This currently involves guiding students in the management of two real money stock portfolios.

Moazzem Hossain is a senior lecturer in the School of International Business, Griffith University, Australia. He obtained his Ph.D. from the University of Western Australia in 1986. He worked for the Australian Public Service as Research Economist in Canberra for almost five years before he joined Griffith University in 1990. Dr Hossain has been awarded the first Bangabandhu Sheikh Mujibur Rahman Chair of the University of Hull, United Kingdom, in March 2000. Over the last ten years he has visited various institutions in Europe and the United States. He published several journal articles and research monographs. Most recently, Routledge has published two of his books: *South Asian Economic Development: Transformation, Opportunities and Challenges* in 1999 with Islam and Kibria and *Who Benefits from Privatisation?* with Justin Malbon (eds.) in 1998. A research paper with Mukhpadhaya entitled "Currency

Crisis: A South Asian Perspective" has been published in the *Review of Asian and Pacific Studies*, Tokyo, in February 2001.

Derek P. J. Hum is a professor in the Department of Economics and the, Center for Higher Education Research and Development and a fellow of St. John's College, University of Manitoba. He is a graduate of Mount Allison, Oxford University, University of Toronto, and a former Rhodes scholar. He was formerly research director of Mincome, Canada's experimental guaranteed income program. Dr. Hum has published extensively in a wide variety of disciplines and subjects, and is currently researching labor market issues, university and training issues, and matters concerning immigrants and visible minorities. He is a member of Canada's National Statistics Council.

Mobinul Huq is an associate professor of economics at the University of Saskatchewan, Canada. He received his Ph.D. in economics from the University of Western Ontario, Canada, in 1987. Dr. Huq's research interest is in labor market issues, urban economics, and economic development. He published his research work in refereed U.S. as well as international journals. Dr. Huq received the R.E. Olley Award for excellence in teaching at the University of Saskatchewan.

Ihsan Isik received his Bachelor of Science degree in management from Middle East Technical University (METU), Ankara, Turkey, in 1992. Upon graduation, he joined the largest commercial bank in Turkey, T.C. Ziraat Bankasi, as a security specialist and attended its Banking and Insurance School, which was jointly organized by the University of Manchester, UK. Later, he worked for Arthur Andersen Worldwide as an auditor in the Istanbul office in 1993. As a result of his distinguished performance in a nationwide examination, he was awarded a scholarship to pursue graduate studies in the United States. He earned his Master of Science degree in finance from Texas Tech. University, Lubbock, Texas, in 1995. He joined the University of New Orleans in 1996, where he received his Master of Arts degree in economics in 1997 and his Ph.D. in financial economics in 2000. Dr. Isik is currently working at New Jersey Institute of Technology (NJIT) in Newark, New Jersey, as an assistant professor of finance and accounting. His research and teaching interest is in the field of financial markets and institutions. He is presently working on technical progress, efficiency change, and productivity growth in international financial institutions. He has several research papers on banking that appeared in quality finance journals like *Journal of Banking and Finance*.

Faridul Islam is an assistant professor of economics, finance, and enterprise strategy at the Utah Valley State College. He completed his master's degree from the London School of Economics and earned his Ph.D. from the University of Illinois at Urbana, working under Professor Paul Newbold. Prior to joining Utah Valley State College, he served as an economist at the World Services of the Wharton Econometric Forecast Associates, Pennsylvania, where he worked as the country expert on Spain, Australia, New Zealand, and India. As a graduate student, he taught at the University of Illinois at Urbana, as Adjunct faculty at the University of Illinois at Springfield, and as visiting assistant professor at the Illinois Wesleyan University. While in Bangladesh, he worked as a research economist/fellow and also as the secretary at the Bangladesh Institute of

Development Studies (BIDS), Dhaka. He came to know Professor Sen personally while working in BIDS. Dr. Islam's research interests are in the areas of time series econometrics, development economics, and international trade. He has published in professional journals and presented papers in conferences. As teaching assistant in Illinois, he was on the dean's list of excellent teachers for several years, and received an honorable mention and the Robert Demarest Teaching Award for teaching excellence.

M. Mahabub-ul Islam is a professor of economics and finance in the Department of Business Administration/MBA at Saint Francis University, Pennsylvania. He received his Ph.D. in economics in 1989 from Northeastern University, Boston, Massachusetts. Dr. Islam has taught economics and finance at Chittagong University, Northeastern University, and University of Rhode Island. He served as a member of the dissertation committee and advised students at both graduate and undergraduate levels. He has been recognized for his excellence in teaching with a number of awards, including the Sesquicentennail Year Distinguished Faculty Award at Saint Francis University. His primary area of research has been financial markets and institutions. Several of Dr. Islam's articles have appeared in various journals and edited books. He is currently acting as the president of an investment club.

S. Hussain Ali Jafri is a professor of Economics at Tarleton State University, in Stephenville, Texas. Professor Jafri has been on the faculty of economics at Tarleton since 1989. He received his master's degree from Cornell University and a Ph.D. from the University of Wisconsin-Madison. Dr. Jafri has several publications, some of which were published in *Thunderbird International Business Review, Journal of Food Distribution Research, Midsouth Journal of Economics and Finance,* and the *Southwestern Journal of Economics.* He also served as program chair and president of the Southwestern Economics Association. Dr. Jafri's current research interests are in environmental and regional economics.

A. Eric Kam is an assistant professor of economics at Huron College, University of Western Ontario. He received his Ph.D. from York University in 2000. Professor Kam's research interests include macroeconomics with special emphasis on the real sector implications of monetary growth in open and closed economies.

Lewis L. Laska is a professor of business law at Tennessee State University. He received his J.D. from Vanderbilt University Law School in 1972 and his Ph.D. from George Peabody College in 1978. He is the author of numerous books and articles on constitutional law and is a columnist for the *Nashville Business Journal.* In 1984 the *Tennessee Bar Journal* awarded him a prize for the best article published in it that year; it dealt with commercial arbitration. Dr. Laska is author of *The Tennessee State Constitution: A Reference Guide.* His other areas of research include personal injury litigation and legal history.

Irwin Lipnowski is an associate professor in the Department of Economics, University of Manitoba, Canada. He received his Ph.D. from the London School of Economics, England, in 1976. Dr. Lipnowski held a Lady Davis Postdoctoral Fellowship at the Hebrew University of Jerusalem during 1979-1980 and the

Technion-Israel Institute of Technology for the period 1980-1981, and was a visiting senior fellow in economics at Princeton University in 1983. He has published articles in leading journals including *Economica, Journal of Public Economics, Mathematical Social Sciences, Canadian Journal of Economics, Journal of Environmental Economics and Management*, and *Canadian Journal of Law and Society*, and has co-edited and co-authored several papers in *Macroeconomics* and *Social Institutions*. In 1999, he was honored with a teaching excellence award "in recognition of significant influence and contributions to the education of outstanding graduate students." Dr. Lipnowski is also a FIDE Chess Master, and in 2000, was captain of the Canadian team at the World Youth Chess Festival in Oropesa, Spain.

Hasina Mohyuddin received her MBA in electronic commerce and healthcare from Owen School of Management, Vanderbilt University, and her BA in economics from Yale University. Since then, Ms. Mohyuddin has worked as Chief Operating Officer at the Evelyn Frye Center, a behavioral healthcare group in Nashville, Tennessee. Her research interests include healthcare information systems, healthcare delivery systems, and healthcare and economic development.

Muhammad Mustafa is a professor of economics at South Carolina State University. He received his Ph.D. from Wayne State University, Michigan, in 1988. Prior to joining South Carolina State University in 1989, he taught at several universities in the United States and Bangladesh. He specializes in financial economics, quantitative methods, macroeconomics, and economic development. He published several articles in Applied Economics, Applied Financial Economics, Journal of Asian Business, Journal of Economics and Finance, Research in Finance, and others. He has received research grants from USDA and USDA Cooperative State Research Service. He received faculty excellence awards for intellectual contribution in 1996, 1998, and 2000, teaching excellence awards in 1993 and 1998, and the Distinguished Professional Development Award in 1995 from the School of Business at South Carolina State University. He received the Levin Award for Best Research Paper in 1987 and the Mendelson Research Award in 1986 from Wayne State University, the Southwestern Society of Economists Distinguished Paper Award in 1997, and the Irwin/McGraw Hill Distinguished Paper Award in 2000.

Hollis F. Price is the executive assistant to the president of Tennessee State University, Nashville, Tennessee. The University of Colorado awarded him the Ph.D. in economics in 1972, and his professional career has encompassed both teaching and administrative appointments at majority institutions and historically black colleges and universities. The Preponderance of his career was spent at the University of Miami, Coral Gables, Florida. Most of his research has examined and assessed the impact of the suburbanization of affluent metropolitan population cohorts and "old economy" businesses on employment opportunities for the low-income, ethnic minority center city residents.

Halima Qureshi received her Ph.D. in economics from Vanderbilt University. Since then, Dr. Qureshi has taught at Austin Peay State University, Cumberland University, Middle Tennessee State University, and Vanderbilt University. In addition, she has worked as an economic consultant for Data

International. Her research interests include health care and economic issues, and she is currently preparing a research grant to study the relationship between health status and economic development in Bangladesh.

Marisa A. Scigliano is the acting university librarian at Trent University in Canada. An experienced academic librarian, she holds an M.L.S. from Dalhousie University and an M.A. from Concordia University. Scigliano was the recipient of Trent University's merit award for excellence in librarianship in 1988, 1991, and 1999. Her research interests are in economics as well as library science and include the economics of fine art at auction and the evaluation of Internet resources for academic institutions.

Norman Schofield is the William Taussig Professor of Political Economy at Washington University. In 1990 he took over from Douglass North as director of the Center in Political Economy at Washington University. He received Ph.D. in both government and economics from Essex University and a Litt. D. from Liverpool University. He has taught at Yale University and the University of Texas at Austin. He has been Hallsworth Fellow at Manchester University, Fairchild Fellow at Caltech, and a fellow at the Center for Advanced Study in the Behavioral Sciences, Stanford. His books include *Social Choice and Democracy*, *Multiparty Government* (with Michael Laver), and various co-edited and co-authored volumes. His field of research is the application of social choice theory to political economy.

Shamim Shakur is currently a senior lecturer in economics at Massey University in New Zealand. He received his doctoral degree with concentration in international economics from Boston College, Massachusetts in 1989. Prior to his taking of the current position at Massey University in 1994, he taught at Okanagan University College, Brock University, and University of Saskatchewan in Canada. Dr. Shakur specializes in agricultural trade and has published research papers in trade and agricultural policy. He obtained research grants from the ASIA 2000 Foundation, Venture Trust and Massey University and consulting contracts from regional councils and government ministries in New Zealand.

Mohammed Sharif is a professor of economics at the University of Rhode Island. He received his Ph.D. from Boston University in 1984. Prior to joining the University of Rhode Island in 1984, he taught at the University of Chittagong, Chittagong College, and Gouripur College in Bangladesh. Sharif specializes in economic development and applied microeconomics–poverty, subsistence, labor supply, unemployment, nutrition, environment, and advertising in less developed countries. He has published his research in various journals and edited collections. He is a member of the American Economic Association, Econometric Society, American Association of Muslim Social Scientists, Union of Concerned Scientists, and Scientists' Action.

Baker A. Siddiquee is an associate professor of economics at the University of Illinois at Springfield (UIS). Prior to joining the UIS in 1987, Dr. Siddiquee taught economics at the University of Manitoba, Canada, and Jahangirnagar University, Bangladesh. Dr. Siddiquee holds a B.S. degree with honors in economics (minors: mathematics and statistics) and an M.S. degree in economics from Jahangirnagar University, and an M.A. and a Ph.D. in economics from the University of Manitoba. At UIS, Dr. Siddiquee has served as chair of the economics department from 1989 to 2000 (except 1995-1997). Dr. Siddiquee teaches courses in economic theory, international trade and finance, development economics, and econometrics. His current research interests include trade and globalization, exchange rates economics, and financial crises.

M. Muin Uddin is an associate professor of economics and management at Wells College and a visiting professor of economics at Syracuse University. He received his Ph.D. in economics from Syracuse University in 1989. He also has taught at other institutions, including Oswego State University and Hobart and William Smith colleges. Professor Uddin has worked and researched for several organizations, including the World Bank and USAID. His research and publication interests include government finances and health economics. His manuscript focusing on local government finances has been accepted for publication. He is a recipient of research grants from various national and international organizations.

Mahbub Ullah is a professor of economics at the University of Chittagong, Bangladesh. He studied at the University of Dhaka, Boston University, and Jawaharlal Nehru University, Delhi. He has been teaching in the Department of Economics, University of Chittagong, since 1976. He also worked as a researcher for two years at the Bangladesh Institute of Development Studies, Dhaka. He was also involved in research programs sponsored by IDRC, Canada, Center for Development Research, Copenhagen, and the United Nations University. He received research grants from Ford Foundation, Winrock International, University Grants Commission (Dhaka), Indian Council for Social Science Research, and ICIMOD, Katmandu. He has authored a book and written many research articles and monographs. Three books by him containing writings on contemporary issues on society, politics and economics was published in February 2001. His research interest includes agrarian economics and resource and environmental economics.

Ian K. Wilson is the dean of the School of Business at the Utah Valley State College (UVSC). He completed his master's degree at the Brigham Young University, Utah, and his Ph.D. at the University of Calgary, Canada. Prior to joining Utah Valley State College, he served as both a member of faculty and an administrator in the capacity of chair of the Department of Business Administration and acting dean at Mount Royal College, Canada, for several years. He also taught at Brigham Young University as a visiting professor. He has wide-ranging experience in consulting and industry. Ian enjoys teaching and regularly teaches a course in business and marketing ethics at UVSC. He is married to Jeanne and they have four children.

Sajjad Zahir is a professor of decision sciences and information systems at the University of Lethbridge, Canada. Prior to joining the faculty, Sajjad was an assistant professor in information systems and management science at Saint Mary's University in Halifax and held postdoctoral research positions in the universities at Victoria, McGill, and Regina. His current research interests are in expert systems, production and inventory management, applications of the analytic hierarchy process in decision analysis, data mining, Internet technologies, and simulation. He has published papers in the *European Journal of Operational Research*, *SIGNUM Newsletter*, *Journal of the Operational Research Society*,

International Journal of Operations and Quantitative Management (IJOQM) and *Canadian Journal of Administrative Sciences (CJAS)*. He has contributed an invited article to *the Encyclopedia of Library and Information Science*.

The Economics Nobel Prize at a Glance (1969 -1999)

Year	Laureate(s)	Affiliation at the Time of Award	Broad Field	Major Contributions
1969	Ragnar Frisch Jan Tinbergen	Oslo University, Norway The Netherlands School of Economics, The Netherlands	Macroeconomics	Development and application of dynamic models for the analysis of economic processes.
1970	Paul Samuelson	Massachusetts Institute of Technology, USA	Microeconomics	Innovation of static and dynamic theory and activity contributed to raising the level of analysis in economic science.
1971	Simon Kuznets	Harvard University, USA	Economic Growth	Empirical foundation and interpretation of economic growth which has led to new and deepened insight into the economic and social structure and process of development.
1972	Kenneth Arrow John Hicks	Harvard University, USA All Souls College, Oxford University, UK	Microeconomics	Pioneering work to general economic equilibrium theory and wefare theory.

Year	Laureate(s)	Affiliation at the Time of Award	Broad Field	Major Contributions
1973	Wassily Leontief	Harvard University, USA	Microeconomics	Development of input-output method and its application to important economic problems.
1974	Friedrich Hayek Gunnar Myrdal	University of Freiburg, Germany University of Stockholm, Sweden	Monetary Economics	Contributions to the theory of money and economic fluctuations and penetrating analysis of the interdependence of economic, social, and institutional phenomena.
1975	Leonid Kantorovich Tjalling Koopmans	Academy of Science, Russia Yale University, USA	Microeconomics	Ingenious work to the theory of optimum allocation of resources.
1976	Milton Friedman	University of Chicago, USA	Macreconomics	Achievements in the fields of consumption analysis, monetary history and theory, and demonstration of the complexity of stabilization policy.
1977	James Meade Bertil Ohlin	Cambridge Unniversity, UK University of Stockholm, Sweden	International Economics	Pathbreaking contributions to the theory of international trade and international capital movement.
1978	Herbert Simon	Carnagie Mellon University, USA	Microeconomics	Research into the decision-making process within economic organizations.
1979	Arthur Lewis Theodore Schultz	Princeton University, USA University of Chicago, USA	Economic Development	Economic development research with particular consideration of the problems of developing countries.
1980	Lawrence Klein	University of Pennsylvania, USA	Econometrics	The creation of economic models and their application to the analysis of economic fluctuations and economic policies.

Year	Laureate(s)	Affiliation at the Time of Award	Broad Field	Major Contributions
1981	James Tobin	Yale University, USA	Macroeconomics	Analysis of financial markets and their relations to expenditure decisions, employment, production and price.
1982	George Stigler	University of Chicago, USA	Microeconomics	Studies of industrial structures, functioning of markets, and causes and effects of public regulations.
1983	Gerard Debreu	University of California-Berkeley, USA	Microeconomics	Innovation of new analytical methods into economic theory and reformulation of the theory of general equilibrium.
1984	Richard Stone	Cambridge University, UK	Macroeconomics	Contributions to the development of systems of national accounts and, hence, improvement of the basis for empirical economic analysis
1985	Franco Modigliani	Massachusetts Institute of Technology, USA	Macroeconomics	Pioneering analysis of saving and financial markets.
1986	James Buchanan	George Mason University, USA	Public Economics	Development of the contractual and constitutional bases for the theory of economic and political decision.
1987	Robert Solow	Massachusetts Institute of Technology, USA	Economic Growth	Contributions to the theory of economic growth.
1988	Maurice Allais	Ecole Nationale Superierure des Mines de Paris, France	Microeconomics	Development of the theory of markets and efficient utilization of resources.
1989	Trygve Haavelmo	Oslo University, Norway	Econometrics	Clarification of the probability theory, founddations of econometrics, and analysis of simultaneous economic structures.

Year	Laureate(s)	Affiliation at the Time of Award	Broad Field	Major Contributions
1990	Harry Markowitz Merton Miller William Sharpe	City University of New York, USA University of Chicago, USA Stanford University, USA	Financial Economics	Development of the theory of portfolio choice and contributions to the theory of price formation for financial assets, the so-called Capital Asset Pricing Model(CAPM).
1991	Ronald Coase	University of Chicago, USA	Microeconomics	Discovery and clarification of the significance of transaction costs and property rights for the institutional structure and functioning of the economy.
1992	Gary Becker	University of Chicago, USA	Microeconomics	Extension of the domain of microeconomic analysis to a wide range of human behavior and interaction, including nonmarket behavior.
1993	Robert Fogel Douglass North	University of Chicago, USA Washington University, USA	Economic History	Renewed research in economic history and application of economic theory and quantitative methods in order to explain economic and institutional changes.
1994	John Harsanyi John Nash Reinhard Selten	University of California-Berkeley, USA Princeton University, USA Rheinisece Friedrich-Wilhelms Universitat, Germany	Macroeconomics	Analysis of equilibria in the theory of noncooperative games.
1995	Robert Lucas Jr.	University of Chicago, USA	Macroeconomics	Development and application of the hypothesis of rational expectations and transformation of macroeconomic analysis and deepening of our understanding of economic policy.

Year	Laureate(s)	Affiliation at the Time of Award	Broad Field	Major Contributions
1996	James Mirrlees William Vickrey	Cambridge University, UK Columbia University, USA	Microeconomics	Contributions to the economic theory of incentives under asymmetric information.
1997	Robert Merton Myron Scholes	Harvard University, USA Stanford University, USA	Financial Economics	Development of a new method to determine the value of derivative.
1998	Amartya Sen	Cambridge University, UK	Microeconomics	Contributions to welfare economics
1999	Robert Mundell	Columbia University, USA	International Economics	Contributions` to the analysis of monetary and fiscal policy under different exchange rate regimes and analysis of optimum currency area.

1

The Nobel Prize in Economics:
A Brief Overview

Abu N. M. Wahid

INTRODUCTION

The official name of the Nobel Prize in economics is The *Sveriges Riksbank* (Bank of Sweden) Prize in Economic Sciences in Memory of Alfred Nobel. The economics Nobel Prize, in some ways, differs from the traditional Nobel Prize awarded for physics, chemistry, medicine/physiology, literature, and peace because the science of economics was not included in the original list of subjects for which the Nobel Prize began in 1901. Economics was added as a specialty only in 1969. Furthermore, funds for the Nobel Prize in economics do not come from the foundation that was established by Alfred Nobel in 1900 following the famous will that he signed in 1895. Rather, money for the economics Nobel Prize is drawn from an endowment generously donated by the Central Bank of Sweden. Thus officially the award bears the name of the Bank of Sweden.

The Nobel Prize in economics is equivalent to the others in the sense that it is administered in accordance with the same rules, criteria, standards and principles as the original Nobel Prize in the five other fields. Thus the economics Nobel Prize carries the same honor and prestige as the other Nobel Prizes that are mentioned in the will of Alfred Nobel. Over and above, the monetary value of the economics Nobel Prize is quite in line with those of the others. The Nobel Prize cannot be awarded posthumously as enunciated in the will. This is true for the economics award as well.

HISTORY

The very idea of introducing the Nobel Prize in economics came from the mind of the then governor of the Swedish Central Bank, Per Asbrink, in 1968 to mark the 300th anniversary of the bank. Regarding this matter, the governor first consulted with Assar Lindbeck, Erick Lundberg and Gunnar Myrdal, who at that time were the economic advisors for the Bank of Sweden Tercentenary Foundation (BSTF). The advisors were overwhelmingly positive about the idea of this new award. Accordingly, the Royal Swedish Academy of Sciences (RSAS) was asked to launch and administer the new award for economics. The bank also made a firm long-term commitment to provide the prize money for the economics Nobel Prize.

The non-economist academy members opposed the idea of an economics Nobel Prize. They thought that economics was not precise and scientific enough compared to hard sciences and hence that it did not warrant this award like physics, chemistry, and other sciences did. However, the economists who were on the board of the Royal Swedish Academy of Sciences were strongly in favor of this award. Among them Gunnar Myrdal was primarily instrumental in convincing the RSAS, after a thorough debate, to initiate the new award in economics. Following that, all legal formalities were completed by the academy, the Nobel Foundation, the Swedish Central Bank, and the government of Sweden, and The Central Bank of Sweden Prize in Economic Sciences in Memory of Alfred Nobel came into being in 1969.

CONTROVERSY

The Nobel Prize originally was instituted to give recognition to specific scientific inventions/discoveries or achievements/contributions rather than to recognize the individuality of the brilliant achievers. The nature of the science of economics is such that it is not as easy to isolate specific achievements as in other hard sciences. This fact raises some fundamental questions about the legitimacy of the economics Nobel Prize. Keynes believed that "Economics depended as much on values, intuition, ethics, and introspection as it did on the scientific method." Myrdal, an early advocate of the award, also raised some concerns. He asserted that economics was a "soft" science, had no "constant" and no "laws of nature," and was a "confused admixture of science and politics." He went as far as accusing the RSAS of politicizing the award by jointly giving it to him with Friedrich Hayek. In this joint award, he believed that the RSAS attempted to balance his twentieth-century liberalism with the classical liberalism of Hayek. The tone of Myrdal's criticism suggests that it is based more on personal resentment than on substantive grounds. Perhaps it was Myrdal's conviction that the academy had undermined his contributions by recognizing him along with Hayek.

The supporters of the economics Nobel Prize have counterargued that some of the Nobel laureates in economics were themselves natural scientists. For example, Tinbergen and Koopmans were physicists and Kantorovich and Debreu were well-established mathematicians. Moreover, most of the economics Nobel laureates have successfully incorporated pure scientific methods in their research. In line with the original stipulation of the will of Alfred Nobel, the RSAS' early choice of the economics Nobel laureates reflects more of the scientific aspects of modern economics, such as quantitative methods and econometrics. Later on, however, the RSAS did not seem to adhere strictly to this scientific principle. The choice of Herbert Simon in 1978 best reflects this slackness. Simon believed that economics was a social as well as a behavioral science. His formal education was in the department of political science. Although Simon's broad field was cited to be microeconomics, his main contribution was in the specialty of administrative science, an area closer to business administration than economics.

NOMINATION AND SELECTION PROCESS

The Royal Swedish Academy of Sciences oversees the nomination and selection process of the laureates for economics as well as for physics and chemistry. The academy forms an Economics Selection Committee with five internationally reputed scholars belonging to the discipline of economics. This committee seeks nominations for the economics Nobel Prize from the eminent members of the profession around the world and also receives recommendations from those who were previously awarded this prestigious award. This is done normally around October of every year for the following year's selection. On the average, nearly one hundred economists are nominated every year from different countries representing different fields of specialization. Then the committee appoints a team of experts who helps the committee make a short list of twenty to thirty candidates. The experts' opinions about the strength and weaknesses of the candidates are then thoroughly debated by the committee. Around springtime of the award year, the committee makes its final recommendation to the Social Sciences Class, which endorses the recommendation and sends it to the full academy by late summer or early fall. Finally, the Royal Swedish Academy of Sciences selects one or more nominees for the economics Nobel Prize by a simple majority vote and announces the results in October. Thus, the whole nomination and selection process takes nearly a year.

AWARD GIVING CEREMONY

Like the Nobel Prize in all other categories, the economics Nobel Prize consists of a diploma, a medal, and a prize amount of money. Every year on December 10, the economics Nobel Prize is ceremonially given to the designated laureate(s) along with that of physics, chemistry, literature, medicine/physiology. The date is so chosen to commemorate the death anniversary of Alfred Nobel. The ceremony of the Economics Nobel Prize takes place at the Stockholm Concert Hall. At this event, His Majesty the king of Sweden, hands each Laureate a diploma, a medal and a document confirming the prize money. The Nobel Peace Prize is presented on the same day at the Oslo City Hall by the Chairman of the Norwegian Nobel Committee in the presence of the monarch of Norway.

MONETARY VALUE

The Nobel Foundation does not give a fixed amount of money to the Nobel laureates every year. It varies from year to year, depending on the earnings of the foundation. In 1901, the year the Nobel Prize was given for the first time, the value of the award was 150,000 Swedish crowns. Since then, the smallest amount ever disbursed was only 115,000 Swedish crowns in the year 1923. The Nobel Foundation was granted tax-exempt status by the Swedish government in 1946. Since then, the value of the award has been mounting steadily. In 1953, the foundation's investment policy was changed, and since then there has been a significant increase in the value of the award.

In 1969, Ragnar Frisch of Norway and Jan Tinbergen of the Netherlands – the first Nobel laureates in economics shared only 375,000 Swedish crowns. By 1999, the award amount had increased several times to 7,900,000 Swedish crowns, and went to Robert Mundell alone.

RECIPIENTS' BROAD FIELDS OF RESEARCH

All Nobel laureates in the science of economics are/were basically theoreticians. However, in establishing their theories, most of them did lots of empirical work. Those whose citations are broadly categorized as microeconomics are/were Paul Samuelson, Kenneth Arrow, John Hicks, Wassily Leontief, Leonid Kantorovich, Tjalling Koopmans, Herbert Simon, George Stigler, Gerard Debreu, Maurice Allais, Ronald Coase, Gary Becker, John Harsanyi, John Nash, Reinhard Selten, James Mirrlees, William Vickrey, and Amartya Sen.

Those who won the Nobel Prize in macroeconomics are/were Ragnar Frisch, Jan Tinbergen, Milton Friedman, James Tobin, Richard Stone, Franco Modigliani, and Robert Lucas Jr. Those who were awarded this prestigious award for their illuminating contributions in financial economics are/were Harry Markowitz, Merton Miller, William Sharpe, Robert Merton, and Myron Scholes.

Those who got the Nobel Prize for their theories of economic growth are Simon Kuznets and Robert Solow. The two who received this prize for their pathbreaking work on the quantitative interpretation of economic history (Cliometrics) are Robert Fogel and Douglass North. Friedrich Hayek and Gunnar Myrdal were awarded the economics Nobel Prize for their contributions on monetary economics.

Those who received the award for their works on economic development were Arthur Lewis and Theodore Schultz. Three of the laureates secured the prize for their research in international economics. They are/were James Meade, Bertil Ohlin, and Robert Mundell. Two got the Nobel Prize for their contributions in econometrics; they are Trygve Haavelmo and Lawrence Klein. Only one - James Buchanan-was awarded the economics Nobel Prize for his pioneering work in public economics.

AFFILIATION OF THE LAUREATES
AT THE TIME OF THE AWARD

At the time of the award, eight laureates were from the University of Chicago. They are/were Milton Friedman, Theodore Schultz, George Stigler, Merton Miller, Ronald Coase, Gary Becker, Robert Fogel, and Robert Lucas Jr. Those who were affiliated with Cambridge University, England, are/were James Meade, Richard

Stone, James Mirrlees, and Amartya Sen. The laureates of Harvard University are/were Simon Kuznets, Kenneth Arrow, Wassily Leontief, and Robert Merton. Paul Samuelson, Franco Modigliani, and Robert Solow were associated with the Massachusetts Institute of Technology at the time of the award. The prize winners attached to Oslo University, Norway, are/were Ragnar Frisch and Trygve Haavelmo. Princeton University has two Nobel laureates: Arthur Lewis and John Nash. The laureates affiliated with Stanford University are William Sharpe and Myron Scholes. Gerard Debreu and John Harsanyi were at the University of California – Berkeley at the time of the award. The laureates with Yale University are/were Tjalling Koopmans and James Tobin. Those who got the Nobel Prize from the University of Stockholm, Sweden, were Gunnar Myrdal and Bertil Ohlin. Being affiliated with Columbia University, two economists received this prestigious award. One of them was William Vickrey who passed away within three days after his award was announced for him and the other one is Robert Mundell.

The single laureates and their affiliations are as follows: Leonid Kantorovich-Academy of Sciences, Russia; Herbert Simon-Carnegie Mellon University, James Buchanan-George Mason University, Harry Markowitz-City University of New York, Maurice Allais-Ecole Nationale Superieur des Mines de Paris, France; Jan Tinbergen-The Netherlands School of Economics, the Netherlands; Friedrich Hayek-University of Freiburg, Germany; John Hicks-Oxford University, England; Reinhard Selten-Rheinische Friedrich Wilhelms Universitat, Germany, Lawrence Klein-University of Pennsylvania, Douglass North-Washington University, St. Louis.

NATIONALITIES AT BIRTH AND COUNTRIES OF ORIGIN

From 1969 until 1999, 44 economists in total won the Nobel Prize. Out of them, 19 were Americans by birth. They are/were Paul Samuelson, Kenneth Arrow (parents are of Rumanian origin), Milton Friedman (parents were born in Carpatho-Ruthenia – a province of the then Austria-Hungary), Herbert Simon, Theodore Schultz, Lawrence Klein, James Tobin, George Stigler (father came from Bavaria and mother was from Hungary), James Buchanan, Robert Solow, Harry Markowitz, Merton Miller, William Sharpe, Gary Becker (father came from Montreal, Canada, and mother immigrated from Eastern Europe), Robert Fogel (parents immigrated from Odessa, Russia), Douglass North, John Nash, Robert Lucas Jr., and Robert Merton. Five of the Nobel laureates are/were of the British origin. They are/were John Hicks, James Meade, Richard Stone, Ronald Coase, and James Mirrlees. Three laureates were born in Canada. They are/were Myron Scholes, William Vickrey, and Robert Mundell. Two of the Nobel Prize winners were born in Russia. They are/were Wassily Leontief and Leonid Kantorovich. Jan Tinbergen and Tjalling Koopmans were of the Dutch origin, Gerard Debreu and Maurice Allais were born in France. Ragnar Frisch and Trygve Haavelmo were Norwegians. Gunnar Myrdal and Bertil Ohlin were Swedish by birth. One each was born in Ukraine, Austria, Germany, Hungary, India, Italy, and St. Lucia. They are Simon Kuznets, Friedrich Hayek, Reinhard Selten, John Harsanyi, Amartya Sen, Franco Modigliani, and Arthur Lewis, respectively.

IDENTITY PROBLEM

If we carefully scrutinize the list of the economics Nobel laureates, it will be very difficult to ascertain who is/was an economist and who is/was not. Some of the laureates were physicists such as Koopmans and Tinbergen. Some were mathematicians such as Kantorovich and Debreu. Some were lawyers, political scientists, and/or psychologists such as Hayek and Simon. Some were financial experts such as Markowitz, Miller, Sharpe, Merton, and Scholes. Some were computer scientists such as Markowitz and Simon. Allais is as much an economist as he is a physicist and historian. In general, all economics Nobel laureates, have been very strong in terms of their training and practice of mathematics. The frontier-level material of modern economics is so quantitative that it is often difficult to determine whether economics is a hard science or a social science. It is also true that a large part of the contributions of the economics Nobel laureates in their original forms are not even understandable to economists holding Ph.D. degrees.

CONCLUSION

The Nobel Prize in economics is the most prestigious and commendable award to which an economist can aspire in his lifetime. Although the selection process for this award is quite thorough and scientific, it cannot be guaranteed that the Royal Swedish Academy of Sciences has always been one hundred percent fair in making the difficult choice of selecting the prize winners. Based on expert opinions, once the candidates are short-listed, the final selection process is more subjective and political than objective and fair. Every year the academy makes the final choice in the face of tremendous pressures emanating from different quarters. Sometimes, the candidates themselves become "shameless self-promoters."

In our judgment, some of the laureates, such as Amartya Sen and Robert Mundell, should have received this recognition earlier than they actually did. In 1998, Sen's selection was regarded as "new economists' choice." In 1999, with Mundell, Zvi Griliches, Dale Jorgenson, and George Akerlof competed shoulder to shoulder. It is known that Gary Becker and Robert Lucas Jr. made it to the shortlist several times before they were honored with the economics Nobel Prize. It has also been shocking to observe that some of deserving economists, such as Joan Robinson, Harry Johnson, William Baumol, and others, did not get this award. The first two are already deceased and will never get it. Many original economic theorists did not get this prize just because they expired before the beginning of the award in 1969. The most notable modern economists in this category are John Maynard Keynes, Irving Fisher, and Joseph Schumpeter.

The Royal Swedish Academy of Sciences is also subject to criticism because of their preference to older economists for this prestigious award. The average age of the economics Nobel laureates is nearly seventy. Most of the laureates receive the award for their contributions made some thirty years earlier. This trend should be changed.

Although the Nobel Prize selection process is not perfect, it is a recognized criterion to determine the importance and rigor of the contributions that economists are making to their science. Within the profession, the great economists are recognized and respected according to the quality, significance, and importance of their works. Winning or not winning the Nobel Prize does not make much difference. However, there is no doubt that the Nobel Prize has an enormous impact on the acceptability and honor of the prize winners among the general public. Herbert Simon once said, "The Nobel does not certify scientists to their scientific communities. It certifies them to the wider public."

RECOMMENDED READINGS

Katz, Bernard S. (ed.) (1989). *Nobel Laureates in Economic Sciences: A Biographical Dictionary.* New York: Garland.

Lindbeck, Assar. (1985). "The Prize in Economic Science in Memory of Alfred Nobel," *Journal of Economic Literature.* Vol. 23, No. 1, pp. 37-56.

———. (1992). (ed.). *Nobel Lectures Including Presentation Speeches and Laureates' Biographies of Economic Sciences 1969-80.* Stockholm: Institute for International Economic Studies, University of Stockholm.

The Nobel Foundation Web site.<http//:www.nobel.se.laureates/economy-1975-1autobio.html>.

Sichel, Werner. (1989). *The State of Economic Science: Views of Six Nobel Laureates.* Kalamazoo: W.E. Upjohn Institute for Employment Research.

Wirtz, Ronald. (1999, September). "The Beauty (Pageant?) of Economics," *The Region.*

2

Ragnar Frisch (1895-1973):
A Founding Father of Econometrics
and a Laureate of 1969

Lewis L. Laska

BIOGRAPHICAL PROFILE

Ragnar Frisch was born in Oslo, Norway in 1895 to a family of German goldsmiths and jewelers. He began an apprenticeship in an internationally known workshop in Oslo. His mother was unhappy that Frisch would become merely a goldsmith and encouraged him to seek a university education while doing the apprenticeship. Accordingly, Frisch enrolled in the economics undergraduate program at Oslo University's Law School. The reason he chose economics was because it was the shortest – only a two year program. He received his economics degree in 1919 and became a certified jeweler in 1920, a trade which he promptly abandoned. For the next four years Frisch sought education in economics which he could not receive in Norway. He attended lectures in economics in France (for three years), Germany, Britain, Italy and the United States. Frisch returned home to continue his studies at Oslo University and received a Ph. D. in mathematical statistics in 1926. Following that he joined the Oslo University faculty. In the late 1920s, he received a three-year fellowship from the Rockefeller Foundation and spent 1927-1928 in the United States. He returned again to Oslo University where he became a full professor and later director of the newly established Economic Institute.

Although Frisch was an international lecturer, he remained rooted to his native Norway and had enormous influence on its post-World War II economic planning. Frisch was married to Marie Smedal from 1920 until her death in 1952, and married Astrid Johanssen in 1953. Marie gave birth to Frisch's only daughter, Marie Ragna Antonette, in 1938. Frisch had interesting hobbies; for fifty-seven years he was engaged in beekeeping, focusing on raising queen bees. He was an avid mountain hiker. At the time he was supposed to give his Nobel acceptance speech, he could not attend because of a broken leg. Frisch died in 1973. (Bjerkholt:1995, pp. xiii-lii; Samuelson: 1974, pp. 7-23.)

INTRODUCTION

Ragnar Frisch, along with Jan Tinbergen, received the economics Nobel Prize in 1969 for "having developed and applied dynamic models for the analysis of economic processes." Ragnar Frisch was one of the first choices of the Nobel Committee when it inaugurated the Nobel Memorial Prize in Economic Sciences in 1969. The committee awarded Frisch the prize because Frisch had pioneered the realm of economic theory and method development. Indeed, in his first published economics paper, "Sur un probleme d'economie pur" ("On a Problem of Pure Economics,") in 1926, Frisch began, "Intermediate between mathematics, statistics, and economics, we find a new discipline which, for lack of a better name, may be called *econometrics."* (Bjerkholt:1995, pp.3-40.) In short, Frisch is credited with coining the term econometrics, and most give him credit for the first widespread use of the terms macroeconomics and microeconomics in 1933. Likewise, Frisch's acknowledgement of Knut Wicksell's famous "rocking-horse" analogy, placed in the context of a 1933 mathematical explanation of business cycles, was his most celebrated article and the one for which he was awarded the Nobel Prize, although the work itself was not explicitly mentioned in the official announcement (Bjerkholt: 1995, p. 338.) Frisch shared the prize with the Dutch economist and his former student, Jan Tinbergen. The choice and the rationale behind it were welcomed by all who were familiar with Frisch's extensive academic and scientific works. Besides Norwegian, Frisch has published original articles in English, French and German. His contributions to the fundamental aspects and early direction of both micro and macroeconomics, in addition to the methodological development of the economic quantitative science, econometrics, are hard to overstate.

ECONOMIC THEORY

Although his formal economics education lasted for only two years and his doctoral degree was in statistics, Frisch had undertaken significant studies in pure economics during his stays abroad. As a statistician, he became, at an early stage, aware of the pitfalls of uncritical and unrestricted data mining. Although a great admirer of Alfred Marshall and Knut Wicksell, Frisch was painfully aware of "the rudimentary state, logically and systematically, of economic theory compared to the theory of other, more mature, empirical sciences." (Kvantitiativ: 1926, pp. 299-334.) Frisch wanted to make economics the conceptual and logical foundation for quantitative analysis. For today's economists, this seems self-evident. In the 1920s and 1930s, however, the German tradition of the more descriptive-oriented "Begriff and Wesen" (concept/definition and nature) analysis had deep roots in Western European economic thinking. Closest to Frisch's views of the role of economic theory were the American economist Irving Fisher and the Austrian economist

Joseph Schumpeter. These two contemporaries, who Frisch met and corresponded, were proponents of the basic philosophy that theoretical economics should serve the same purpose theoretical physics did in physics. Thus, the theoretical concepts and relationships should have real quantifiable counterparts in any economic study. Later, Frisch felt the necessity to warn mathematical economists against defining economic concepts for mathematical convenience rather than real economic content, a problem frequently encountered even in today's literature.

In the late twenties, Frisch came to regard some of the sub-disciplines of economics as having progressed further than others toward his philosophical/methodological ideal. In Frisch's opinion, macroeconomics (or monetary theory as it was called then), production theory, and value theory had reached some maturity. In these three areas Frisch concentrated his theoretical efforts. In macroeconomics, Frisch worked extensively to put an appropriate empirical frame of reference, that is, a national income accounting (NIA) system, in place. Here, Frisch developed his own terminology. The NIA system was referred to in Norwegian by Frisch as the "okosirk" system, an acronym for the economic circulation system, or "ecocirc." Like many other linguistic novelties, Frisch developed the optimal substitution expansion path for the theory of the firm. Other Frischian abbreviated concatenations, like "econometrics" are now firmly established in both the economics terminology and the general vocabulary. The first English reference to the *ecocirc* system was in Frisch. Later this system played a pivotal role in establishing the Norwegian NIA system which also influenced the international alignments in the United Nations on NIA systems. Frisch served as the Norwegian member on the UN Sub-commission on Employment and Economic Stability from 1947 onwards. Here, he felt a need to structure the economic analysis behind the policy directives emanating from this commission and get the commission's discussions to concentrate on something more than the evils of inflation. Consequently, Frisch put together, with assistance of his research associates at the Institute of Economics at the University of Oslo, an NIA system that was presented to the commission in 1948.

During the early years, Frisch's philosophy on theoretical economics developed rapidly. His contributions to the definitions and clarifications of the difference between dynamic and static theories are many. Frisch described clearly what, in his opinion, was a dynamic theory as opposed to a static theory: "Every theoretical law that includes the concept of growth rate or velocity of reaction (with respect to time), is a dynamic law. All other theoretical laws are static. The static law is a comparison of alternative outcomes, the dynamic law is an analysis of growth rates." (Bjerkholt:1995, p. 294.) Thus, Frisch emphasized that in a theoretical context, dynamic and static refer to modes of analysis rather than aspects of the object under study. Frisch introduced and defined macro-economic dynamics. This conceptual definition later initiated the definitions for the whole body of economics into micro and macro economics. Any review of Frisch's works on economic theory would not be complete without mention of his approach to consumer theory. Throughout his life, Frisch adhered strongly to the view that the utility function was measurable. Frisch postulated an ordering principle of the commodity bundles that implies the existence of a utility function uniquely determined up to an increasing linear transformation. Frisch outlined statistical methods on how to estimate the shape of the utility function from survey data. Other economists of the era soon followed Hicks and Samuelson in viewing the utility function as a theoretical auxiliary concept that does not need qualification. Frisch, however, remained steady in his belief of the usefulness and importance of a measurable utility function, and it is easy to understand his reluctance to give it up. One of his basic aims with economics, theoretical and applied, was to guide economic policies. Thus, Frisch, a model builder and ardent proponent of macro-economic planning, needed a consumer based objective function. What would be more theoretically and politically satisfying than an objective function based on consumer preferences revealed through consumer surveys?

In his works on consumer theory, Frisch contributed significantly to the new theory of price indices. In this work, spurred by Fisher, Frisch connected the level of utility to the cost-of-living index. This was based on his initial work on index numbers. His final work in this field was "a complete scheme." Here, in the pre-personal computer era, Frisch used his assumptions of want independence to develop a simple scheme for estimating all elasticities, including the cross-elasticities, of a system of demand equations.

ECONOMETRICS

Despite all of Frisch's pathbreaking endeavors in economic theory, it is in econometrics that he has had the most profound impact. No one disputes the fact that Frisch originated the word "econometrics." Frisch's pioneering efforts in quantitative economics were born out of necessity and raised by his mathematical and statistical prowess. Given his basic philosophical views of how the economic science should develop, somebody had to provide the statistical methodology to move the science forward. For this task, Frisch was eminently qualified. He was mathematically astute and had studied statistics during his earliest European travels, most notably in Paris, the leading center for mathematics and statistics during the first half of the 20th century. His doctoral thesis in statistics at the University of Oslo was mostly shaped during his stay in Paris in the early 1920's.

Together with Charles Roos, a mathematician at Princeton University, and Irving Fisher, a professor of economics at Yale University, Frisch was one of the co-founders of the Econometric Society that began in 1930. When the Econometric Society started publishing its quarterly journal, *Econometrica*, in January 1933, Frisch became the editor in chief, a position he held for twenty-two years until December 1954. Frisch's work in econometrics can most appropriately be grouped in two epochs: the inter-war years and the post-World War II years. In fact, most of Frisch's published works in econometrics were done prior to World War II.

After the war, Frisch became increasingly involved in macroeconomic planning. He had great confidence in himself and trust in this effort. Frisch was convinced that macroeconomic planning was the only way for the world to proceed if general prosperity and peace were to prevail. Consequently, he was a great admirer of the Soviet Union's macroeconomic planning efforts. The scientific and personal connection between Frisch, the department of economics at the University of Oslo, and the Soviet planning hierarchy was very good. In that relationship, Frisch forged his views of the world and the role applied economics should play.

Not surprisingly, Frisch fought hard to keep Norway out of the Common Market (European Community). In that, he succeeded beyond his wildest dreams, with Norway turning down both the European Economic Community (EEC) in 1972 and the European Union (EU) in 1994. Still, while Frisch's grand hopes for economic planning became as anachronistic as the Iron Curtain itself, some of his tools remain vital. For example the use of a cost-of-living index, urged by Frisch and others, was first put into practice in a peacetime setting when the Norwegian trade unions agreed to resolve disputes without strikes by incorporating the cost-of-living index into wage negotiations. Today, the concept of a cost-of-living index is so much a part of popular economic discussion that it is hard to imagine political discourse in the United States without it.

Frisch's early works in quantitative economics were essentially in business cycle theories and time series analysis as described in great detail by Jens Andvig. It is evident that this earlier research, fueled by Frisch's interest in statistics, is somewhat at odds with his basic philosophy of the science of economics. This work, relatively unknown to most business researchers and largely forgotten by the econometrics profession, displays a dichotomy that is hard to explain. On the one hand, Frisch continued the more mechanistic tradition of the business cycle research. Business cycle research, a very popular branch of empirical economics in the pre-depression era, was basically a data mining exercise without much macro-theoretic underpinning. On the other hand, as discussed above, Frisch wanted economics to develop along the lines of physics. While research in business cycles basically followed the data mining tradition, his knowledge of statistics made him skeptical of much of the work taking place in this area at that time. He was, inter alia, opposed to the common practice of assuming constant periodicity. For example, he saw the need to allow for varying periodicity, the amplitudinal shape of the cycles. In the early thirties at a meeting in Stockholm, Sweden, Frisch seems, however, to have made an effort to align business cycles research more with theoretical economics. In this lecture he distinguished between the endogenous (free oscillations) and exogenous (forced oscillations) forces that impact an economic system. Frisch asserted that the explanation of the cyclical character of the oscillations must be sought in the inner structure of the system. Here, he meant that one should not solely rely on the forced oscillations to explain business cycles, but rather take into consideration the endogenous repercussions (free oscillations) in order to fully understand the phenomenon.

Another of Frisch's endeavors during these early years was published in 1934. In the "statistical confluence" paper, Frisch devised methods to get at the true structural parameters of a given model. Paradoxically, the inherent philosophy of confluence analysis seems to clash with Frisch's own scientific principles concerning theory and measurement.

Frisch may be contrasted with Trygve Haavelmo, his most famous student. Frisch, instead of expounding the underlying theoretical basis, went directly to the set of data and wanted to discover which equations were hidden in them.

Haavelmo, on the other hand, demanded researchers start from an economic theory specified in the form of algebraic equations and probability laws. Frisch's earlier works in econometrics have, to date, had a more profound impact on the science of econometrics than did his later works. In the "correlation and scatter" paper, he provided a comprehensive methodology for data analysis and for the use of multiple regression. In this paper, Frisch used the compact language of linear matrix algebra and introduced the problem of "multiple collinearity." In this period, Frisch became alarmed over, as he witnessed, the careless use of regression methods particularly when the practitioners neglected the potential problems arising from the presence of multicollinearity in econometric models. Frisch used Leontief as an example of the abuses he saw in quantitative economics at the time. Leontief, in his attempt to estimate demand and supply curves, made the assumption of independent shifts in both curves to circumvent the identification problem. The written exchanges between the two Nobel laureates became needlessly sharp. This was neither the first time nor the last time Frisch lashed out at people with different approaches to what he saw as the scientific truth.

It is hard for people unfamiliar with the academic culture prevailing at the University of Oslo to understand these sharp attacks on different minded individuals. In an environment where only one truth can exist at a time, an academic arrogance tends to build and permeate the whole institution. It is exceedingly difficult for outsiders to understand and deal with this phenomenon. The Danish-Norwegian author Akset Sandemose, very familiar with the Norwegian academic and cultural life, formulated brilliantly these sentiments in his description of the "Law of Jante," which can best be described as an insidious form of political correctness. Because opposition to the prevailing truth is dealt with swiftly and severely, it seems unexplainable and out of context, but a closer analysis reveals all too familiar patterns. This disregard for other opinions and arrogance toward other researchers became painfully clear during Frisch's long tenure as editor in chief of *Econometrica*. Even admireres refer to Frisch as "an editor in the old style." In fact, Frisch's autocratic style became, on various occasions, an embarrassment to the leadership of the Econometric Society which belatedly discovered that no limits had been put on the length of time an editor could remain in office. Frisch's stature in the econometric science was so strong that it kept him in charge of *Econometrica* for twenty-two years, despite serious misgivings about his editorial style. One of the more peculiar editorial privileges Frisch granted himself was the habit of inserting editorial comments and assertions into articles accepted for publication in *Econometrica* which frequently made reference to works by Frisch himself. In one infamous example, Frisch even published comments on an article by Kalecki in the issue before the article appeared.

One episode that illustrates this conflict between Frisch and contributors to *Econometrica* is reported by Olav Bjerkolt. When Frisch told Harold Hotelling that he was preparing a comment to append to Hotelling's "General Welfare...," the author retorted that he had worked on the topic for six to seven years and brushed the editor off rather brusquely: "Under these circumstances, I do not think it likely that any criticism conceived within a few days and published immediately is likely to have much force" (Bjerkholt: 1995, p. xxxv). Unperturbed, Frisch completed his comments but conceded a point by not publishing it in the same issue.

Frisch was not above self-promotion. He allowed the misperception that he was Jewish to serve as an explanation for his internment by the Nazis in World War II, some biographers even noting that he "shared a cell with the Norwegian chemist, Odd Hassel," who also won the Nobel Prize (Wasson: 1987, p. 356; Bjerkholt: 1995, p. xx.)

As the years went by and the science of econometrics deviated more and more from the narrow path favored by Frisch, he grew disenchanted with the developments. Frisch did not acknowledge the trial and error aspect so crucial to the development process of any new science. On various occasions he referred to the developments as *playometrics*. In fact, the science of econometrics was moved forward to a large degree by economists, statisticians and mathematicians that did not attempt to claim the science as their eminent domain. The current revival of econometrics as a relevant tool for practical applications is due in large part to the severe criticism and failure of econometrics that occurred during the 1970s and 1980s.

Frisch used the phrase "unenlightened financialism" in many contexts, particularly during his campaign against Norwegian membership in EEC. Putting the kindest possible spin on "unenlightened financialism" (*det uopplyste pengevelde*), Frisch can be interpreted to mean "market economies" or "free competitive markets" as defined in the above quote. The connotations in Norwegian are, however, much stronger. The expression literally translates to "the government of the uninformed/unenlightened financial interests." This seems to be the real base of Frisch's philosophy of regulation of the economy. His experience during the depression in the 1930s led him to believe that markets should not be left to their own devices. Strict government control of the economy was necessary in order to avoid "feast and famine" chaos. This Frischian legacy still prevails in Norway where the government's share of GDP is close to 60 percent and regulation of the economy is persuasive. His reason for control was, however, much more Platonic than Machiavellian. Frisch believed his models could significantly improve the economic fortunes of his fellow Norwegians and the rest of the world. He was convinced that the application of his econometric models for planning and policy was far superior to anything else mankind could come up with at this stage of the economic science.

When reviewing Frisch's predictions on the demise of the Western democracies, the kindest thing that comes to mind is Danish humorist Storm P's famous lament that "It is extremely difficult to predict, particularly about the future." The best that can be said about some of Frisch's bombastic predictions is that they were royally wrong. The Soviet Union planned itself into oblivion and the Western democracies that planned the least, in other words those that practiced "unenlightened financialism," like the USA, prospered the most. Countries with extensive macroeconomic planning and regulations prospered the least. For example, India and Egypt are two developing countries that experimented heavily in economic planning with the help of Frisch. In those countries stagnation and unemployment have been rampant for years.

According to Frisch, the tools of successful macroeconomic planning were available; only the will of the Western democracies was lacking. He seemingly was not worried by the enormous amount of information such planning would require, even in a society of static preferences. He was convinced that his survey approach to preference function estimation would yield the right results. Frisch was convinced that the preference function problem for an economy at large could be solved when it was approached in an intelligent and cautious way and liked to refer readers and listeners to various Oslo memoranda–several that were never published and others that remained unfinished. Frisch was still alive during the beginning of the information age and was a sophisticated user of computers and computer technology. He did not, however, consider the possibility that constant bombardment of information by an increasing set of information media could change consumer preferences, and consequently, decision makers' preference functions. Thus he could not visualize a very dynamic and moving economy where consumer preferences changed rapidly and where budget shares of even broad-based consumer goods categories would change from month to month. In such an economic environment, the information requirements to correctly plan all goods and services would be overwhelming.

CONCLUSION

Ragnar Frisch's place in history of economic thought is clearly one of a pioneer with strong convictions of the inherent truths carried by his own theorems and conclusions. His contribution to the economic science is well appreciated. Although his theoretical and methodological contributions to economic theory and economic quantitative science were many, Frisch will probably be judged by history as one who initially gave direction to modern economics. Together with Irving Fisher and Joseph Schumpeter, he charted a new course for economics away from descriptive institutional analysis and toward more general scientific principles of theory building and quantitative proofs.

RECOMMENDED READINGS

Bjerkholt, Olav. (ed.) (1926). *Foundations of Modern Econometrics: The Selected Essays of Ragnar Frisch*. Vol. 1 , Brookfield, pp. xiii-lii.

Frisch, Ragnar. (1926). *Sur les semi-invariants et moments employes dans l' etude des-distributions statistiques*. Doctoral thesis. Oslo: University of Oslo.

——. (1929). "Correlation and Scatter in Statistical Variables," *Nordic Statistical Journal*. pp. 36-102.

——. (1929). *Statikk og Dynamikk I den Okonomishe Teori*. Kobenhavn: Nationalokonomisk Tidskrift.

——. (1930). "Necessary and Sufficient Conditions Regarding the Form of an Index Which Shall Meet Certain of Fisher's Tests," *Journal of the American Statistical Association*. Vol. 25, No. 4, pp. 397-406.

——. (1933). *Propagation Problems and Impulse Problems in Dynamic*

Economics, Essays in Honour of Gustav Cassel. London: Allan and Unwin, pp. 171-205.

———. (1933). *Pitfalls in the Statistical Construction of Demand and Supply Curves*. Leipzig: Hans Buske Verlag, pp. 1-39.

———. (1934). *Statistical Confluence Analysis by Means of Complete RegrEssion Systems*. Oslo: Institute of Economics, University of Norway.

———. (1936). "Annual Survey of General Economic Theory: The Problem of Index Numbers," *Econometrica*. Vol. 4, pp. 1-38.

———. (1945). "The Responsibility of the Econometrician," *Econometrica*, Vol. 13, reprinted in O. Bjerkholt, (ed.), *Foundation of Modern Econometrics: The Selected Essays of Ragnar Frisch*. Aldershot: Edward Elgar Publishing, Ltd. Chapter 22.

———. (1959). "A Complete Scheme for Computing All Direct and Cross Demand Elasticities in a Model with Many Sectors," *Econometrica*. Vol. 27, pp. 96-117.

———. (1959). *Practical Rules for Interview Determination of One-Sided and Two-Sided Preference Coefficients in Macroeconomic Decision Problems*, Memorandum of 25 June.

———. (1961). *Preface to the Oslo Channel Model-A Survey of Types of Economic Forecasting and Programming*, Memoramdum from Institute of Economics: Oslo: University of Oslo.

———. (1981). "From Utopian Theory to Practical Applications: The Case of Econometrics" (Nobel Prize lecture), *American Economic Review*, Vol. 71, No. 6, pp. 1-6.

Kvantitiativ, A. (1926), "Quantitative Formulation of the Laws of Theoretical Economics," *Statsokonomisk Tidsskrift*. Vol. 40, pp. 299-334.

Samuelson, Paul. (1974). "Remembrances of Frisch," *European Economic Review*. Vol. 5, pp. 7-23.

3

Jan Tinbergen (1903-1994):
Who Integrated Physics, Mathematics, Statistics, and Economics and Was a Laureate of 1969

M. Mahabub-ul Islam

BIOGRAPHICAL PROFILE

Jan Tinbergen was born in the Hague, The Netherlands, in 1903. He was the son of a schoolteacher. His early education started in a school designed for middle class children. He learned Latin and Greek and entered into the University of Leiden, where he studied mathematics and physics, in 1921. Through his academic advisor at Leiden, professor Ehrenfest, Tinbergen came in contact with great scientists like Albert Einstein. During student life, Tinbergen was inclined toward left-wing socialist politics. Under the supervision of Ehrenfest, he completed his Ph.D. thesis, in which he integrated mathematics, physics, statistics, and economics, and submitted it in 1929. He was one of the pioneers of mathematical modeling. After his education, from 1929 to 1945, he worked as a statistician with the Bureau of Statistics of the Dutch government. There he tested many of his theories with empirical observations. Later, he became a professor of economics at the Netherlands School of Economics. Tinbergen was the only economics Nobel laureate whose brother, Nikolaas Tinbergen, also got the Nobel Prize in medicine/physiology in 1973. Tinbergen held important positions with the League of Nations and the Dutch Planning Bureau. Tinbergen and his wife, Tine De Wit, got married in 1929 and had four daughters. Tinbergen died in 1994.

INTRODUCTION

Jan Tinbergen, along with Ragnar Frisch, got the Nobel Prize in economics in 1969 for "having developed and applied dynamic models for the analysis of economic processes." Tinbergen was one of the pioneers who combined the disciplines of physics, mathematics, statistics, and economics and used mathematical formulae and econometric models to develop economic theories and their applications in practice. Tinbergen's groundbreaking development of quantitative-dynamic models by applying mathematical and statistical methods to economic analysis was built on his background in physics. He earned a doctorate in physics at Leiden University with the thesis "Minimum Problems in Physics and Economics." After completing his formal education, Tinbergen devoted himself to the advancement of economic theory, its application, and economic policy analysis for developed, as well as developing, economies. Tinbergen's scholarly works are characterized by his unique and distinctive approach to scientific investigation, integrating major social and economic issues. His works and interest in scientific analysis were guided by his idealistic views on mankind and his devotion to humanitarian activities and human welfare.

ECONOMETRIC METHODS

Tinbergen was one of the founding fathers of the science of econometrics– a marriage between economics and statistics. In the 1930s, Jan Tinbergen, Ragnar Frisch, and Irvin Fisher founded the Econometric Society. According to its constitution, the Econometric Society is an international society for the advancement of economic theory in its relation to statistics and mathematics. The Econometric Society serves as a pioneering center for the quantitative approach to economic research, promoting unification and application of mathematical and statistical methods to economic analysis.

Tinbergen made significant and pioneering contributions to econometrics. In the field of econometrics, he was particularly known for the discovery of the "Cobweb Theorem" and the related dynamic theory and for the contribution of econometric modeling to statistical testing of business cycles theories. In 1930, Tinbergen authored a monumental article entitled "Bestimmung und Deutung von Angebotskurven: ein Beispiel," which was published in *Zeitschrift fur Nationnalokonomie* in which he developed the Cobweb Theorem. The theorem explains the short-term cyclical fluctuations of price and quantities of agricultural products with fixed demand and supply curves, provided that supply reacts to prices with a one-year time lag, while the demand reacts immediately. Tinbergen's use of difference equations in analyzing business cycles made him a key founder of economic dynamics, and this technique has been the standard in economic analysis since the late 1930s.

Tinbergen made great contributions to econometrics by developing the methods for empirical testing of mathematically formulated economic theories and by constructing econometric models for the entire economy. In the first major endeavor in 1936, Tinbergen developed a macroeconometric model for the Dutch economy. The model consists of twenty four simultaneous equations with more than fifty interrelated variables and includes equations for income generation and consumption expenditures consistent with the Keynesian explanation. Consumption is explained as a positive function of disposable income. Tinbergen suggests that investment depends upon profit, contrary to the conventional wisdom, in which investment is considered to be an inverse function of the rate of interest. The model also includes foreign trade equations and export and import functions. The volume of exports depends on the world demand and relative competitiveness, while the imports are determined by domestic demand and competitiveness. The model splits money-flows into prices and quantities, and prices are explained by a number of mark-up equations. The 1936 model explains the inverse relationship between wage inflation and the level of employment, consistent with the widely known Phillips curve of the late 1950s. Tinbergen also explains the dynamic relationship between wage inflation and price inflation by suggesting that the wage rate is directly related to the rate of change of consumer prices with a one-period time lag.

The main objectives of Tinbergen's 1936 model were to investigate the dynamic properties of the Dutch economy and to provide a framework for policy decisions. However, Tinbergen's first attempt at macroeconometric modeling failed to attract   adequate attention from the professionals until the 1950s due to its quantitative nature, advanced   technical expression, and the fact that it was not translated into English until 1959. In response to the invitation of the League of Nations, in 1936-1938, Tinbergen provided an empirical analysis of the business cycles theories within the macroeconometric framework of the complete dynamic model of interrelated variables. The project produced a two-volume work, *Statistical Testing of Business Cycles Theories*. The first volume, *A Method and its Application to Investment Activity*, analyzes investment activity using standard classical multiple regression analysis combined with new methods, known as "confluence analysis," developed by Frisch. This study explains the empirical methods used and provides examples of their applications.   Tinbergen's investigation did not find much empirical evidence to support the contemporary wisdom suggesting the acceleration principle was the key determinant of investment cycles. Instead, he formulated an alternative hypothesis known as the "Profit Principle," showing that the level of profit, not change of profits, is an important factor in private investment cycles.

In the second volume, *Business Cycles in the United States of America 1919-1932*, Tinbergen focuses on the macroeconometric modeling of the business cycles in the United States. The model provides a complete macroeconomic model consisting of forty eight equations. In this research, Tinbergen investigates business cycles as a single unified phenomenon within the framework of a complete dynamic model instead of following the tradition of the time, in which each phase of any cycle was considered a separate phenomenon. The dynamic model explains the development of the past and also allows prediction of future development. Tinbergen duplicated the American model for the British economy in his book, *Business Cycles in United Kingdom, 1870-1914*. Tinbergen's pio- neering work on econometric modeling was received with skepticism by many economists, including Keynes. However, since the late 1950s, econometric model building has revolutionized the economics profession. The work of Tinbergen gave birth to a completely new branch of economics– empirical macroeconomics. In recent decades, the application of the macroeconometric model for predictions is highly valued, although somewhat controversial, among professional economists, business decision-makers, and public policy planners.

QUANTITATIVE ECONOMIC POLICY ANALYSIS

Tinbergen's emphasis in scientific research shifted to quantitative economic policy analysis with his appointment in 1945 as director of the newly established Netherlands Central Planning Bureau. During this time, he studied the general theoretical questions of economic policy planning and developed a quantitative framework capable of reliable forecasts of short-term developments and rational calculations of policy measures required to achieve policy targets. Tinbergen's research efforts in the area of economic policy produced a number of publications, including his books *On the Theory of Economic Policy, Centralization and Decentralization in Economic Policy, and Economic Policy: Principles and Design*. In these studies, Tinbergen categorized policy variables as targets, data, and instruments. He argued, in order to achieve a set of targets (such as a stable price level, full-employment, balance of payments, income distribution, etc.), it is necessary to have an equal number of policy instruments (such as fiscal, monetary, and exchange rate policies, etc..) He also addressed the issues of fixed and flexible targets. Tinbergen advanced the thesis of multitarget problems. Traditionally, economists dealt with a particular economic policy separately in relation to a specific target without any consideration of simultaneity among various types of economic policies. Tinbergen viewed economic policy as consisting of multiple related targets which must be analyzed simultaneously within a framework of multi-target problems. He developed a quantitative framework to deal with several targets subject to a sufficient number of appropriate instruments simultaneously. Tinbergen's investigation involving economic policy planning was concerned with actual macroeconomic policy targets in existing economies. His book *Economic Policy: Principles and Design* presented many examples of practical problems and their solutions using the theoretical foundation of economic policy making. Tinbergen also developed a quantitative framework to address the issues of centralized and decentralized policy-making. He analyzed the advantages and disadvantages of centralized versus decentralized policy planning under specific situations. He suggested that a mixture of centralized and decentralized policy making was the optimal regime.

ECONOMIC DEVELOPMENT AND COOPERATION

In the mid-1950s, Tinbergen left the Dutch Central Planning Bureau to become a full-time professor of development planning at the Netherlands School of Economics. After that he focused his attention on investigating the problems of long-term growth and development and on issues of international cooperation and integration. Tinbergen's scientific contributions to the theory and practice of long-term growth and development, particularly focused on developing countries, was driven by his idealistic views of mankind, deep devotion of humanitarian activities, and serious awareness and acute concern of the problems of developing countries.

In this work, Tinbergen applied quantitative analysis to understand and promote long-term growth and development. He analyzed the practical problems of economic development, formulated models and methods to deal with these problems, and provided recommendations for solutions. Tinbergen submitted numerous memorandum and papers to governments and international organizations. He also published a series of books such as *The Design of Development*, *Mathematical Models of Economic Growth*, *Econometric Models of Education*, *and Development Planning*.

Tinbergen designed the models for developing countries on the assumption that the availability of required statistical data and the skills of administrators, planners, and politicians are limited. He developed three main models. The macro model consists of three planning stages. In the first stage, the target for economic variables is determined, and plans are made for the levels of output, savings, investments, capital, and exports and imports of the economy. In the second stage, the aggregate activities are broken down by regions, sectors, and industries using input-output models and sectoral capital-output coefficients. The final stage involves choosing investment projects based on the policy targets of the economy. The second type of model, known as the semi-input-output model, is constructed by starting with large investment projects and integrating them into the macro plans. Each project is appraised using the input-output model, shadow prices, and international prices. The third type of model is a large system of simultaneous equations derived from the types of econometric models. Tinbergen applied it in the empirical investigation of business cycles. In this system, the policy instruments are incorporated explicitly in the solutions. The macro model is a widely used method for policy planning in developing countries, although it is unable to ensure economic efficiency.

In addition to his scholarly contributions to the economic advancement of developing countries, Tinbergen was active in helping to solve their other problems. He traveled widely and lectured extensively on the problems and policy options of development. He served as an advisor to the governments of a number of countries, including Chile, Egypt, India, Indonesia, Iraq, Libya, Turkey, Suriname, and Syria. He has helped these countries identify problems, define various types of macroeconomic requirements, such as investment and savings, and develop methods of planning. Tinbergen suggests that the developing countries emphasize labor-intensive industries and techniques in order to maximize employment and income. On the other hand, the developed countries should focus on capital-intensive industries to maximize productivity, income, and efficiency. He emphasizes that the government has the significant role of creating favorable conditions for development through publicizing the advantages of development, providing basic investment, and encouraging private investment.

In addition to his concern with economic development, Tinbergen made significant contributions in the area of international cooperation and integration. His interest in this area was accelerated by the creation of Benelux and the European Economic Community (EEC.) He wrote extensively, served as a consultant to various United Nations agencies, and advised a number of international organizations such as The World Bank and The European Coal and

Steel Community. Tinbergen was the chairman of the United Nations Committee for Development and Planning during 1966-1972. He traveled and lectured around the world, focusing on the nature and structure of international cooperation and attempting to design an international development policy to close the gap between developed and developing countries. In his book *International Economic Integration*, Tinbergen argued that economic integration was necessary to ensure good international relations among independent countries and to overcome the political problems regarding short-term national interests. He advocated for designing a framework for international integration based on applied quantitative analysis rather than on theoretical discussion.

Tinbergen's deep concern and commitment to a broad-based integrated approach of international cooperation and integration were also reflected in his contributions to *Reshaping the International Order*, a report to the Club of Rome coordinated by Tinbergen and several other authors. The study addressed the problems with the existing system of international relations and issues and the structure of a new international order, the armament race, population control, and food supply were identified as the main problems. The authors advised that the social responsibility to satisfy collective needs and more equitable distribution of wealth among individuals are required to have a better world. Tinbergen's contribution to quantitative planning methods and its application to promote development in developing countries and his efforts toward international cooperation and integration made him an important frontiersman in economics.

DISTRIBUTION OF INCOME

Tinbergen made significant contributions to the issue of distribution of income among individuals and nations. He wrote extensively on income distribution, including a pamphlet in 1946 and a classic article, "On the Theory of Income Distribution," published in 1956. However, in the 1970s, Tinbergen focused on the personal distribution of income in developed countries and published several articles and a book entitled *Income Distribution: Analysis and Policy*. Tinbergen viewed the reduction of income inequality as a generally accepted objective of economic policy and analyzed the issues of income distribution at both the philosophical and the economic points of view, although his emphasis was on determining the factors of inequality. He investigated the existing pattern of personal income distribution, identified the problems involved in it, and provided direction toward an equitable distribution of income. According to Tinbergen, equity implies equal welfare for all individuals, and level of welfare depends on the level of schooling, occupation, and income.

Tinbergen analyzed the phenomenon of income distribution within the framework of the economic model of demand and supply. He suggested that the excess supply of a particular group of labor, not the lack of specific skill, leads to lower wages for that group and, thus, results in inequality of income in the society. Tinbergen was explicit in his recommendation to reduce income inequality. He advocated for the modification of the education system and the tax structure to improve the distribution of income. He believed a system of education that expands the educational facilities reduces the inequality of income in the society and he advocated for a tax structure that would tax individuals' capabilities instead of their outcomes. However, in absence of such a tax system, he suggested a higher tax on wealth, capital gains, and inherited estates in order to reduce inequality in the personal distribution of income.

Welfare Economics and Comparative Economic System

In all of his professional career, Tinbergen was concerned with social justice and economic welfare of human beings. His resonant concern and commitment for the well-being of individuals and societies directed his interest to welfare economics. In the field of welfare economics, the tradition has been to formulate welfare functions expressing the conditions for maximizing social welfare. The outcome of the theoretical investigations was not widely understood and failed to draw adequate attention, due to its lack of relevance in practical application. Tinbergen criticized the existing studies on welfare economics, based on the argument that the issues of income distribution and social justice had not been adequately addressed in relevance to the field's practical application. In the article *Welfare Economics and Income Distribution,* Tinbergen argued that successful welfare economics should direct political thought and attempted to formulate a social welfare function incorporating alternative economic systems. This method determines an optimal regime, which creates the conditions for optimal economic welfare. The findings of his investigation suggested that the optimal regime lay between the two extremes–capitalism and socialism. According to Tinbergen, the concepts of complete free market economy and totally planned economy are unrealistic, and they are not consistent with human nature. Tinbergen perceives, in reality, two extreme economic systems converging toward a mixed system by compromising their extreme principles.

CONCLUSION

Jan Tinbergen was one of the few economists who brought the discipline of economics forward with his outstanding contributions. He contributed to economic theories and applications concerning both developed and developing countries. He was a pioneer in modern economic dynamics and the founder of empirical macroeconomic modeling. He made significant contributions to modern techniques of economic forecasting and predictions. Tinbergen laid the foundation of modern economic policy and development planning and contributed decisively to the issues of income distribution, welfare economics, and comparative economic systems. He also wrote extensively on many other areas of economics. Tinbergen successfully applied quantitative techniques involving mathematical and statistical formulations in scientific investigations. Although he emphasized the usefulness of quantitative tools as a means of economic analysis, he never allowed tools to overshadow the ends–understanding economic and social phenomena. He emphasized practical problems and empirical analysis within a broader interdisciplinary approach of scientific investigation interrelating economic, institutional, social, and political issues. Tinbergen is considered the intellectual model to the younger generation of economists, and his works have inspired further studies in many areas of economics.

RECOMMENDED READINGS

Tinbergen, Jan. (1951). *Business Cycles in the United Kingdom, 1870-1914.* Amsterdam: Elsevier-North Holland.

———. (1952). *On the Theory of Economic Policy.* Amsterdam: Elsevier-North Holland.

———. (1954). *Centralization and Decentralization in Economic Policy.* Amsterdam: Elsevier-North Holland.

———. (1954). *International Economic Integration.* Amsterdam: Elsevier-North Holland.

———. (1956). *Economic Policy: Principles and Design.* Amsterdam: Elsevier-North Holland.

———. (1958). *The Design of Development.* Baltimore: Johns Hopkins University Press.

———. (1964). *Central Planning.* New Haven: Yale University Press.

Tinbergen, Jan, and Hendricus Bos. (1965). *Econometric Modeling of Education.* Paris: Organization for Economic Cooperation and Development.

———. (1967). *Development Planning.* New York: McGraw-Hill.

———. (1975). *Income Distribution: Analysis and Policy.* Amsterdam: Elsevier-North Holland.

———. (1975). *Reshaping the International Order: A Report to the Club of Rome.* New York: Dutton.

4

Paul Samuelson (1915-   ):
An Economist's Economist
and the Laureate of 1970

Derek P. J. Hum

BIOGRAPHICAL PROFILE

Paul Samuelson was born in Gary, Indiana in 1915. He completed his undergraduate studies at the University of Chicago in 1935 and received his master's and Ph.D. degrees from the prestigious Harvard University in 1936 and 1941, respectively. His doctoral dissertation, later published as *The Foundations of Economic Analysis,* has been a monumental work that brought him an international reputation even before he started his professional career. In his writings, he uses rigorous mathematics and believes that mathematics is not a cure for all but is indispensable to understanding economics. Samuelson joined the Massachusetts Institute of Technology (MIT) faculty in 1940 and became a full professor in 1947. Maintaining his MIT position, he also worked at the Radiation Laboratory, Fletcher School of Law and Diplomacy and many other institutions and organizations in various capacities.   His principles book, *Economics: An Introductory Analysis*, was first published in 1948. It was a bestseller for many years and sold more than a million copies in various languages around the world. Samuelson served as a consultant for several organizations, such as the National Resources Planning Board, the War Production Board, the Office of War Mobilization and Reconstruction, the U.S. Treasury, the Bureau of the Budget, the Research Advisory Panel to the President's National Goals Commission, the Research Advisory Board Committee for Economic Development, the National Task Force on Economic Education, the Rand Corporation and others. He was economic advisor to senator, candidate, and president-elect Kennedy. He received honorary doctor of laws degrees from many academic institutions. He was awarded the David A. Wells Prize by Harvard University and the John Bates Clark Medal by the American Economic Association. Samuelson is one of the greatest living economists and is still contributing. He has published more than one hundred scientific papers and many major books both as author and co-author.

INTRODUCTION

Paul Samuelson was awarded the Nobel Prize in economics in 1970 for "the scientific work through which he has developed static and dynamic economic theory and activity contributed to raising the level of analysis in economic science." Samuelson was the first American to be honored with the prestigious economics Nobel Prize. Upon hearing this, academics instinctively thought of his Harvard doctoral dissertation, *Foundations of Economic Analysis*, a brilliant compact work completed in 1941 but not published until 1947 due to the war. Mark Blaug describes it as "a milestone in the conversion of modern economists to the view that all economic behavior can be fruitfully studied as the solution to a maximization problem." Samuelson himself, in his Nobel address; "Maximum Principles in Analytic Economics," reinforces this interpretation of his achievement and place in the history of economics. But for those who are not professional economists, what probably leapt to mind was Samuelson's *Economics* textbook, their introductory acquaintance with the subject. Perhaps others remember his regular contributions to *Newsweek* during the 1960s, or less likely, his published testimony before Congress and other bodies, including his report to President Kennedy on the state of the American economy.

The judgment of economists is often different from those outside the profession, as Samuelson remarked in his 1961 presidential address to the American Economics Association (AEA). He observed that any pronounced influence on the affairs of men by economists likely would be indirect rather than direct, and might even have little to do with technical correctness. Samuelson has been called a wunderkind, labeled an enfant terrible emeritus, and referred to as the Paganini of economics. His undeniable technical talent has, perhaps, overshadowed his considerable contributions to policy making and issues of concern to the general public. This chapter sketches Samuelson's contribution to economic understanding "outside" the profession and his impact on public policy discussion from the start of his career until his receipt of the Nobel Prize (i.e., his writings in only the first three volumes of *The Collected Scientific Papers of Paul A. Samuelson*). This arbitrary focus is, of course, clumsy but defensible. Well before his Nobel Prize in 1970, Samuelson noted in his 1961 presidential address to the AEA : "The split, between 'the inside look' ... in terms of the logic and experience of its professional development and its implications for the man-in-the-street or the academician down the campus, is well recognized. No one gets a Nobel Prize for an essay on the relationship of quantum mechanics to free will and God; but one who has already received such a prize will get a better hearing for his random or systematic thoughts on the topic."

ANNOUNCING THE ARRIVAL

Samuelson's first professional articles, now classics in the field, were written while he was still a graduate student at Harvard. They were a fitting announcement of his originality and creative flair as well as a harbinger of his philosophical stance. One piece, written when he was twenty three years of age and entitled, "A Note on the Pure Theory of Consumer's Behavior," was no less than an attempt to alter the first principles of consumer behavior as then understood. The notion of utility, which economists then mainly conceded as a useful heuristic device to explain consumer choice, was already much discredited. Samuelson demonstrated that the familiar and popular demand curve of modern economics could be obtained from observing actual purchases at known prices in markets without resorting to any psychological concepts involving pleasure, utility, or ideas about the difficulties of substituting one commodity for another. How far ahead of his time and how sophisticated his approach was can be gauged by noting that even today, senior level undergraduate economic texts still retain the vestiges of the pre-Samuelson approach (involving utility, indifference curves, and the like). Not only was Samuelson's conceptualization novel, but it also signaled his life long allegiance to the modernist method in economics. Over the years, Samuelson would come to embody the Cartesian program in economics; he would supply the rigorous theoretical foundations of the discipline; he would demand a new level of precision; he would establish a new mathematical standard for economic conversation; and he would attempt to banish introspection when discussing economic propositions capable of testing under ideal circumstances. He would come to exemplify the economist as scientist and to dominate the mainstream portions of the profession. His approach would exemplify the break from the purely literary tradition in economics.

FREE TRADE

Samuelson's brilliance was not without application, or relevance, to the great public policy concerns of the day. During the Great Depression and before World War II, international trade topics loomed large among the economic problems of the day, with debate centering on the benefits of universal free trade and whether some group might not do better under a protectionist policy. While mediating a dispute between two of his teachers, Jacob Viner and Gottfried Haberler, on the costs and value of free trade, Samuelson provided in 1939 the framework that remains the standard analysis of the welfare gains from free trade. The core of the demonstration observes that a country without trading partners but wanting an extra widget must necessarily shift resources from producing something else, thereby giving up, say, three apples.

The cost to this society of the extra widget is reckoned, therefore, as the three apples given up. Since this society can produce widgets or apples at a "price" ratio to itself of one-to-three, it would not suffer if it traded with others at this ratio. If, however, some trading partner were willing to offer a widget in return for two apples, that country could gain through trade by specializing in apple production and importing its widget by paying two apples to its trading partner, thereby obtaining the widget by sacrificing two apples instead of three. Samuelson established that the introduction of outside relative prices differing from those established in an economy without trade would lead to the result that every individual could be better off through trade. Though this result was apprehended by many, it was Samuelson who provided the first rigorous proof. Samuelson would eventually go on to establish the stringent conditions linking factor inputs to free trade in other work, but it is perhaps a 1941 paper stating the Stolper-Samuelson theorem that is most frequently relied upon for examining the winners and losers from a protectionist policy. The broad outline of the argument is as follows: Nations will invariably have differing amounts of productive factors such as labor, land, or capital. Further, countries with an abundant amount of a factor, say labor, will enjoy a cheaper price for that factor.

Consequently, a country can expect to produce more cheaply than its trading partners those goods which use a lot of the abundant factor. Therefore, this nation will export these goods. In essence, traded goods are simply bundles of production factors, hence trade will increase the demand for the abundant factors, thereby increasing its price. The equivalent statement is to note that trade will decrease the return to the scarce factor. To prevent this from occurring, owners of the scarce factor may attempt to prevent free trade by lobbying for tariffs or other protectionist policies. Thus, if one believes that the United States is a capital-abundant (or labor-scarce) nation, this would explain why labor would want to support and lobby for protectionist trade policies. Of course the real-life trade strategies of countries is much more complicated than the simple Stolper-Samuelson model. Nevertheless, Samuelson's insights establish a broad template for overlaying issues of politics, power relations, trading customs, and the like. His framework allows a systematic addressing of important policy issues such as: Why should a nation trade? and what's in it for our group if we don't?

PUBLIC ECONOMICS

Samuelson's contributions to trade theory may be seen as paving a deductive path from economic theory to policy analyses concerning the gains from universal free trade and the rewards to scarce productive factors from a protectionist strategy. It was left to others to shape the argument for tariffs or quotas in particular national circumstances; Samuelson's part was to fashion the intellectual weapons for the policy battles about free trade. On the other hand, Samuelson's 1954 contribution on pure public goods can be likened to a linchpin of public economics, a field more broadly conceived than just public finance or taxation matters, and presently taken to mean the study of government's effect on the economy.

In this seminal article and others that followed, elaborating and explaining its nuances, Samuelson introduced the distinction between private goods and public goods. Private goods are simply the familiar ones, like apples and shoes; only the individual eating the apple or wearing the shoes is said to consume or enjoy the good in question. No other person can eat the apple or wear the same pair of shoes at the same time. In contrast, Samuelson referred to another class of goods, termed pure public goods, which have different characteristics. Public goods or collective consumption goods, in fact, may be consumed by more than one individual at the same time (joint consumption); there is also the difficulty of preventing others from consuming (non-excludability), and it is possible to add other consumers without cost (zero marginal cost). The textbook example of a public good is the lighthouse. Its light beacon is able to guide one ship to safety amid darkness without diminishing its capacity to provide this service to another vessel simultaneously without additional cost; furthermore, it is not feasible to stop this second vessel from consuming its benefits if it is provided to the first ship.

The subtlety and wide-ranging impact of Samuelson's seemingly esoteric distinction for public policy matters may be glimpsed by listing some of the obviously important questions that the notion of public goods raised. Samuelson himself noted that the central issue was the "impossibility of decentralized spontaneous solution," in short, the inability of the market mechanism or price system to determine the appropriate level of public goods to produce. This being so, a wide range of difficult questions must now be considered, each question virtually giving rise to a different branch of public economics. For example, with the inability of the market to provide public goods in the right amount, how should a nation pay for its public goods? What should be its taxation principles to determine whether a certain public good should be provided? And if provided, how much should each taxpayer pay, since the principle of relating each individual taxpayer's amount to his individual benefit received is clearly insufficient. Or, if public goods are determined instead by voting procedures, what are the rules governing voter eligibility and procedures? An individual may choose not to reveal truthfully their willingness to pay or otherwise subscribe to the cost of providing a public good, with the knowledge that once the public good is provided (and paid for) by others (e.g., a clean air environment), the impossibility of excluding others from consumption gives that individual a "free ride" on their fellow taxpayers.

Additionally, some public goods have limits to their capacity to accommodate extra consumers at no cost, as frustrated campers to national parks have learned on busy holiday weekends. This "crowding or congestion effect" raises the issue of the best size of unit for particular public goods, much like the decision concerning the membership size of a club. A club should be large enough to enable it to extend its common resources to additional beneficiaries when the cost of doing so is negligible. On the other hand, it must not expand beyond the point where additional members interfere with the enjoyment of present members. Highways, national parks, museums, and so on are examples of public goods subject to crowding. As a final example, consider that different public goods have different limits of service. A small library may serve a town well, or a regional park may be quite adequate for the population of nearby counties. However, national defense or flood prevention measures require greater sums and affect a wider and more dispersed group of citizens. Which order of government should be entrusted with the responsibility to provide particular public goods and services? Or, to phrase matters in constitutional idioms, to which order of a federal or multitiered government should we assign jurisdiction for the various government functions?

The issues above seem a surprising distance from the theory of public expenditure and the idea of a pure public good explored by Samuelson. In retrospect, however, it is plain that the notion of a public good, with its attendant features and difficulties, lies at the analytic heart of much of the controversies of public expenditures.   Samuelson forever changed the landscape of public economics.

UNEMPLOYMENT AND INFLATION

The problems of inflation, unemployment, economic growth, and the like worry everyone. When a family member cannot find a job, or when the prices of household items rise more rapidly than wages increase the failings of the economy are apparent to the general public. Something is terribly wrong when national economies experience unemployment of such depths, and for such long periods, as the world witnessed during the thirties. Furthermore, classical theories had no explanation for the obdurate lack of jobs during the Great Depression, which stands as the ultimate emblem of economic impotence. The British economist Keynes, in 1936, published *The General Theory of Employment, Interest and Money*, which would revolutionize our understanding of the role of government and the operation of the economy. The central insight revolved around the concept of aggregate demand, comprised of the demand for goods and services from household consumption, industry investment, government spending, and foreign trade. If total demand for goods and services from all sources falls too low for firms to operate at full capacity, this would lead in turn to mass unemployment. Further, there is no natural mechanism to guarantee the economy's return to full employment. Under these circumstances, Keynes suggested that government had both the means and the duty to intervene to provide full employment by directly stimulating demand for goods and services through public spending. This stance was diametrically opposite to the prevailing orthodoxy of laissez-faire, since Keynes preached the necessity of government intervention through fiscal policy.

Keynes' book was anything but easy to understand, even by professional economists of the day, to put it mildly. Nonetheless, Keynes' ideas would cross the Atlantic and find a friendly reception from Samuelson, the leader of a younger generation of economists who enthusiastically embraced Keynes' message, and Alvin Hansen, head of the older generation, who became America's champion of Keynesian economics. Hansen published *Fiscal Policy and Business Cycles* in 1941. Samuelson was Hansen's student in his seminar on fiscal policy and immediately absorbed the message of *The General Theory*. He even wrote a mathematical appendix for Hansen's book. But Samuelson did more than merely absorb.   Leonard Silk relates that a piece Samuelson wrote as a mere "finger exercise" for Hansen was published as "Interactions Between the Multiplier Analysis and the Principle of Acceleration" in 1939.   This piece brought Samuelson worldwide fame, for the article " succeeded in transforming Keynes's static analysis of the forces that depressed an economy and produced high unemployment into a dynamic description of the factors causing capitalist economies to swing up as well as down." That same year, Samuelson introduced in a second article on the same topic the famous "Keynesian Cross," or 45-degree line, that is now standard in teaching undergraduates the determination of national income. In a 1959 note celebrating the twentieth anniversary of the original article, Samuelson gave his teacher, Alvin Hansen, full credit for the theory, even trying to have it designated the Hansen-Samuelson model. By this time, Samuelson had achieved a position as the preeminent economist in America. He continued to push the frontier forward at a dizzying pace, and single-handedly spread the message everywhere through his *Economics* text. Samuelson's text for undergraduates, first published in 1947, has been translated in many languages, and with its many editions, is unquestionably the best selling economics text of all time. Its impact, however, cannot be captured in mere royalties. Rather, Silk reports that Samuelson's text may actually represent his greatest contribution because it gave the world a common economic language.

Samuelson's policy writing, as well as his advice to government, was conditioned by his synthesis of classical and Keynesian ideas. He therefore advocated a balanced mix of discretionary fiscal and monetary policies, depending on the circumstances. What was not acceptable was inaction when the circumstances required activism, or hesitancy in the face of uncertainty. For example, Samuelson, who was President Kennedy's initial choice for chairman of the Council of Economic Advisors, supported the Kennedy tax cut of 1964 on the grounds that it would stimulate the economy. However, when inflationary pressures afflicted the U.S. economy a few years later, Samuelson advocated a tax increase. Pragmatism, so much the hallmark of his great teacher, Alvin Hansen, also became Samuelson's credo. At the same time, he witnessed the difficulties of merging economic reasoning with political actions, calling the result "upside-down economics" whenever the Congressional politics would bundle together proposals whose effects tended to offset one another.

Samuelson was at the center of the mainstream new economics. The Keynesian analysis spoke to the problems of the Great Depression, but in the 1960s, rising inflation was becoming meddlesome. In a 1960 paper before the AEA, Samuelson and Robert Solow introduced to American audiences the Phillip's Curve formulation for examining modern economic policy. The curve reflects the trade-off between inflation and unemployment facing an economy by depicting the extra unemployment an economy must bear for a given reduction in inflation. Coming before the advent of powerful computers, the estimates of the trade-off reported by Samuelson and Solow appear crude today. But the thoughtful distinctions between policies that move the economy from one point on the curve to another and those that move the entire curve, as well as the careful attention to the time period under discussion, are as lively and relevant to contemporary discussions of inflation and unemployment.

CAPITAL AND GROWTH

The distinction between the "short-run" and the "long-run" is a perennial source of tension for economists. The short-run, for convenience, is simply a period of time during which certain aspects of the economy, for example, the capital stock are taken as fixed. On the other hand, much of Samuelson's modeling concern the long run equilibrium position, whereby magnitudes are permitted to vary but do not change over time. The Keynesian model was a short-run framework; it held fixed the capital stock of the economy, among other things. But from a longer run perspective, today's saving and investment will alter tomorrow's capital stock, thereby resulting in growth. Samuelson, along with Solow, made seminal contributions to the literature examining economic growth.

This literature is highly technical and is read mainly by academics, but two contributions stand out. In 1958, Samuelson returned to a topic addressed in his very first published article in 1937. The article bore the complicated title, "An Exact Consumption Loan Model of Interest with or without the Social Contrivance of Money." In this article, Samuelson set forth a general model economy in which an infinite succession of consumers (called generations) overlap in their lifetimes so that intergenerational trade is possible. Young consumers in each generation are motivated to trade a portion of their output in order to receive output when old, since the ability to produce is confined to the young. Samuelson established that such a mutual-aid compact cannot be guaranteed with a free market, and that some legislated social collusion arrangement is necessary, or alternatively, that a grand consensus on the use of a socially contrived "money" is required to "give workers of one epoch a claim on workers of a later epoch" Samuelson's insights, now dubbed the overlapping generations model, has become the workhorse of modern macroeconomics, monetary theory and public finance with relevance to the analysis of pensions, an aging society, savings behavior, economic growth, and the like.

Samuelson was also at the center of what has come to be known as the "reswitching" or capital controversy. The debates were highly esoteric, but the issue concerned no less than the validity of the mainstream approach to economics. If consumable output is produced by combining factors such as labor and capital, then today's sacrifice of consumption (i.e., current savings) will enlarge tomorrow's capital stock. The "price" of today's sacrifice must therefore be linked to the profitability of extra capital, and as the capital stock increases, profit (or the rate of interest) must decline. This is necessary to tell consumers to stop saving, and to signal producers to select the appropriate capital-to-labor technique to employ in production. The pivotal relationship in this model hinges on the concept of aggregate capital being a meaningful one, and whether "more capital" necessarily leads to a lower interest rate. This capital controversy debate centered around the two Cambridges (England and Massachusetts). The sharp exchanges surrounding whether or not a concept of aggregate capital stock is meaningful is too technical to relate here. But again, this episode serves as a reminder of how central a protagonist was Paul Samuelson, and the "MIT School," to the advocacy of mainstream neoclassical economics.

CONCLUSION

Paul Samuelson wrote so much, on so wide a variety of subjects, and with such depth and virtuosity, that even concentrating only on his contributions to the time of his Nobel award is no small task. Much could be said of his concern with welfare economics, economic growth, the mixed economy, the ethics of the economic outcomes, or the careful attention and respect that Samuelson unfailingly credited to past scholars and teachers. Even more mention could be made of his advisory services to government, commissions, and the Oval Office. In Samuelson's own reflection of his life philosophy and policy credo, he declares he is "primarily a theorist" whose "first and last allegiance is to the facts." His method is that of an unrepentant modernist who produces "beautiful models."

He remains a self-described "eclectic economist," "blessed with an abundance of interesting problems" and "addicted to writing." This addiction, combined with his prodigious talent, produced about one scientific paper a month over a long career addressed to professional "insiders" on such fundamentally important policy questions as: Will free trade bring about an improvement in nations' well-being? What are the role and limits of government spending? How can we stabilize modern capitalist economies at full employment with stable prices? Samuelson brought to bear his considerable gifts, energies, and moral sense of purpose to these questions, benefitting both professional insiders and those outside the economics guild. Paul Samuelson is an economist's economist to insiders, but besides being expert advisor to government bodies and private tutor to a president, he is also the world's teacher of freshman economics. Quite coincidentally, his *Foundations of Economic Analysis* was published in 1947, the same year as the first edition of his *Economics* text. Since being awarded the Nobel Prize in 1970, Paul Samuelson continues to explore new areas and to write. His scientific papers have since filled two more thick volumes.

RECOMMENDED READINGS

Samuelson, Paul A. (1947). *Foundations of Economic Analysis*. Cambridge: Harvard University Press.

——.(1966). *The Collected Scientific Papers of Paul A. Samuelson*, (ed.) Joseph E. Stiglitz. Cambridge: The MIT Press (Vol. 1, Chapters. 1, 21, 28; Vol. 2, Chapters 113, 61, 62, 92, 93, 94, 82, 83, 84, 102, 146, 148).

——. (1972). *The Collected Scientific Papers of Paul A. Samuelson*. Vol. 3. (ed.) Robert C. Merton. Cambridge: MIT Press (Chapters. 130, 146, 148).

——. (1993). "My Life Philosophy: Policy Credo and Working Ways," In *Eminent Economists: Their Life Philosophies,* (ed.) M. Szenberg. Cambridge: Cambridge University Press.

Silk, Leonard. (1976). *The Economists*. New York: Basic Books.

5

Simon Kuznets (1901-1985):
An Originator of the National Income Accounting Method and the Laureate of 1971

M. Mahabub-ul Islam

BIOGRAPHICAL PROFILE

Simon Kuznets was born in 1901 in Harkiv (pronounced as Kharkiv), Ukraine. He joined his father, who left Europe before the First World War in the United States in 1922. Much about Kuznets' early life is not known. His education started in Russia and was completed at Columbia University, New York, where he received his Ph.D. in economics in 1926. At Columbia, he came in contact with Wesley Mitchell, who influenced Kuznets' life in many ways. After graduation from Columbia, Kuznets worked at the National Bureau of Economic Research, the Social Science Research Council, the Bureau of Planning and Statistics, the War Production Board in the United States and the Maurice Falk Institute of Economic Research in Israel. He taught economics and statistics at the University of Pennsylvania from 1931 through 1954. He also worked as a professor of political economy at Johns Hopkins University from 1954 to 1960. In 1960, he joined Harvard University as a professor of economics and remained there until 1971. He held important positions at the American Economic Association, the American Statistical Association, the Economic History Association, the International Statistical Institute, the Royal Statistical Society of England and many other professional organizations. He received honorary degrees from Harvard, Princeton, and Columbia universities, among others. Kuznets' wife, Edith Handler, was also an economist at the National Bureau of Economic Research. Kuznets was a fan of classical music and was very modest in his personal life. Kuznets died in 1985 leaving behind his wife, a daughter, and a son, and four grandchildren.

INTRODUCTION

Simon Kuznets received the economics Nobel Prize in 1971 for "his empirically founded interpretation of economic growth which has led to new and deepened insight into the economic and social structure and process of development." Kuznets' contributions to economics over a period of more than sixty years resulted in over 200 publications, including thirty books, a great many major articles, and contributions to collections. All of Kuznets' scientific work is unified by his unique and distinctive methodological and philosophical approach—empiricism, gathering, measurement, and interpretation of statistical data for the understanding of economic and social phenomenon. Kuznets was an original thinker, and his interests in scientific inquiries were diverse. He developed, established, and popularized the empirical approach to economic analysis. Kuznets' interest focused on business cycles, national income, and economic growth. His scholarly works resulted in pioneering and significant contributions in several areas of economic science, including national income accounting and product measurement, economic and social growth processes, seasonal and cyclical fluctuations, economic demography, income distribution, and empirical macroeconomics. In addition to the above-mentioned areas, he made scholarly contributions to other fields of economic science as well. The profession of economics is also indebted to Kuznets for his significant contributions in teaching and supervising and for his service in professional activities.

THE KUZNETSIAN APPROACH

Kuznets employed systematic steps in his scientific investigations in order to obtain a consistent and coherent picture of an economic phenomenon. In all his scientific studies, Kuznets used an inductive rather than a deductive approach. He emphasized the importance of empirical research in economic studies based on explicitly stated economic theory expressing the strategic relationships to selected variables under consideration. Although Kuznets recognized the usefulness of a theoretical framework consisting of formal mathematical and econometric models, he considered economic theory to be the foundation of economic analysis and empirical investigation. Kuznets provided a clear view of his approach to economic theory by formulating testable relations among empirically identifiable factors. In his view, a theoretical framework must be preceded by careful accumulation and arrangement of the evidence in order to identify all of the relevant factors involved.

Kuznets himself described the methodological steps of a research project as moving "from measurement to estimation to classification to explanation to speculation." The first step in the Kuznetsian methodology is the systematic investigation—the search for and collection, evaluation, refinement, tabulation, classification, and estimation of the existing statistical data. In the second step, the available statistical data and the involved variables and concepts are critically examined to check on consistency, plausibility, and the relevance of the entities in the study under consideration. The final step involves "analytical description"—

explanation, interpretation, and speculation. Kuznets always went to great lengths to provide explanations of the empirical findings, defining the relations between the variables involved in the analysis. Furthermore, he provided interpretations indicating the implication of his findings for understanding the economic and social phenomena. Speculations about the future possibilities, based on his findings, with reservations and notes of caution are common in the many scientific inquiries of Kuznets.

NATIONAL INCOME ACCOUNTING AND PRODUCT MEASUREMENT

Simon Kuznets is considered to be one of the originators of modern national income accounting and product measurement. Kuznets' scholarly work in this field, over which he exerted tremendous influence, has become one of his principal contributions to economic science. The first attempt to measure national income was made in 1669 by Gregory King of Great Britain by measuring the country's national revenue. Further work in this area was done in Great Britain by Richard Stone and James Meade, and in Norway by Ragnar Frisch, Petter Bjerve, and Odd Aukrust.

W.I. King and O. Knuth made the first attempt to estimate the U.S. national income for the period of 1909-1918. Their findings were published by the National Bureau of Economic Research (NBER) in 1921 and 1922. Kuznets' first work on national income accounting, entitled *National Income 1929-32,* provided the U.S. national income estimates and was published in 1934 by the United States Department of Commerce. This was followed by a series of NBER publications, including *National Income and Capital Formation 1919-1935* in 1937, *Commodity Flow and Capital Formation* in 1938, *National Income and Its Composition, 1919-38* (two volumes) in 1941, *National Income: A Summary of Findings* in 1946, and *National Product Since 1869* in 1946. These works provided national income estimates for the United States since 1869.

Kuznets' research on national income accounting and product measurement rested upon the foundation of economic theory and his unique approach to investigation. He first clarified the underlying assumptions, discussed the definitions, described the relevant concepts and variables, and then hypothesized an analytical framework. Next he collected, evaluated, refined, and measured existing data in order to obtain a coherent and consistent estimate of national income. Finally, the national income series and their components were interpreted. The statistical data were critically evaluated for validity and reliability, and directions were provided for making use of the data and shedding light on the problems one may encounter in the practical application of the data.

Kuznets addressed at length the debatable issues of social philosophy and empirical problems involving national income estimates and product measurement. He distinguished between the gross and net national income and advanced the arguments and methods to deal with the concepts of market value, economic life, and depreciation. He also provided the exclusive analysis of the concepts of final goods and intermediate goods. Kuznets analyzed the risk of double counting, over estimation, and underestimation of national income, particularly where the intermediate goods, unreported income, underground economy, and services were involved. In the analysis of the national income and product measurement, Kuznets clarified the crucial concepts of gross and net investment and their measurements. He paid special attention to the connection between the measured value of national output and the economic welfare resulting from it. Kuznets viewed measurement of national income accounting is not only an exercise in social accounting but also an attempt to measure changes in economic welfare.

The framework of national income and product measurement developed by Kuznets is indispensable to policy makers and the government. National income statistics are the basic source of data required to prepare macroeconomic and econometric models and analysis and, hence, the basis for business and government policy decisions and operations. Kuznets' national income measurement technique has been used throughout the world during the past five decades. Kuznets himself assisted several countries, including the United States, in estimating their national incomes. Kuznets' contribution to national income and product measurement inspired further work in this field in the United States and in other countries. Kuznets created the International Association for Research in Income and Wealth to spread the message of national income accounts. He inspired further studies in this field and enhanced the application of the technique of national income accounts and product measurement throughout the world.

THE KUZNETS CYCLES

Simon Kuznets' intellectual growth took place in the midst of the emergence of econometrics and the rise of Keynesianism, yet, he was neither an econometrician nor a Keynesian. He was far more influenced by Mitchell's *Institutionalism*—as elucidated in his 1930 works on economic methodology. Kuznets' initial work was on the empirical analysis of business cycles (1930.)

Kuznets made significant contributions to economic science by analyzing the pattern of fluctuations in economic activity over time. Business cycles are defined as recurrent ups and downs in the levels of economic activity extending over a period of several years. Usually, the business cycles occur at intervals of five to six years, but they can extend over a period of ten to twelve years. Business activity also displays a secular trend, which refers to the recurrent ups and downs of business activity over a long period of time, such as fifty or hundred years. Kuznets identified intermediate cycles of economic fluctuations with an average duration of fifteen to twenty years, and these cycles are popularly known as Kuznets cycles.

Kuznets examined several economic time series for the U.S. and a number of other countries and found a variety of empirical regularities. The findings of this study provide evidence that there are long swings of altering rapid and slow growth in the economic activity consistent with Kuznets cycles. The unemployment rate is the key element for these ups and downs of business activity. When aggregate demand increases, the unemployment rate decreases, and the economy expands toward full-employment and vice versa. In *Capital in the American Economy* (1961), Kuznets provided evidence of similar long swings in labor resource, capital, residential construction, and railroad capital expenditures. He also investigated the relationship between the fluctuations in economic activities and change in demographic variables such as immigration, the rate of population growth, and the growth rate of the labor force. His evidence suggested the positive relationship between economic activities and immigration.

ECONOMIC GROWTH AND RELATED ISSUES

Economic Growth

Simon Kuznets was a pioneer in analyzing the economic growth process of nations, and his empirical interpretation of economic growth provided new insights in understanding the economic and social structures of growth. In his book, *Secular Movements in Production and Prices*, Kuznets emphasized the importance of investigation of the long-term dynamic growth process toward enhancing the understanding of economic phenomenon. Instead of developing a formal model, Kuznets' investigation was empirical in terms of understanding the mechanism of economic growth. He analyzed empirical records to identify and determine the relative importance of, and connections and interconnections among, the contributing factors of economic growth. He identified several connected and interconnected contributing factors of economic growth: the size of population and its composition by age and occupation, increase in production and productivity, structural change in the economy leading to a shift from agriculture to manufacturing and service sectors, technological advancement, quality and proficiency of labor force, the composition and quality of capital, changes in the social and ideological environment, international interdependence through communication technology, international trade and capital movement, and changes in the forms of the market. In the analysis of economic growth processes, Kuznets made original and significant contributions. They may be discussed under the following heads.

Population and Economic Growth

Kuznets paid a great deal of attention to understanding the relationship between economic growth and population. In a number of studies, including *Economic Growth and Structure: Selected Essays* and *Population, Capital, and Growth: Selected Essays*, Kuznets emphasized the benefits of growing populations, both in developed and developing countries, to the growth process, in contrast to the popular neo-Malthusian view suggesting that a higher rate of population growth has negative effects on economic growth. In order to counter the neo-Malthusian arguments, Kuznets argued that according to empirical evidence, growing populations encourage and enhance economic growth. He suggested that a growing population requires more consumer goods, provides incentive for material gain, encourages entrepreneurial activities and large scale production, and creates an environment for urbanization. Kuznets added that increased populations result in larger and younger productive labor forces, including young scientists and technicians. Since the younger work force is more mobile and innovative, they can create a more productive, creative, and stable society. Thus, further economic growth is encouraged and enhanced. Kuznets noted that growing populations in developing countries may impede capital formation. However, in developed countries, they create an environment of more saving, investment, and capital formation.

Economic Growth and Resources, Productivity, and Technology

Kuznets focused his attention on determining the contributing factors of economic growth and their relative importance to the growth process. Kuznets examined data for a number of countries and suggested that labor and capital input contributed to economic growth and productivity. However, the contribution of capital to growth and productivity was relatively low, and over time, the contributing share of both labor and capital have declined in relative terms. He showed that technological change significantly contributed to economic growth. He concluded that the reallocation of labor between more and less productive sectors improved the quality of labor and that technological advancement is a major contributing factor of higher productivity and economic growth.

Economic Growth and Income Distribution

Kuznets examined various aspects of income redistribution in the process of economic growth. However, he primarily concentrated on the redistribution of income between the two major factors of production, labor and capital, and the redistribution of national income among different income groups at the various stages of economic development. Kuznets' analysis suggests that in the long run, the distribution of income shifts to labor's advantage. Over time, the size of the capital output ratio increases, and the relative return of capital declines, resulting in increased shares of labor in national income.

Kuznets formulated a hypothesis, popularly known as Kuznets' inverse-U hypothesis, showing the relationship between per capita income and income inequality at different stages of economic development. Kuznets' inverse-U hypothesis suggests that income inequality increases in the early stages of development, levels in the intermediate stage, and finally moves toward equalization of income. The implication of this hypothesis is that the developing countries experience a sharp increase in income inequality during early stages of development and eventually move toward equalization as it is experienced by developed countries. Kuznets suggested that inequality of the level of assets and savings among different socioeconomic groups and the shift of production and employment from the agriculture sector to manufacturing and service sectors are major factors that result in increased income inequality in early stages of development. At the developed stage, the dynamism of the growing and free economy leads to more equal distribution of assets and income.

Comparative Studies of Economic Growth

Simon Kuznets was a pioneer of comparative studies of many countries' economic growth over time. As the chairman of the Committee of Economic Growth of the Social Science Research Council, he directed an extensive comparative study. The findings of the study resulted in a series of ten articles entitled "Quantitative Aspects of the Economic Growth of Nations," published in *Economic Development and Cultural Change* between October 1956 and January 1967. In the comparative studies of economic growth, Kuznets classified the countries under investigation into groups based on their per capita incomes. The findings suggested that there are certain empirical regularities in the patterns of growth between countries at different levels of development. The empirical regularities are, with respect to distribution of income and expenditure, share and contribution of factors of production, the shifting structure of the economy and the relative combination of various sectors of the economy, such as agriculture, manufacturing, and service. Kuznets broadened his research in this area and published many of his findings in such books as *Modern Economic Growth: Rate, Structure, and Spread* and *Economic Growth of Nations: Total Output and Production Structure.* In these studies, he emphasized the thesis of common patterns of growth, suggesting that the factors and effects of economic growth are similar for different countries. Kuznets also analyzed the sources of errors involved in comparative studies of economic growth.

MACROECONOMIC ANALYSIS

Kuznets made weighty contributions to empirical macroeconomics. Specifically, he provided the empirical foundation for the Keynesian approach to macroeconomics. The statistical data on national income and product measurement provided by Kuznets opened the opportunities for empirical investigation of Keynesian macroeconomic theory. In his work entitled *The General Theory of Employment, Interest and Money,* published in 1936, Keynes shook the foundation of the classical theory of the self-correcting mechanism. The aggregate model of Keynesian economics suggests that the total amount of goods and services, and therefore the level of employment, depends directly on the level of aggregate demand. Aggregate demand is the sum of consumption expenditures, private domestic investment, government expenditures, and net foreign export. The Keynesian theory suggests that it is necessary to stimulate aggregate demand through public spending to increase employment during high unemployment resulting from recession or depression. Kuznets developed the methodology to measure the national income from two perspectives: national income as the sum of total expenditures, which provides the Keynesian aggregate demand, and national income as the sum of the resource payment such as wages, interest, rents, and profits. Thus, Kuznets' national income accounting provided the statistical background for Keynesian macroeconomic policy.

Kuznets studied and empirically established the relationships among the major macroeconomic variables such as income, consumption, saving, investment, and capital formation. In his work, published in 1946, entitled, *National Product Since 1869*, Kuznets analyzed and empirically tested the consumption function and established two important points about consumption behavior. First, consumption is positively related to income, and the consumption/income ratio varies inversely with income during cyclical variation. Second, a stable long-term consumption function indicates the long-term stability of the ratio of consumption to income as income grows along a trend. Kuznets analyzes the gravity of the inventory variations for cyclical fluctuations. In doing so, he rejected the strict application of the acceleration principle. Kuznets suggested that there are wide variations in the accelerator during the business cycles. He also shed light on the actual size and cyclical variations of total inventory investments. Work continues by other economists on the various empirical macroeconomic phenomena based on the initial contributions of Kuznets.

CONCLUSION

Simon Kuznets was one of the few scholars who made a fundamental difference in economics by their outstanding contributions. He developed and established the empirical methodology of economic research and provided new direction for economic analysis. Kuznets was a major originator of modern national income accounting and product measurement, the developer of a new system of seasonal and cyclical measurement, the discoverer of Kuznets cycles, a pioneer in studies of economic and social growth processes, a distinguished scholar in studies of income distribution and economic demography, and a frontiersman of empirical macroeconomic analysis. In addition, Kuznets made momentous contributions to many other areas of economics, including consumption, savings, capital formation, migration, econometrics, industrial structure, international trade, capital movements, and economic efficiency.

RECOMMENDED READINGS

Blaug, Mark. (1985). *Great Economists Since Keynes*. Sussex: Wheatsheaf Books.

Easterlin, Richard and Simon Kuznets (1979). *In International Encyclopedia of the Social Sciences*. Vol. 18 (ed.) David Sills. New York: The Free Press.

Hinck, Harriet and Simon Kuznets. (1989). *Nobel Laureates in Economic Sciences: A Biographical Dictionary*. (ed.) Bernard S. Katz. New York: Garland.

Kuznets, Simon. (1930). *Secular Movements in Production and Prices*. Boston: Houghton Mifflin.

——. (1946). *National Product Since 1869*. Assisted by Lillian Epstein and Elizabeth Jenks. New York: National Bureau of Economic Research.

——. (1953). *Economic Change: Selected Essays in Business Cycles, National Income, and Economic Growth*. New York: W.W. Norton.

——. (1961). *Capital in the American Economy: Its Formation and Financing*. New York: National Bureau of Economic Research.

6

Kenneth Arrow (1921-): The Father of the Arrow's Impossibility Theorem and a Laureate of 1972

Shamim Shakur

BIOGRAPHICAL PROFILE

Kenneth Arrow was born in 1921 in New York City to a middle class family. His father, Harry Arrow, was a self-starter with a poor background. George Feiwel narrates the humble beginnings of young Harry: "It was a case of genuine and harsh economic trade-off: to go to this (Townsend Harris High) school young Harry would have to take the subway; the fare was 5 cents each way which would mean that there would be no meat on the dinner table every day." By the time Kenneth Arrow was born, the Arrow house became relatively affluent but when Kenneth was a young boy, he experienced the devastating effects of the great depression. His father, by then a banker, lost his job with bank closures, and the good life came to an abrupt end. Young Kenneth attended the publicly funded City College of New York (CCNY), from which he graduated in 1940 at the age of nineteen. To this day, Arrow remains an avowed supporter of public education and has mentioned that his college education "was made possible only by the existence of that excellent free institution (CCNY) and the financial sacrifices of my parents." Arrow studied mathematics for both his bachelor's (CCNY) and master's (Columbia University) degrees. It was at the advice of his mentor, the statistician and mathematical economist Harold Hoveling, sweetened by the offer of a fellowship, that Arrow switched to economics. His doctoral studies were interrupted by World War II, in which he served as a weather officer in the U.S. Army Air Corps. Returning from the war, Arrow earned his doctorate from Columbia in 1949 and took office as an assistant professor at Stanford, where he quickly was promoted to a professorship in 1953. Prior to this, he worked at the famous Cowles Commission at the University of Chicago, where he had the opportunity to work with Tjalling Koopmans and Jacob Marschak. Arrow's subsequent jobs took him to Harvard University in 1968 and then back again to Stanford in 1979. He received the John Bates Clark Award of the American Economic Association in 1957. He was also associated with the National Academy of Sciences, the American Philosophical Society, the American Academy of Arts and Sciences, the Econometric Society, the Institute of Mathematical Statistics, and the American Statistical Association. He received honorary degrees from the University of Chicago, the City University of New York, and the University of Vienna, Austria. Arrow married Selma Schweitzer. They have two sons.

INTRODUCTION

Kenneth Arrow shared the economics Nobel Prize with John Hicks in 1972 for "his pioneering contributions to general economic equilibrium theory and welfare theory." Arrow is undoubtedly one of the most brilliant economists of all time. He has a very strong mathematical mind, which allowed him to do so much pathbreaking work in theoretical economics. When his doctoral dissertation was published as *Social Choice and Individual Values* in 1951, the thesis raised questions and controversies that, to date, remain unresolved. The great specialty of Arrow is his passionate mathematical and theoretical insight and its articulate application to social, political, and economic issues. At the beginning of his career, while he worked for the Cowles Commission at the University of Chicago, Arrow was deeply influenced by Jacob Marschak and Tjalling Koopmans–two great economists of the modern age. They were the mentors who stimulated Arrow's mathematical aptitude and directed his quantitative talent to develop theoretical economics.

WHY GENERAL EQUILIBRIUM?

To understand general equilibrium, we should start with the easier, partial equilibrium analysis. In partial equilibrium models, we study individual markets in isolation. We deliberately abstract them from interrelationships that exist between the single market under study and all the other markets in the rest of the economy. In doing so, we are explicitly or implicitly using the *ceteris paribus* (meaning "other things remaining unchanged") assumption. For example, in the case of the law of demand, with respect to the market for a single product, bread, the law would state that "other things remaining same," as the price of bread increases, the quantity demanded for bread will decline. This is clearly a plausible statement, to which real world observations will conform in almost all situations. The problem is that the statement falls short of reality. An increase in the price of bread will invariably affect the demand for and prices of flour and yeast (inputs), cereals and potatoes (substitutes), butter and jam (complements), as well as wages and employment in these industries. To make the story longer, but realistic, changes in these secondary markets will, in turn, affect the original market, that of bread.

To put it simply, "everything depends upon everything else." Neglecting these spillover or feedback effects does not do proper justice to the full impact of the original disturbance, an increase in the price of bread.

What is needed is a model that is capable of identifying this interdependence among all markets and then providing an explicit, simultaneous solution to all variables. A general equilibrium analysis exactly does this. By its very nature, general equilibrium analysis is complicated, time consuming, and expensive. Partial equilibrium analysis remains the method of choice in, by far, the majority of economics research endeavors. But the appeal of simplicity is not defensible when the spillover or feedback effects from other markets are significant. At least that would be the view of an economist of Kenneth Arrow's caliber.

Mathematically, the interdependencies sought in the general equilibrium model are represented as a (rather huge) simultaneous equation system. The solution to this system will produce a set of relative prices, at which the quantity demanded will equal the quantity supplied in each of the markets. This is what is viewed as competitive market equilibrium. The existence of such equilibrium is not a trivial matter. Beyond existence, Arrow, in his Berkeley Symposium paper, showed not only (1) that a competitive equilibrium was Pareto efficient, but (2) that starting from any initial distribution, a Paretoefficient allocation could be obtained by competitive market process. These are known to be the first and second theorems of welfare economics. The policy implications of Arrow's discovery are far reaching. Among other things, it implies that governments wishing to redistribute income from the rich to the poor should not interfere directly with people's consumption behavior (similar analysis applies to input choice in production.) Governments and social institutions cannot be as well aware of individuals' preferences as individuals are of themselves. Thus policies like food stamps, subsidized housing, or low interest student loans are Pareto inferior to neutral policies like lump-sum transfers and capital levies in that the latter do not interfere with the operation of competitive market forces.

THE ARROW'S IMPOSSIBILITY THEOREM

Arrow used his mastery over binary relations theory and his clever wit to challenge the most fundamental of free democratic institution, that of majority voting rule. Arrow's impossibility theorem shows that there is no ethically acceptable method for translating individual preferences into collective societal preferences. The theorem casts doubt on the ability of the political institution we dearly call democracy to function. Naturally, Arrow's theorem, which originally appeared as a monograph in 1951, kicked off a long and serious debate among economists, philosophers, and political scientists alike. Their research has not been successful to break the stalemate. To understand the impossibility, we should start by stating the minimum conditions that social choices must meet in order to reflect individual preferences. Arrow originally listed four such conditions, which attained the status of being "four axioms," as transitivity, Pareto efficiency, interdependence of irrelevant alternatives, and non-dictatorship.

Transitivity

Social choices must be consistent. In other words, if building a hospital is preferred to building a college, and building a college is preferred to building a correctional facility, then building a hospital will be preferred to building a correctional facility.

Pareto Efficiency

If every individual prefers having a hospital built in his locality over building a college, then society's ranking must prefer building a hospital over building a college.

Independence of Irrelevant Alternatives

Society's ranking of two alternatives should depend only on individuals' rankings of these alternatives and not on any other irrelevant alternative. Thus, the collective ranking of a publicly funded healthcare plan and free college education should not depend on how individuals rank either of these alternatives relative to sending a peacekeeping contingent to the Middle East.

Non-dictatorship

Social preferences must not reflect the preferences of only a single individual. In other words, an alternative that would otherwise have been the society's choice must never be rejected just because some individual came to regard it favorably. For democratic decision making, these criteria all seem only logical. However, Arrow has demonstrated that violation of at least one of these four criteria becomes inevitable as one tries to choose among all possible sets of alternatives. In other words, democratic social choice becomes impossible. The difficulties encountered can be illustrated as follows:

Table 6.1 Paradox of Voting

	Hospital	College	Correctional Facility
A	High	Medium	Low
B	Low	High	Medium
C	Medium	Low	High

IMPOSSIBILITY OF DEMOCRATIC DECISION MAKING

According to the above preference table, (1) both A and C prefer building a hospital to building a college; (2) both A and B prefer building a college to building a correctional facility; (3) both B and C prefer building a correctional facility to building a hospital. Thus, the majority (two out of three) prefers building a hospital to building a college, and building a college to building a correctional facility. According to Arrow's first axiom, transitivity, the majority would rank the building of a hospital higher than that of a correctional facility. But then look at the preference table one more time. It also says, the majority (two out of three) prefers the building of a correctional facility to that of a hospital. Confused? The majority voting rule that lies at the core of democratic decision making can very well lead to intransitive patterns in social choice. Rankings of the majority are inconsistent with the rankings of the individuals making up the majority. We, especially the policy makers, frequently talk about improving society's aggregate welfare (what economists refer to as the social welfare function). Yet Arrow pointed out, as demonstrated in the above preference table, that such social welfare functions cannot be arrived at consistently by democratic voting principles.

It should be noted that the voting paradox illustrated in the preceding paragraphs is rooted in Arrow's fourth axiom (non-dictatorship), which requires that only the voters' rankings of alternatives be admissible, not the intensity with which the alternatives are preferred. Thus if half (or any given percentage) of the society only mildly prefers that a local government expenditure be directed at organizing an exhibition football match, while the other half (or the same percentage) strongly prefers spending the money toward the city's homeless population, Arrow's fourth axiom would require that these intensities be disregarded in decision making. Dictatorial decision, which would be in violation of axiom four, is the only panacea of this stalemate. Despite its discomforting outcome, Arrow's *Social Choice and Individual Values*, where this impossibility theorem was written, remains his most frequently cited work. Another Nobel laureate, Paul Samuelson, called Arrow's impossibility theorem to "a first-rate contribution to man's body of knowledge." Between 1966 and 1983, the publication had been cited 1,203 times, more than twice the number for his second most cited publication, *General Competitive Analysis*, which was co-authored by Frank Hahn.

EXISTENCE OF GENERAL EQUILIBRIUM

After the impossibility theorem, Arrow's next assault was on the fundamental question of the existence of competitive general equilibrium and the validity of its conclusions widely accepted in the economics literature. Like many of Arrow's works, the proof is difficult to comprehend, even to the hard-core, mathematically inclined economists. Arrow's contributions in this area may be simplified for general readers in the following manner. To be fair, Arrow was not the first to introduce a general equilibrium model to economics profession. That accolade goes to the nineteenth-century French economist Leon Walras. Walras, however, was not a sophisticated mathematician. According to Walras, the existence of simultaneous equilibrium in all markets was a simple matter of counting the number of equations rendered by the demand and supply relations and the unknowns, which are the prices. If the numbers match, a solution exists that is also unique. Economists, including Walras himself, had a hunch that an adequate proof of existence of competitive equilibrium must involve more than a mere counting of equations and unknowns. As expected, it turned out that, this conception is too naive. The equality of the number of equations and unknowns does not guarantee that a solution exists, and when it does, there is no guarantee of its uniqueness. Though abstract, the existence of equilibrium is fundamental to any economic analysis. The concern here is whether an economic model that is used extensively to draw various conclusions about equilibrium can itself ensure the possibility of an equilibrium under the conditions it specifies. For if it does not, all conclusions drawn from the model are, as Tjalling Koopmans calls them, "vacuous." And yet, the profession simply lacked the mathematical tools necessary to take the proof of existence to its recognized level.

Arrow teamed up with Gerard Debreu to complete the task. Together, they published their results in a seminal paper titled, "Existence of Equilibrium for a Competitive Economy" in *Econometrica*. The Arrow-Debreu model, as it has come to be known, provides the modern proof for the existence of competitive equilibrium using new mathematical techniques, in particular, the fixed point theorem. In essence, Arrow and Debreu discovered the necessity of forward markets for the existence of an equilibrium. In forward markets, participants can make a spot (current) payment for a future (forward) delivery, or accept a spot delivery against promise of a future payment. Such markets exist in many commodities in financial exchanges throughout the world. But the Arrow-Debreu proof of existence requires such forward markets in all goods and services, a requirement that cast doubt on the usefulness of the general equilibrium theory. Much to the relief of the profession, Arrow later went on to show that the general equilibrium theory was quite robust in its content, such that it had relevance even to economies where forward markets are missing. This time, Arrow was aided by a well-known English economist from Cambridge University, Frank Hahn.

ADVERSE SELECTION AND MORAL HAZARD

Although a theoretician by all measures, Arrow showed an exceptional ability to apply general theorems to specific, practical situations. In Arrow's own words, "The tasks of economic theory include but are certainly not confined to the abstract development of very broad principles. Indeed, even to one whose interests are largely theoretical, specific problems have frequently suggested new general principles. Thus, my work contains both successive developments of large themes and much that is opportunistic and specific." One of Arrow's colleagues from Harvard, Jerry R. Green, comments: "Arrow's leadership in choosing abstract theoretical models to analyze questions in applied economics and policy analysis is surely one of the most important impetuses behind the ready acceptance of theory in the applied fields. Arrow never forces a theoretical model on a particular subject just because of its higher level of abstraction. He understands very well the basic economics and institutional features, and then chooses the model carefully without theoretical overkill, to address exactly the main economic point.

One such example can be found in the twin principle of adverse selection and moral hazards, and its application to the insurance industry. Let's take Arrow's example of life insurance to explain adverse selection. A population at risk of an untoward event can be divided into segments (alcoholic, smoker, multiple sex partners, etc.) with differing probabilities of occurrence of the event. An individual contemplating purchasing a life insurance policy may know the segment to which he belongs and hence the risk factor associated with himself. If the insurers cannot distinguish the insured by respective risk, because of lack of full information, they are then constrained to offer a uniform premium for all. At any uniform premium, the high-risk individuals will buy excessive coverage, and the low-risk individuals will buy less. The actuarial expectation thus becomes more adverse for the insurer, than it would be with equal participation by all, or under a discriminatory premium that reflects risk associated with each segment. This necessitates the creation of a much wider array of insurance premiums based on differential risk.

A related problem that applies to even wider areas, including public policy, is that of moral hazard. In this case, for example, an insurance policy may induce changes in the behavior of the insured in a way that increases the risk against which the insurance is written. In case of health insurance, it may mean over consumption of health care services (as the price of health services to the insured decrease). This may also reduce incentive on the part of both the physician and the patient to shop for cheaper hospitalization or diagnostic procedures. In case of auto or home insurance, it may mean being negligent in locking the doors. The moral hazard problem is accentuated if the book value of the automobile or the house is perceived by the insured to be greater than its expected resale value. Recognizing such moral hazard issues, the insurer frequently attempts to minimize the adverse effects by soliciting information on the insured, putting a ceiling on the sum that can be insured, imposing a deductible, or requiring that the insured obtain multiple quotations from potential service providers. The insurer wants to make sure that the event against which the insurance policy is sold is completely exogenous to the insured, something that cannot be made foolproof. In the case of public policy, for example, guaranteed old age provision may create disincentive to save for retirement, or unemployment insurance may discourage the seeking of employment.

In all of the above examples of adverse selection and moral hazards, insurance produces disincentive effects, which cost the society as, ultimately, premiums will have to be increased for all. The paradox is this: the most socially desirable insurance scheme would be the one that has the most discriminatory premium structure. And yet, politically, it is appealing to equalize premiums on equity grounds. This is misleading. As Arrow points out, in the case of health insurance, for example, "This constitutes, in effect, a redistribution of income from those with low propensity to illness to those with a high propensity. The equalization, of course, could not in fact be carried through if the markets were genuinely competitive."

DISTRIBUTIVE JUSTICE

Arrow was critical of societies that accept the prevailing distribution of material goods as unquestionably right. He called them static societies where religious beliefs led people to accept existing distribution of material rewards as the work of a divine justice. In his 1976 speech to the University of British Columbia in Vancouver, Arrow asserted that as members of a more dynamic society, we cannot unthinkingly assert that "what is, is just." His concern for social justice led him to cry out against discrimination in the job market. While staying within the framework of the standard neoclassical analysis, Arrow demonstrated that discrimination is costly for firms. By channeling capital to nondiscriminatory firms, which ceteris paribus has less cost, competitive markets actually fosters social justice. To use Arrow's own words, "Only the least discriminatory firms survive. Indeed, if there were any firms which did not discriminate at all, these would be the only ones to survive the competitive struggle." Arrow blames imperfect information for the perpetuation of wage and income gaps between the advantaged and the disadvantaged groups in society. If employers have a preconceived notion (because of lack of information) that women or members of certain ethnic groups have lower productivity, then they will offer them a lower wage. The victims of discrimination, believing that high paying jobs are not for them, are then discouraged from developing the skills necessary for high productivity. When the belief passes on to the next generation, it becomes a vicious circle. But then, it cannot happen in a perfectly competitive market which assumes full information.

CONCLUSION

Arrow is one the very few economists (like Samuelson and Debreu) whose works have been so technical in nature that they are hardly accessible even to economists holding Ph.D. degrees. Thus Nobel laureates like Kuznets, Leontief, and Myrdal denounced the use of high-level mathematics by Arrow, Debreu, and Samuelson. However, Arrow's mathematics is not emanated from his passion for complex equations; rather, it comes from his deep concern to understand the nature of social and economic issues. For example, he modeled the competitive equilibrium process not to impress the profession with mathematical jargons but to understand the balance between the amounts of goods and services some individuals want to supply and the amounts the others want to buy. Arrow has made significant contributions to a wide range of theoretical issues in economics. His works are highly original and of superb quality. Arrow has been an economist of an exceptional caliber, no doubt, but he is also known to be a man of great personality. George Feiwel, who has summarized the life and achievements of Arrow in two volumes, writes: "Great scholars are not always admirable individuals. This is not true of Arrow."

RECOMMENDED READINGS

Arrow, Kenneth J. (1949)."On the Use of Winds in Flight Planning," *Journal of Meteorology*. Vol. 6, pp. 150-59.

——. (1951). *Social Choice and Individual Values*. New Haven: Yale University Press.

——. (1951). "An Extension of the Basic Theorems of Classical Welfare Economics," *Proceedings of the Second Berkeley Symposium on Mathematical Statistics and Probability*. (ed.) J. Neyman. Los Angeles: University of California Press, pp. 507-32.

——. (1963). "Uncertainty and the Welfare Economics of Medical Care," *American Economic Review*. Vol. 53, pp. 941-69.

——. (1971). *Essays in the Theory of Risk Bearing*. Chicago: Markham.

——. (1973). "The Theory of Discrimination," *Discrimination in Labor Markets*. (ed.) Orley Ashenfelter and Albert Rees. Princeton: Princeton University Press, pp. 3-33.

——. (1982, January). "Risk Perception in Psychology and Economics," *Economic Inquiry*.

——. (1984). *Social Choice and Justice–Collected Papers of Kenneth J. Arrow*. Oxford: Blackwell.

Arrow, Kenneth J., and Gerard Debreu. (1954). "Existence of Equilibrium for a Competitive Economy," *Econometrica*. Vol. 20, pp. 265-90.

Feiwel, George R. (ed.) (1987). *Arrow and the Foundations of the Theory of Economic Policy*. New York: Macmillan.

7

John Hicks (1904-1989):
An Architect of the Famous IS-LM
Framework and a Laureate of 1972

Shamim Shakur

BIOGRAPHICAL PROFILE

John Hicks was born in Leamington Spa, Warwick, England, in 1904. His father, Edward Hicks, used to work for a local paper as journalist. Early academic achievements won Hicks a scholarship to study mathematics at Clifton College (1917-1922), and to the University at Balliol College, Oxford (1922-1926). After his first year of study at Oxford, Hicks shifted his interests away from mathematics and toward politics, philosophy and economics. His performance in college was quite average. In Hicks' own words, "I finished with a second-class degree and no adequate qualifications." Market forces had their influence on Hicks' choice of career. During the period when Hicks was attending college, the demand for economists was very strong. As Hicks later confessed, "I was advised that economics was an expanding industry, so I would have a better chance of employment if I went that way. So I did." Hicks was quite correct in his choice. His first professional job came immediately after he completed college. It was a temporary lectureship at the prestigious London School of Economics (LSE) in 1926, where he remained until 1935. It was at LSE that Hicks came into contact with heavyweights in economics like Roy Allen, Friedrich Hayek, Nicholas Kaldor, Abba Lerner and Lionel Robbins, to name a few. The next three years, Hicks spent as a fellow at Cambridge University, where he was also married to an economist, Ursula Kathleen Webb (1896-1985). Together, they wrote extensively on applied policy matters. Besides economics, they also shared their passion for gardening. His three years of work at Cambridge also produced Hicks's most recognized piece, *Value and Capital* (1939). In 1938, Hicks was appointed to the

Jevons Chair at Manchester University, and in 1946, Hicks returned to Cambridge, this time to spend the rest of his professional career, first as a fellow and then as a professor at Nuffield College. A year after he was knighted (1964) for his services to economic science, Sir John Hicks retired from active service. Hicks died in 1989.

INTRODUCTION

John Hicks, along with Kenneth Arrow, got the economics Nobel Prize in 1972 for his "pioneering contributions to general economic equilibrium theory and welfare theory." Although the two economists made their marks in the areas cited, they belonged to different generations and certainly did not work together. It was, however, Hick's *Value and Capital* (1939) that laid the foundation for Arrow's subsequent developments of the general equilibrium theory in the fifties. As Arrow admits, "Ever since I encountered Hicks's *Value and Capital* while I was still a graduate student, I had the aim of completing and extending his vision of the economic system in its purest form. The idea that the economic world was a general system, with all parts interdependent, seemed to me to be an essential of good analysis." Like Arrow, Hicks made fundamental contributions in areas that go far beyond the domain of general equilibrium and welfare theory.

A MODERN THEORY OF AN OLD TOPIC

Even more celebrated than the constant elasticity of substitution (CES), production function is the concept of indifference curves, another Hicksian invention. There is probably not a single textbook in economics that does not employ this venerable tool. In his classic paper with R.G.D. Allen, Hicks brought the doomsday for the then prevalent marginal utility theory of consumer behavior and firmly established the new indifference theory, which has stood the test of time. The Hicks-Allen paper laid the foundation for the modern demand theory. Until then, the consumer demand theory was based on the notion of cardinal utility–that utility could be quantified on a cardinal scale. Utility was to be measured in units called "utils." Thus, if consuming an apple gave a consumer 200 utils while an orange produce 100 utils, the former was said to render twice as much satisfaction to the consumer than the latter. Although considered crucial for demand analysis, the cardinal approach to utility always bothered economists since utility is, by its very nature, subjective. This was considered unduly restrictive. Using the new concepts of indifference curves and budget lines, Hicks and Allen were able to derive all standard conclusions of cardinal demand analysis without relying on objective measures. Enter the world of ordinal utility. Under this later approach, consumers need only to rank their preferences, say which basket of commodities they rank higher compared to alternative baskets, and need not say by how much. "To take an arithmetic illustration: successive positions might be numbered 1, 2, 3, 4, 5; or 1, 4, 9, 16, 25; or any increasing series we like to take. So far as the actual behavior of any individual can possibly show, any such series would do absolutely as well as any other."

As an added bonus, the Hicks-Allen indifference curve-budget line framework is capable of clearly demonstrating the substitution and income effects of a price change with relative ease. Hicks acknowledged the similarity in the works published earlier by Eugen Slutsky. However, it did not create much impact until Hicks and Allen's paper surfaced. "How Slutsky, a Russian, came to publish his paper in an Italian journal does not seem to be known; neither in Italy, nor in Russia, nor anywhere else, did it make any impact. It had to be rediscovered after our work had come out." The Hicks-Allen approach to demand analysis is as pervasive today as it was when their 1934 *Economica* paper was published. The indifference curve-budget line apparatus is possibly the most widely used diagnostic tool used in economics textbooks and scholarly publications alike.

THE GENERAL EQUILIBRIUM MODEL

The most acclaimed piece of Hicks' work was *Value and Capital*. "They gave me a Nobel Prize for my work on 'general equilibrium and welfare economics.' The former, I took it, referred to *Value and Capital*; the latter to a number of papers between 1939 and 1946, which laid down main lines of what came to be called the 'New Welfare Economics' or Kaldor-Hicks Welfare Economics'–for it was Kaldor's note on 'welfare propositions in economics' that my work started." The book addressed several fronts. It started by way of exposition of the theory of household and firm behavior and their interrelationships. Any change in the price of a commodity, Hicks argued, will have a "substitution effect" that is invariably negative (quantity demanded moving in opposite direction to the price change.) For a given money income, agents always move toward the (substitute) product which is now more attractive, price-wise. The second component from the price change, the income effect, can have either sign, depending on the "normality" (positive income effect) or "inferiority" (negative income effect) of the commodity. This is what now is taught in almost all intermediate microeconomics courses, and a more rigorous mathematical treatment is usually reserved for advanced courses.

Later in the book, Hicks introduced time into the general equilibrium analysis to examine the more difficult area of dynamic stability of such models. Specifically, Hicks derived the conditions under which an economic system would return to equilibrium from a disequilibrium state (dynamic stability). Hicks invented the concept of "temporary equilibrium" to explain an inherently difficult dynamic process. Hicks conceived of time as a stream of short periods, called "weeks." At the start of the week, on "Mondays," agents would form their expectations (about the relevant economic variables) for that week. The agents would then optimize their activities (production, consumption, money demand, etc.) for the week based on these expectations. This is how the economy would work to a temporary equilibrium during the week. At the start of the following week, the next Monday, agents would revise their expectations, based on new information or learning from previous week's mistakes. The economy would leap forward toward a new temporary equilibrium. The process would continue.

Hicks was aware of the shortcomings of such a simplistic model. "I wanted to avoid so much happening, so that my markets could reflect propensities (and expectations) as they are at a moment. So it was that I made my markets open only on a Monday; what actually happened during the ensuing week was not to affect them. This was a very artificial device, not (I would think now) much to be recommended." Using such an artificial method, Hicks was able to demonstrate the inevitability of economic fluctuations whenever expectations were elastic with respect to price changes. There was nothing automatic in the free market economy that would guarantee its return to equilibrium. The preceding statement could easily pass as a quotation from Keynes. But the reasons put forward by the two for such dynamic instability were quite different. Hicks saw some "special reasons" that give the economic system "a sufficient amount of stability to enable it to carry on, but it is not inherently and necessarily stable." Some of these special reasons Hicks cited are jobless workers, long-term contracts and rigid prices. Quite unhappily, Hicks found the best (price) stabilizer in unemployment.

HICKS ON KEYNES

The 1930s was a time when John Keynes revolutionized macroeconomics with his publication of *The General Theory of Employment, Interest and Money* in 1936. Hicks was prompt to write two reviews on Keynes' *General Theory*. The first failed to make much impact, but the second article, "Mr. Keynes and the Classics," did. It was in this later paper that Hicks introduced the famous IS-LM diagram, which has found its place in to almost every macroeconomics textbook until now. Keynes' *General Theory* is a difficult book to read, and an enormous volume of literature has been written since its publication to make its contents more palatable to aspiring economists. The central theme of Keynes' book is an attack on "classical economics," which believes in the magical powers of the "invisible hand" (meaning free markets) to guarantee full-employment equilibrium in the economy. With the Western economies going through their worst recession, Keynes saw the world around him in equilibrium at less than its full-employment level, something he coined as "unemployment equilibrium." But maybe because of his confusing writing style, Keynes' message was not hitting home with the more average reader.

Hicks understood that Keynes was trying to draw a clear distinction between the goods (and services) market and the money market. To be in equilibrium, the former requires an equality between planned saving and investment, to be brought about by changes in total income. The latter (money market) equilibrium requires an equality between the demand for money (what Keynes coined as liquidity preference) and the supply of money, to be brought about by changes in the interest rate. For the overall economy to be in equilibrium, at the classical full employment or the Keynesian-under employment, both the markets will have to be in equilibrium simultaneously. So Hicks invented this diagram with income (GDP) on the horizontal axis and interest rate on the vertical axis. The IS (investment equal saving) curve plots all combinations of income and interest rate at which the goods market is in equilibrium, whereas the LM (liquidity preference or money demand equal money supply) plots all combinations of the variables on axes at which the money market is in equilibrium. The mathematical counterpart of the

IS-LM geometry was shown by Hicks in the form of two reduced form equations (one in which the right-hand side variables are exogenous, that is, determined outside of the model), representing equilibrium in the goods market and the money market.

Hicks then went on to point to the conflict between Keynes and the classics, in terms of their beliefs on the shapes of these IS-LM curves. Keynes' belief would translate into a completely flat LM curve, because of "liquidity trap," a situation in which interest rates are at their historical lows such that people believe they cannot go any lower. Thus, at any rate of money supply, people only hold on to the extra cash, rendering money supply ineffective. Such a situation (Great Depression) possibly prevailed during Keynes' writing of *The General Theory*. No wonder Keynes advocated expansionary fiscal policy, which will shift the IS curve to the right, as a cure for the depression. Hicks showed that in the intermediate situation, when both the IS and the LM curves have finite slopes, an expansionary fiscal policy will also raise the interest rate, thereby crowding out some of the private investments.

NEO-KEYNESIANS ON HICKS

Most of the Keynesians do not seem to like the IS-LM framework. Robert Clower, one of Hicks' students, is critical of the IS-LM framework as being a static equilibrium model that cannot justifiably explain the dynamic, disequilibrium nature of Keynes' theory. In his subsequent paper on the theory of the trade cycle, Hicks aptly demonstrated the adaptability of his model to dynamic developments, especially with respect to the determination of investment. As always, Hicks is humble about his contributions: "The IS-LM diagram, which is widely, though not universally, accepted as a convenient synopsis of Keynesian theory, is a thing for which I cannot deny that I have some responsibility. For it first saw the light in my own paper 'Mr. Keynes and the Classics.' I have, however, not concealed that as time has gone on, I have myself become dissatisfied with it. 'That diagram,' I said in 1975, 'is now much less popular with me than I think it still is with many other people.' "

Apart from the analysis of the IS-LM, Hicks and Keynes had important differences in their modeling approaches. Hicks had a flex-price model under perfectly competitive conditions, in which all prices (including wages) are flexible. In Keynes' model, prices are relatively "sticky"and the level of wages was determined exogenously. Perfect competition was replaced by highly organized labor unions in the input market and powerful monopolies with administered prices in the output market. In other words, Keynes' was a fix-price model. The flex/fix price controversy was elaborated by Hicks in his later book, again on Keynes, *The Crisis in Keynesian Economics*, published in 1974. Thus, in the Keynesian model, which is consistent with unemployment, an increase in government expenditure, for example, has the direct and almost immediate impact on (real) output and employment, rather than on (nominal) prices and wages. Hicks' was a full-employment model, where such fiscal stimulus will impact on (flexible) prices.

WELFARE ECONOMICS

Besides contributions to the general equilibrium theory, Hicks was also cited for his work in welfare economics. His first essay on the subject appeared in *The Economic Journal*. Three years later, Hicks wrote his own textbook, *The Social Framework*. Hicks' concern was how to come up with a measure of welfare change such that a change in the economy can be described, unambiguously, as an improvement in productive efficiency. The dominant criterion for welfare change is the Pareto criteria (named after the Italian economist, Vilfredo Pareto). According to this criterion, a change in the economy can be regarded as a Pareto improvement if it leaves no person worse off and at least one person strictly better off compared with the initial state. Uncontroversial, but hardly useful for practical policy purposes.

Hicks teamed up with Nicholas Kaldor to develop some compensation criteria for welfare change. Any economic policy, no matter how noble, will always leave some section of the population worse off compared to the initial state. A policy to cut defense spending, for example, will free up public funds to finance healthcare or social welfare projects, which will benefit most American people. But it will also mean layoffs in the defense sector, which will lobby actively to block such a move. If the benefit to most American people exceeds the loss to those in the defense sector, and the former (majority of Americans) compensate the latter (those currently employed in the defense sector), then everyone would be better off with reduced defense spending. He argued that such policy measures should not be abandoned just because interpersonal comparisons of utility require value judgment. "When any considerable improvement, in our sense, is made, it ought to be possible actually to give compensation, out of the gains of the gainers, to cover the losses of the losers." Pareto would not agree with this, which also renders Pareto improvement criteria quite impractical. With appropriate compensation criteria, it would be within the government's power to compensate the losers to raise net welfare to the society. By developing such a criteria, the equivalent variation measure, Hicks also laid the theoretical foundation of the modern cost-benefit analysis, which has become the tool of choice of project appraisers and policy makers.

Hicks used the Marshallian concept of consumer's surplus to measure the loss for compensation purposes. Marshall defined consumer's surplus as the excess of the price that which he would be willing to pay rather than go without the thing, over the price he actually does pay. Diagrammatically, it turns out to be the curvilinear triangle under the demand curve, called the Marshallian Triangle. This measure ran into a great deal of criticism, as it crucially depends on the assumption of constancy of the marginal utility of money. But Hicks had too much respect for Marshall and his measure of consumer's surplus to let such criticism pass. In a separate chapter titled "The Rehabilitation of Consumer's Surplus," Hicks states, "The discovery is being made that consumer's surplus is an analytical tool of great power, whose use is perfectly legitimate if proper precautions are taken. Some of the newer developments in economic theory have been made much poorer and less significant than they might have been made, as a result of the fashion of avoiding consumer's surpluses." Hicks salvaged the Marshallian measure by showing that constancy of marginal utility of money is justified whenever the consumer spends only a small proportion of his total income on the commodity in question or when the particular change does not involve a large net change in real incomes. Hicks then went on to adjust the Marshallian ordinary demand curve so as to allow for the effects of the changes in real income as one passes along the curve. The result is the Hicksian compensated demand curve, a tool that has found a permanent place in welfare economics literature.

CONCLUSION

After the end of World War II, Hicks, it seems, took some time away from theory to concentrate on more applied work. Together with his wife, Ursula, he wrote several books and articles on public finance. They advised the British government on its tax policy. They also counseled the governments of several commonwealth nations, including India and Jamaica, in running their finances in their postcolonial transition. The year Hicks retired from his professorship also witnessed the publication of another of his landmark books, *Capital and Growth.* It was in this book that Hicks introduced the distinction between fix-price and flex-price markets, which he used to explain the differences between Keynesians and the classical economists. Another new label, the theory of the traverse, he used to study stable and optimal growth paths. Criticisms on Hicks' methods led him to refine the concept twenty years later in *Methods of Economic Dynamics. A Theory of Economic History* provides the reader with an analysis of economic institutions and events over centuries. He draws insights into the emergence of money and the decline of the slave trade. His view that modern economic growth is led by a series of impulses coming mainly from science-based technological improvements is ingrained in this book.

Hicks is considered to be one of the most outstanding economic theorists of this century. As the great toolmaker, Hicks is remembered by graduate students as the prescription for passing the doctoral comprehensive exams. The IS-LM diagrams, the indifference curve analysis, the compensated demand curve, the equivalent variation measure of welfare change and the flex/fix price model are all components of Hicks' tool kit. Anyone who has a grasp of this tool kit definitely has an excellent grasp of economics.

RECOMMENDED READINGS

Hicks, John R. (1932). *The Theory of Wages.* New York: Macmillan.

Hicks, John R. and Allen, R.G.D. (1934, February). "A Reconsideration of the Theory of Value," *Economica.* February, pp. 52-76.

——. (1937)."Mr. Keynes and the Classics," *Econometrica.* Vol. 5, pp. 147-59.

——. (1939). *Value and Capital.* Oxford: Clarendon Press.

———. (1939, December). "The Foundations of Welfare Economics," *The Economic Journal*. Vol. 49, pp. 696-712.

———. (1942). *The Social Framework*. Oxford: Clarendon Press.

———. (1950). *Contribution to the Theory of the Trade Cycle*. Oxford: Clarendon Press.

———. (1974). *The Crisis in Keynesian Economics*. New York: Basic Books.

———. (1981-1983). *Collected Essays on Economic Theory*. Vols. 1-3. Oxford: Basil Blackwell.

8

Wassily Leontief (1906-1999):
The Founder of Input-Output
Analysis and the Laureate of 1973

Lorenzo Garbo

BIOGRAPHICAL PROFILE

Wassily Leontief was born in Saint Petersburg, Russia, in 1906. When he was very young he witnessed the impact of the First World War in Russia and the political turmoil resulting from the socialist revolution there. He entered the University of Leningrad in 1921 and studied philosophy, sociology and then economics. He received the degree of Learned Economist at the University of Leningrad in 1925 and completed his doctoral studies in 1928 at the University of Berlin, Germany. He received his Ph.D. at the age of 22. Before completing the terminal degree, he joined the University of Keil. As a member of the staff of the Institute for World Economics at the University of Kiel from 1927 to 1930, Leontief engaged in research on the derivation of statistical demand and supply curves. This academic work was interrupted in 1929 by a twelve-month stay in China as advisor to the Chinese Ministry of Railroads. In 1931, he immigrated to the United States and got a job with the National Bureau of Economic Research and the department of economics at Harvard University, where he received a $2,000 research grant to begin the compilation of the first input-output tables of the American economy. In 1946, after the publication of "Structure of the American Economy, 1919-1929," he became a professor of economics at Harvard University, where he organized the Harvard Economic Research Project in 1948 and served as its director until the closure of the project in 1973. From 1953 until his resignation at Harvard in 1975, Leontief held the Henry Lee Chair of Political Economy. After his resignation from Harvard, he continued his studies at the Institute for Economic Analysis at New York University, where he became a university professor in 1983. Leontief received honorary doctoral degrees from the universities of Brussels, York, Louvain and Paris. He was a member of the National Academy of Sciences, the American Academy of Arts and Sciences, the British Academy and the Royal Statistical Society in London. He served as the president of the Econometric Society in 1954 and of the American Economic Association in 1970. Leontief died in 1999, leaving his wife–writer Estelle Marks–his daughter, Svetlana Alpers, and two grandsons.

INTRODUCTION

Wassily Leontief got the economics Nobel Prize in 1973 "for the development of the input-output method and for its application to important economic problems." Leontief, the fourth American to receive the Nobel Prize in economics, stands as one of the fathers of the "new" methodology for economic analysis of the twentieth century, bridging the philosophical world of economics of the 1800s with the rigor of mathematical and statistical investigation of more recent research. Robert Solow, one of his pupils in the years of Harvard, describes his mentor as: "I learned from him the spirit as well as the substance of modern economic theory." The most important and pervasive heritage of Leontief's work is the balance between impeccable philosophical and anthropological reasoning and technical sophistication. Clearly Leontief was not only an economist. Being aware that so much still had to be discovered, he extended his philosophical understanding to the acceptance of interdisciplinary work as a means for scientific progress and to the use of the technical tools of modern economic analysis without ever losing the ultimate task of scientific investigation, that is, to explain and illuminate reality. Leontief introduced to economic analysis the importance of understanding the specific components of reality before attempting a general grasp, an approach that anticipated by fifty years what is today known as the "microfoundation" of economics, asserting that the unreality of the aggregative approach could be reduced only through the use of less aggregative models. More specifically, since the 1930s, Leontief's work has become synonymous with *input-output*, the analysis that lent the title to his Nobel lecture, "Structure of the World Economy: Outline of a Simple Input-Output Formulation."

His contributions became so central in the economics literature that it is almost impossible to find economics chapters where something is not of a Leontief type. A few examples include The Leontief Production Function, that describes a technology where factors of production are combined in fixed proportions; The Leontief Utility Function, which indicates that the consumption goods under investigations are complements, giving satisfaction only if they are made available in given proportions (one more right shoe gives some satisfaction only if accompanied by one more left shoe); The Leontief Paradox, which became the shortcut for the results of the complex empirical investigation that showed that the United States in 1947 was not, as commonly believed, a country relatively more endowed with capital than labor with respect to the rest of the world. Though he was the son of a professor of labor economics, Leontief modestly "refers to luck as a deciding influence on choosing economics." At the early age of twenty-five he joined the department of economics at Harvard University and the National Bureau for Economic Research. Luck made him publish *The Economy as a Circular Flow*–his doctoral dissertation–in 1925. By luck, he also published his first article in economics: "The Balance of the Russian Economy: A Methodological Investigation."

A COURAGEOUS INTERPRETATION
OF ECONOMIC THOUGHT

The subtitle for this section could have been: "Leontief and the Theory of General Interdependence." As mentioned earlier, Leontief reached the National Bureau of Economic Research and Harvard University in 1931, in the aftermath of the Great Depression and during the stimulating academic debate between Cambridge, England, and Cambridge, Massachusetts. The titles of his sharp and elegant writings of those years are by themselves a clear indication of how actively Leontief participated at the highest intellectual peaks of those developments of economic thought; examples are "The Fundamental Assumption of Mr. Keynes' Monetary Theory of Unemployment," "Implicit Theorizing: a Methodological Criticism of the Neo-Cambridge School," "The Significance of Marxian Economics for Present-day Economic Theory," "Postulates: Keynes' *General Theory* and the Classicists."

Leontief's contribution to the economic science, therefore, began in years of academic turmoil, years in which several attacks were directed to disqualify the classical apparatus of economics. It was an ideal intellectual environment in which imperfectly structured new approaches could find enthusiastic followers even in high academic circles. Meanwhile, Leontief stood as an unforgiving filter of ideas lacking in substance. The common denominator of his contributions certainly can be summarized by intellectual honesty, logical perfection and consistency of purpose. His disqualification of the neo-Cambridge approach, for instance, is mostly based on methodological inconsistencies. He wrote: "The difference between the two lines of thought (Neo-Cambridge and Classical) appears to be neither a disagreement in final scientific outlooks, nor a divergence in identification of the immediate objects of observation–the economic realities of common experience. With both, the point of departure and the ultimate goal are essentially the same. What is different is the intermediate path." He made clear that while a skillful use of definitions allows deductive analysis to reach the "remotest stages of implication," an unskillful use of them leads to logical mistakes and dangerous "implicit theorizing."

Leontief's concern was not restricted to his criticism of the neo-Cambridge school. He concluded his 1947 article, which reviews both Keynes' and classical approaches: "The liberal economist of the past century was prone to overlook the troublesome distributive aspects of economic change. Keynes, as Karl Marx before him, did well in pointing out this indeed most serious omission. They seemed to press, however, for reconstruction of the whole foundation in order to mend a leaky roof."

Leontief's main critique of Keynes' *General Theory* referred to the expedient used by Keynes to theoretically justify the possibility of involuntary unemployment: "monetary unemployment, which could not exist under the classical assumptions. The expedient consists in the remotion of the orthodox assumption of the homogeneity of degree zero with respect to all prices of every demand and supply function, and in particular of the supply function of labor. Leontief pointed out that the orthodox theory does not postulate the homogeneity characteristic of such functions, but derives it from "fundamental assumptions concerning the economic behavior of individuals and business firms." Keynes did not discredit those basic assumptions, but he did try to contest the postulate. "In order to be successful in this endeavor, he would have to find a series of empirical situations in which all the prices which might exercise a direct influence upon the size of the labor supply, although constant in their relative magnitude, would differ from case to case in absolute height. The non-homogeneity of the labor supply function would be proven if, under these conditions and in absence of friction and time lags, the amount of labor employed would change (in a significant degree) with the variation of the price level, instead of remaining constant as expected by 'orthodox' theorists. No demonstration of this kind is given in the pages of the *General Theory*."

Another courageous attempt to serve as interpreter of the economic thought is found in "The Significance of Marxian Economics for Present-day Economic Theory," published in the *American Economic Review Supplement* in 1938, where Leontief praised Marx's realistic and empirical knowledge of the capitalist system well beyond his analytical and methodological accomplishments. In particular, Leontief focused on two aspects of Marx's writings: the accusation of "fetishism" Marx raised against the "vulgar" economist, the today neoclassical economist, and his explanation of "economic crises," currently known as business cycles. In regard to the first point, Leontief protected the neoclassical economist and argues for some form of "fetishism" of both consumers and producers themselves. He asserted the neutrality of the neoclassical economist with respect to the procedure that leads to the cost and demand functions by recalling that what the orthodox economist does is simply, first, to take the behavior of individual entrepreneurs and households in terms of their own economic incentives, and next, to allow all these individual behaviors to interact with each other behind their originators' consciousness, leading to the shape and the position of the cost and demand curves. Leontief conclude; "Should the Marxian theory of fetishism be understood as a forthright condemnation of the first stage of our theoretical analysis–the stage which deals with conscious reactions of individual entrepreneurs and householders–his objection must simply be turned down as fundamentally wrong."

In contrast, Leontief celebrated the modernity of the Marxian apparatus in regard to the theory of business cycles: he asserted that no other contribution in the economic science has done as much as the three volumes of *The Capital* in bringing the problem of "economic crises" to the forefront. Marx's interpretations of the "ups and downs" of economic activity still represent the foundation on which the modern approach to business cycles develops: the theory of underinvestment, based on the law of the falling rate of profits, and the theory of underconsumption. As anticipated in the introduction, in his philosophical writings Leontief kept a standpoint that, even if sometimes sharply critical with respect to any attack against the classical approach to the economic science, always emphasized the possibility for such apparatus to embrace viewpoints only superficially different. In his pages there is always the struggle to accept different perspectives, as long as they satisfy a deeply rooted logical procedure and a meaningful interpretation of facts, which in Leontief, as in very few others, are the only acceptable ways to proceed in science.

ACCOUNTABILITY OF ECONOMIC ACTIVITY: INPUT-OUTPUT ANALYSIS

By far the most important of Leontief's scientific achievements, which more than any other of his contributions led to the Nobel Prize, the input-output method of economic analysis consists in "an adaptation of the Neo-classical theory of general equilibrium to the empirical study of the quantitative interdependence between interrelated economic activities." The fundamental justification and motivation for such analysis was Leontief's desire to describe and thoroughly understand what actually happens inside an economy in a certain period of time, and the basic flows that characterize and distinguish different economic realities. Because the observation of the whole set of transactions becomes meaningless for the multitude of them, the first objective was to classify and aggregate them into clusters in order to allow the analyst to identify and understand the structure of production by the simple observation of a numerical table. In the input-output matrix that Leontief calculated for the American economy on the basis of data collected by the Bureau of Labor Statistics for the year 1947, for instance, "transactions are grouped into 42 major departments of production, distribution, transportation and consumption." Such sectors, reported both horizontally and vertically, compose the forty-two rows by forty-two columns of the input-output matrix.

The number at the intersection of a row and a column is the result of empirical computation, and represents the output of the sector indicated in the row, which is absorbed by the sector reported in the column. The number at the end of each row represents the total output of the row-sector, which is the aggregate typically used to evaluate the size of an industry and to compare it with the size of other sectors (the numbers at the end of the other rows of the table) in order to judge its importance in the aggregate economic activity of the country. The sum of the totals of each row gives the national output, provided that the classical double-counting issue that arises in the calculation of national income is taken into account.

If the application and interpretation of an input-output table seems very intuitive and simple, the same cannot be said about its construction and computation. Once production and consumption data are collected, the input coefficients of each cluster of products into the other sectors need to be calculated. The mathematics required is simple linear algebra: because the level of output of each sector depends on the levels of production of all the others, the problem consists of the solution of a system of a number of simultaneous equations that is always equal to the number of sectors in which the economy is disaggregated. The amount of calculations depends on how specific the desired solution is, varying between the square and the cube of the number of sectors. As an example of the magnitude of the task, a typical general solution of the 42-sector United States table that Leontief calculated for 1939, required fifty-six hours of processing by the Harvard Mark II computer. The input-output method of describing aggregate economic activity became soon the most popular tool to analyze the flows of goods and services within an economy and, therefore, to describe the overall structure of the economy. The first table was calculated by Leontief and his associates at Harvard University in the 1930s for the United States, on figures of 1919 and 1929, and the results are published in the first edition of *The Structure of American Economy: 1919-1929*. The 1939 matrix was completed only in 1944. In 1965, the U.S. Department of Commerce published the input-output table of the U.S. economy for 1958.

The technique also has an important strategic use, as it allows economists to pin down and numerically determine the effects of a production change in one sector on other industries and on the whole economy, thus becoming an essential instrument for accurate policy tuning. *The* Leontief coefficients, which are derived from the input-output table and are the fixed proportions in which each industry's output enters the other sectors, per unit of total output, represent an additional shortcut that enormously simplifies economic planning. Leontief's input-output analysis is the first operational tool introduced in the economic science for the static and dynamic analysis of economic systems, and has been adopted widely in the course of the century by both academics and governmental statistical agencies. Historical analyses, aimed at a complete understanding of the interrelations within economic systems, have been pursued, among others and apart from Leontief himself, by Carter, Vaccara and Simon, and Bezdek and Wendling. Examples of the dynamic version, where the structure of the economy is allowed to change through time because of technological progress, changes in the relative supply of factors of production, and so on, are in Leontief, Carter, and Petri, Osterreichisches Institut, and the U.S. Department of Labor.

INTERNATIONAL TRADE:
THE LEONTIEF PARADOX

Starting with the two seminal articles that Leontief published in 1953 and 1956, which can be considered the most far-reaching application of the input-output analysis, an important line of economic research has been devoted to possible explanations of the so-called Leontief Paradox. In those articles, Leontief showed that, contrary to the common belief, in 1947 the United States was a relatively labor-abundant country, "as an average million dollars worth of its exports embodied considerably less capital and somewhat more labor than would be required to replace an equivalent amount of its competitive imports." His relevant results are summarized in the following table:

Table 8. 1 Domestic Capital and Labor Requirements per Million Dollars of American Exports and of Competitive Import Replacements, 1947

Factor	Exports	Imports
Capital ($:1947 prices)	2,55,780	3,091,339
Labor (many years)	182,313	170,004

The table shows that in 1947 the ratio between capital and labor embodied in American exports (14.014966) was lower than the corresponding ratio in American imports (18.183919), which proves that American imports were in that year relatively capital intensive with respect to exports. The theory of comparative advantage based on relative factor abundances across countries (the well-known Heckscher-Ohlin theorem of comparative advantage) states that a relatively labor (capital) abundant country exports relatively labor (capital) intensive products. The trade-revealed comparative advantage obtained by Leontief, therefore, proves that the United States, just after World War II, was a country more endowed with labor than with capital and more endowed with labor than the rest of the world, which is clearly a paradoxical result, stating the opposite of what was generally believed.

The result opened streams of research not yet settled. Leontief himself gave two possible hints to explain his paradox: one consisted in removing the assumption of technological parity between the United States and the rest of the world, which was assumed in order to calculate the input coefficients for imports, and the other was the potential role of natural resources and human capital, which were left out of the picture in his original work. The issue is only indicated and not in fact pursued. Leontief, however, also suggested that the recognition of natural resources within his framework would not require much of a change, involving "nothing more than a straight-forward generalization of the two factors–two commodities analysis." Many scholars tried to look for possible mistakes and shortcomings of Leontief's analysis, always with debatable success. It can be said, with little generalization, that all the work on the paradox can be reconnected to the two avenues suggested by Leontief himself. Each avenue, however, has a different flavor for trade economists: While an explanation through technological differences would remove one of the basic assumption of the Heckscher-Ohlin model, the attempt to include natural resources and human capital was in fact an attempt to reconcile Leontief's findings with the factor abundance theory of comparative advantage. In conclusion, more than forty years of continuing research have not been able to provide a general and satisfactory explanation of the Leontief's findings, and his paradox remains one of the most studied and debated puzzles in the field of international trade.

ECONOMIC DEVELOPMENT

The application of the dynamic input-output analysis serves as a guide in reviewing Leontief's contributions in two of the most important aspects of economic development and structural change: the raising of standards of living and the effects of the mechanization of production processes on labor. The dynamic input-output analysis allows economists to develop a general equilibrium system that, moving from the known economic conditions of the base year, traces different possible development paths of the economy, depending on the assumptions made on the proportions in which the national product is divided into consumption and investment, and on the investment coefficients in each sector. Typically, different scenarios are formulated depending on the assumption made on the allocation patterns and technological change, thus identifying the most desirable and/or attainable development strategy.

In his Nobel lecture, Leontief asserted: "The subject of this lecture is the elucidation of a particular input-output view of the world economy. This formulation should provide a framework for assembling and organizing the mass of factual data needed to describe the world economy. Such a system is essential for a concrete understanding of the world economy as well as for a systematic mapping of the alternative paths along which it could move in the future." The passage refers to the gigantic project that Leontief sponsored at the United Nations as part of the "Action Program of the General Assembly for the Second United Nations Development Decade." Targets for growth of the entire developing region were fixed at 6 percent per annum for GDP (gross domestic product) and 3.5 percent per annum for per capita GDP. Leontief's analysis focused on the consistency between those targets and the distribution of resources around the world. Leontief and his team constructed a dynamic input-output model of the world, distinguishing fifteen regions on the basis of income and geographical-climatic characteristics, and forty-five sectors of economic activities, many of which further subcategorized in more disaggregated industries (for instance, manufacturing was divided in twenty-two subsectors). The results are represented in Table 8.2. Among the most important conclusions and policy implications of the analysis are the necessity to increase the target rates of growth of gross products in the less developed countries, if the objective of increasingly closing the gap between North and South has to be fulfilled; the identification of political, social and institutional, more than physical, limits to sustained growth for the developing world; and the important indication that the costs of pollution abatement do not necessarily represent a threat for economic development. The United Nations study was not, however, the first occasion in which Leontief approached the field of development in such a systematic way. A first attempt to quantify the jump in investment necessary for less developed regions to begin growing at the average rates of the industrialized countries dates back to 1963 and was presented at the "Study Week on the Role of Econometric Analysis in Economic Development Plans in Controlling Economic Fluctuations," organized by the Political Academy of Sciences. Later, he completed two main applications of his dynamic input-output analysis in the several projections of the demographic,

Table 8.2 Hypothetical Scenarios of World Economic Development

	Developed Countries		Developing Countries	
	Scenario 1	Scenario 2	Scenario 1	Scenario 2
Growth Rates % GDP	4.50	3.60	6.00	6.90
Population	1.00	0.60	2.50	2.00
Per-capita GDP	3.50	3.00	3.50	4.90

Income Gap in the Year 2000	Scenario 1: 12 to 1
	Scenario 2: 7 to 1

Source: W. Leontief, et al., (1977). *The Future of the World Economy.* Oxford: Oxford University Press, p. 3.

Scenario 1: GDP targets as established by the International Development Strategy of the United Nations.

Scenario 2: GDP growth rates assumed by Leontief in order to considerably reduce the gap between developed and developing regions

economic and environmental alternatives for the world in the benchmark years 1980, 1990 and 2000 (*The Future of the World* (1977)) and in the study of the impact of technological change in the U.S. economy, with forecasts for the year 2000 (*The Future Impact of Automation on Workers* (1986)).

Such interest began with the beautiful and evocative article, "Machines and Man" published in 1952, which dates the outset of the issue back to the very first industrial revolution of the late 1700s, thus deemphasizing the fear, burst in the years after World War II, that modern technological progress embodied the tragic fate of causing forever increasing rates of unemployment. Leontief considered the problem serious enough, but his historical, almost Schumpeterian, approach gave the problem a perspective that is still actual more than forty years later; his first essay, in fact, recommended the necessity for labor to keep the pace of technological change by continuous training and education, in order to speed up the intersectoral mobility of labor and smooths the impact of technological progress on employment.

CONCLUSION

Leontief is one of the first economists who was deeply concerned about the impact of unabated economic activities on the global environment. In his Nobel lecture, he outlined a simple input-output model where pollution was treated explicitly as a separate sector. His input-output analysis has become a classic technique of economic behavior, and some go as far as comparing him with John Maynard Keynes. One would never want to conclude a review of the contributions that Leontief offered to economic science, any possible list would always fall short of the overall message to the reader, a message of search, even more than research, for some pattern, some code hidden behind the surface of social and economic appearances, able to explain what happened and why, and what to expect, a message that springs from the synthesis of an immense and reasoned background which melts history, anthropology, philosophy, and certainly all the possible economic knowledge at the service of the humanity.

RECOMMENDED READINGS

Leontief, Wassily. (1936). "The Fundamental Assumption of Mr. Keynes's Monetary Theory of Unemployment," *Quarterly Journal of Economics.* Vol. 51.

——. (1937). "Implicit Theorizing: A Methodological Criticism of the Neo-Cambridge School," *Quarterly Journal of Economics.* Vol. 51.

——. (1938). "The Significance of Marxian Economics for Present-day Economic Theory," *American Economic Review Supplement.* 28(1).

——. (1941). The Structure of the American Economy. *1919-1929.* Cambridge: Harvard University Press. (Second edition, 1951: *1919-1939*). New York: Oxford University Press.

——. (1947) "Postulates: Keynes' *General Theory* and the Classicists," in *The New Economics: Keynes' Influence on Theory and Public Policy.* (ed.) S. Harris. New York: Knopf.

——. (1948). "Note on the Pluralistic Interpretation of History and the Problem of Interdisciplinary Co-operation," *The Journal of Philosophy.* 45(23).

——. (1952). "Machines and Man," *Scientific American.* 187(3).

——. (1954). "Mathematics in Economics," *Bulletin of the American Mathematical Society.* 60(3).

——. (1956). "Factor Proportions and the Structure of American Trade: Further Theoretical and Empirical Analysis," *The Review of Economics and Statistics.* Vol. 38, pp. 386-407.

——. (1963–1964). "Modern Techniques for Economic Planning and Projection," in *La scuola in azione.* ENI-Ente Nazionale Idrocarburi, Scuola Enrico Mattei. Vol. 23.

——. (1966a). *Essays in Economics.* New York: Oxford University Press.

——. (1966b). *Input-Output Economics.* New York: Oxford University Press.

——. (1974). *Les Prix Nobel en 1973.* Stockholm: Norstedt & Soner.

Leontief, Wassily, et al. (1953). *Studies in the Structure of the American Economy.* New York: Oxford University Press.

Leontief, Wassily, Anne P. Carter, and Peter A. Petri. (1977). *The Future of the World Economy.* New York: Oxford University Press.

Leontief, Wassily, et al. (1978). "Preliminary Study of Worldwide Economic and Social Implications of a Limitation on Military Spending (An Input-Output

Leontief, Wassily, et al. (1978). "Preliminary Study of Worldwide Economic and Social Implications of a Limitation on Military Spending (An Input-Output Approach)," New York: *Institute for Economic Analysis*. Prepared for the United Nations Centre for Disarmament.

Leontief, Wassily, and Faye Duchin. (1980). "Worldwide Implications of Hypothetical Changes in Military Spending (An Input-Output Approach)," New York: *Institute for Economic Analysis*. Prepared for the U.S. Arms Control and Disarmament Agency.

——. (1983). *Military Spending*. New York: Oxford University Press.

——. (1986). *The Future Impact of Automation on Workers*. New York: Oxford University Press.

9

Friedrich Hayek (1899-1992):
Who Combined Psychology, Physiology, Philosophy, and Economics and Was a Laureate of 1974

Mussaddeq Chowdhury

BIOGRAPHICAL PROFILE

Friedrich Hayek was born in Vienna in 1899. His father, August Hayek, was a local health official and a part-time teacher of biology at the University of Vienna. Hayek's maternal grandfather was a law professor at the same university. After graduating from high school, Hayek joined the Austrian army in 1917 and was stationed in the Italian front during the First World War. The following year, returning from the army, Hayek entered the University of Vienna and studied law, economics, philosophy and psychology. He was one of the very few economists who had two earned Ph.D. degrees–one in law and the other in economics–from the University of Vienna in 1921 and 1923, respectively. During these years, Hayek worked at the Austrian War Claims Settlement Office under Ludwig Mises–a famous Austrian economist. He stayed in the United States for some time to work as a research assistant of Jeremiah Jenks at New York University. At that time, he also attended a lecture series delivered by Wesley Mitchell and John Clark on business cycles at Columbia University. Thus he developed his research interests in economic fluctuations and business cycles. On his return to Austria, Hayek persuaded his government to initiate research on business cycles, and he became the pioneer of this research in Austria. In 1929, he went to England and gave four invited lectures at the London School of Economics (LSE). In 1931, he joined LSE as professor of economics and statistics. In the 1930s, Hayek became intensely entangled in a series of intellectual debates with Keynes and Keynesian economics that made him famous there. In 1946, he visited Stanford University for a year, and in 1950, he came back to the United States as a visiting professor at the

University of Arkansas. Then he joined the University of Chicago as a professor of social and moral science and remained there until 1962. Later on, he worked for the University of Freiburg and the University of Salzburg in Germany and the University of California, Los Angeles. Hayek received the Austrian government's Medal of Honor for Arts and Science in 1976. He was a member of many academic societies. He married Helen Fritsch in 1926. They had a son and a daughter. After the dissolution of their marriage, he married Helene Bitterlich. Hayek became a British citizen in 1938. He died in 1992.

INTRODUCTION

Friedrich Hayek, along with Gunnar Myrdal, received the economics Nobel Prize in 1974 for his "pioneering work in the theory of money and economic fluctuations and for [his] penetrating analysis of the interdependence of economic, social and institutional phenomena." Hayek was one of the most celebrated Austrian economists of the twentieth century. He was the student of Friedrich Wieser and a colleague of Ludwig Mises. Hayek was instrumental not only in developing but also in spreading Austrian economic thought to the rest of the world. Hayek's theory of business cycles was overshadowed by the Keynesian revolution. However, it eventually received full international recognition. He was one of the very few economists who had successfully integrated different branches of knowledge such as psychology, physiology, philosophy, economics, etc. He made valuable contributions to our understanding of fluctuations of economic activities and the role of money and monetary policy in explaining business cycles. He also shed light on social and political processes and their interrelationships with economic performance of a society.

HAYEK, THE PHILOSOPHER

In the 1960s and 1970s, Hayek focused on issues in political philosophy and the liberal tradition. Hayek argued that because the human's mental ability is limited, individual freedom is essential. Human knowledge is not only limited, but an individual is not even aware of all the knowledge (s)he has. A central government would, therefore, at best have access only to the conscious knowledge, that is, the part of knowledge that can be expressed in logical propositions. Hayek distinguishes between a "spontaneous order" and an "organization," the latter being a group that intentionally comes together for a particular purpose. He views the former as an order that simultaneously expands and limits human control over the social environment. The spontaneous order develops as individuals adapt to circumstances known only to some of them, with the entirety of circumstances unknown to anyone because such circumstances may be "so complex that no mind can comprehend them all." Hayek states that, "in a free society the general good consists principally in the facilitation of the pursuit of unknown individual purposes." The rules or laws of a free society help, not hinder, general welfare. Distributive justice attempts to force society–as opposed to individuals–to behave in a just manner. But since society is an impersonal entity, this implies that only organized individuals who are able to command obedience can perform this role. Thus the attainment of distributive justice means the sacrifice of individual liberty. Hayek expresses concern about the tyranny of the majority and about the coercive power of the government. While he concedes that coercion is necessary, he warns that it should be used "only for the purpose of ensuring obedience to rules of just conduct approved by most, or at least by a majority." This is "the essential condition for the absence of arbitrary power and therefore of freedom."

HAYEK, THE PSYCHOLOGIST-PHYSIOLOGIST

Though relatively unknown among economists, Hayek's book, *The Sensory Order: An Inquiry into the Foundations of Theoretical Psychology,* is perhaps one of his most important works. Gerald Edelman–a Nobel laureate in physiology/medicine–wrote: "I must say that I have been deeply gratified by reading a book–Hayek's *The Sensory Order.* I was deeply impressed... I recommend this book to your (The American Academy of Arts and Sciences) attention, as an exercise in profound thinking by a man who simply considers knowledge for its own sake." In this book, Hayek studies the correspondence between our sensations (Sensory Order) and the external physical world (Physical Order). Our sensations, perceptions and beliefs emanate from stimuli transmitted by the central nervous system which is the common "structure of the mind" shared by everyone. Each stimulus generates neural firings to the central nervous system and these firings differ; this means that the same stimulus may trigger different patterns of such firings and thus cause qualitative differences in perception and sensation in different people. Thus, although our minds may be the same, there is a physiological basis for differences in perception, sensation, belief, experience, and, ultimately, and perhaps most importantly for Hayek, knowledge.

Hayek was sharply critical of the attempts to incorporate scientific methodology in the study of social sciences. Pure science uses models to study empirically verifiable phenomena while a social science like economics has a psychological aspect. The latter makes it difficult, if not impossible, to make predictions. The economic order is complex and–as explained in Hayek's *The Sensory Order* arbitrary, because the same stimulus may cause different sensations in different people. Thus, using the methodology of pure science in a social science is inadequate.

HAYEK AND THE MARXISTS

The 1930s and 1940s saw Hayek involved in a war of words and ideas with the Marxist economists Maurice Dobb and Oscar Lange over the possibility of central planning. Dobb had argued that if a central authority were to control consumption decisions, the problems of central planning, such as the inability to replicate the automatic adjustments that occur in a free market, would be solved. Hayek offered two objections to Dobb's idea: (1) consumer sovereignty would be nullified, and (2) even if (1) were somehow made acceptable–unthinkable in Britain in those days–prices would still be required to ration scarce goods. Hayek also offers a critique of Dickinson's view that any economy could be represented by a Walrasian system of equations, the difference being that, in a capitalist system, the equations are solved by the market, while in a socialist system, they are solved by the planners. As in his later writings, it is important to note that Hayek does not criticize the Marxist position from the usual static equilibrium approach. Rather he points out the tremendous amount of information that would be required, the difficulty of formulating and solving the correct system of equations (perhaps consisting of hundreds of thousands of equations) and the impossibility of such a price planning system to adjust to constant change.

Hayek's objection to Lange's position was in a similar vein. Lange had argued that prices did not have to be determined in the market but could be calculated by the central planners, who could then use these as parameters for their work. If the original set of (shadow) prices did not reflect relative scarcities adequately, a trial-and-error method–not unlike the one prevalent in a capitalist economy–could adjust prices up or down until they were "correct." Hayek observed that Lange displayed "an excessive preoccupation with problems of the pure theory of stationary equilibrium." He thus took issue with Lange's idea that the movement toward a set of equilibrium (accounting or shadow) prices would be a one-time adjustment; in the real world, Hayek notes, "constant change is the rule."

HAYEK AND KEYNES

Hayek was involved in a long debate with the writings of John Keynes. He severely criticized Keynes' *Treatise on Money*, to which Keynes replied by retracting and modifying the system outlined therein. When, in 1936, Keynes published his seminal work, *The General Theory of Employment, Interest and Money*, Hayek offered no criticism. Although Hayek found the work somewhat misleading, he apparently thought that Keynes would change his mind again. Perhaps more significantly, Hayek's disagreement with Keynes was over the very essence of macroeconomics and its analytical approach and not merely the details of fiscal policy. Hayek counterargues with Keynes and asserts that it is not the deficiency of aggregate demand that causes depression; rather it is a result of overconsumption and deceptive policy measures. Misguided policies with regard to money supply may distort relative prices that, in turn, cause imbalances in labor supply and demand throughout the economy. According to Hayek, only market forces can bring the economy back to equilibrium. Here Hayek may be regarded as a forerunner of Milton Friedman and monetarism. However, sound as his arguments may be, it appears that Hayek underestimated both the analytical power of Keynesian theory and its attraction to policymakers faced with high unemployment. The result was that, from 1936 to the 1970s–until the emergence of Margaret Thatcher and Ronald Reagan–Keynesian economics was triumphant, and Hayek was relegated to the wilderness.

HAYEK AND THE CLASSICAL LIBERALISM

In the 1940s, Hayek turned his attention to the relationship between political order and economic organization. The problem of how to rescue liberal democracy from recurrent depression led to a serious and unbridgeable schism between Hayek on the one hand and Keynes on the other. The latter's system was seen as the middle way, with the best of the Soviet system of planning and of the classical liberalism. To Hayek, however, as Cockett observes, "'Liberal Socialism' was a contradiction in terms and the 'middle way' a dangerous fallacy." Planning would ultimately destroy freedom; without the operation of a (free-market) price mechanism, the government would have to intervene at such a micro level that the individual's freedom to choose would be abrogated: this is the road to serfdom.

Hayek published two years before George Orwell's *Animal Farm* and five years before 1984 was addressed to "The Socialists of all Parties." The picture painted by Hayek is as bleak (and inevitable) as that painted by Orwell. Even if a democratic form of socialism were to be put in place, it would, due to the absence of a shared set of values, - inevitably expand beyond the economic, and into the political arena and, thus, turn authoritarian. The human race had to choose between "two irreconcilable types of social organizations," one commercial, the other military. He thus saw no third or middle way, noting, "The last resort of a competitive economy is the bailiff; the ultimate sanction of a planned economy is the hangman."

HAYEK VERSUS THE NEOCLASSICISTS

Hayek's opposition may lead one to think that he was sympathetic to the neoclassical orthodoxy. Caldwell summarizes why this was clearly not the case. First, there is a crucial difference between the neoclassical concept of information and Hayek's concept of knowledge. The latter includes tacit knowledge that cannot be transmitted and is important because it affects entrepreneurial decisions and, thus, is reflected in the prices in a free market system. Replacing the market by a planner implies that the prices in such a system would contain less information. Second, Hayek rejected the idea of given data and perfect competition in favor of a dynamic market process where rivalry ensures the generation and discovery of knowledge. There is no guarantee of coordination; a free market, however, is one which is least likely to hinder coordination. Third, Hayek rejected the idea of *Homo Economicus*, a crucial construct in the neoclassical literature. As discussed above, Hayek posited the mind of the individual as a complex adaptation of self-organizing neural order with unique sensations, perceptions, beliefs, and knowledge. Thus, the neoclassical world, with rational individuals maximizing an objective function subject to one or more constraints, makes little or no sense.

Hayek ridiculed the tendency among mainstream economists to use the methodology of the physical sciences, an attempt, he warned, that may lead to "outright error." In the physical sciences, the investigator can measure what (s)he considers important on the basis of theory. It is often the case that, in the social sciences, what is considered important is what can be measured. The difference between the physical and social (and biological) sciences is that the latter has to deal with structures of essential complexity, which can only be captured by a model of numerous variables. Furthermore, the complexity is organized, that is, "the character of the structure depends not only on the properties of the individual elements and the relative frequency with which they occur, but also on the manner in which the individual elements are connected with each other." Thus, the best we can do is to make "pattern predictions," that is, predictions regarding some of the general attributes but not individual elements contained therein.

Thus, Hayek regarded the mathematical technique of representing the economy (or a part thereof) by a system of algebraic equations useful because it allows us to observe the interdependencies between different markets. But he rejected the notion that we can ever know all the parameters of this system to be able to solve the system of equations for the equilibrium prices. This depends on "so many particular circumstances that it could never be known to man but was known to God." The mimicking of the methodology of the physical sciences thus leads to a situation where only measurable variables are regarded as important and gives us the illusion of perfect knowledge. Hayek, on the other hand, preferred "true but imperfect knowledge, to a pretense of exact knowledge that is likely to be false."

HAYEK AND THE BUSINESS CYCLES

Hayek's theory of business cycles is regarded as his most illuminating contribution to the science of economics. He demonstrated that the economy's capital structure is inextricably intertwined with the fluctuations of economic activities of a country. In his famous "Hayekian Triangles," Hayek explained the complex relationship between the present value of capital goods and the future value of final goods and services that the capital produces. Once capital is ready to be used for producing a certain combination of final goods and services, it cannot be reused readily for any other purpose if the demand for the original set of final goods and services changes. Thus macroeconomic stability and equilibrium crucially depend on the "intertemporal coordination" between the present use of capital goods and the future demand for consumer goods. Capital goods are heterogeneous, so the production structure of the economy depends on the "durability, complementarity, substitutability and specificity" of capital goods.

Hayek's business cycle theory also states that if expansionary monetary policy reduces the interest rate below the "natural rate," then it can distort the economy's intertemporal structure of production. As a consequence of monetary expansion, the fall of the interest rate is accompanied by a change in relative prices, which in turn gives a false signal to the market, causing economic instability and distortion in consumers' intertemporal preferences. The expansion in economic activities and growth in output resulting from increased investment is merely artificial. Soon economic agents realize that enough savings would not be generated in the economy to complete the pending projects. Thus every artificial boom is finally ended in a bust. Recovery may again be underway if the artificial investments are liquidated.

NEANDARTHAL CONSERVATIVE
OR RADICAL ANARCHIST?

Let us now turn to the rhetorical question of whether Hayek was a neanderthal conservative or a radical anarchist. Hayek's political views may be summarized as follows: an endorsement of free markets, operating within a liberal democracy with established and enforceable property rights, all protected by a strong constitution. As noted above, he sought to minimize the role of the government in economic life not because it is inefficient (the neoclassical argument) but because it has insufficient knowledge to do so. Hayek, however, was no anarchist; he saw useful roles for the government to play. Hayek stated that there is no reason " why in a society which has reached the general level of wealth which ours has attained the first kind of security should not be guaranteed to all without endangering general freedom." Furthermore, he advocated state assistance for the "common hazards of life," which are uncertain. Thus, Hayek clearly was not adverse to some elements of a "safety net" policy.

Hayek offered two main reasons why he was not a conservative. First, a conservative opposes change, while Hayek supported spontaneous change, which he viewed as a necessary condition for the growth of society. Second, a conservative is unable to work with people whose moral values differ from his own for "a political order in which both can obey their convictions." Hayek was also critical of the position that conservatives often take; they often are not opposed to unlimited government and favor governmental pursuit of what they would prefer to have done. There is, thus, no difference between a conservative and a collectivist. Hayek toyed with the idea of calling himself a liberal in the classical sense of the term but discarded it as too confusing because of the different things the term implies to different people. He thought the answer may have been to call himself a libertarian but felt that "It carries too much the flavor of a manufactured term and of a substitute." Finally, he settled on calling himself an unrepentant Old Whig, " with the stress on the 'old.'" He thus identified himself with the party of liberty in England that had an important role in inspiring the liberal movements in Europe.

CONCLUSION

Hayek was one of the most illustrious economists of our time. His talents were diverse and his contributions to economics were multifaceted. Regardless of the controversy, Hayek will remain as a giant figure in the economics profession, particularly in the fields of economic fluctuations, business cycles, comparative economic systems, etc. He also established himself as a solid authority on legal theory, political and social philosophy and cognitive psychology. Hayek was a prolific writer and he published continuously throughout his life, though his works have not been very easy to follow. There are multiple interpretations of his theories, and it might take several decades for the profession to digest the literature produced by Hayek. He will remain as a fascinating and prodigious figure to us for ages to come.

RECOMMENDED READINGS

Hayek, Friedrich, (ed.) (1935). *Collectivist Economic Planning: Critical Studies on the Possibilities of Socialism*. London: Routledge.

———. (1948). "Socialist Calculation: The Competitive 'Solution.'" 1940. Reprinted in *Individualism and Economic Order*. Chicago: University of Chicago Press.

———. (1944). *The Road to Serfdom*. London: Routledge.

———. (1952a). *The Sensory Order: An Inquiry into the Foundations of Theoretical Psychology*. Chicago: University of Chicago Press.

———. (1952b). *The Counter-Revolution of Science: Studies on the Abuse of Reason*. Glencoe: Free Press.

———. (1960). *The Constitution of Liberty*. Chicago: University of Chicago Press.

———. (1973, 1976, 1979). *Law, Legislation and Liberty: A New Statement of the Liberal Principles of Justice and Political Economy*. Vols. 1-3. Chicago: University of Chicago Press.

———. (1984). "Why I Am Not a Conservative," in Chiaki Nishiyama and Kurt R. Leube, (eds.) *The Essence of Hayek*. Stanford: Hoover Institution Press.

———. (1989). "The Pretense of Knowledge," (The Nobel Memorial Lecture, December 11, 1974), *American Economic Review*. Vol. 7, No. 6.

10

Gunnar Myrdal (1898-1987):
An Economist, a Social Thinker, a Politician, and a Laureate of 1974

S. Hussain Ali Jafri

BIOGRAPHICAL PROFILE

Gunnar Myrdal was born in a small village called Solvarbo in Sweden in 1898. His father, Karl Myrdal, was a railroad worker. Myrdal spent his early life in a farming community and then started university education in 1919 at Stockholm University. He earned his first degree in law in 1923 and started practicing law while continuing his education. He received his Ph.D. degree in economics in 1927 from the same university. During 1925-1929, he studied in Germany and England for some time. For the period 1929-1930 he came to the United States with a Rockefeller Fellowship. On his return from America, he joined the Post Graduate Institute of International Studies in Geneva, Switzerland as associate professor. In 1933, he came back to Sweden and took a position at Stockholm University as Lars Hierta Chair of Political Economy and Public Finance to replace Gustav Cassel, a famous Swedish academician of that time. Myrdal also was involved in Swedish politics. In 1934, he was elected to the Swedish senate. From 1945 to 1947, he served the government of Sweden as the cabinet minister for commerce. He also worked for the United Nations as executive secretary of the Economic Commission for Europe. In the 1970s, he worked for the University of California-Santa Barbara and New York University as a visiting research fellow and visiting professor, respectively. He received dozens of honorary degrees, including one from Harvard University. In 1924 he married Alva Reimer, who was a very educated and distinguished lady. She held a high position in the United Nations and was Swedish ambassador to India. As of now, Myrdal is the only economics Nobel laureate whose wife was also glorified with the same prize for peace. She was recognized for her "commitment to the service of disarmament." The Myrdals' only son and both of their daughters have been very successful in their respective professional fields. Gunnar Myrdal died in 1987.

INTRODUCTION

Gunnar Myrdal, along with Friedrich Hayek, received the economics Nobel Prize in 1974 for his "pioneering work in the theory of money and economic fluctuations and for [his] penetrating analysis of the interdependence of economic, social and institutional phenomena." Myrdal had a fascinating and eventful career. He was an unconventional economist with many other rare qualities in politics and diplomacy. Throughout his distinguished career of public service and contributions to the economics profession, Myrdal studied some of the most complex and perplexing problems facing society. His two influential and controversial publications, *An American Dilemma* and *Asian Drama* suggest that Myrdal, far from being a conventional economist, was a pragmatic social thinker and a social scientist. Throughout his professional assignments, he included several interdependent economic and noneconomic (cultural, political and social) variables when analyzing economic problems. The models that he used were not always "neat" and "precise," and like John Galbraith, Myrdal was also mocked by his peers. Perhaps Myrdal had the attitude that it is better to be vaguely right than "precisely" wrong. He made some significant breakthroughs in economics and introduced some very abstract concepts to the profession. He consistently stressed searching for reality and desired that abstraction of real world problems follow relevant rather than narrowly preconceived lines. Even when he was young, Myrdal challenged the establishment and the status quo and was truly an independent thinker.

ECONOMIC THEORY

Doctoral dissertations rarely make a contribution to the literature and come to advance the understanding of a discipline. However, Myrdal's was one of the few exceptions. Studying economics under such giants as Knut Wicksell, Eli Heckscher and Gustav Cassel, Myrdal wrote his dissertation entitled, *Prisbildningsproblemet och foranderligheten* (The Problem of Price Formation Under Economic Change) and introduced the term expectations systematically into the analysis of prices, profits and changes in expected values. His dissertation examined how the expectation of uncertain future market conditions might influence the behavior of firms at the microeconomic level. Myrdal's characterization of this problem led to further research on the economics of risk and uncertainty. By introducing expectations into the analysis of economic phenomena, he also extended the scope of introducing the term dynamics, into which time, uncertainty and expectations enter in an essential way. Therefore, from the onset of his career, Myrdal's work, like Samuelson's *Foundations,* was setting the stage for breakthroughs in the advancement of economic science.

Myrdal continued his interest in the ideas and concepts he had developed in his dissertation by expanding his mentor Wicksell's theory of interest rate and cumulative processes. The concept of "cumulative causation" became one of the main tools in Myrdal's arsenal for examining economic and social phenomena. Basically, this concept departs from static models as it links future events to past events and recognizes interdependencies in both spatial and temporal dimensions, combining general equilibrium in a dynamic context. The final result would either converge in equilibrium or remain in a state of disequilibrium, as demonstrated in the Cob-Web theorem or the physical theory of chaos, depending on the flow of events and the presence or absence of intervening factors. In general terms, the concept of cumulative causation is analogous to cliches such as "success begets success," the "vicious cycle," "the poverty trap," and in economic applications, "the paradox of thrift" and the "multiplier effect." Initially, Myrdal applied the concept of cumulative causation in explaining the difference between the "natural" rate and the money rate of interest and monetary equilibrium. He later applied this concept in his study of American blacks, reported in *An American Dilemma,* by applying noneconomic variables, such as racial prejudice, to their level of economic performance. Using the same concept, he also predicted that the gap between the first- and- third world countries will grow as rich countries, by their growth and trade patterns, expand while poor countries will remain poor as long as they maintain their precolonial growth and trade patterns.

Myrdal was a pioneer in introducing and differentiating the concepts of *ex-ante* and *ex-post* in economic analysis. *Ex-ante* refers to the anticipated values of a given economic variable, while *ex-post* refers to the realized (or actual) values of that variable. Before Myrdal, confusion reigned, due to a failure to differentiate between expectations and results. Myrdal clarified these concepts in the discussion of savings, investment and income, and their effects on prices. He was the first to have asserted that only in equilibrium will both the *ex-ante* and *ex-post* values be equal. Expectations play an important role in consumers' and producers' decisions and help to shape the actual, or *ex-post* values. Indeed, Lucas' "Rational Expectations" hypothesis, which assumes a "rational" behavior of economic participants when they make decisions for the future as well as the present, may have its roots in Myrdal's introduction of expectations. Myrdal considered this distinction to be his main contribution to economics. Myrdal, demonstrated his independent and bold thinking at a relatively young age. He questioned the very foundations of economic theory and refused to follow conventional (neoclassical) approaches to the study of problems faced by society. Myrdal's latent desires to seek realism in his work and to accurately build real world models was reinforced by his "special assignments" to conduct comprehensive studies of the racial problems in the United States and the process of economic development in South Asia. As both of these monumental works involved analyzing very complex issues, he realized and exhorted the profession to seek relevance in their work and to recognize the limitations of using only economics in finding solutions to the real world problems of the day. In *Against the Stream: Critical Essays in Economics–* published in 1973, Myrdal criticized mainstream economists for slighting the moral bases of economic theory and asserted that the belief in optimality of competitive markets is justified only if distributional issues are ignored. He felt that an economist who ignores the effects of political and social forces on economic events is dangerous. His criticisms of mainstream economic theory is summarized by Streeten as: (i) Irrelevant features are selected and relevant ones ignored–what Myrdal termed as "opportunistic ignorance." (ii) The narrow or abstract definitions of development, economic growth and welfare are too limited. Myrdal was interested in finding the actual needs and valuations of people and also challenged the assumption of interpersonal comparisons of utility. He considered this unexamined assumption to be a major methodological weakness and argued that ideological preferences and value judgments be stated explicitly and openly. (iii) The narrow definition and limits of the discipline. Myrdal advocated the institutional approach including all relevant knowledge and techniques, economic, political or social, in dealing with a problem. (iv) The biases and twisted terminology evident in terms such as "welfare," "values," "developing countries," "free world" and so on.

THE PUBLIC POLICY

Myrdal made several significant contributions to economic policy formulation and implementation. He was an adviser to the new Social Democratic government in 1932 and was elected to the Swedish senate in 1934. He had the unique distinction of putting his own theories to the test as chairman of the planning commission, director of the Central Bank, federal minister of commerce and finally as secretary general of the Economic Commission for Europe.

The Stockholm School, based on the cumulative process, studied the economy in a manner similar to Keynes. Due to lack of communications, the English economists were unaware of the simultaneous developments in economic thinking in Sweden. The Swedish economists paralleled and, on some important points, even anticipated the Keynesians. Myrdal, in *Monetary Equilibrium*, written in 1931, provided a new conception of monetary equilibrium, in which stability occurs when there is a correspondence between the actual and anticipated course of events, and actually anticipated some significant aspects contained in Keynes' *General Theory*. Playfully, Myrdal chided Keynes for his "unnecessary originality." Actually, the relationship between the Swedish and the English was of a more complementary nature. When Keynes, in his *Treatise on Money*, had discussed the inequality between savings and investments as causing changes in the level of income and employment, he meant ex-ante and when in *The General Theory*, he wrote about the equality of these two categories, he meant *ex-post*, which, thanks to Myrdal's clarification, helped economists later to recognize this distinction in Keynes' work as well.

Like Keynes, Myrdal was a fiscal conservative and advocated using counter cyclical fiscal policy measures. Myrdal's policies emphasized the use of public-works programs and budgetary reforms as tools to counteract fluctuations in business cycles. In the Swedish case, he cautioned against the use of these programs for more than only for a limited time and interestingly (and implicitly) warned that these programs do not have the negative crowding-out effect, "so that they (public-work programs) do not displace the private sector and cause fiscal problems that will necessitate hiking tax-rates or cause doubts in the government financing and banking system." He was also skeptical of the legislators' ability to self-discipline and worried about the politicization of fiscal policy. In agreement with his fellow co-winner of the Nobel Prize, Friedrich Hayek, Myrdal felt the need for "legislating the legislators," especially in the area of economic affairs.

Myrdal was perhaps one of the first to challenge the classical or conventional thinking of his time that the budget should always be balanced. His view contrasts with those that prevailed, and the balanced-budget rule was followed strictly in the United States by President Hoover even in the midst of the Great Depression. He felt like Keynes, or even before Keynes, that the concept of deficit financing is a most crucial factor in establishing a reformed budgetary system. However, he anticipated the problems associated with the abuse of deficit financing and proposed an "automatic process" through which budget deficits remain within control. Myrdal advocated separating the national budget into two totally separate and distinct parts–a "Running Budget" financed through tax revenues, and a "Capital Budget" financed through bonds, which would be repaid from the profits that would be generated from public enterprises. He insisted that all previous debts be repaid before a government could claim to have a surplus in any given year. Thus, Myrdal was essentially proposing to reduce the national debt from the public sector before any new spending program was initiated.

These examples demonstrate that even in the matter of macroeconomic policy, Myrdal was not only a pragmatist but was ahead of his time in anticipating problems that most economies have later faced with budget deficits, politicization and abuse of fiscal policy. Myrdal studied human behavior from different angles, could anticipate these flaws and forewarned of the potential abuses. It appears, however, that he also advocated protectionist "Beggar Thy Neighbor" policies in dealing with domestic economic problems. He felt that a tool of an expansionary fiscal policy could be found in what he termed "international space." In a monograph entitled *Economic Effects of Fiscal Policy*, he discussed various methods to exploit the international space, such as import restrictions, devaluation of the national currency and subsidies to areas that produced goods that either had a higher rate of import substitutability or were suitable for exporting.

Myrdal also influenced public policy in the area of social reform. He advocated a pragmatic social policy by developing deliberate, rationally conceived policies whereby the state would actively intervene to correct social and economic problems, believing that "well-planned egalitarian reforms would be preventive, prophylactic and thus productive." To reverse a declining birthrate in Sweden, Myrdal recommended instituting several programs such as larger tax deductions for families with children, subsidies for expectant mothers, public housing, school lunch programs, free public daycare facilities, aid to orphans, widows and disabled men and so on. These recommendations eventually resulted in the establishment of the Royal Population Commission in Sweden, which served as a model for social reform for other European countries as well.

ECONOMIC DEVELOPMENT

Although Myrdal had lectured and written books on the economic development of the third world (for example, Cairo lectures on development and *Economic Theory and Underdeveloped Regions*), his interest deepened in this subject by a coincidence. Gunnar Myrdal received a grant from the Twentieth Century Fund to direct a comprehensive study of economic trends and policies in Asia. This study, which was indeed comprehensive (in three volumes and over 2,300 pages), considered the history and prospects of eight Asian countries: India, Pakistan, Burma, Thailand, Malaya, Indonesia, the Philippines and Ceylon, with the inclusion of South Vietnam, Cambodia and Laos. Myrdal's thoughts on third-world problems had three major themes: (1) The economic gap between rich and poor countries is widening. (2) Standard economic theory is inadequate to explain or help narrow the gap. (3) Governments in third-world countries must play a larger role in promoting economic development.

At first glance, Myrdal's diagnoses and prescriptions of the problems of the third world sound like Raul Prebisch's characterization with his Center-Periphery argument. Applying his now familiar principle of circular and cumulative causation, Myrdal assessed that the upper classes of rich nations are growing richer, while the poorer countries trapped in their poverty will be spiraling ever downward with the result that the gap between the rich and the poor will widen even further than in the preindependence period. He also had little faith in the relevance of standard economic theory to solve these problems, since according to Myrdal, it (1) focuses on production and is weak on distribution of wealth, which according to Myrdal is a precondition for development, (2) emphasizes laissez-faire economics and free trade, which were biased against third world countries because they were producing and exporting generally low-priced commodities or simple goods, while the rich countries were producing and exporting the high-valued manufactured goods, and (3) assumes that an economy tends toward a stable equilibrium. In contrast is Myrdal's view, wherein the cumulative and circular causation process will make matters worse and pull the economy away from a "stable" equilibrium.

Myrdal's characterization of these problems places him as an early intellectual architect of the "New International Economic Order." He also criticized third-world countries, attributing their problems to three factors: (1) population explosion, (i2) deforestation and (3) overemphasis on the industrial sector at the expense of labor-intensive agricultural and simple manufactured goods. He expressed frustration and was particularly critical of the third-world countries' failure to institute political, economic and social reforms as well as reform of the "soft state." Myrdal used the term "soft state" to the governments that he characterized as corrupt and dominated by opportunistic members of the upper class who regularly practiced nepotism and favoritism while discharging their duties toward the poorer segments of their populations. Among the measures that he proposed for third-world countries were: (1) Promote a more equal distribution of income locally to create purchasing power among the masses, a precondition for creating markets for domestic producers. He implicitly recognized that the marginal propensity to consume is higher for the poor masses than the wealthier class, so any income distribution moving in favor of the poor will result in a higher multiplier effect due to changes in autonomous spending. He also felt that increasing income and improving standards of living improve health and living conditions for the poor and as such are precursors for increasing productivity. (2) Invest public funds in infrastructure projects such as highways, irrigation projects, ports and so on. (3) Engage in comprehensive institutional reform: land ownership and tenancy, educational reforms and quality of life changes needed to uplift the masses. He advocated the use of a "Basic Needs" approach to development.

He was also critical of the rich countries for ignoring the plight of the poor arguing that their neglect was for sociopolitical reasons, and consistently maintained that advanced countries should increase their economic aid to third-world countries. He particularly chided the U.S. foreign aid decisions, saying aid "is not distributed according to needs but according to the U.S. interests in the Cold War." Expressing frustration at the third-world countries' failure to root out corruption and institute political reforms, Myrdal advocated that foreign aid be (1) given for relief and humanitarian purposes rather than earmarked as development aid and (2) channeled through international agencies such as the Red Cross since he had a basic mistrust of the integrity of third-world governments. He further argued that any concessions to the third world's demand for a new international economic order be conditioned upon their instituting domestic reforms.

INSTITUTIONAL ECONOMICS

Gunnar Myrdal's conversion and contributions to institutional economics can be traced to at least five factors: (1) Myrdal's quest and insistence on seeking relevance to his work, (2) his perception of the weakness of the conventional (classical) approach in analyzing and solving realworld problems, which was exemplified to Myrdal by the failure of the German and American schools to cope with the Great Depression of the 1930s, (3) his early work with the Swedish government's move toward social reform, (4) special assignments to study the problems facing American blacks (*An American Dilemma*), followed by a comprehensive study of the process and politics of development in South Asia (*The Asian Drama*), and (5) the influence of his wife, Alva Myrdal-a world renowned political activist and sociologist.

Myrdal insisted that real-life problems are complex and thus "disciplinary boundaries make no sense beyond pragmatic criteria of problem solution." For example, in development theory, Myrdal believed all "relevant" factors should be included, be they economic or non economic, within the scope of a study, without apology. In *An American Dilemma* as well as in *The Asian Drama*, Myrdal saw the relevance and the application of his early work on the principle of circular and cumulative causation-that everything affects everything else in a dynamic context. For example, in the case of the study of the American blacks, he analyzed the interaction and mutually reinforcing forces affecting this group, which include occupational distribution, income levels, consumption patterns, segregation and discrimination. Myrdal identified these factors as causal variables in explaining poverty among blacks. In a dynamic context, any change within any of these factors (economic, socio-cultural or political) will bring about changes within the other factors, and through mutual interaction, change the course of movement within the whole system. These movements, through "circular cumulative causation," could improve matters (virtuous cycle) or worsen them (vicious cycle).

Myrdal's study had tremendous social and political implications, since it exposed for perhaps the first time not only the overt and covert discrimination against blacks but also diagnosed (and perhaps prescribed) in a comprehensive manner, the real causes of the existence as well as the perpetuity of discrimination against the blacks in the American society in the 1950s and the 1960s. It showed, for example, how discrimination in education meant fewer blacks will become doctors, and how, through negative feedback, the blacks were relatively less knowledgeable about health and sanitation, which resulted in their poorer overall health (Pressman). Consequently, as the blacks found it harder than the whites to obtain and keep jobs and with lower incomes, black education would suffer. To break this cycle, segregation had to end, and indeed, Myrdal's work was cited as a basis in the Supreme Court's decision on school desegregation that "separate cannot be equal."

Within the context of studying economic development, Myrdal again felt the need for adopting an institutional approach. He argued that the problems of the third world were unique, complex and interrelated and that they stemmed from several sources. Therefore, using an institutional approach was both rational and realistic to accurately identify and solve them. According to Myrdal, "any other approach will not be adequate to the realities of development because it will abstract away from precisely the conditions fundamental to development: attitudes and institutions." Myrdal identified a mix of these attributes, ranging from a purely economic perspective regarding production and income, to attitudes toward life and work, to institutions and policies that in an interrelated way, affect the process of development. For example, he prescribed institutional reforms for redistributing wealth, political power bases, and education leading to a more equitable distribution of education resources among society's haves and have-nots. According to Myrdal, these changes will bring about not only an expanded market base (essential for producers to achieve economies of scale and efficiency) but also improve efficiency as the masses develop the skills, health and motivation to succeed and progress in society.

Myrdal once again applied the institutionalist concept of cumulative circular causation in describing problems in third-world countries. For example, he contrasted the "spread-effects" that reinforce equilibrating and equalizing tendencies with the "back-wash effects" that reinforce the opposite disequilibria in a cumulative fashion. Initial disparity between regions will grow even more as the more prosperous region will attract capital and labor from other regions. Myrdal further applied this principle of circular causation by basically arguing that if the masses are trapped in low standards of living (due to lack of educational and employment opportunities), this will lead not only to lower productivity, which will make this segment less employable and low-wage employable, but also to higher rates of fertility, which will also perpetuate poverty. He never lost his desire to help make such change more likely. You could see it in his eyes and hear it in his voice, even when he made the most drastic pronouncements about the present state of the world.

CONCLUSION

Myrdal did not have as much influence on the mainstream economic theory as Arrow, Debreu and Samuelson. However, he left a towering impact on the political, institutional, moral and ethical aspects of economics. According to him, an economist who ignores the effects of political and social forces on economic events is dangerous. Myrdal put absolute emphasis on a balance between optimality of competitive markets and egalitarian distribution of income. He had a tremendous international experience and influence and a very clear vision about society and socioeconomic development of the third-world nations. Myrdal was a humanist, a pragmatist and a problem solver. Throughout his life, he sought ways to improve the human condition and used economics as a framework to solve societal problems. He was, even at the expense of his own prestige, unwilling to settle for sanitized and simple models but sought real solutions to "real-world" problems. In a memoir after Myrdal's death, a younger colleague and friend, Lars Ingelstam summarized Myrdal's life as follows: "Gunnar Myrdal wanted to see himself as an analytical intellectual, but there was in him, an insistence that the world could be rearranged in a more rational manner."

RECOMMENDED READINGS

Angresano, James. (1997). *The Political Economy of Gunnar Myrdal.* Cheltenham: Edward Elgar

Assarsson-Rizzi, Kerstin and Harold Borhrn. (1984). *Gunnar Myrdal: A Bibliography 1919-1981.* New York: Garland.

Dopfer, Kurt. (March 1998). "In Memorium: Gunnar Myrdal's Contribution to Institutional Economics," *Journal of Economic Issues.* Vol. 12, No. 1.

Dostaler Gilles, Diane Ethier and Laurent LePage. (1992). *Gunnar Myrdal and His Works.* Montreal: Harvest House Ltd.

Dykema, Eugene R.(1986). "No View Without a Viewpoint: Gunnar Myrdal," *World Development.* Vol. 14, No. 2, pp. 147-63.

Hagewood, Cathy J. (1982). *Contributions of the 1974 Nobel Prize Winners in Economics.* Coe College, Cedar Rapids , Iowa.

Myrdal, Gunnar. (1939). *Monetary Equilibrium.* London: Hodge.

——. (1944). *An American Dilemma: The Negro Problem and Modern Democracy.* 2 Vols. New York: Harper.

——. (1958). *Rich Lands and Poor: The Road to World Prosperity* (a revised edition of Myrdal's *Cairo Lectures*). New York: Harper

——. (1968). *Asian Drama: An Inquiry into the Poverty of Nations.* 3 Vols. London: Penguin.

——. (1974). *Against the Stream: Critical Essays in Economics.* New York: Pantheon.

——. (1985). "International Inequality and Foreign Aid in Retrospect," in Gerald M. Meier, and Dudley Seers, (eds.) *Pioneers in Development.* New York: Oxford University Press.

Pressman, Steven. (June 1994). "An American Dilemma: Fifty Years Later," *Journal of Economic Issues*. 28(2).

Streeten, Paul. (1990). "Gunnar Myrdal," *World Development*. 18(7), pp. 1031-37.

11

Leonid Kantorovich (1912-1986):
A Pioneer of the Theory of Optimum
Resource Allocation and a Laureate of 1975

Khashruzzaman Choudhury

BIOGRAPHICAL PROFILE

Leonid Kantorovich was born in 1912 in Saint Petersburg, Russia. His father died when he was only ten years old. At the age of fourteen he started his undergraduate education at Leningrad University, where he took courses in mathematics, political economy and modern history. His mathematical genius was evident from a paper he presented on set theory at the First All-Union Mathematical Congress in 1930. Kantorovich graduated from Leningrad University in 1930. Following that, he started teaching mathematics at Leningrad University. By 1934, he was promoted to the rank of full professor, and only a year later, he received his doctoral degree in mathematics from the same university. In the 1930s, Kantorovich witnessed an unprecedented growth in the industrial sector of the Russian economy. He made contributions to that through his theoretical and applied knowledge of mathematics. In 1938, he took a consultancy with the laboratory of the Plywood Trust. In solving some optimization problems there, he got interested in economics. Kantorovich invented the technique of linear programming in economics. During the Second World War, he taught at the Higher School for Naval Engineers. In that capacity, also, he continued advanced applied economic research. In 1944, he became the head of the department of approximate methods at the Mathematical Institute of the Soviet Academy of Sciences. There he did research leading to the efficient use of resources in socialist planning. As Kantorovich kept doing his research in mathematics, his achievements grew. From 1958 to 1964, he was a corresponding member of the Soviet Academy of Sciences, and from 1964, he became a full member. He published a number of works in various areas of mathematics. Kantorovich received the (then) Stalin prize for his contribution in mathematics in 1949. In 1965, along with two other Soviet economists, he was awarded the Lenin Prize for his path-breaking work in economic science, particularly for applications of mathematical methods to economic research and planning. In addition to working in Leningrad, for a long period, Kantorovich directed the department of mathematical-economic methods at the Siberian Division of the Academy of Sciences of the (former) Soviet Union.

Kantorovich received honorary degrees from many universities, including Glasgow, Grenoble, Nice, Helsinki and Paris. He was member of the American Academy of Arts and Science. In 1938, he married Natalia Ilyina, a physician. Their son and daughter are both economists. Leonid Kantorovich died in 1986.

INTRODUCTION

Leonid Kantorovich, along with Tjalling Koopmans, won the economics Nobel Prize in 1975 for his "contributions to the theory of optimum allocation of resources." Until 1975, Kantorovich was the first and only economics Nobel laureate from the then Soviet Union. Although Wassily Leontief and Simon Kuznets were born in the Soviet Union, at the time they received this prestigious award, both of them had already become American citizens. Kantorovich's other distinction was that he was one of the few mathematicians who received the Nobel Prize in economics. He became an economist by accident. Being a professor of mathematics at Leningrad University, he once took a consultancy with the Russian Plywood Trust. There solving a complex constrained optimization problem, he developed an interest in economics. He worked under unfavorable political and economic situations, yet he achieved a lot. He invented linear programming–a sophisticated tool in economics to make efficient utilization of resources under constraints.

ALLOCATION OF RESOURCES

During the 1930s, the Soviet Union was going through a period of rapid economic and industrial development. According to the philosophy of economic growth through planning, Kantorovich could foresee his role in applying, in a variety of cases, mathematical methods in solving optimization of production problems under a given set of constraints. Kantorovich had his first opportunity in 1938 to apply his mathematical knowledge to solve such problems when he was appointed a consultant to the laboratory of the Plywood Trust. His primary task was to suggest a technique for distributing raw materials to different production lines in order to maximize equipment productivity. Kantorovich cast the problem in mathematical terms–which later was known as linear programming: maximization of a linear function subject to a large number of constraints. Kantorovich could anticipate that solving this problem would open doors for using this technique in many other optimization cases, for example, in the cases of determination of optimum sowing area or the most efficient distribution of transport flows.

In the Plywood Trust case, Kantorovich aimed at maximizing the sum of the values of the output of all machines. His constraints were represented by equations that related quantities of each input employed–such as power, wood, labor and time–to output of each machine. Of course, the total quantity of each input in no way exceeded the total quantity available. Kantorovich then introduced new variables called *resolving multipliers* as the coefficient of each input in the constraint equations and showed that the values of the input and output variables could easily be determined, once the values of the multipliers were known. These multipliers were essentially the marginal values, or shadow prices, of the critical limiting factors, equivalent to the scarcity price of each input in a perfectly competitive market.

Kantorovich's original work in the Plywood Trust case laid the foundation of all such work in the field in the Soviet Union and elsewhere. His original insight into the economical and mathematical significance of the multipliers led the way to further developments in constrained optimization problems, and especially in linear programming. Kantorovich demonstrated that all economics allocation problems could be framed as maximization problems subject to multiple constraints, and therefore, could potentially be resolved using linear programming–a technique he developed. In his presentation address at the award ceremony, Ragnayo Bentzel of the Royal Swedish Academy of Sciences presented the work of Kantorovich and Koopmans as evidence that the basic economic problems could be addressed in a scientific manner, which was independent of the political organization of the society under consideration.

Optimum Allocation of Resources

Based upon his experiences of applying mathematical linear programming methods to solve allocation of resources problems, Kantorovich extended his work into the entire economy. In his book, *The Best Use of Economic Resources*, Kantorovich analyzed efficiency conditions for optimum production in the entire economy. He worked toward establishing the connection between the allocation of resources and the price system, not only for a stationary economic system but also for a growing economy. Kantorovich demonstrated in his analysis that potential decentralized decisions in a planned economy were clearly dependent on the existence of a rational price system, including a uniform accounting interest rate, to suggest appropriate criteria for sound investment decisions. Kantorovich's contribution to economics, especially his insight into the basic nature of the optimization problem in all production situations, earned him worldwide recognition and respect when the English translation of his work reached other countries, including the United States. Although superior techniques were later formulated in linear programming, Kantorovich was the first mathematician-economist to formulate the basic linear programming problem involved in optimization very precisely. He also provided a wide range of examples of practical problems, which could be addressed and solved by his approach.

A pioneer in the field of linear programming, G.B. Dantzing, casts Kantorovich's contribution to allocation of resource problems in the following words: "Kantorovich should be credited with being the first to recognize that certain important broad classes of production problems had well-defined mathematical structures which, he believed, were amenable to practical numerical evaluation and could be numerically solved. The report contains an outstanding collection of potential applications."

In his evaluation of Kantorovich, Leif Johansen enumerates different aspects of Kantorovich's contribution to economics. According to him, if all of Kantorovich's contributions could be grouped under one heading, the appropriate heading would be optimization of the use of limited resources, that is, the most central of all economic problems. Johansen concludes his evaluation of Kantorovich with the following remarks: "From reading Kantorovich's books and papers, it is clear that he has acquired a profound understanding of economic problems and many of his expositions are marked by penetrating economic considerations and realistic references to practical problems. Kantorovich is a distinguished mathematician, but there is no doubt that we also have the right to include him among the ranks of the most outstanding economists of the last decades."

CONCLUSION

Kantorovich will always be remembered for his fundamental contribution to the theory of optimum allocation of resources. For the Soviet economy, his research provided direction and guidance for better economic planning, then rigorously in practice in the Soviet Union. Kantorovich showed how his technique could be applied to individual plants and industries, and also to the entire economy. His research on the price system, uniform accounting interest rate and criteria for sound investment decisions paved the way for somewhat decentralized but rational decision-making in the Soviet economy. Such decentralization was the demand of the time in former Russia, and Kantorovich's contributions were thus critical in bringing about the required changes in such decentralized Soviet decision-making regarding what to produce and how to produce. Kantorovich himself was very optimistic about the application of mathematics to solving problems of dynamic economic systems. He was aware of the difficulties inherent in the somewhat unavoidable loyalty to old ways of thinking and operation, but he was still optimistic about things to come: "In spite of mentioned difficulties, I am looking optimistically on the prospects of wide spread of mathematical methods, especially those of optimization, in economic science and in all-level economic control. It can give us a significant improvement of planning activity, better use of resources, increment of national income and living standards."

RECOMMENDED READINGS

Dantzing, George B. (1962). *Linear Programming and Extensions,* Princeton: Princeton University Press.

Johansen, Leif (1976). "L.V. Kantorovich's Contribution to Economics," *Scandanivian Journal of Economics.* Vol. 78, pp. 61-80.

Kantorovich, Leonid. (1989, December). "Mathematics in Economics: Achievements, Difficulties, Perspectives." (Nobel Memorial Lecture, December 11, 1975). Published in *American Economic Review*. pp. 18-22.

———. (1958). "On the Translocation of Masses," *Management Science*. Vol. 5, pp. 1-4.

———. (1965). *The Best Use of Economic Resources*. London: Pergamon Press.

Katz, Bernard S., (ed.) (1989). *Nobel Laureates in Economic Science: A Biographical Dictionary*. London: Garland Publishing.

Koopmans, Tjalling, (ed.) (1951). *Activity Analysis of Production and Allocation*. New York: John Wiley and Sons.

Lindbeck, Assar, (ed.) (1992). *Nobel Lectures, Including Presentation Speeches and Laureates' Biographies*. Stockholm: Institute for International Economic Studies, University of Stockholm.

12

Tjalling Koopmans (1910-1985):
The Originator of Activity
Analysis and a Laureate of 1975

Abul Hasnat Dewan

BIOGRAPHICAL PROFILE

Tjalling Koopmans was born in 1910 in Graveland, the Netherlands. His father was the principal of a Protestant school. His eldest brother, Jan, who died during the World War II, was a minister of the Dutch Reformed Church, and his elder brother, Hendrijk, was a chemical engineer. At the age of fourteen, Koopmans received the St. Geertruidsleen fellowship that supported his studies for the next 12 years. It gave him the much needed financial support, "and therefore, intellectual independence and the opportunity to explore various fields of knowledge" as Koopmans put it. Initially, Koopmans concentrated on mathematics. Later, he considered becoming a psychiatrist, but in order to apply his mathematical training, he chose the field of theoretical physics. Koopmans acknowledged that his teacher Hans Kramers' style of mathematical application had great influence on his later work. Koopmans received his master's degree in mathematics and physics from the University of Utrecht in 1933, and published a paper in quantum mechanics in 1934. His passion for a subject "closer to real life" and the Great Depression in the 1930s drew his attention to the field of economics. Through some of his socialist friends, he came across Karl Marx's *Das Kapital*, which was the first economics book that he read. The exposition of Marxian thought had an everlasting effect on Koopmans in the sense that in later years, when he became a mathematical economist, he tried to make the fundamental part of his economic theory independent of any institutional-setting. In 1933, Koopmans came to know about the field of mathematical economics. He moved to Amsterdam to learn from the then leading mathematical economist, Jan Tinbergen. In 1935, Koopmans spent four months with the "giant of mathematical economics," Ragnar Frisch, but they differed in their econometric approaches. Koopmans received his Ph.D. from the Faculty of Mathematical and Physical Sciences at the University of Leiden for his dissertation "Linear Regression Analysis of Economic Time-Series" in 1936. At the news conference following the award of the Nobel Prize, he stated: "I first aspired to being a mathematician and then to being a theoretical physicist .... I was halfway with math and halfway with physics when I found economics more challenging." (Katz: 1989). From 1936 to 1938, Koopmans taught at the School of Economics at Rotterdam as a replacement teacher for Tinbergen. Then, he worked for the Financial Section of the League of Nations in Geneva until he moved to the US in 1940. He assumed the "humble role" of statistician for the Combined Shipping Adjustment Board in 1942. Koopmans left the Board in 1944, joined the Cowles Commission for Research in Economics at the University of Chicago and was there until 1955, when he moved to Yale University as a full professor. He remained with Yale until his death. He served as director of the Cowles Foundation at Yale from 1961 to 1967. He taught at Harvard University in 1960-61, and spent 1968-69 at the Center for Advanced Study in the Behavioral Sciences at Stanford University. Because of his interest in the area of energy-supply, he served a year at the International Institute for Applied Systems Analysis in Austria. In 1936, a month before receiving his Ph.D. degree, Koopmans married an economics student, Truus Wanningen, who he had tutored. After winning the Nobel Prize, Koopmans praised her as an economic bibliographer and "an advisor on important decisions." Koopmans enjoyed playing violin and occasionally wrote musical compositions. His life, full of great work, ended on February 26, 1985 in Yale University Hospital at the age of 74. He left behind his wife, three children – Anne, Henry and Helen, and brother, Henrijk.

INTRODUCTION

Tjalling Koopmans, along with Leonid Kantorovich, won the economics Nobel Prize in 1975 for his "contributions to the theory of optimum allocation of resources." Dutch-American economist Koopmans and Kantorovich of Russia, through their independent research, proved that the economic problem faced by all societies (regardless of their political color)... fundamentally the same. That is the efficient utilization of scarce resources under a set of constraints. Koopmans invented activity analysis for the purpose of optimum resource allocation, which is similar to the technique of linear programming that was developed by Kantorovich in Russia. Koopman's basic training was in mathematics and physics, yet he became a great economist, not only making monumental contributions to the mainstream economics but also guiding and directing the research of several other brilliant economists who established themselves in the economics profession with same stature as Koopmans. They are Lawrence Klein, Milton Friedman, Robert Solow, Herbert Simon, Harry Markowitz and many more.

ACTIVITY ANALYSIS

In a 1942 memo, *Exchange Ratios Between Cargoes on Various Routes*, Koopmans first described the activity analysis technique. Koopmans showed, that when a firm has a limited amount of inputs at its disposal, and these limited inputs can be combined in a finite number of mixes to produce goods, that the appropriate method to choose the optimal mix of inputs involves linear programming or activity analysis.

For example, assume that a firm can use one of the following two processes, or combinations of capital and labor, to make a maximum of 100 pair of jeans per day: (i) 3 units of capital and 5 units of labor or (ii) 4 units of capital and 4 units of labor. If the firm produces 100 pair of jeans per day, its activity level is 100. The firm can operate each of the two processes at different activity levels, e.g., 0, 25, 50, 100 etc. Different activity levels with different processes will yield different amounts of profit. Koopmans' methodology is applied to find the profit-maximizing process and the activity level in such cases.

Koopmans used activity analysis to find the most cost-effective cargo delivery route for Allied Shipping during the World War II. He showed that in case of non-availability of market prices for some routes, the potential values or shadow prices could be used in his methodology to determine the cost-effective allocation of ships. Koopmans applied activity analysis to transportation economics and inter-temporal resource allocation problems. His methodology has improved the criteria for investment project evaluations.

Activity analysis is a powerful tool for summarizing technological choices and production possibilities under a particular set of conditions. It also gives an indication of the welfare losses due to the use of improper or inferior technology. The efficient allocation of resources, achieved by using his methodology, yields a set of prices that are equivalent to the input prices in a perfectly competitive market. Therefore, even planners in centrally controlled economies can use activity analysis to determine "competitive" prices for various inputs.

THEORY OF OPTIMAL ECONOMIC GROWTH

While activity analysis considers productive activities in a short planning horizon, Koopmans' other major research interest, economic growth theory, seeks to find an optimal consumption path in a very long, or infinite, time horizon. The objective of optimal growth model is inter-temporal allocation of scarce resources to maximize utilities for all generations. By handing over capital stock, a current generation partly determines the range of choices of possible consumption paths for later generations. "Each generation's choice thus involves a weighing of a little more consumption for itself against a little wider range of choice (including higher consumption paths) for its descendants " (Koopmans: 1967).

In the same 1967 article, "Objectives, Constraints and Outcomes in Optimal Growth Models," Koopmans further argued that "too much weight given to generations far into the future turns out to be self-defeating ... How much weight is too much has to be determined ...." Koopmans recognized the impact of technological progress on the optimal growth path. However, he asserted that humankind needs to be aware of the productive capacity limits of the planet. Population cannot go on increasing exponentially forever, because the rate of technological progress has an upper bound, too.

Koopmans also made major contributions in the areas of efficiency in growth and preference orderings. A rational consumer's objective is to maximize satisfaction (or utility) given her budget constraint. Therefore, she has to rank different bundles of consumption goods. In his 1972 paper "Preference Orderings in Consumption," Koopmans showed how a given preference ordering can be represented by a function. In another paper "Preference Orderings Over Time," he talked about the preference ordering of an individual's lifetime consumption program, and also about the aggregation of individual preferences over time. The consumers' finite life spans, their bequest motives and population growth rates are important considerations in such cases. Koopmans discussed relevant utility functions, or objective functions, and their significance in optimal growth models.

In his Nobel lecture, he stressed that various strands of ethical, political or social thought could be incorporated in the objective function of a growth model. He also emphasized the need for incorporating various aspects of an economy such as exhaustible resources, technological change, and population growth as policy variables in economic models. However, in a paper, Koopmans noted that the contributions of growth models are still limited in practical decision-making processes due to the simplified assumptions used in building such models.

EFFICIENT ALLOCATION OF RESOURCES

Allocation of Resources and the Price System (1951b)

This is the first essay of Koopmans' seminal work, *Three Essays on the State of Economic Science*. Here, he emphasized "a need for the evaluation of institutional arrangements as well as for the prediction of production capabilities in any particular institutional setting." He pointed out that under certain conditions, an efficient set of activities would be sustained forever in a competitive market. The required conditions are: (i) a system of prices that is compatible with a given technology, (ii) non-negative prices for desired commodities, (iii) non-usage of a process with negative profit, and (iv) the continued usage of break-even processes at the same level of activity.

In many allocation problems such as resource development, municipal services, or national defense no market valuation exists. However, data on input prices, or prices of scarce resources used to serve these objectives, might be available. Linear programming methods can be used for computational purposes in such cases.

Efficient Allocation of Resources (1951b)

Efficiency in production requires the additional cost, or marginal cost, of production be equal to price. The problem, however, is that the marginal cost may not necessarily be known quantitatively to the manager of individual production process. Koopmans' methodology can be used to find an efficient outcome in such a case. The prerequisites for productive efficiency in an economy are: "(A) the attainment of efficiency by each process manager within the set of activities controlled by him, and, in particular, (B) the selection of such an efficient activity composition by each process manager that an associated set of efficiency prices exists which is the same for all process managers."

Once efficiency is attained, it can be maintained if each process manager behaves according to the following simple rules: "Any activity yielding a negative profit is to be contracted. Any activity yielding a zero profit is to be maintained at a constant level. Any activity yielding a positive profit is to be expanded, if necessary by bidding up prices of its input commodities." Such a behavior could be enforced through administrative rules that are binding for the managers, or it could simply be the result of the competition among independent entrepreneurs.

OPTIMAL GEOGRAPHICAL
DISTRIBUTION OF INDUSTRY

Optimal Utilization of the Transportation System (1949a)

In this article, Koopmans explored a theory of optimal transportation rates, which laid the groundwork for a theory of the optimal geographical distribution of industry. Koopmans formulated a criterion for determining the marginal cost of a given change in the routing of ships, which is equally applicable to other modes of transportation.

An example can be cited from his article to explain this. Assume that two terminals A and B are connected with a railroad. Everyday there is a demand for five trainloads of goods from A to B, but only three trainloads of goods from B to A. If the demand for goods from A to B increases by one more trainload, the cost of that transportation in terms of time is the sum of the times spent loading in A, moving to B and unloading in B, by a train. Not only that, we must account for the cost of the train coming back empty from B to A. In this case the marginal cost is the whole turn-around time of one train: loading, moving, unloading, and coming back to the point of origin. The marginal cost of an additional trainload from B to A is, however, only the time spent loading in B and unloading in A, since the train has to return anyway. Therefore, a sizable difference in marginal cost can be found depending on the direction of transportation. In the real world, transportation systems connect many terminals, not only two. Koopmans formulated a rule for determining the marginal costs in a general network of routes.

PRODUCTION, EXHAUSTIBLE
RESOURCES, AND THE DOOMSDAY

Koopmans tried to find optimal level of consumption and investment, and discussed the roles of exhaustible resources and discount factor with this regard.

The followings are three such selective articles that also appear in the second volume of his *Scientific Papers.*

Production (1977)

Using the optimization technique, Koopmans tried to find a capital stock which, "if put in the place of the given initial stock, will be reproduced precisely at the end of each period." He used different models to find the amounts of invariant optimal capital stocks, and showed that they are functions of available technology, resource constraints and preferences of the people.

Optimal Economic Growth and Exhaustible Resources (1973)

To maximize social welfare, output at all times need to be optimally divided between consumption and net investment. "In the exhaustible resources model, discounting of future utilities favors an earlier generation over any surviving later generation, and shortens the period of survival." In this paper, Koopmans cited an example of a group of stranded sailors in a barren island. Assume that the sailors have pooled their resources, R, to be allocated over time to maximize their utility. The sailors know that a subsistence level, r, of consumption of resources is needed for survival. The maximum survival time for the group is $T = R/r$. A higher than subsistence level of consumption means a shorter period of survival for the group.

A competitive market with infinitely long foresight would exhibit a sustained exponential increase in the scarcity price, or shadow price, of an exhaustible resource if no substitute were available.

The Doomsday (1974)

Consumers maximize present and discounted future utility from their inter-temporal consumption levels. If it is assumed that the consumption of a certain amount of a resource is essential for human life, all human lives will cease upon its exhaustion. Koopmans showed that a larger discount rate would make the survival period shorter. In other words, if people put less weight on future consumption, doomsday comes sooner.

PARAMETER ESTIMATION AND IDENTIFICATION OF ECONOMETRIC MODELS

Econometric models are used to predict the future course of various economic variables and also, to analyze various policy-impacts. An econometric model is an equation, or a set of equations, that embody some aspects of the economy. For example, a consumption function can be written as:

$$C = a + bY$$
where,   C = consumption spending;

$$Y = \text{after-tax income;}$$
$$a, b = \text{parameters.}$$

Assume that, when using data from an economy, the parameters of this model are estimated to be:

$$C = \$500 \text{ billion} + 0.8Y$$

This equation indicates that consumer spending in that economy is $500 billion plus 80 percent of disposable or after-tax income. This very simple model can then be used to predict the nation's consumption expenditure given disposable income.

In the past, many researchers and policy makers expected that such econometric models would allow the government or the appropriate authority to respond with precise quantitative measures to minimize cyclical variations of economic variables around the trend. The works of Koopmans and several other econometricians helped establish the theoretical basis for large-scale macroeconomic models of an economy. Koopmans led a team of econometricians at Yale University, which developed useful new estimation procedures, particularly in cases of limited information.

Any statistical inference or prediction regarding a parameter of economic behavior is conditional upon the correct choice of a model. Koopmans argued that economic data alone could support too many plausible hypotheses unless the data were supplemented with *a priori* information. *Identification* issues affect the possibility or impossibility of obtaining meaningful estimates of the structural parameters of a model. In his 1949 article, "Identification Problems in Economic Model Construction," Koopmans emphasized the need for identification of parameters, in particular when there is a change in structural parameters between the period of observation and the period to which the prediction applies. For example, assume a model that shows consumers' demand for jeans depends on prices and on their incomes. If there is any change in consumers' preferences, future expectations, or a change in the tax rates between the period of observation and the period to which the prediction applies, there will certainly be some effect on the parameter values of this model. In such a case, knowledge of the earlier values of the variables may not be sufficient for predictions. Predictions are possible ".... if the known structural change can be applied to identifiable structural parameters, i.e., parameters of which knowledge is implied in a knowledge of the 'old' distribution combined with the *a priori* considerations that have entered into the model." (Koopmans: 1949b)

ECONOMIC SCIENCE

Economics Among the Sciences (1979)

In this paper, Koopmans identified some common errors made by researchers in other fields of sciences. As an example, he pointed out that the proposals of the Helium Study Committee on helium storage program could not be satisfactory to an economist, for it had failed to provide cost or benefit estimates for the program.

"... because of the importance of energy supply processes among the increased uses of helium ..., the benefits cannot be estimated without comparable cost and fuel availability estimates for alternative energy supply and use technologies which have low or zero helium requirements." Another limitation is the failure of recognizing the need for "discounting" future benefits and costs. Koopmans noted that in the presence of considerable uncertainty, economists also prefer to add an allowance for risk to the discount rate.

The Construction of Economic Knowledge (1957)

This is the second essay of the *Three Essays* where Koopmans explored various directions in which ".... the postulates of economic theory could be modified and refined in order to recognize more aspects of reality." Economic theory is a sequence of conceptual models that express different aspects of a complicated reality in simplified form. Koopmans emphasized more systematic observation and direct or indirect testing of postulates, rather than casual empiricism. In this essay, he also discussed increasing returns to scale (or decreasing cost) and location problems, uncertainty, and interaction of preferences.

The Interaction of Tools and Problems in Economics (1957)

The third essay of the *Three Essays* examined several developments of the tools of economic analysis and their implications "in regard to the problems of achieving a stable rate of growth of the economy." Koopmans accentuated the need for *a priori* knowledge, or assumptions through observation, in econometric models. He also emphasized the importance of disaggregated data. For example, in order to use engineering knowledge in the production models, a high degree of disaggregated data would be required.

THE NOBEL LECTURE

Koopmans defined economics as a discipline capable of assuring the "best use of scarce resources." The optimization models, therefore, have useful applications in different areas of economics. For example, productive sectors of an economy, where managers and supervisors try to achieve the best use of scarce resources; economic growth models, where "best allocation" means maximization of the sum of utilities for all generations; and development programming, that involves the construction of programming models for extended time frames.

Koopmans argued in favor of using positive discount rates in economic growth models. He said, "the impatience expressed by a positive discount rate merely denies to uncounted distant generations a permanently higher level of consumption because that would necessitate a substantially smaller present consumption. Perhaps a pity, but not a sin " (Zahka: 1991).

CONCLUSION

Koopmans' contributions in economics were varied and extensive. As a mathematical economist, Koopmans' work demonstrated mastery of sophisticated techniques and arguments. Nonetheless, he made conscious effort to minimize the communication gaps between the mathematical and non-mathematical economists. In this paper, I have focused mainly on his contributions in economic growth theory, economic planning and policy analysis. A modest and careful scholar, Koopmans as Scarf puts it: "consistently displayed .... intellectual freshness, conceptual originality, and stylistic clarity over .... an extended period of time" (Introduction to *Scientific Papers*).

NOTE

The author is grateful to Drs. F. T. Jannuzi & G. Tarzwell for their helpful comments. Any remaining errors are solely the author's responsibility.

RECOMMENDED READINGS

Blaug, Mark. (1983). *Great Economists Since Keynes*. Sussex: Wheatsheaf Books.

Brownlee, O. H. (1952). "Book Review of T. C. Koopmans' Activity Analysis of Production and Allocation," *Econometrica*. Vol. 20, No. 1, pp. 111-12.

Jungenfelt, Karl G. (1976). "Koopmans and the Recent Development of Growth Theory," *Scandinavian Journal of Economics (SJE)*.

Katz, Bernard S. (1989). *Nobel Laureates in Economic Sciences: A Biographical Dictionary*. London, New York: Garland Publishing.

Koopmans, T. C. (1985). *Scientific Papers of Tjalling C. Koopmans*. Vol. II, Cambridge: MIT Press.

_____ . (1979). "Economics Among the Sciences," *American Economic Review*. (69)1.

_____ . (1970). *Scientific Papers of Tjalling C. Koopmans*. New York: Springer Verlag.

_____ . (1967). "Objectives, Constraints, and Outcomes in Optimal Growth Models," *Econometrica*. Vol. 35, No. 1.

_____ . (1957). *Three Essays on the State of Economic Science*. New York: McGraw-Hill Inc.

_____ . (1951). *Activity Analysis of Production and Allocation*, Proceedings of a Conference, (ed.) Koopmans, T. C., Chicago: Cowles Commission.

_____ . (1951). "Efficient Allocation of Resources," *Econometrica*. Vol. 19, pp. 455-65

_____ . (1949). "Optimum Utilization of the Transportation System," *Econometrica*. Vol. 17, pp. 136-46.

_____ .(1949). "Identification Problems in Econometric Model Construction," *Econometrica*. Vol. 17, No. 2, pp. 125-44.

Scarf, Herbert. (1975). "The 1975 Nobel Prize in Economics: Resource

Werin, Lars. (1976). "Activity Analysis, Methodology and Econometrics," *Scandinavian Journal of Economics.* Vol. 78.

Zahka, William J. (1992). *The Nobel Prize Economics Lectures.* Avebury Publishing.

13

Milton Friedman (1912-   ):
The Leader of the Monetarist School of Thought and the Laureate of 1976

Muhammad Mustafa

BIOGRAPHICAL PROFILE

Milton Friedman was born in 1912 in Brooklyn, New York. His parents immigrated to the United States from the then Austria-Hungary at a young age. His father did not have any solid job. His mother used to run a small retail store. He did not grow up in affluence, but there was not much hardship in the family. His father died before he was a high school graduate. He started his undergraduate studies at Rutgers University, New Jersey, with a scholarship and received his first degree in 1932. He majored in mathematics hoping to become an actuary, a dream that did not materialize. Then he became interested in economics. The same year, he started his graduate program in economics at the University of Chicago, where he came in contact with Jacob Viner, Frank Knight, Henry Schultz and others. After obtaining his M.A. in Chicago in 1933, he moved to Columbia University with an attractive fellowship. At Chicago, he was exposed to economic theory by Jacob Viner, and at Columbia, Harold Hotelling opened the door of mathematics and statistics for him. The following year he returned to Chicago again. He worked for Henry Schultz as a research assistant and became friendly with George Stigler and W. Allen Wallis. In the summer of 1935, his work at the National Resources Committee in Washington, DC, shaped his theory of Consumption Function. In 1937, he worked with Simon Kuznets at the National Bureau of Economic Research, the outcome of which constitutes his doctoral dissertation. He received his Ph.D. from Columbia in 1946. Prior to that, during 1941-1943 he worked for the U.S. Department of Treasury, and from 1943 to 1945 he worked at Columbia University on problems of weapon design and military tactics. In 1945, he joined the University of Minnesota, and the next year he moved to the University of Chicago to succeed Jacob Viner who left for Princeton. At Chicago, he led the work to develop the School of Monetarism, which is also known as the Chicago School of thought. In 1950, he spent some time in Paris as a consultant to administer the Marshall Plan. He spent 1953-1954 in Cambridge University, England, as a Fulbright professor. In the 1960 he also served as economic advisor to Senator Goldwater and President Nixon. In 1977, he retired from the University of Chicago and became a senior research fellow at the Hoover Institution of Stanford University. Friedman received the John Clark Medal of the American Economic Association and honorary degrees from many universities, including Harvard, Rutgers, Lehigh, Loyola, and others. In 1938, he married Rose Director, who is also an economist. They have a son and a daughter.

INTRODUCTION

Milton Friedman received the economics Nobel Prize in 1976 for "his achievements in the fields of consumption analysis, monetary history and theory and for his demonstration of the complexity of stabilization policy." Friedman's research in theoretical and empirical economics has been very diverse and provocative. Until the early 1970s, Keynesians had the upper hand on macroeconomic policy matters in the Western world. Following the Arab-Israel war and the oilcrunch of 1973-1974, the capitalist world was suffering from the simultaneous presence of inflation and unemployment. Keynesians could not come up with a correct explanation and solution to the problem. Friedman termed it as "stagflation," gave his supply-side solution and became popular among the policy people.   Friedman is one of the very few economists who know how to communicate effectively with noneconomists.   In lectures, debates, the TV documentary series *Free to Choose*, several best-selling books and a column in Newsweek, he has persuasively presented his ideas to his audience. Friedman's conservative ideas about the importance of a free market had a tremendous influence on many politician including the U.S. presidents Richard Nixon and Ronald Reagan and the British prime ministers Margaret Thatcher and John Major. Even his critics recognize the significance of Friedman's contributions to the areas of empirical research, methodology, macroeconomic theory, monetary history and public policy analysis. Although many of Friedman's policy prescriptions are controversial, John Burton, a British economist, says, "[Friedman] provided us with an agenda for the future of macroeconomic research."

METHODOLOGY OF POSITIVE ECONOMICS

In 1953, Friedman published an essay on "The Methodology of Positive Economics,"   which has given rise to a persistent set of methodological controversies. In this essay, Friedman contrasts normative and positive economics. Normative economics refers to "what ought to be," whereas positive economics examines the facts to determine "what is." Friedman favors positive economics, with its ability to predict consequences, rather than the normative approach, which provides inconclusive results. Friedman believes that the free market helps to reconcile normative conflicts over values. Friedman argues that most traditional criticism of economic theory has criticized assumption, instead of testing implications. He contends that the validity of a theory is to be established by the accuracy of predictions, not by the description of realism at the premise. "A hypothesis is important if it 'explains' much by little."

THE PERMANENT-INCOME HYPOTHESIS

Working with Dorothy Brady, Margaret Reid and Rose Director, Friedman formulated and empirically tested his "Permanent Income Hypothesis" of consumption. Friedman, in his book, *A Theory of Consumption Function*, published in 1957, reinterpreted the Keynesian consumption function by relating it to a lifetime instead of current income. Keynes postulated that current consumption spending has a stable relation to current income and that a larger proportion of income is saved as real income rises. Friedman and others were puzzled by two apparently contradictory empirical facts: (1) time-series data from World War II and cross-sectional data from surveys of individuals and families confirmed that current consumption was highly correlated with income and the percentage of income saved increased with rising income; and (2) the ratio of saving to income in the United States since 1899 has been relatively constant despite increases in real income. Friedman's theory helps resolve this apparent contradiction.

Friedman argues that Keynes' consumption function, which relates consumption to current income, is misleading. Instead, Friedman maintained that consumers base their consumption decisions on their expected long-run or lifetime income. Friedman calls his theory the Permanent Income Hypothesis (PIH). If at any time income rises above or falls below the permanent level, an individual considers the increase or decrease to be only temporary; Friedman calls it transitory. Any transitory increase in income causes an increase in savings and vice versa. Consumption remains constant in both situations where income increases or decreases. Thus, Friedman's PIH provides testable hypotheses regarding policy prescriptions such as permanent changes in taxes versus temporary changes, for instance, tax rebates. Empirical data in the United States and Europe were found to be consistent with PIH's prediction.

THE QUANTITY THEORY OF MONEY

Friedman, in his essay "A Monetary and Fiscal Framework for Economic Stability," turned his attention to monetary affairs and stabilization issues. Friedman calls for various reforms in the areas of monetary and fiscal policies designed to create stability and prevent inflation in the macroeconomy. Some of the measures are: limiting the powers of the Federal Reserve System over the money supply, reducing the ability of the government to take counter-cyclical fiscal policies, and allowing the money supply to change only in response to changes in the federal budget deficits. In his *Studies in the Quantity Theory of Money* (1956),

Friedman attempted to give new life to the anti -Keynesian doctrine that "money matters". According to the quantity theory of money, the price level in the economy depends on the money supply. In the equation form, the quantity of money is as follows:

$$MV = PY$$

where,
M = money supply consisting of currency,
coins and checking balances,
V = average number of times the money is
exchanged during a period of time or the
velocity of money,
P = price level and
Y = real income.

Classical theorists assume that the velocity of money is stable. Therefore, price level is proportional to the stock of money. In his essay "The Quantity Theory of Money: A Restatement," Friedman presents a new version of demand for money. In a functional form, the Friedman's demand for money can be written as:

$$md = a\ (Yp, w, i, p^*, p, z)$$

where the demand for money (md) is a function
of (a) permanent income (Yp), the proportion
of human to non-human wealth (w), the nominal
interest rate (i), expected changes in the rate of
change in the price level (p*), the actual price
level (p), and the preference function for money
versus other goods (z).

Friedman's reformulation is a theory of demand for money, not a theory of prices. This approach is similar to that of Keynes. However, there is an important difference between them. In Friedman's restatement, permanent income, rather than actual income is used. Using the concept of permanent income, Friedman is able to resolve an apparent empirical contradiction: over time, as real income rises, the velocity of money declines. However, during short periods of expansion, velocity rises and during contractions it falls. Friedman maintains that people make their money demand decision based on their permanent income. In the long run, both velocity and demand for money are stable functions of permanent income. In the long run, as permanent income rises and demand for money increases, expanding the money supply helps the price level remain stable. Thus, in the long run, money is neutral. However, changes in the money supply can have short-run effects on income, employment and interest rates. Friedman's finding has implications for monetarists' policy: as the money supply is a crucial factor to ensure economic stability and prosperity, the government should establish a constant rate of growth of the money supply equal to the desired rate of growth of output.

In a controversial work with Meiselman published in *Stabilization Policies*, Friedman argues that monetary velocity is more stable than the Keynesian investment multiplier. They calculated the correlation between consumption spending and investment spending. Their finding suggests stronger correlation between consumption and money stock. But these findings were challenged in the profession.

MONETARY HISTORY

Friedman's classic work, *A Monetary History of the United States, 1897-1960*, co-authored with Anna Schwartz of the National Bureau of Economic Research, had a profound influence on the economics profession. The authors compiled monetary statistics dating back to the American Revolution and recorded the pervasive role of changes in the nation's money supply on its inflationary evidences. Perhaps the most important period covered in the study is between 1929-33. To the Keynesians, the Great Depression was a proof that laissez-fair did not work and intervention by government is essential for economic stability. The most striking finding of the book: the major cause of the Depression was the Federal Reserve System's failure to prevent the money supply from shrinking by one-third. With respect to the Great Depression, Friedman concludes: "The Great Depression in the United States, far from being a sign of the inherent instability of the private enterprise system, is a testament to how much harm can be done by mistakes on the part of a few men when they wield vast power over the monetary system of a country." "The Great Contraction (of money supply,)" they wrote, "is tragic testimony to the power of monetary policy - not, as Keynes and so many of his contemporaries believed, evidence of impotence." The finding confirmed Friedman's contention that changes in the money supply have significant short-term effects on real income and employment. This clashed sharply with the Keynesian view that government fiscal policy is the key to economic stability.

INFLATION AND UNEMPLOYMENT

Friedman's presidential address to the American Economic Association, "The Role of Monetary Policy," introduced the profession to the now famous concept of "natural rate of unemployment." Friedman defines the natural rate of unemployment in the following terms: "It refers...to that rate of unemployment which is consistent with the existing real conditions in the labor market. It can be lowered by removing obstacles in the labor market, by reducing friction. It can be raised by introducing additional obstacles. The purpose of the concept is to separate the monetary from the non-monetary aspects of the unemployment situation–precisely the same purpose that Wicksell had in using the word natural in connection with he rate of interest."

The natural rate of unemployment is some rate of equilibrium unemployment consistent with the market structure of the economy. Any attempt to reduce the unemployment rate below this level will lead to ever-increasing inflation. Friedman maintains that there is no long-run trade-off between inflation and unemployment. However, due to workers' inaccurate assessment of actual rate of inflation, short-run trade-offs between inflation and unemployment are possible. Friedman's concepts of real and anticipated variables and natural rate of unemployment became so well-known and widely accepted that all intermediate macroeconomic theory texts include them. These concepts are essential to the understanding of modern macroeconomics. Furthermore, Friedman's initial research stimulated a tremendous amount of research, which examined the influence of expectation and the natural rate of unemployment on other macroeconomic variables.

In his *A Theoretical Framework for Monetary Analysis* and "Nobel Lecture: Inflation and Unemployment," Friedman continued to defend and analyze his concept of natural rate of unemployment. Then he explained a new problem, not "stagflation" but "slumplation"–rising level of unemployment occurring simultaneously with rising rates of price inflation. That means the long-run Phillips Curve is positively inclined. He admitted that the natural rate hypothesis alone cannot explain this problem. He suggested that supply-side shock such as increases in oil prices may be responsible in addition to the interventionist policies of government along with changing environment.

PUBLIC POLICY ISSUES

Friedman gave a series of lectures and wrote many articles on policy issues for the general public. Friedman's views on social policy became widely known through the publication of *Capitalism and Freedom* (1962), *Dollars and Deficits* (1968), *Bright Promises, Dismal Performance* (1972), and series of television documentaries. In *Capitalism and Freedom*, Friedman made policy suggestions including to discontinue price supports for agriculture, tariffs and quotas on imports, rent control, minimum wages, regulation of industries, compulsory old-age retirement programs, licensing of professions or occupations, public housing, national banks, and the prohibition of carrying first-class mail for profits.

CONCLUSION

Friedman is one of the greatest empirical economists of this time. "His work has become popular because it helps in practice to make predictions." He firmly believes that economic models should be judged by the ability of their predictions, not by the soundness of their assumptions. According to him, a single equation model may be more meaningful than the multiple equation model that Keynesians favor. Friedman is almost solely instrumental in reestablishing the role of money and monetary policy to explain and interpret economic fluctuations and the process of inflation. The words "money matters" or even "only money matters" are the gifts of Friedman to macroeconomics literature. Friedman's criticism about the so-called inflation unemployment trade-off portrayed by the Phillips Curve left a lasting impact on the macroeconomic policy controversy. Friedman's assertion that "uncertainty and time lag are involved in stabilization policies" also has a very strong standing in modern macroeconomic literature. Friedman is not only a brilliant economist and a great scholar but also a terrific teacher in the classroom. His clarity of exposition and power to persuade and convince people is unparalleled. He is one of the most articulate men in speech and writing the economics profession has ever produced.

RECOMMENDED READINGS

Friedman, Milton. (1937). "The Use of Ranks to the Assumption of Normality Implications of the Analysis of Variance," *Journal of American Statistical Association*. Vol. 32, pp. 675-701.

——. (1948). "A Monetary and Fiscal Framework for Economic Stability," *American Economic Review*. Vol. 38, pp. 245-64.

——. (1953). *Essays in Positive Economics*. Chicago: University of Chicago Press.

——. (1953). "It All Depends of What You Mean by 'Money Supply," *Business Week*.

——. (1953). "The Methodology of Positive Economics," *In Essays in Positive Economics*. Chicago: University of Chicago Press.

——. (1956). *Studies in the Quantity Theory of Money*. Chicago: University of Chicago Press.

——. (1957). *Theory of Consumption Function*. Princeton: Princeton University Press.

——. (1962). *Capitalism and Freedom*. Chicago: University of Chicago Press.

——. (1968). *Dollars and Deficits*. New York. Prentice-Hall.

——. (1968). "The Role of Monetary Policy," *American Economic Review*. Vol. 55.

——. (1968). "The Role of Monetary Policy," *American Economic Review*. Vol. 58, pp. 4-17.

——. (1971). *Readings in Microeconomics*. Ed. William Breit and Harold Hochman. Second Edition. New York, Holt: Rhinehart and Winston.

——. (1972). *Bright Promises, Dismal Performance*. New York: Harcourt Brace Jovanovich.

——. (1975). *There's No Such Thing as a Free Lunch*. Chicago: University of Chicago Press.

——. (1977). "Nobel Lecture: Inflation and Unemployment," *Journal of Political Economy*. Vol. 85, pp. 451-72.

——. (1984). "Lessons from the 1979-1982 Monetary Policy Experiment," *Papers and Proceedings, American Economic Association*. pp. 397-401.

14

James Meade (1907-1995):
A Pioneer of the Theory of the Second
Best and a Laureate of 1977

Khashruzzaman Choudhury

BIOGRAPHICAL PROFILE

James Meade was born in Bath, England, in 1907. His early education was concentrated on Greek and Latin. When he entered Oriel College, Oxford, in 1926, he continued the same line of education until 1928. Then he started to study philosophy, politics and economics. His interest in economics was triggered by high unemployment in England during the interwar period. In 1930, he won a fellowship to Hertford College, Oxford, to study economics, but soon after he moved to Trinity College, Cambridge, at the invitation of Dennis Robertson. That was the most exciting time for him, because at Cambridge, he came in contact with Richard Kahn, Peiro Sraffa, Joan Robinson and above all John Maynard Keynes. He taught economics at Hertford College, Oxford during 1931-1937. At that time, he was deeply involved in the study of economics of unemployment and international trade. Presumably being persuaded by his wife, toward the end of 1937, he joined the Economic Section of the League of Nations and moved to Geneva because his wife had some acquaintances in Geneva. There he edited two issues of *the World Economic Survey*. At the outbreak of the Second World War, Meade left Geneva for England with his wife and three young children and joined the Economic Section of the War Cabinet Secretariat of the British government. He held this position until 1947. With the cooperation of Lionel Robbins and John Keynes, this became a very prestigious agency. There he, along with Richard Stone, for the first time estimated the national income and expenditure of the United Kingdom. He was also actively involved with the preparation of the British White paper on employment policy and the ideas concerning the origination of the post-World War International Monetary Fund, the International Bank for Reconstruction and Development and the General Agreement on Tariffs and Trade (now known as the World Trade Organization). In 1947, he joined the London School of Economics as a professor of commerce. For the period 1957-1967 he held a chair of political economy at the University of Cambridge. From 1967 until his retirement in 1974, he was a senior research fellow at Christ's College, Cambridge. Meade was an honorary fellow of the London School of Economics, Oriel and Hertford Colleges of Oxford and Christ's College, Cambridge. He was a member of the Belgian Royal Society of Political Economics, the American Economic Association and American Association for the Advancement of Sciences. In 1933 he got married to a lady named Margaret Wilson. James Meade died in 1995.

INTRODUCTION

James Meade, along with Bertil Ohlin, won the economics Nobel Prize in 1977 for his "pathbreaking contribution to the theory of international trade and international capital movements." Meade's contributions to the shaping of modern international economic order is immense. His writings, discussions, seminar presentations and so on are pivotal in devising the post–World War international financial and economic settlements. He is one of the strong proponents of the International Monetary Fund (IMF), the International Bank for Reconstruction and Development (The World Bank) and the General Agreement on Tariffs and Trade (GATT)–now transformed into the World Trade Organization (WTO). James Meade made significant contributions to several branches of economics, including national income accounting along with Stone, the theory of international trade, the theory of customs unions, a hypothesis concerning internal and external balance of an economy, a preliminary theory of the second best, a welfare theory, a geometry theory of international trade, theories of fair distribution and more. His contributions to these areas were varied but substantial.

INTERNATIONAL TRADE

Meade made enormous contributions to the field of international trade, as represented by the two volumes of his *Theory of International Economic Policy*, published by Oxford University Press in 1951 and 1955. Meade was concerned about a country's internal and external balance and the relationship between these two balances in a general equilibrium framework. In the first volume of the *Theory of International Economic Policy, The Balance of Payments* (1951), Meade explored this relationship in a general equilibrium setting that allowed for including both price effects (pre-Keynesian ideas) and income effects (Keynesian ideas) into analysis. In this book, Meade also systematically explored a large number of both theoretical and practical possibilities of relationships involving internal and external balances. It took some time for his ideas on intern about trade to gain ground because of the technical nature of his analysis, but they did spread soon and bolstered the status of international economics as a discipline. However, in his

Nobel memorial lecture, Meade himself recognized one deficiency of his analysis: "The basic analysis in *The Balance of Payments* was conducted in terms of static equilibrium models, rather than in terms of dynamic growing or disequilibrium models." In the second volume of his *Theory of International Economic Policy, Trade and Welfare*, published in 1955, Meade examined the arguments for controls in trade and their effects on external balance. This examination led to his discovery of "the theory of the second best," which basically stipulates that piecemeal corrections of distortions may worsen, rather than improve, a country's economic welfare. Meade's discovery of the theory of the second best was a significant addition to the literature on welfare economics. This theory was later further developed by other economists, notably Lipsey and Lancaster.

Meade also made other contributions to the field of international trade. His work titled, *A Geometry of International Trade*, published in 1952, explored presentations of international trade problems through the tools of geometric analysis of such problems. He also investigated the conditions pertaining to the formation of a customs union, the creation of a region without trade barriers, such as import tariffs and the effects of such unions on trade creation and trade diversion. His ideas were presented forcefully in his book, *The Theory of Customs Unions*, which was published in 1955. Meade's contributions in the field of international trade are characterized by both the importance and the novelty of his ideas. Several observations are warranted here. First, prior to the publication of his first volume on trade in 1951, economists had treated income and price movements separately and had analyzed mainly automatic mechanisms for adjustment in a country's balance of payments, deficits or surpluses. Meade considered both price and income effects jointly in his model within a general equilibrium framework. In so doing, he integrated Keynesian analysis, with its concern for income changes, with a classical analysis emphasizing relative price movements. Meade pointed out that the policy objective should be not just external balance but internal balance as well, which means and includes full- employment as a cherished objective. Meade rightly emphasized the need for examining two-policy instruments to achieve internal and external balance simultaneously.

Second, Meade also examined the role of the impact of capital movements on internal and external balance. This was a novel approach, since till that time, the effects of capital movements on internal and external balance were not adequately treated. Third, Meade also did the preliminary work in his book regarding the interrelationships of various currencies. The theory of optimum currency areas, which was later fully developed by others, owed a great deal to Meade's preliminary analysis in his first volume. Fourth, Meade's examination of controls in trade and factor movements in his second volume was an original approach. He showed how both types of controls could and should be included in a single analysis. Finally, Meade's geometrical portrayal of international trade and its problems and prospects was a brilliant contribution. Here he developed the geometrical tools for creating what came to be known as "offer curves." These curves showed for a two-country, two- government case the combination of goods and services that a country is willing to import and export at alternative values of the terms of trade. As Bernard Katz points out, "Using the concept of a 'trade-indifference curve,' Meade was able in a single diagram to represent a free trade equilibrium involving two countries, each with its own production possibility frontier and consumption indifference curves" (Katz:1989, pp. 195-96).

WELFARE ECONOMICS AND THE THEORY
OF THE SECOND BEST

Meade's discovery of the "theory of the second best" has already been cited. This theory was developed further later by Lipsey and Lancaster, with immense possibilities of application to both domestic and external sectors of an economic system. Meade's discovery of this theory arose from his concern for welfare for a country's population. This concern is reflected in several contributions by Meade to the field of welfare economics. Unlike many economists of his time, or several preceding him, Meade was concerned about a fair distribution of income in the world and about unequal distribution of capital in Great Britain and the United States. This concern is reflected in his books *Efficiency, Equality and the Ownership of Property* (1964), *The Inheritance of Inequalities* (1974) and *The Intelligent Radical's Guide to Economic Policy* (1975). This concern had also earlier been reflected in his book *Planning and the Price Mechanism*, published in 1948. Unlike many of his critics, Meade regarded his book *Efficiency, Equality and the Ownership of Property* (1964) as his best book. In this book, as well as in the others cited, Meade explored the relationship between earned and unearned income and the factors that promoted capital accumulation. Meade, however, did not advocate redistributionary policies, such as high rates of direct tax, since he was reluctant to support any policy that interfered with the price mechanism. He instead argued for the use of redistributionary death and gift taxation. During the period of 1965-1976, Meade authored a four-volume economics text titled *Principles of Political Economy*. The third and fourth volumes also reflects his concern for fair income and capital distribution in society.

THE DEVELOPMENT OF KEYNESIAN THOUGHTS

Since his early days in 1930, as a fellow of Hertford College, Oxford, Meade had been very active as an inner-circle (called "Circus") member surrounding Keynes. The other members were young economists such as Kahn, Piero Sraffa and Joan and Austin Robinson. This group deliberated on Keynes' ideas and did constructive research for him on important theoretical and policy issues. As the youngest member of the group, Meade was very instrumental in the development of Keynesian thoughts, contributing to these thoughts, for example, his own ideas on the relationship between savings and investment. One may argue that Keynes' *General Theory* was a product of collective efforts, to which the contribution of Meade was substantial by any criterion. Meade's book *An Introduction to Economic Analysis and Policy* published in 1936, was the first text-book that systematically presented the Keynesian approach to economics. Meade then went one step further in a paper published in 1937 in the *Review of Economic Studies*.

Meade introduced the main arguments of *General Theory* in simple algebra. However, more elegant versions of *General Theory* were later developed by Hicks.

CONCLUSION

James Meade is one of the greatest international economic theorists. It is he who integrated economic theory with policy instruments. He showed how internal (full-employment) and external (equilibrium in the balance of payments) balances could be achieved through the instruments of fiscal and monetary policies. Assar Lindbeck says, "[Meade] laid the foundation for the modern theory of employment in open economies." He is the one who dealt with the complex relationships among employment, wages, prices and foreign exchange. Domestic policy issues became Meade's interest when he joined the League of Nations in Geneva in 1937 where he worked for three years. Meade was more successful with regard to the setting up of a new international monetary system. Meade, Robertson and Fleming constantly provided Keynes with information and arguments so that he could support the agreements drawn up at the Bretton Woods conference in 1944. The International Monetary Fund (IMF) was subsequently setup to oversee the world monetary system.

RECOMMENDED READINGS

Katz, Bernard S. (ed.) (1989). *Nobel Laureates in Economic Sciences: A Biographical Dictionary*. New York: Garland.

Meade, James. (1951). *The Balance of Payments*. London: Oxford University Press.

———. (1955, September). "The Case for Variable Exchange Rates," *Three Banks Review*. pp. 3-27.

———. (1952). *A Geometry on International Trade*. London: Allen & Unwin.

———. (1983). *A Neoclassical Theory of Economic Growth*. Westport: Greenwood Press.

———.(1965). *The Stationary Economy*. London: Allen and Unwin.

15

Bertil Ohlin (1899-1979):
A Co-founder of the Celebrated Heckscher-Ohlin Theorem of Factor Endowment and a Laureate of 1977

Khashruzzaman Choudhury
Abu N. M. Wahid

BIOGRAPHICAL PROFILE

Bertil Ohlin was born in a village in southern Sweden in 1899. His family was well-to-do and he was one of seven children. After some home tutoring, he entered school at the age of seven. He was very fond of mathematics from boyhood, as he enjoyed computing the cost of cakes that his mother used to bake at home. Ohlin started his undergraduate studies at the University of Lund with a concentration in mathematics, statistics and economics. While in university, he read a book review by Eli Heckscher on the economics of World War I and was encouraged to study at the Stockholm Business School, where Heckscher was teaching. He moved there accordingly and finished a two-year course of business. In 1918, he became a member of the Political Economy Club, where he learned a great deal by interacting with Sven Brisman and Knut Wicksell. In 1920, he served as assistant secretary to the Economic Council under the Swedish Ministry of Finance. There he had to work with representatives from the banking and agriculture industries. He served one year in the Swedish navy, then studied at Grenoble in France and presented his thesis on the theory of international trade to Gustav Cassel in 1922 for the degree of *licentiatus philosophiae*. Further developing the same thesis, he received his doctoral degree in 1924. In 1922, with a stipend from the Swedish-American Foundation, he visited Cambridge University, England and Harvard University, USA. In late 1923, Ohlin was asked by Heckscher to apply for the position of department chair of economics at the University of Copenhagen. After a long selection process, he was appointed and joined the faculty there in January 1925. In 1931, he returned to Sweden and succeeded Heckscher in the Stockholm School of Business. However, he spent most of the year of 1931 he spent in Geneva to prepare a report, "The Course and Phases of the World Economic Depression." Following that, he concentrated his research on monetary theory and economic expansion, following the path of Knut Wicksell, Erik Lindhal and Gunnar Myrdal. While continuing teaching at Stockholm University, Ohlin led the Liberal Party of Sweden, the leading opposition party of the country, for more than twenty years. Bertil Ohlin died in 1979.

INTRODUCTION

Bertil Ohlin, along with James Meade, received the economics Nobel Prize in 1977 for his "pathbreaking contribution to the theory of international trade and international capital movements." Ohlin was one of the few eminent Swedish economists who was honored with the celebrated Nobel Prize in economics. He was not only an economist but also a politician and he left many positive impacts on liberal Swedish politics. Although Ohlin was known as an international economist, his contributions to the overall science of economics were diverse, and he wrote on a wide variety of burning economic issues. Ohlin was one of the founders of the modern theory of international trade. He made significant contributions to several branches of economics, such as the theory of interregional and international trade, the empirical testing of this theory, the development of employment theory, the quantity theory of money, theories of saving investment equality, business cycles, ...theories of money... and credit markets and interest rates and, finally, the development of theories involving monetary and real movements arising from capital transfers. His contributions to these areas were varied but significant and substantial.

THE THEORY OF TRADE AND EMPIRICAL TESTS

Ohlin's views and ideas were originally presented in his 1924 Ph.D. dissertation and were partly derived from the 1919 writing on trade by Eli Heckscher, his teacher at the University of Stockholm, Sweden. Ohlin developed ideas that were presented finally in his most important book *Interregional and International Trade*, which was published in 1933. Until the publication of Ohlin's book in 1933, international trade was thought to be guided by what Ricardo had called the Labor Theory of Value. Under several restrictive assumptions, including the same patterns of demand in the trading countries and different technologies, Ricardo's theory indicated that trade would take place by a country that had a comparative advantage in the production of a good, judged by its labor value. A country would export goods in which it had comparative advantage and import goods in which it had comparative disadvantage.

In his final arguments presented in his book in 1933, Ohlin developed the thesis that interregional or international movements of goods and factors of production across regions or countries lead to a tendency towards factor price equalization as intuitively argued by many others before him. Earlier, his teacher, Eli Heckscher, had studied the conditions under which factor prices would be equalized by trade. Later on, Paul Samuelson outlined and proved factor equalization under certain assumptions. However, subsequent research has indicated that complete factor price equalization across countries was unattainable, and one could only argue, like Ohlin, for a tendency toward such equalization. What is the basis of trade? Economists have long argued that trade is profitable for countries when relative prices of goods and services differ between countries. Superlative price differences result from interactions of supply and demand in autarky. Heckscher and Ohlin examined the basis of trade by further investigating the supply side: factor endowments in different countries.

Based upon the work of Heckscher in 1919, Ohlin further developed the idea that relative prices in different regions or countries depended on the relative scarcity of factor endowments in these regions or counties. This fundamental observation led to the formulation of what has come to be known as the Heckscher-Ohlin (H-O) theorem. This theorem has two versions, weak and strong. The weak version is a virtual restatement of why trade takes place: a country tends to export those commodities that would be relatively cheap without any trade. The strong version of the H-O theorem brings into play both Heckscher's and Ohlin's fundamental ideas about the role of factor abundance in trade. According to this version, a nation tends to export those goods and services that utilize in production large quantities of its relatively abundant factor, and tend to import those commodities that require large quantities of its relatively scarce factor. This statement assumes that demand patterns are identical or similar in the two countries considered.

Although the credit for fundamental ideas about relative factor abundance, the tendency toward factor price equalization, composition of trade, the H-O theorem, and their role in trade can and should be given to both Heckscher and Ohlin, the latter deserves more credit for at least five reasons. First, Heckscher's ideas were not published in English. Ohlin publicized his ideas through some of his English writings, especially interregional and international trade. Second, Ohlin presented the fundamentals of the new trade theory in a brilliant manner synthesizing past and his own knowledge. At first, Ohlin presented the celebrated Heckscher-Ohlin theorem with restrictive assumptions. Later on, he further investigated and analyzed theorems by deleting all restrictive assumptions such as absence of transport cost, no import tariffs, absence of economies of scale in production, and so on. Third, it was Ohlin who developed and demonstrated in his book, as clearly as one could, the intimate and crucial connections between location theory, regional economics and international trade. Fourth, credit is due to Ohlin for making his presentation suitable for further extension and empirical research. The latter works in the international trade area by Paul Samuelson and Wassily Leontief owe much to Ohlin's presentation of his ideas in a testable framework. Finally, in a later section of his book *Interregional and International Trade*, Ohlin himself set out to test his trade theories presented in the earlier parts of his book. However, it should be pointed out that these tests are not formulated as tightly as present-day empirical tests, and statistical procedures are not used. Ohlin used causal reasoning and examined large data sets to test his propositions.

CAPITAL TRANSFERS AND BALANCE
OF PAYMENTS ADJUSTMENT MECHANISM

When capital is transferred from one country to another, how does the balance of payments adjust? Ohlin made fundamental contributions with regard to this question in the context of Germany's reparations due to Great Britain and France after World War II. In doing so, he approached the problem in an entirely different way than did Keynes. In an article published in 1929, Keynes had argued that real resource transfers perhaps would not work, because such transfers implied a generation of a trade surplus for the transferring nation. Keynes was of the view that a reasonably large surplus was unlikely. Ohlin argued that real transfers, to begin with, were not necessary. Germany could transfer the required financial resources. Ohlin pointed out that such a financial transfer would induce a real transfer of goods and services. Unlike Keynes, Ohlin stressed that a monetary transfer would ultimately bring about the desired real transfer. In doing so, he helped unravel a new adjustment mechanism not highlighted earlier.

THEORY OF EMPLOYMENT: MONEY,
INTEREST, INVESTMENT, AND SAVINGS

The great economist John Keynes published his classic book, *The General Theory of Employment, Interest and Money,* in 1936. This theory developed ideas about the crucial relationship among money, interest rate, credit, investment and savings. The primary thesis of *The General Theory* was that adequate savings and investment may not automatically come forth in the economy to initiate and ensure full employment. Thus the government may have to increase investment when private savings and investment are not enough to generate and maintain full employment. Keynes' ideas have dominated macroeconomics for a long time. Modern critics point out that several Swedish economists of the so-called Stockholm School, including Wicksell, Heckscher and Ohlin, were precursors of Keynes, and much of what Keynes said later had been already presented by them. Here, Ohlin made important contributions, although since most of these writings were published in the Swedish language, they remained unknown to the English speaking world for a long time. What were the main contributions of Ohlin here? They were several. First, in an article published in 1933 in Swedish (later translated into English), Ohlin suggested that monetary disturbances (e.g., changes in the supply of money) influence the price level, as well as income and production. He also hinted at the idea of a multiplier in this article.

OHLIN AND THE ECONOMIC
SCIENCE SYMPOSIUM

It gave Ohlin great satisfaction when the Nobel Foundation–using a grant from the Bank of Sweden as well as grants from the Marcus Wallenberg and the Handelsbanken Research Foundations–in 1974 decided to add a symposium in economic science to the symposia in natural sciences, international peace problems, and literature, which had been organized in the preceding decades. The prize committee in economic science decided to choose as its subject the International Allocation of Economic Activity. As chairman of the organizing committee of the symposium, Ohlin was grateful for the friendly reception of their invitations. The symposium took place in Stockholm in 1976, and a volume edited by P.O. Hesselborn, P. Wijkman and Ohlin himself appeared toward the end of the following year. It contained contributions from a large number of the most prominent economists in this field. However, monetary aspects of international trade relations found no place on the agenda, as several international symposia had in recent years taken up this subject for debate. On the other hand, scientists who had come from economic and social geography to study international division of labor or who had specialized in regional economics were well represented. One of the chief aims of the symposium was to avoid arbitrary borderlines between different approaches to research into local aspects of production and trade. To sum up in Ohlin's own words: "It has not been easy to combine scientific work, teaching, journalistic writing and political leadership. All of these types of activity have no doubt suffered from my attempts to do too many things at the same time. However, I have found it all to be a fascinating business."

CONCLUSION

As the volume of international trade grew and the process of globalization accelerated after the Second World War, Ohlin's importance increased in the economics profession. Ohlin, through his writings and speeches, made it succinctly clear that the problems associated with resource allocation, economic fluctuations, income distributions, and so on were more international than national problems. However, economists at large did not take these issues seriously until the 1960s. Ohlin was one of the architects who brought these issues into public policy consideration in almost all open economies of the world. In the citation about Ohlin, the Nobel Foundation says, "He has developed a theory that demonstrates which factors determine the pattern of foreign trade and the international division of labor on the one hand, and on the other, shows what effect foreign trade has on the allocation of resources, price relations and the distribution of income. Ohlin has also demonstrated similarities and differences between interregional (intra-national) and international trade, and the connection between international trade and the location of industries" (www.nobel.se).

RECOMMENDED READINGS

Choudhury, K. (1980). *Evaluation of Comparative Cost and Expenditure Data: Some Conceptual and Statistical Problems—A Note.* (ICED) Internal Note. Essex, Ct: International Council for Educational Development (ICED).

Coombs, Philip H. (1985). *The World Crisis in Education —The View from the Eighties.* New York: Oxford University Press. Chapter 5.

Hutlin, Mats. (1975, May). *Costing and Financing Education in LDCs: Current Issues.* Washington, D.C. : World Bank Staff Working Paper, No. 216.

——. (1980, March). *The Allocation of Resources to Education Throughout the World.* Paris: UNESCO.

——. (1982, February). "Costs and Financing Obstacles to Universal Primary Education in Africa," *UNESCO Educational Financing, Occasional Paper.* No. 6.

UNESCO. (1977). *Trends and Projections of Enrollment by Level of Education and Age.* Paris: UNESCO.

Van Dijk, C.P., (1976, May). "Recent Trends in Public Education Expenditure in a Sample of Developing Countries," (unpublished paper). Rotterdam, the Netherlands.

The World Bank. (1979). *The World Development Report.* Washington, D.C.

Zymelman, Manuel. (1976, November). "Patterns of Educational Expenditures," *The World Bank Staff Working Paper.* No. 246, Washington, D.C.

16

Herbert Simon (1916-2001):
One of the Most Versatile Talents of the Twentieth Century and the Laureate of 1978

Sajjad Zahir
Abu N. M. Wahid

BIOGRAPHICAL PROFILE

Herbert Simon was born in Milwaukee, Wisconsin, in 1916. His father was an electrical engineer and a patent lawyer who immigrated to the United States from Germany in 1903. Simon's father was a noted person of the area and was awarded an honorary doctorate degree by Marquette University of Milwaukee. His mother's family also came from Europe some generations ago. Simon received a good education from the Milwaukee public school system, and there was a congenial academic atmosphere in his family. In the dining table, they used to have regular intellectual discourse of political and scientific topics. He used to enjoy his studies at school and at home. He was also a very playful and joyful boy. At school, Simon developed a keen interest in science and mathematics. Simon was very intimate with one of his maternal uncles, who was a student of economics. From this man and the books left by him, Simon was exposed to economics and social science, and he finished reading some good economics books before entering university. His undergraduate education began at the University of Chicago in 1933. At Chicago, he took courses in economics, mathematics, physics, statistics, and logic, with a major in political science. He graduated in 1936. During his undergraduate studies, he wrote a term paper on organizational decision making that brought him a research assistantship from Clarence Ridley in municipal administration. This, in turn, made him director of a research group at the University of California–Berkeley, for 1939-1942. In that capacity, with special permission from the University of Chicago, he took his doctoral examinations and completed his Ph. D.

thesis on administrative decision making under the political science department. In 1942, he joined the faculty of the political science department at the Illinois Institute of Technology. In the early 1940s, he used to take part in the Cowles Commission staff seminars at the University of Chicago. This was intellectually very rewarding to him, stimulating his interest in mathematics. In 1949, he joined the Carnegie Institute (now Carnegie Mellon University) to develop the newly established School of Industrial Administration. During the early 1950s, he developed the Hawkins-Simon Conditions of the input-output analysis. At Carnegie Mellon, he had the opportunity to work with Franco Modigliani and John Muth to develop dynamic programming methods. In 1952, he met Allen Newell at the RAND Corporation, with whom he later developed computer simulations. Simon also worked in administering the Marshall Plan in 1948 and served as economic adviser to the Nixon and Johnson administrations. He was married to Dorothea Pye in 1937. Herbert Simon died in February 2001.

INTRODUCTION

To the surprise of traditional economists, Herbert Simon won the economics Nobel Prize in 1978 for his "pioneering research into the decision-making process within economic organizations." Simon himself was equally surprised. He admitted soon after hearing the news, "It was a little like being struck by lightning." The Swedish Academy of Sciences specifically recognized his research for the contributions he made during the 1940s and 1950s. While presenting the award, Sune Carlson of the academy stated that "the study of the structure and the decision making of the firm has become an important task in economic science. It is in this new line of development that Simon's work has been of the utmost importance, Simon's theories and observations on decision making in organizations apply well to the systems and techniques of planning, budgeting, and control that are used in business and public administration. They are, therefore, excellent foundations of the empirical research"(www.nobel.se).

SIMON AND OTHER SCIENCES

As expected, when Simon entered the University of Chicago in 1933 at the age of seventeen, he decided to be a mathematical social scientist. Hard sciences had such an influence on him that he did not intend to study social sciences as an extension of humanities. Instead, his desire was to study them as disciplines enriched with the rigor and mathematical foundation of hard sciences. He was motivated to investigate human behavior as a scientific discipline. Through formal training and self-guided study, Simon gained a broad-based knowledge in economics, political science, advanced mathematics, and statistics. To strengthen and practice his mathematical skills, and to obtain an intimate taste of the hard sciences, he took graduate-level physics courses. Since then, he developed a lifelong interest in the philosophy of physics. Later, he even published several papers on this subject. He greatly appreciated and enforced the synergy between social and natural sciences throughout his life. In an autobiographical sketch,

Simon noted, "In the 'politics' of science, which these other activities have entailed, I have had two guiding principles to work for the 'hardening' of the social sciences, so that they will be better equipped with the tools they need for their difficult research tasks; and to work for close relations between natural and social scientists, so that they can jointly contribute their special knowledge and skills to those many complex questions of public policy that call for both kinds of wisdom."

INVOLVEMENT WITH THE COWLES COMMISSION

While working at the Illinois Institute of Technology, Simon was a regular participant in the intellectual discourse at the Cowles Commission for Research at the University of Chicago. During that time, through the Cowles Commission, Simon could come in close contact with Kenneth Arrow, Leo Harvey, Lawrence Klein, and Don Patinkin, who were the graduate students of Jacob Marshak and Tjalling Koopmans at the university. There, he also had the opportunity to meet Oscar Lange, Milton Friedman, and Franco Modigliani, who were frequent visitors. This association that Simon had with the Cowles Commission, introduced him to new ideas of research in human decision making. He also wrote two chapters on the macroeconomic aspects of atomic power for a book on the *Economic Aspect of the Atomic Power* by Jacob Marshak.

AT THE CARNEGIE INSTITUTE OF TECHNOLOGY

Simon left the Illinois Institute of Technology in 1949 to become a professor of administration at the newly formed Graduate School of Industrial Administration at the Carnegie Institute of Technology. The new location gave him an opportunity to further expand the research he had done on administrative behavior under a new program on empirical research in organization. Simon, LeBach, and Bill Coops worked together to develop the curriculum of the school as well as a whole new faculty. Although Simon headed the area of organizational behavior, he was also working as a management scientist and a business school administrator. As associate dean, he played a pivotal role in making the Graduate School of Industrial Administration at Carnegie-Mellon a leading business school in the United States.

At the Carnegie Institute, Simon further developed the theories originally set forth in *Administrative Behavior* by writing *Models of Man* in 1957 and *Organization* in 1958. In these books, he expressed his thinking, that the behavioral and cognitive properties of human beings were integral parts of decision making and problem solving. He emphasized that, since a human being is limited in memory and computing powers, he, as a decision maker cannot be fully rational. Under these conditions, "satisficing," not optimizing, behavior becomes the accepted norm.

ON THE COGNITIVE PSYCHOLOGY
AND ARTIFICIAL INTELLIGENCE

Drawing on the same line of thoughts, Simon explored the reason for consensus and dissension among economists in his essay "The State of Economic Science." When economists have applied their knowledge to explain various contemporary issues, they seem to agree on some and to disagree on others. Simon explained that "The reason economists are able to agree on their conclusion is that they apply to the problem a common set of assumptions and inference procedures." However, while applying the standard core theory to the real-world problems, economists have to make assumptions about the real world. Besides, they have to deal with uncertainty and their limited computational power. Consequently, they end up disagreeing with each other although they apply identical modes of reasoning. To avoid this problem, he suggested a new kind of research training for them. According to Simon, cognitive psychology and organizational theory should play a very important role. Economists must learn about the internal and external factors affecting an organizational decision-making process. In addition, empirical data are also very important. "When theories and facts are in conflict, theories must yield," Simon commented.

As he explored the cognitive basis of decision making, Simon slowly moved into two new fields–cognitive psychology and computer science. His pioneering contributions helped Carnegie-Mellon University to become the leading institution in these two fields. Indeed, Simon's work in the later part of his life mostly concerned artificial intelligence and computer science. After 1965, he was the Richard King Mellon Professor of Computer Sciences and Psychology at Carnegie Mellon University. He discussed the idea of artificial intelligence as early as 1952 with Alan Newell, who was a research scientist at the RAND Corporation. *Business Week* magazine wrote in a recent issue about this episode as follows: back in the days when computers were as big as house trailers, Herbert Simon, Professor of psychology and computer science at Carnegie-Mellon University (CMU) and a future Nobel laureate, had a flash of inspiration. He was strolling through a park in October 1955, when it suddenly dawned on him how he could program a computer to reason on its own. He and fellow CMU computer scientist Alan Newell spent Christmas vacation writing a small program to prove the concept. Dubbed Logic Theorist, the software enabled a computer to work out independently the proofs for simple math theorems. When school resumed in January, Simon walked into his mathematics class and dropped a blockbuster. 'Over the Christmas holiday,' he told his students, 'Al Newell and I invented a thinking machine'"

Later, Newell formally joined Simon at Carnegie Mellon in 1961 as a university professor. Simon wrote his book *Science of the Artificial* in 1969. On a similar topic, he and Newell wrote another book, *Human Problem Solving,* in 1972. The book *Science of the Artificial* is based on Simon's invited lectures at two universities. These were the Karl Taylor Compton lectures at MIT and the H. Rowan Gaither lectures at the University of California-Berkeley, in 1968 and 1980, respectively. In these lectures, Simon set out to explore a deeper and more universal meaning of the word artificial. He pointed out the significance of the dynamics of the interface that divides any environment we work in into an inner and an outer environment: "The artificial world is centered precisely on this interface between the inner and outer environments; it is concerned with attaining goals by adapting the former to the latter."   This idea has been central to his original research, at first in organization theory, and later in economics and management science and psychology. In this book, he further extended it to engineering, architecture, business, and medicine. To Simon, "The topic of artificiality and complexity are inextricably interwoven." The natural sciences study the knowledge of natural objects and phenomena. He asked whether there could also be "artificial" science–knowledge of artificial objects and phenomena. He explained the "nature of artifacts" as follows: "Central to their description are the goals that link the inner to the outer system. The inner system is an organization of natural phenomena capable of attaining the goals in some range of environments, but ordinarily there will be many functionally equivalent natural systems capable of doing this. The outer environment determines the conditions for goal attainment. If the inner system is properly designed, it will be adapted to the outer environment, so that its behavior will be determined in large part by the behavior of the latter, exactly as in the case of 'economic man.'"

Following the same thread of thoughts about the bounded rationality of the "economic man," Simon explained that the economic man also operates in an artificial system which is strongly influenced by the limits of its adaptive capacities. Thus, "the economic man is in fact a satisficer, a person who accepts 'good enough' alternatives, not because he prefers less to more but because he has no choice." He called engineering the "design" tasks responding to the complexity of the outer environment in which we all seek to survive and achieve. However, Simon wanted to preserve the harmony between the natural sciences and the science of the artificial. "If we regret that fragmentation, then we must look for a common core of knowledge that can be shared by the members of all cultures–a core that includes more significant topics than the weather, sports, automobiles, the care and feeding of children, or perhaps even politics. A common understanding of our relation to the inner and outer environments that define the space in which we live and choose can provide at least part of that significant core."

Simon was keen on the developments in expert systems, an application of artificial intelligence. In reference to an expert system called Bacon, Simon called it a model of data-driven theory formation in science. Given basic data on the solar system, plus a few hints, Bacon could produce Kepler's Third Law of Motion. It could also generate Ohm's Law of electricity. "What this shows," said Simon, "is that great scientific discoveries can be produced by feeding known data to a fairly simple set of rules." Until the end of his life, Simon was optimistic about computers being more intelligent than humans. *Business Week* quoted him as saying, "Why people feel threatened by that, I don't know. We all know someone who is smarter than we are, and can run faster than we do. Why is this so different. Our species can stand some improvement — and we can use all the assistance we can get."

CONTRIBUTIONS TO MANAGEMENT
AND DECISION SCIENCES

Simon also had a special interest in management science, especially the study of decision making in hierarchal organized institutions with multiple objectives. He always felt that traditional economies failed to address the issue of "micro-microeconomies" that encompasses economic decision making processes in households, firms, and government agencies. As an expression of this line of thinking, he and some of his associates at Carnegie-Mellon University launched a new journal, *The Journal of Organizational Behavior*. Other books he has written in this area are *New Science of Management Decision and The Shape of Automation for Man and Management*. Although Simon's main research was in the areas of decision making and artificial intelligence, his intellectual interests were beyond these specializations.

In decision sciences, Simon's major contribution is the behavioral analysis of the decision-making processes in large economic organizations. He had carried this out in contrast to the thinking of the traditional economists. In the conventional way, economists have been used to thinking that a large organization functions in a manner as though it makes decisions. But Simon, in an attempt to build a bridge connecting a real world to an economic model, emphasized that it was the people in the organizations who processed information and made decisions. The traditional economists have often assumed an "extravagantly" ideal picture of the real world. In contrast, Simon had pointed out through his research that human decision makers hardly possessed enough accurate information on which to base decisions. Neither do they have enough memory to store all this information. He described what he called "administrative man," who functioned within "bounded rationality" due to lack of knowledge about the uncertain future. Thus, it is impossible for the "economic man" to maximize the profits and the utility functions even if he wants to. Instead, Simon argued, a typical administrator was most likely to reject risky but profitable steps in favor of risk-free choices that might even bring fewer gains. That was what Simon called "satisficing." In other words, decision makers in an organization would settle for a certain aspiration level, which they would occasionally adjust either upward or downward. They usually would make the adjustments to adapt the outcomes against the target. These are the outlines of the main concepts that he put forth in his magnum opus, *Administration Behavior*. His findings occasionally placed him at odds with conventional economists. While praising the merits of Simon's behavioral theory of decision making, notable economists like Edward Mason, Fritz Machup, and Milton Friedman questioned its usefulness for economic analysis. While Simon considered the behavioral factors in decision making, other economists chose to ignore them.

CONCLUSION

To most of us, Simon is best known not as an economist, but as a pioneering expert in artificial intelligence, a decision scientist, an applied mathematician, a cognitive psychologist, a philosopher, and a political scientist. When Simon earned his bachelor's degree in 1936, the major of the degree was not in economics but in political science. He had completed all the courses except one for an economics degree. That was an accounting course, and he thought accounting was such a dull subject that he simply did not like to take it. Simon earned his Ph.D. degree in political science. In 1977, he took over a first-year history course, simply because he wanted to learn about the French Revolution, and he has even taught graduate-level courses in psychology.

Simon's successful ventures in several disciplines could be termed as rare human efforts to achieve the ultimate nirvana of the intellectual minds that glide through the barriers of specialization at the highest level. While describing Simon, Robert Cyert, the president of Carnegie-Mellon University, once said that he " is the one man in the world who comes closest to the ideal of Aristotle or a Renaissance man." An introverted and bookish child, Simon was proud of his ability to learn on his own. However, it was his uncle, Harold Merkle, who had played a profound influential role on the intellectual developments of Simon. Harold Merkle, who had earned degrees in economics and law from the University of Wisconsin, died early at the age of thirty. His collection of books became Simon's possession and satisfied the learning curiosities of the young nephew for a long time. In high school, Simon was a great debater, just like his uncle. Besides, he had also expressed great interests in hard sciences, especially physics, mathematics, chemistry, and biology.

Simon's research ranged from computer science to psychology, administration, economics, and philosophy. The thread of continuity through all his work was his interests in human decision-making and problem-solving processes, and the implications of these processes for social institutions. For more than forty years, he made extensive use of the computer as a tool for both simulating human thinking and augmenting it with artificial intelligence.

RECOMMENDED READINGS

Blaug, Mark. (1985). *Great Economists Since Keynes*. Sussex: Wheatsheaf Books.

Katz, Bernard S. (ed.) (1989). *Nobel Laureates in Economic Sciences: A Biographical Dictionary*. New York: Garland Publishing.

Simon, Herbert A., (1947). *Administrative Behavior*. New York: Macmillan.

———. (1989). *The State of Economic Science: Views of Six Nobel Laureates*. (ed.) Werner Sichel. Kalamazoo: Upjohn Institute for Employment Research.

17

Arthur Lewis (1915-1991):
The Founder of the Theory of Unlimited Supplies of Labor and a Laureate of 1979

Mohammed Sharif

BIOGRAPHICAL PROFILE

Arthur Lewis was born in St. Lucia in 1915. Among the economics Nobel laureates, he is thus far the only one with a black racial background. His parents were schoolteachers. From his very early childhood, Lewis was a gifted student. In elementary school, he was promoted from grade 4 to grade 6. He wanted to be an engineer, but under the British rule at that time, it was hard for a black to get a government job nor was it likely that any white firm would hire him. He did not like the independent professions, such as medicine or law. Thus he decided to study business, and for that purpose, he went to England and entered the London School of Economics (LSE) with a scholarship. He did very well at LSE and graduated with first class honors in 1937. Subsequently, he completed his Ph.D. in industrial economics. Before finishing his terminal degree, he taught at LSE which was an unusual honor for him. Then he moved to the University of Manchester and became a full-professor in 1948 at the age of 33. He came back to LSE and taught there when Friedrich Hayek was the acting head of economics. In the 1950s, he published a series of articles on world production, prices, and trade for the period 1870-1914. Then he was in administration for six years. In 1963, he returned to academia and joined Princeton University in the United States. In 1952, Lewis discovered his great theory of the unlimited supplies of labor while he was walking down a street in Bangkok, Thailand. In the 1960s, he made some monumental publications, including his famous book on development planning. Lewis served as an adviser to the United Nations, the prime minister of Ghana, and as deputy director of the UN Special Fund and vice chancellor of the University of the West

Indies. In the early 1970s, he set up the Carribean Development Bank. He married Gladys—a Grenadian woman in 1947. His two daughters are Elizabeth and Barbara. Arthur Lewis died in 1990.

INTRODUCTION

Arthur Lewis, along with Theodore Schultz, won the Nobel Prize in economics in 1979 for his "pioneering research in economic development with particular consideration of the problems of developing countries." Lewis' contributions are mainly in the field of development economics. In fact, it is his theory of economic development with "unlimited supplies of labor" that has led to the growth of extensive literature on development economics and its development as an important branch of economics. More importantly, his work has generated unprecedented interest, both at scholarly and policy levels, in studying the conditions of poverty of the majority of world's population in less developed countries (LDCs) and in devising and implementing measures for its alleviation. To Lewis, economic growth through generation and reinvestment of capitalists' surplus provides the process of transforming the subsistence economies of LDCs, and thereby achieves economic development for improving the living conditions for the majority of their populations. Analyzing the historical process of economic growth in developed countries (DCs) and the conditions of stagnation in LDCs, Lewis concluded that it was the use of surplus labor at a virtually constant low wage rate that led to the generation of capitalists' surplus and, thus, to the achievement of economic growth in DCs, and offered the key to economic growth in LDCs. Thus his works are directed toward identifying the process of transferring surplus labor from the subsistence to the capitalist sector, utilizing this labor to generate and reinvest capitalists' surplus, and devising measures for retaining the generated resources within the economies of LDCs. A less discussed but no less important aspect of his work was in the field of political economy.

THE THEORY OF
ECONOMIC DEVELOPMENT

In his analysis of the history of economic growth, Lewis identified two key sectors of the economy—a subsistence sector holding a large pool of surplus labor and a capitalist sector playing the "engine of growth." The surplus labor depresses the wage rate (return to labor) to its minimum subsistence level, which remains constant as long as the surplus persists, and the capitalist sector employs the surplus labor at a wage marginally higher than its subsistence level and generates sizable amounts of profit for reinvestment. This process of employing low-wage labor in capitalist production continuously increases the share of profit in national income, which is saved, invested, and reinvested, thereby leading to sustained economic growth. The history of industrial revolution in Western Europe substantiates this contention; there the real wage rate in the capitalist sector remained almost constant and below its pre industrial level for over fifty years.

Evidence of similar historical processes of growth has also been identified in the case of the *United States of America,* Japan, and other countries. The conditions prevailing in LDCs are postulated to offer a stronger case for a similar process of economic growth. The economy displays dualism consisting of a vast subsistence sector and a small capitalist sector. The subsistence sector holds "unlimited supplies of labor," produces only for subsistence consumption of those living and working in it, and saves and invests virtually nothing, thus creating stagnation. The capitalist sector produces for the market with an objective to make profit, generates savings and investments, and thereby leads to economic growth. Lewis proposed for LDCs a model of growth in the capitalist sector through utilization of the surplus labor drawn from the subsistence sector. Since the pressure of surplus labor keeps returns to labor in the subsistence sector at very low levels, the capitalist sector can attract and employ this labor at a marginally higher, but still very low, wage rate. This means a significant margin of profit and reinvestment and, thereby, expansion of the capitalist sector. Since the pool of surplus labor is very large, by the time the surplus is exhausted, this process of expansion in the capitalist sector will lead to growth in the whole economy.

Lewis' subsistence sector is traditional, unorganized, and informal, and it is found in both rural and urban areas in the forms of peasant family farming, casual labor employments, feudal retaining, petty trading, low-production self-employment activities, and domestic services. His capitalist sector is modern, organized, and formal, and it is given by profit seeking enterprises in industries, plantations, and governments. While the prime motive for employment and production in the former sector is consumption, that in the latter is generation of profit and "reproducible capital."

Although this model is general and broad, Lewis presents his formulation with examples of peasant family farming and feudal retainers in the traditional rural sector, and industrial production in the modern capitalist sector. The peasant agriculture is assumed to have many more workers than it requires; however, because of lack of alternative employment opportunities, the excess labor is absorbed through some kind of social arrangements of work-sharing. In family farming, all the members of the household are engaged part-time, or through inefficient use of their labor, full-time. Either way, a sizable segment of the labor force is redundant in the sense that it can be removed from the farm without reducing farm productivity, assuming full-time employment and efficient utilization of labor-time of those remaining on the farm. This implies that, on the family farm, the marginal productivity of labor, not necessarily of labor-time, is negligibly low or even zero. Thus the redundant segment of the labor force is basically unemployed, although in disguise.

However, the arrangement of family farming for sharing the work and consuming the farm income equally (the average productivity) perpetuates the situation of disguised unemployment. While most of the rural families do farming either through ownership or tenancy rights, there are households that are landless and rely on casual or retainer employment by the farmers and landlords, or on self-employment activities of various types. Lewis' second category of illustration is with retaining employments. If labor were already redundant and disguisedly unemployed on the family farms, why would the farmers hire the landless workers? Similarly, why would the landlords employ more workers than the minimum needed? Lewis' answer is a social "code of ethical behavior" on the part of the landowners to make provision for the employment of all in the society and ensure satisfaction of their minimum needs of subsistence consumption. The result is absorption of all the workers through a work-sharing arrangement and the provision of subsistence to them and their families through the payment of a subsistence wage, which is obviously higher than their marginal productivity.

The subsistence in this model, however, has no reference to biological nutritional needs — it is a socially perceived minimum standard of decent living, thus, a social datum determined in the context of overall conditions of living in the society. Since the rural economy absorbs all of its labor in self- or wage-employment with zero or near-zero marginal productivity, the average productivity in this economy is also very depressed and offers a very low standard of living. It is this average productivity that gives the socially determined minimum subsistence wage for the workers. As to the workers who fail to obtain employments with the landlord or farm households and are forced to engage in low productive self-employment activities, such as handicrafts work and petty trading, the return to their labor is generally lower than this average standard. However, the number of workers in these categories is not sizable, and therefore, is implied not to affect this subsistence wage significantly.

There are two important implications of this subsistence living in the traditional economy — stagnation in the subsistence sector and potential for growth in the capitalist sector. The absorption of redundant labor through the social arrangement of work-sharing with the result of reducing the average product to the minimum of social subsistence and the provision of this subsistence to all in the economy eliminate the potential for saving in the traditional sector, thereby causing stagnation. This subsistence wage rate, however, creates the potential for growth in the capitalist industrial sector that can attract labor from the subsistence sector by paying them a marginally higher but still low wage rate, and without losing any output in the subsistence sector. This employment of surplus labor can generate for the capitalist employers a significant amount of profit that, reinvested, will increase labor productivity, raise profits, and expand employment and output further. More importantly, the low wage rate might be expected to remain constant for a long time, as the pool of surplus labor is significantly large. Thus, the process of utilization of the surplus labor in the modern sector will lead to the generation and regeneration of reproducible capital and its use in increasing industrial production to the growth of the economy. As this process of growth in the industrial sector is based on "unlimited supplies" of cheap labor, the technology to be used in industrial production is implied to be labor-intensive. Hence, growth in national income is expected to be accompanied by expansion in employment, diffusion of the benefits of growth across the population, and thereby, the achievement of economic development.

THE TRADE POLICY

While Lewis proposed economic development with "unlimited supplies of labor" through the use of labor-intensive technology, he strongly recommended against the policy of exporting labor- intensive goods by LDCs. He insisted that trade cannot be used as an "engine of growth" by LDCs, as their comparative advantage dictates the export of low-valued labor-intensive goods and the import of high-valued capital-intensive goods, which turns the terms of trade against them and causes transfer of income to DCs in the long-run, and thereby perpetuates their own underdevelopment. Thus he recommended a policy of import substitution for LDCs in both industrial and agricultural production. Here again, Lewis' conclusion is based on his analysis of the history of trade relations between the rich "core" and the poor "periphery" countries. In his work on the evolution of the world economy, he recognized that the expansion of manufacturing played the "engine of growth" in the "core" countries of Western Europe and the *United States of America* and that international trade worked as the vehicle in sending "growth pulsations" to the rest of the world. However, he showed that trade relations with core countries exerted contradictory growth effects on two groups of countries in the periphery — favorable effects on countries in the temperate region and unfavorable effects on those in the tropical region. He cited the examples of Argentina, Australia, Canada, and New Zealand in the former group and most of the LDCs of today in the latter. These contradictory effects are especially important because both of these groups of countries were exporting primary goods to the core countries and importing manufactured goods from them. Lewis convincingly showed that differences between the two regions in the levels of wages for unskilled labor are responsible for these contradictory effects. The temperate zone countries were populated by migrant labor from Europe, land was relatively abundant, and the wage level was high enough to provide a standard of living comparable to that of the core countries. This resulted in a high marginal productivity of labor in food in this zone. In the tropical zone, labor was available in "unlimited supplies" and land was relatively scarce, which depressed labor productivity, especially in food, to a very low level, thereby reducing the wage rate to its subsistence level. These differences in labor productivity and wages had important implications for the sizes of their domestic markets, their terms of trade, and their potential for industrial development.

Size of the market, both domestic and foreign, is an important determinant of profitability of investment and production, and therefore, of economic growth. The size of the domestic market is determined by the level of income that is, in turn, a function of the productivity of workers and the wages they earn. The gains from foreign trade, given the size of the foreign market, are determined by the terms of trade. Thus, the potential for industrial development of a country or a region is a positive function of the labor productivity and wages and of the terms of trade it enjoys with its trade partner; the higher the labor productivity and wages are, the larger is the domestic market, and the more favorable the terms of trade are, the greater are the gains from trade. While the higher labor productivity and higher wages in the temperate periphery provided a large domestic market for industrial production, the market was lacking in the tropical periphery. This partially explains why the countries in the temperate zone grew, while those in the tropical zone stagnated. The labor productivity and wages also exerted differing impacts of trade on their growth through the opposite terms of trade they enjoyed or suffered in their trade with the core countries. Although both groups of periphery countries were exporting primary goods against the import of industrial products, the temperate countries' exports were reasonably high-valued, which afforded these countries a competitive share in the gains from trade with the core countries. But the tropical countries were exporting lower-valued items that turned their terms of trade against them, offering all the gains from trade to their trade partners in the core and resulting in long-term transfer of income away from them, thereby causing their stagnation.

To stop the "perpetuation of comparative advantage based on low wage labor" and the secular deterioration in the terms of trade, Lewis recommended against the export not only of primary goods, but also of labor-intensive manufactured goods. Thus, he suggested a strategy of import substitution for LDCs in both the agricultural and industrial sectors. In his view, LDCs have two options: to imitate the DCs by having their own technological revolution, or to trade with them by exchanging primary products for manufactured goods. While the trade option seems easier, he insisted that, "the true '...engine of growth...' has to be internal, and can only be installed by having an industrial and associated agricultural revolution of one's own" (Findlay, 1982). He declared that "anything the Europeans could do we could do, " and that "most of these economies, though not all, have what it takes."

Lewis advocates import substitution for the industrial sector for another reason also. The employment in the traditional sector is determined by social consideration, and the wage rate is given by the average productivity of workers. However, in the modern industrial sector, employment and the wage rate are determined by the marginal productivity of labor. This means that the marginal product of labor in industry is equated with their average product in agriculture, while social optimality requires it to be equal to agriculture's marginal product, which is very low. This violation of the optimality rule implies underallocation of labor to the industrial sector, putting the industrial sector at a relative disadvantage. Subsidizing the industrial sector can correct for this suboptimality, and Lewis recommended that protection from foreign competition is an effective solution.

POLITICAL ECONOMY

In an age of ideological polarization, when scholars were generally divided into camps advocating either unmixed laissez-faire or centralized planning, Lewis was a pragmatist and a great champion of prudent public policy. He saw the market as an economic institution of overwhelming importance, but with serious limitations. In his view, the horrendous job the market performs in no way can be supplanted by centralized planning. However, to him the market is not an unmixed blessing — it suffers distortions generated by monopolies, inequities, and externalities, and thereby produces sub-optimal outcomes. Thus he recommended the application of appropriate public policies to correct for these distortions, and to achieve optimal results. More importantly, Lewis' government is called upon to play a catalyst for economic growth by adopting effective policies to mobilize resources, creating an environment favorable to capitalists' investment, and making investment in the public sector in cases where private initiative is lacking.

While advocating vigorous use of public policy in modifying free market outcomes, which he called "planning through the market," Lewis vehemently argued against centralized planning, referring to it as 'planning by direction.' His arguments for planning through the market and against planning by direction are based on availability of information for making decisions, the cost of decision making, flexibility in modifying decisions, product differentiation, innovation, and the implications of democratic control over the economy. Economic decisions require myriads of information regarding the complex production and consumption relations that prevail in the economy and the possible consequences on them of the actions taken based on these decisions.

It is practically impossible to gather all the information and gather it on time for planning by direction, while the market embodies the mechanism for their automatic and instantaneous transmission. Moreover, the cost of collecting information for planning is enormous, while the market performs this job through its price mechanism free of charge. Once decisions are made, plans are rigidly implemented, basically with no consideration for modification for changed circumstances. This is so because "you cannot alter a part of [the plan] without altering the whole, and altering the whole is too elaborate a job to be done frequently." The market, however, adjusts itself regularly as dictated by the price signals. Because the planning process is time-consuming and expensive, excessive product standardization is another problem in planning that the free market never encounters. This not only ignores differences in consumers' taste for differentiated products, but it also reduces a country's competitiveness in foreign trade. Thus Lewis observed that, standardization "is frequently the enemy of happiness, and in foreign trade it is in many lines fatal to success."

Innovation in production — finding out new products and better methods of production — is the key to entrepreneurial success in a market economy and plays a critical role in promoting growth. However, not only is the incentive for innovation lacking under centralized planning, but innovation itself is generally hindered by the bureaucratic control, thus creating a stifling effect on growth. Planning by direction also decreases democratic control over the economy, as planning has to depend on bureaucratic decisions and orders. As Lewis very aptly put it, "When the government is doing only a few things we can keep an eye on it, but when it is doing everything it cannot even keep an eye on itself." The extraordinarily convincing arguments for planning through the market and against planning by direction from a Fabian socialist, at a time when centralized planning is not only a fashionable idea among the socialists, but also a reality in socialist economies, splendidly speak about Lewis' great scholarship and clarity of mind. There is sufficient proof that he was truly an unbiased, realistic, and moderate economist with a great mind.

A CRITIQUE OF THE LEWIS' THEORY

Lewis faced a lot of criticism, mostly against his theory of development. In spite of the stream of attacks, his work has retained its predominance in the literature till today. The most serious criticism of Lewis' model came from Theodore Schultz. Schultz questioned the validity of Lewis' assumption of "unlimited supplies of labor" and thereby tried to destroy the very foundation of his model. Using evidence from India relating to the influenza epidemic of 1918-1919, Schultz contended that there is basically no surplus labor in traditional agriculture. He showed that, as the labor force declined by 8 percent due to influenza deaths, both the observed acreage sown and the predicted output in agriculture in 1919-1920 declined by 3.8 percent and 3.3 percent, respectively, from their comparable levels in 1916-1917. If labor were in surplus and their marginal productivity were zero, this reduction in acreage and output would not have happened. Thus, he concluded that there is no part of the labor force in traditional agriculture that is surplus and can be removed without reducing agricultural output.

The assumption of zero marginal productivity of labor, however, is not essential for the functioning of the Lewis' model. Amartya Sen analyzes this possibility very convincingly. The fact that labor productivity is negligibly low in traditional agriculture, a fact Lewis emphasized and Schultz recognized, is sufficient to provide the mechanism outlined in the model for transferring low-wage labor for use in the industrial sector. The loss of output in the traditional sector, if a segment of the labor force is withdrawn, will be small and can be countered by minor reorganization of the sector. But the gain in output, savings, and reinvestment in the modern sector can be expected to be enormous.

Another criticism of Lewis' model is against his assumption of the economic irrationality of the farmers and landlords, and the resultant inefficiency in the traditional sector. Lewis imposed a "social code of ethical behavior" on the landlords and farmers for the employment and absorption of the surplus labor in the traditional sector, thereby to ensure the provision of subsistence to all through a work-sharing mechanism. Schultz cited David Hopper's work on India and Sol Tax's work on Guatemala to show, contrary to Lewis' assumption, that the traditional sector workers, though poor, allocate their resources very efficiently — indeed, they are found to demonstrate economic rationality as much as the Western capitalists so that Tax finds it fit to call them "penny capitalists." Sen provides theoretical analyses using the assumption of rational behavior to derive Lewis' results.

In fact, the assumption of a social code of ethical behavior is not necessary, although it might play a role in ensuring employment to all in the system. It is a social stigma against physical labor, on the one hand, and a depressed wage rate, on the other, that do the job. While the former eliminates the relatively well-to-do segment of the traditional sector population from the labor force, the latter makes it feasible for them to get the work done by hired labor, thus, making provision for employment of the assetless by the asset-holding (Sharif, 1993a). Recent empirical evidence on differential labor force participation, labor supply, and wage rates earned by workers in different asset-holding households substantiates this contention (Sharif, 1991). The assumption of social provision of subsistence through work-sharing implies that everybody in the system is employed and is offered the minimum requirements of subsistence. While the only implication of this assumption needed for Lewis' model is a low wage for the modern sector, it has an undesirable implication for a section of the traditional sector population. The assetless casual day-laborers, who are not permanently retained, do not always find gainful employment, especially during the slack seasons of farm activities, and are required to engage in very low-productive self-employment activities, working long hours in hard jobs but failing to earn the minimum needs of social subsistence (Sharif, 1993). Lewis' generalization creates the incorrect ideas that everybody in the traditional sector is working part-time and that there is nobody suffering below-subsistence living, thus failing to recognize the problem of "working poor unemployment," a phenomenon of below-subsistence living associated with over work.

For the modern sector, Lewis' model implies that surplus labor will dictate the use of labor - intensive technology, that capitalist surplus will be re invested, and that protection will afford the opportunity for production to be efficient and for the economy to grow. Indeed, this strategy has been pursued by some LDCs, such as South Korea and Taiwan, which have implemented their own agricultural and industrial revolutions, fruitfully utilized import-substitution industrialization for a reasonable period, and developed competitive economies for export production. But in a large number of LDCs, low-wage labor has failed to lead to the adoption of labor-intensive technology– imported Western capital-intensive technology has been extensively applied, industrial profits have not been fully and gainfully reinvested, domestic capitalists have suffered demonstration effects and indulged in conspicuous consumption, production has remained inefficient while enjoying protection through import substitution, and export of primary products has continued to be a common practice. These more or less fit the dependency analysis of the center-periphery relationship generating and perpetuating the underdevelopment of LDCs.

This not only has perpetuated relative stagnation of these economies, but it also has created additional problems: rural-urban migration and modern sector unemployment. The incentive of higher expected income has generated a steady flow of labor from the traditional to the modern sector. But as the modern sector has failed to expand at a reasonable rate and the growth of employment in this sector has lagged behind the growth of the sector itself because of the application of capital-intensive technology, the inflow of labor has created a problem of unemployment. However, since the expected differential wage rates between the two sectors has persisted, the problem of migration and unemployment has continued to prevail. While the failure of the modern sector to grow and, thereby, to absorb the migrated labor is a shortcoming of Lewis' model, it is the LDCs, policymakers and administrators who are responsible for neglecting their rural and agricultural development.

CONCLUSION

Arthur Lewis was one of the most brilliant economists of the modern time. His theories of development have left an enormous impact on the economics literature. Apart from some minor limitations, Lewis' works have survived continuous scrutiny for almost half a century, and they still occupy the center stage in development economics. His research addressed the heart of the problem of economic growth with the historical experience of DCs and the perspective of contemporary LDCs. Moreover, he was both a theorist and a practitioner in economic development, a combination rare in the world of economists.

RECOMMENDED READINGS

Breit, William, and Roger W. Spencer, (eds.) (1990). "W. Arthur Lewis," *Lives of the Laureates, Ten Nobel Economists*. Cambridge: MIT Press.

Lewis, Arthur. (1949). *Economic Survey, 1919-1939*. London: Allen & Unwin.

——. (1949a). *Principles of Economic Planning*. London: Allen & Unwin.

——. (1952). "World Production, Prices, and Trade," *Manchester School*. Vol. 20, No. 2, pp. 105-38.

——. (1954). "Economic Development with Unlimited Supplies of Labor," *Manchester School*. Vol. 22, No. 2, pp. 139-91.

——. (1955). *Theory of Economic Growth*. London: Allen & Unwin.

——. (1958). "Unlimited Labor: Further Notes," *Manchester School*. Vol. 26, No. 1, pp. 1-32.

——. (1966). *Development Planning: The Essentials of Economic Policy*. London: Allen & Unwin.

——. (1969). *Aspects of Tropical Trade 1883-1965; Wicksell Lectures*. Stockholm: Almqvist & Wicksell.

——. (1970). *Tropical Development 1880-1913*. London: Allen & Unwin.

——. (1978). *The Evolution of the International Economic Order*. Princeton: Princeton University Press.

Sharif, Mohammed. (1991). "Landholdings, Living Standards, and Labor Supply Functions: Evidence from a Poor Agrarian Economy," *Journal of Development Studies*. Vol. 27, No. 2, pp. 256-76.

——. (1993a). "Working Poor Unemployment and Wage Rigidity– Evidence of Economic Distress," *Kyklos*. Vol. 46, No. 1, pp. 47-63.

——. (1993b). "Child Participation, Nature of Work, and Fertility Demand: A Theoretical Analysis," *The Indian Economic Journal*. Vol. 40, No. 4, pp. 30-48.

18

Theodore Schultz (1902-1998):
An Expert on Agricultural Economics and Human Capital Theories and a Laureate of 1979

Baker A. Siddiquee
Faridul Islam

BIOGRAPHICAL PROFILE ·

Theodore Schultz was born in Arlington, South Dakota, in 1902. His father's name was Henry Schultz, and his mother was Anna Elizabeth. He was raised in a German farming community. In his early life, he experienced the hardship faced by a typical American farming family. He witnessed precipitous falls in the prices of farm products, severe shortages of credits, and foreclosures of farms. Schultz wanted to study economics to understand the farming crisis. Meanwhile, the World War I broke out, and in the midst of an extreme labor shortage, he withdrew himself from school and worked for some time. In late 1921, he entered South Dakota State College for a short program in agriculture, graduating from college in 1926. Then he started his graduate education at the University of Wisconsin and received M.A. and Ph.D. degrees in 1928 and 1930, respectively, in agricultural economics. During 1930-1943, Schultz worked at Iowa State College, Ames. Within four years at that college, he became the head of a new department called economic sociology and developed the curriculum for that department. Intellectually, his time at Iowa State College was most rewarding for him. He learned a lot from his own personal experiences of the Great Depression. In 1943, he joined the University of Chicago as a professor. Three years later, he was appointed Charles L. Hutchinson Service Professor. During his early years at Chicago, Schultz got involved in research of world agricultural problems. After the World War II, his research interests shifted to the broader issues of development economics. In the 1950s, he led a major development project in Latin

America under the Technical Assistance for Latin America (TALA). During this time, he was gave a concrete shape to his theory of "human capital." According to this theory, the educational level of a population governs its ability to make use of information and technology, for development as well as for redevelopment. Schultz received honorary medals from the American Economic Association and International Agricultural Economic Association. He was a member of many professional associations, including the American Academy of Arts and Sciences and the American Economic Association. He secured honorary degrees from many academic institutions. He married Esther Werth in 1930 and had two daughters and a son. Theodore Schultz died in 1998.

INTRODUCTION

Theodore Schultz, along with Arthur Lewis, received the economics Nobel Prize in 1979 for his "pioneering research into economic development research with particular consideration of the problems of developing countries." The decades of the thirties through the sixties were one of search and analysis of growth of economies and   understanding of the process of development. Chicago economists had a particular interest in the analysis of such economies. A major influence in shaping their perspectives of growth was based on the departure from the obsession that economic development and growth can be wholly explained in terms of additions to the real resources, which include such elements as physical capital and labor which implied the number of workers (labor). This position is very consistent with the Chicago tradition, which had nourished the idea of human capital and accorded a special position to the idea of investing in human capital. Theodore Schultz was an unquestioned pioneer in leading what was later known as the human capital revolution in economics. Schultz's contributions in agriculture and economic development have been fundamental, and they deservedly brought him (jointly with Arthur Lewis) the greatest recognition in the profession–the Nobel Prize in 1979. Schultz studied extensively the productivity problems of agriculture–both in the United States and in the developing countries –that led to his pioneering contributions on the importance of human resources in economic and social development. To Schultz, the decisive factors of production in improving the welfare of poor people are not space, energy and cropland; the decisive factor is the improvement in population quality."

AGRICULTURE AND
ECONOMIC DEVELOPMENT

Schultz was an agricultural economist per excellence. During the thirties and forties, he presented a series of studies on the crises of American agriculture, addressing issues such as the relationship between agriculture and the rest of the economy, the instability of farm income, forward prices for firm products, and problems in agricultural policy. In these studies, Schultz not only emphasized the central policy issues of the immediate postwar years but also analyzed the underlying reasons for the persistence of problems both within agriculture and between agriculture and the rest of the economy. His best-known works from this period are *Redirecting Farm Policy, Agriculture in an Unstable Economy, Production and Welfare of Agriculture,* and *Economic Organization of Agriculture.* Schultz later took up the agricultural problems of those countries and earned international recognition for his penetrating analyses of agriculture and economic development in his book *Transforming Traditional Agriculture.* His other major works on agriculture are *Economic Crisis in World Agriculture, Economic Growth and Agriculture,* and *Distortions of Agricultural Incentives.*

It was no surprise that Schultz began his intellectual curiosity with a big question in his very first publication. In his 1932 paper in the *Journal of Farm Economics,* Schultz raised "the question whether or not the experience of agriculture tends to invalidate the admirable and well qualified interpretation which Marshall placed upon the classical law of diminishing returns." Using farm level data on crop statistics from Iowa for 1890-1930, Schultz demonstrated that the "average farm person of Iowa has in the course of forty years increased his crop output about 130 percent" and that "this increased productivity cannot be accounted for by a greater expenditure of capital per unit of crop production." This increase in productivity was due to what he called "favorable changes in the state of the arts" brought about by technological advancement in crop farming and "those broad progressive influences arising from greater specialization of the interrelated communities as whole." Although Schultz did not reject Marshall's prophecy that ultimately diminishing returns must prevail, he was one of the first to raise the question against such prophecy. He demonstrated quite convincingly how arbitrary and exacting the assumption of a fixed area of land is and that there existed the possibility of increasing returns in agriculture too, not just in industry alone.

In his 1956 paper on agricultural production, Schultz drew attention to the fact that "much of the increase in output in agriculture cannot be explained by additional inputs of the conventional types." Schultz demonstrated the declining importance of additional inputs in the expansion of agricultural output by analyzing data for the period 1920-1950. For example, from 1900 to 1920, virtually all of the increase in output may be attributed to increased inputs, while from 1940 to 1948, only about a fifth to a fourth of the increase in output can be explained by increased inputs. A similar trend was also observable in Brazil and Mexico. Schultz, in his paper proposed a theory of output growth that would incorporate "two major neglected inputs, namely, the improvement of the quality of the people as productive agents and the raising of the level of the productive arts," meaning the advance in technology.

Schultz was a strong advocate for agricultural research and considered it as "public good." In this 1979 paper, he provided estimates of growth and magnitude of agricultural research and attempted to answer an important question: who should pay for agricultural research? Schultz's careful review of the literature led him to conclude that "the rates of return on investment in various specific classes of agricultural research have been much higher than normal rates of return." He concluded that international agricultural research centers were not substitutes for national research enterprises and that "the only meaningful approach to modern agricultural research is to conceptualize most of its contributions as public goods. As such, they must be paid for on public account." Too little was spent on agricultural research, and important crops often received too little research attention. Much of the foreign aid undervalued agricultural research, and the distortions in prices and in agricultural incentives did substantial harm to agricultural research and, thus to economic growth. Finally, he explained the importance of research entrepreneurship.

Contrary to Malthusian doomsayers, Schultz was an optimist. Despite the cruelties and caprices of nature in the forms of drought, bad monsoons, harmful insects, diseases of crops and cattle, and distortions and failures of policy, Schultz believed the fundamental economic potential of the world's agriculture to be such that the food production would outpace the population growth. Schultz followed a disequilibria approach in analyzing the development potential of agriculture. In his opinion, the gap between traditional production methods and the modern effective methods created the conditions necessary for a dynamic development paradigm.

ECONOMICS OF POVERTY

Schultz was the first to challenge much of the conventional wisdom in economics regarding poor countries. Since most of the poor people of the world earned their living from agriculture, it was only natural for Schultz to study traditional agriculture to understand the economics of being poor. He believed that poor people were as much concerned about improving their plight as the rich people. In the tradition of David Ricardo, conventional economics overrated the importance of land and greatly underrated the importance of population quality, assigning too little for improvement in population quality.

Schultz identified two intellectual mistakes of economics regarding poor countries. First, he challenged the presumption that standard economic theory was inadequate for understanding poor countries and that a separate economic theory was needed. Schultz considered these attempts to discover an appropriate theory as, at best, intellectual curiosity. He also discounted the route taken by some to explain the poor economic performance of low-income countries in cultural and social theories. To him the standard economic theory is just as applicable to the scarcity problems that confront low income countries as to the corresponding problems of high income countries. Second, economists in general tended to neglect the study and relevance of economic history to better understand the problems and possibilities of low-income countries. This understanding was far more important than gathering exact knowledge about geology, ecology, or technology. In addition, Schultz drew attention to the lack of historical perception on population issues and dispelled the notion that poor people breed like lemmings headed toward their own destruction.

Schultz was first to address forcefully the follies of both the Ricardian quandary based on the primacy and fixity of land and the Malthusian doom based on population growth in the context of traditional agriculture. Schultz believed that human beings had the ability and intelligence to lessen their dependence on traditional agriculture. For example, substitutes for cropland were discovered by means of research. Also parents revealed a preference for fewer children as their income rose by opting for quality over quantity of children. Economic history demonstrates that advances in knowledge can augment resources and choices, thereby dispelling both the Ricardian quandary and the Malthusian doom. Schultz earned his fame for his path-breaking work in *Transforming Traditional Agriculture*.

SCHULTZ'S HUMAN CAPITAL THEORY

Reference to the importance of human capital and education is not something that can be called original by itself and certainly is not the only modern concept. A small but growing literature on the role of education in the doctrines of English economists existed, but it was rather contradictory in content, if not downright misleading. Adam Smith mentioned this important issue, although it remained largely neglected until it was taken up by J.S. Mill in 1840. It is surprising that the contribution of the classical political economists, by any standard, was not insignificant, contrary to the expectation that they had undermined the very theoretical foundation of this interesting topic. Presumably, they had difficulty in imputing value in human beings as capital goods, except in the context of slavery. It took over a century for a systematic effort to be geared to gain insight in to the field. It was through the works of Schultz, Becker, Mincer, and Denison, which came to be known as the "human capital investment revolution" in economics. Schultz's 1961 article in the *American Economic Review*: "Investment in Human Capital," is considered one of his best and according to H.W. Singer, this flawless article has become the foundation of what is now conventional wisdom, but it was new and needed saying in 1961.

The Logical Framework

Schultz focused on identifying the portion of human capital represented by education. It is now a standard practice in the analysis of economic growth to include human capital formation. Numerous studies examine the requisites for particular countries with due regard to identifying appropriate strategies for developing human resources. One observes that the GDP of the United States has grown, from $2,244 in 1870 to $18,258 in 1990, by a factor of 8.1, which corresponds to a real per capita income growth rate of 1.75 per year at 1985 constant dollars. Three pertinent but perplexing issues need to be raised in this context. First, in the context of behavior of long run capital income ratio, while in the conventional analysis one would argue that a country with more reproducible capital should deepen such cheap factors in combination with labor and land, reality suggests the contrary. Available estimates suggest that less of such capital is employed relative to income as the economy grows. Strangely, it should suggest that the ratio of capital to income has nothing to do with affluence or poverty. Schultz argued, such findings could result from a partial view of capital, leading to an inaccurate estimation of the capital income ratio. In particular, exclusion of human capital may cause such an anomaly if it grows faster than physical capital. This would indicate that not all capital is decreasing. Thus the decline in estimated capital income ratio is a signal that human capital is not only increasing to physical capital but also with income.

A second puzzling question relates to the national income rising faster than growth of resources. That is, the U.S. income is rising faster than the combined rise of land, man-hours worked, and the amount of physical capital combined. It has been argued that the discrepancy is larger from one business cycle to the next. One must be able to provide a logical explanation for this. One may refer to this in terms of the returns to scale or the large improvement to quality of input that has contributed to this. Schultz argued that physical capital may have a part in explaining this, but certainly it is not the most significant factor, much less the only one. These are minor factors compared with the significant growth of human capital that has taken place but, unfortunately been omitted. The third surprise comes from the large but unexplained increase in the income of workers. Schultz pointed out that it is mainly the returns due to increased investment in human beings. While the unit of the individual is constant, the capital content in him has been steadily increasing due to conscious investment decisions. This has increased the pool of human capital component as a result of investment over years and maybe decades. One additional feature that has been observed in the postwar economies is that much of the physical capital was destroyed and, to a large extent, was supplemented with human capital; thus they achieved faster growth following the war.

SCHULTZ ON INVESTMENT

Schultz was the first to introduce the qualitative characteristics of human capital in the form of skill, knowledge, and such features augmenting the human capability to add to productivity. This provided him with the tools to define investment in human capital as any expenditure that contributes to increase the value productivity of human effort in the form of labor, yielding a positive rate of return. He argued that the observed rate of return may take any value due to uncertainty and imperfect knowledge. On the estimation of human capital formation, he suggested that the same approach can be adopted as one uses in the analysis of the formation of physical capital. However, he pointed out that it would be necessary to draw a line between what we can call consumption and investment, and he noted that it involves not only practical but also conceptual difficulties. He talked of three kinds of expenses: (1) those satisfying only consumption needs but not directly adding to "capabilities," implying pure consumption; (2) those augmenting "capabilities" without regard for preference underlying consumption behavior, implying investment; and (3) those having some of each. In a real - life situation, most are classed under the third category. The difficulty in separating consumption and investment expenses has profound implications for measurement of human capital. As a result, an alternative approach has been adopted wherein yields rather than costs are used. The capability increases by investment is embedded in the individual and is reflected in wages and salaries and may be called the yield of investment. Schultz mentioned at least five activities with the potential for increasing the capabilities that shed light on the understanding of the issue of investment, despite problems of measurement. They include health, on-the-job training, organized education, adult education, and immigration.

Investment in Education

Schultz first presented his views on investment in education in a series of papers published from 1959 through 1961 and subsequently leading to the publication of two major books on the topic. In these sources, Schultz proposed what he called "a human wealth hypothesis," later come to be known as the human capital hypothesis, to explain the observed three-to-one divergence between the rate of economic growth and the rate of increase of labor and physical capital. Citing an even earlier work of his, "Gross Capital Formation Represented by High School, College, and University Education in the United States, 1900 to 1956," and preliminary estimates of Gary Becker, Schultz concluded that investment in man through education has increased the stock of human capital and that this not only has the potential to explain the observed economic growth puzzle but also has policy implications for welfare economics and for the poor countries. Schultz explicitly addressed the connection between education and economic growth with the bold statement where he proposed to treat education as an investment in man and to treat its consequences as a form of capital. Referring to it as human capital. He analyzed the data for the United States for 1900-57 on total costs of and returns to education and found that the increase in education per person during 1929-1957 explains 36-70 percent of the otherwise unexplained increase in earnings per worker, depending on which of the three different rates of return estimates one used. He showed that between 1900 and 1965, educational expenditures in the United States increased about three and one-half times, relative to both income and gross physical capital formation. Further, he concluded that when treating education expenditures as investment, using his and Becker's estimates, it can be shown that the rates of return to education were relatively attractive and were larger than the rate of return to investments in physical capital. This implied larger rate of growth of human capital. Schultz had convincingly demonstrated that there has been a considerably higher yield on investment in education (human capital) than on physical capital and that this has resulted in a much faster increase in educational investments compared to other forms of investments. His major contribution was not so much in developing the detailed theories of human capital (this was left for his students, among others, Gale Johnson, Gary Becker, Zvi Griliches, Finis Welch, and Jacob Mincer made notable contributions) but in thinking of expenditures in education and health as "investment" in man and also in terms of rate of return to investment, capital formation, growth, and efficient allocation of resources. Conventional economic theory treats all educational expenditures as pure consumption. Schultz quite convincingly demonstrated the flaws, arguing that schooling and educational expenses be treated as an investment.

He rightly observed that it was misleading to treat public expenditures in schooling as 'welfare' expenditures, and that using resources can have the effect of reducing savings.

Investment in Health

Schultz's conception of human capital formation is much broader than simply investment in education. He would include all expenditures that enhance human capabilities, actual and potential, as investment in human capital formation. Particularly, he considered expenditure on health and disease control as an essential factor in economic development in the third world. He did a number of studies on this and opened up avenues for new and fruitful research in this and many related areas.

SCHULTZ ON THE QUESTION OF COST

On the estimation of cost of education, Schultz made his point very clear. He argued that a measurement of the components of cost should not only include those of providing it but also must include the income foregone during education, which according to him, is not negligible. As an example, this foregone cost may be as high as half of out of pocket cost of education in the United States. Previous estimates suggest that early this century, this cost accounted for a quarter of the total cost of elementary, secondary, and higher education, which rose to about two-fifths of all costs in 1956. The percentage rise in educational cost is a staggering three and a half times the rise in consumer income, implying a greater than unity income elasticity. Educational cost also increased almost three and a half times as rapidly as gross capital formation. This suggests that the returns to education must have been more attractive than those of physical capital. Tentative estimates suggest that the stock of human capital rose eight and a half times, compared to four and a half for physical capital at 1956 constant prices. On the issue of returns, he forcefully argued that returns to education have been rising despite higher enrollment. He substantiated his results with empirical findings. But consumer capital is also a part of this cost. It is interesting to note that the allocation of cost between consumption and investment does not cause a serious problem when we evaluate the contribution of education to earning. This is because a change in allocation alters the rate of return, not the total return.

CONCLUSION

The time at Chicago where Schultz had been since 1943 gave him an ideal opportunity to consolidate and interpret his experience. Schultz valued highly what he had learned about the economic behavior of rural people while abroad. During the summer of 1929, he acquired location-specific information in parts of the Soviet Union. In 1960, when he was president of the American Economic Association, several U.S. economists and he were guests of the Soviet Academy of Sciences. It was a grand opportunity to return to the same locations about which he had acquired information in 1929. Over the years, Schultz had ventured frequently into many low-income countries to do what he did in the Soviet Union. In general, he avoided giving lectures or attaching himself to a university while abroad. To learn what he wanted to know, he instead decided to learn directly from rural communities and actual farms. Talking with university people, government officials, and the U.S. personnel stationed in the country was much less rewarding for him.

The contributions of Schultz have had a profound impact on the theory and policy for both developing and developed economies. His exposition is clear and lucid, but not at the expense of rigor. His writings are insightful and arouse immediate intuition. To refer to his works, one may present his philosophy of economics and the role of economists in the following sentences. While everyone hankers for prestige, often accorded to scientists, as hard as they economists must try, will not and cannot succeed in obtaining a separation from the social attributes of society and humanism. Well-reasoned doubts offer good payoffs for economists. Neither theory, nor data, nor even the rigors of mathematics will ever resolve the diverse issues that pervade a social science. One can say that economic behavior is more complex than our thoughts, and more comprehensive than mathematical economics can model. And whatever is derived from them is always subject to criticisms and doubts.

RECOMMENDED READINGS

Schultz, Theodore W. (1943). *Redirecting Farm Policy.* New York: Macmillan.

——. (1945). *Agriculture in an Unstable Economy*. New York: McGraw-Hill.

——. (1959, June). "Investment in Man: An Economist's View," *Social Service Review*. Vol. 33, No. 2, pp. 109-17.

——. (1960, December). "Capital Formation by Education," *Journal of Political Economy*. pp. 571-83.

——. (1961, March). "Investment in Human Capital," *American Economic Review*. Vol. 60, pp. 1-17. AEA Presidential Address.

——. (1961). "Education and Economic Growth," in Nelson B. Henry, (ed.) *Social Forces Influencing Education, Part II*. Chicago: University of Chicago Press.

——. (1963). *The Economic Value of Education*. New York: Columbia University Press.

——. (1964). *Transforming Traditional Agriculture*. New Haven: Yale University Press. Reprint: New York: Arno, 1976.

——. (1971). *Investment in Human Capital: The Role of Education and of Research*. New York: Free Press.

——. (1972). "Human Capital: Policy Issues and Research Opportunities," *Human Resources*. New York: Columbia University Press (for NBER).

——. (ed.) (1974). *Economics of the Family: Marriage, Children and Human Capital*. Chicago: University of Chicago Press.

——. (1975). "The Value of the Ability to Deal with Disequilibria," *Journal of Economic Literature.* Vol. 13, pp. 827-46.

——. (1980). "Nobel Lecture: The Economics of Being Poor," *Journal of Political Economy.* 88(4), pp. 639-51.

19

Lawrence Klein (1920-):
A Giant of Econometric Modeling
and the Laureate of 1980

Akhter Faroque

BIOGRAPHICAL PROFILE

Lawrence Klein was born in Omaha, Nebraska, in 1920. His parents were Leo and Blanche Klein. Lawrence was one of the three children of the family. He started his education in the public school system of Omaha, where, he had solid training in mathematics, English and history. The Great Depression of the 1930s left a lasting impact on the formative mind of Klein. His first college was the Los Angeles City College. Then he entered the University of California, Berkeley, from which he graduated with a major in mathematics in 1942. Klein started his graduate education at the Massachusetts Institute of Technology (MIT) in economics. At MIT, he worked closely under Paul Samuelson. There, he systematically transformed the fundamentals of Keynesian economics into a large set of equations. In Keynesian line, he estimated the future output of an economy based on the relationship among investment, interest rate, tax and income. In doing so, Klein gained mastery over econometrics and econometric modeling. In 1944, he received his Ph.D. in economics from MIT. Soon after, Klein started his academic career as a research associate with the Cowles Commission at the University of Chicago. There he had the opportunity to work with such great economists as Tjalling Koopmans, Kenneth Arrow, Don Patinkin and Herbert Simon. Jacob Marschak, then director of the Cowles Commission, gave Klein the challenging job of completing the econometric model of the U.S. economy that was started by Jan Tinbergen. Klein did the job brilliantly with a great deal of originality. In 1947, Klein constructed an econometric model for the Canadian economy. Then he spent some time in Norway to work with two other giants, Ragnar Frisch and Trygve

Haavelmo. On return from Norway, Klein joined the National Bureau of Economic Research and then The Survey Research Center of the University of Michigan. There, along with a graduate student named Arthur Goldberger, he developed the Klein-Goldberger model of the U.S. economy. Despite his path-breaking work at the University of Michigan, his tenure was denied at the news broken by Senator McCarthy that Klein was a member of the Communist Party during 1946-1947. In 1954 he left Michigan, joined Oxford University, England, and stayed there for four years. In 1958, he returned to the United States and joined the economics department at the University of Pennsylvania. At Pennsylvania, Klein developed a complex quarterly model for the U.S. economy consisting of 1,000 equations. The powerful computer facility at Pennsylvania helped him estimate the model. In the 1960s, Klein constructed comprehensive econometric models for many other countries. In 1968, he became the Benjamin Franklin Professor of economics and finance at the Wharton School of Business at the University of Pennsylvania. He is now well-known worldwide as a giant in econometric modeling. Klein served as the economic adviser to presidential candidate Jimmy Carter in 1975. Klein received the John B. Clark medal of the American Economic Association and the William Butler Award of the New York Association of Business Economists. He is a member of many academic societies, including the American Economic Association.

INTRODUCTION

Lawrence Klein won the economics Nobel Prize in 1980 for "the creation of econometric models and the application to the analysis of economic fluctuations and economic policies." Klein is an innovator-scholar among economists; his work has been responsible, in large measure, for shaping the development of economics from an abstract, academic science toward a more practical, predictive science. He has created and established a highly successful paradigm for the construction of macromodels and their practical application to forecasting and policy analysis. Although Klein's early hopes of using macroeconometric models to choose policies that would eliminate business cycles has not been fulfilled, there is much evidence that business cycles in the postwar period are generally milder than those experienced in the prewar period. This may largely be a consequence of the emergence of the social institutions that Professor Klein relentlessly promoted and helped create in order to give some built-in stability to the economy.

THE ARCH-APOSTLE OF KEYNESIANISM

Lawrence Klein's very first professional position in the field of economics was with the famous Cowles Commission, a small group of brilliant researchers, from whose midst have emerged five other Nobel laureates in economics. But the precocious Klein first made his mark in the economics profession even before that. As a graduate student at MIT, still in his teens, he published a major paper in the *Journal of Political Economy* (1947) on theories of effective demand. The same year, when his doctoral thesis, The Keynesian Revolution (1947), was published,

Klein gained an instant world readership and international recognition. To quote Paul Samuelson, "Lawrence Klein was too young to vote when he came to our graduate school. His thesis became a classic, The Keynesian Revolution, and it gave the name to an epoch." The problem with John Maynard Keynes' General Theory was its literary style of economic analysis. The work was difficult to read the amenable to alternative interpretations. For several years after its publication, the main message of his seminal contribution remained unclear to the economics profession, and the book remained mired in controversy. It not only sparked a protracted debate between the classics, whose work he attacked, and the Keynesians, who are his followers, but also triggered the so-called "what Keynes-really-meant" debate among his own disciples.

On to this scene came Lawrence Klein. His book, The Keynesian Revolution, clarified and extended Keynes' seminal work in The General Theory to the entire economics profession and has ultimately served to popularize and elevate Keynesian economic principles and policies to the position of the most dominant intellectual force, where they have remained for several decades. With the self-assurance of an authority, young Lawrence Klein stripped The General Theory of its inconsistencies, discarded everything that did not seem to fit its fundamental logic and told, with masterful clarity, the story of Keynes' work. Klein demonstrated how, from the economic dislocations of the 1920s and the 1930s, Keynes' seminal ideas arose, what the new ideas were and how they differed from those of his predecessors. He proclaimed to the world that there had been a revolution in economic thought, one that rejected the classical and neoclassical systems that view the economy as "a big ship with an automatic steering system" and that, under the propulsion of the perfect flexibility of wages and prices, will always achieve full employment, without the help from a captain. More than anything else, the Keynesian ideas were strongly opposed to the attitude of laissez-faire when millions were unemployed.

The Keynesian Revolution showed that Keynes' truly revolutionary idea was that the cause for mass unemployment is not the inflexibility of wages and prices, but rather the lack of demand. When demand for goods and services falls short of the economy's potential output because of business pessimism and consumer uncertainty about the future, businesses lay off workers. Thus, in the parlance of the previous metaphor, in the absence of a helmsman, the economic ship will run off course and may remain there for prolonged periods of time unless active support from government demand management policies returns the economy to full employment. Having set the theory straight, Klein turned to policy for fighting business cycles. And it is here, in the arena of policy, where Klein strongly asserted his own view. "A backlog of planned public work," he wrote, "should always be ready so that unemployed factors can be immediately put to work on useful jobs whenever the private sector of the economy is unable to carry the ball. Government spending should be very flexible and subject to immediate release or curtailment in just that precise amount which will maintain full employment." That maxim will forever remain one of the lasting legacies of The Keynesian Revolution.

Two other aspects of The Keynesian Revolution have had a decisive influence on the course of development of economics as a science. The book specifies, for the first time, the complete Keynesian theory as a system of simultaneous equations and talks about the relevance of parameter values. This observation establishes the precedent for giving empirical content to the parameters of theoretical macro models. In this respect, The Keynesian Revolution lays the foundation for Klein's future contribution to economics: the development of a complete theoretical paradigm for the construction of macro econometric models and their applications in forecasting and policy analysis. Surprisingly, the book also anticipates many of the issues that are of central concern for modern macroeconomists and policymakers. To quote Gerard Adams (1992), "The tenor and focus of macroeconomic theory has changed a good deal in the years since then, but, to a surprising extent, much of the practical work that economists and policy makers do today is still informed by the basic Keynesian framework as described in this book."

"Microfoundations" is one such issue where the tenor and focus of modern research in macroeconomics have changed. The protagonists of the modern Rational Expectations school have argued that only relationships that are explicitly derived from the optimizing behavior of individual agents can be expected to be stable and, thus, usable for forecasting. This has been the basis of the 1970s methodological counter revolution against Keynesian macroeconomics. However, it should be noted that long before the 1970s, Klein had already made some major contributions to the subject. His early papers on "Macroeconomics and the Theory of Rational Behavior" and "Remarks on the Theory of Aggregation," published in Econometrica in 1946, are important contributions to the development of modern thinking on the subject and will remain two of Klein's enduring contributions to economic theory.

Supply-side economics is another area where the tenor and focus of modern research have changed. Supply management is now at the centerstage of the modern macroeconomic research agenda, ostensibly because supply (productivity and cost) shocks are now viewed as the predominant cause of business cycles. Important world events in the 1970s seem to have confirmed this view, discrediting the traditional Keynesian demand-oriented economics. The huge oil price shocks of the 1970s and the ensuing simultaneous rise in inflation and unemployment broke down the traditional Phillips curve trade-off relationship between inflation and unemployment. Since the evidence of a trade-off between inflation and unemployment has traditionally provided the justification for the Keynesian policy activism, the apparent disappearance of the Phillips curve in the 1970s put the Keynesians in a state of disarray. Many economists declared Keynesian economics dead, some switched camps, and others felt that it was time to replace Keynesianism with the economics of the Monetarists or the Rational Expectations school of thought.

It is in this backdrop that   Klein made another important contribution to economics. This time, however, it is not to extol the virtues of demand management but to draw attention to the supply side of the economy. Although many of Klein's early works included explicit analyses of production function and factor markets and an embryonic Phillips curve appeared in his Economic Journal paper, it was not until the publication of The Economics of Supply and Demand that his deep commitment to the supply side was fully appreciated by the economics profession. The book is a collection of Klein's thoughts on current controversies in macroeconomics, and his central message is a reminder to macroeconomists around the world that managing supply is not an antithesis of managing demand but, rather, the logical corollary.

Klein is convinced that supply-side difficulties are our most pressing macroeconomic problem, and he makes a convincing case that these problems are sectoral and structural, that is to say, microeconomic in nature. (Morely:1984). He then offers a practical solution to the problem. He proposes that if the effects of supply shocks, including energy shock, pollution control, government regulation, productivity shock and capacity constraints are to be successfully tracked and predicted, then we must integrate our demand-side models with a much higher level of sectoral and structural detail. In one chapter of the book, Klein and two of his associates present such a model and demonstrate the power of the Klein approach to economic modeling by simulating the world wide impact of an unexpected increase in the price of oil.

As the chief economic advisor to President Jimmy Carter during the 1976-1980 period, Klein put into practice the supply management policies that he recommends in this book. He encouraged the administration to pursue such supply-side policies as training programs to improve the productivity of workers, tackling youth unemployment by, perhaps, lowering the minimum wage rate, and the selective deregulation of energy and food prices. As Frances Cairncross (1983)aptly puts it, "If these sound rather familiar goals, then that may reflect the influence Klein has already had on economic teaching."

THE KLEIN REVOLUTION

The Keynesian revolution gave the world a theoretical framework for thinking about macroeconomic policy. The Klein revolution that ensued has taught the world that economic theory must be formally written down as a set of behavioral (structural) equations of the macroeconomic actors, that the parameters of the system must be estimated from real data using probability theory and statistical estimation methods and that the estimated model must be analyzed and tested in various ways, before the theory contained in the model can be used for practical decision making and as an instrument for policymaking. This unique approach to modeling the economy, which Klein has helped develop and popularize, became the most dominant methodology of macroeconomics during the 1950s and the 1960s and, to this day, remains the most widely used methodological paradigm for econometric model-builders around the world.

It is hard to exaggerate Klein's contribution to each of the three stages of the theory of econometric modeling, namely, specification, estimation and testing. Many of his contributions appeared in various scholarly and technical journals in the profession, and some of the original ideas also appeared in his books. The pioneering and pathbreaking nature of these contributions has had a deep and profound impact on the course of the development of economics as a science. Indeed, it is predominantly due to Klein's work on econometric modeling that quantitative methods are now widely used as standard tools in economic analysis as well as in many other disciplines. His work was a major impetus in the formation of a subdiscipline in economics, called econometrics, which is devoted exclusively to quantitative work and applied research in economics. On the balance, applied work in economics using econometric methods has grown at least as rapidly as theoretical research since the inception of the Klein revolution.

THE GREATEST
FORECASTER OF ALL TIME

Applied econometrics has been the primary theme of Klein's professional work. Among his numerous gifts of innovative ideas to economics, none has had a greater practical impact on industry and government than his contribution to the field of econometric forecasting. Though hardly without its critics, the diffusion of econometric forecasting is truly impressive. A recent study by Faulhaber and Baumol (1988) concludes that among all of the inventions of economic research that have found beneficial practical applications, econometric forecasting ranks along with marginal analysis, capital budgeting, peak-load pricing, the portfolio selection model and the options pricing model as being the most widely used by business and government. In the same vein, Gerald Adams writes, "Econometrics has thoroughly invaded, if not captured, the world of business. Most large corporations and banks use econometric forecasts. Many major firms have hired their own econometrician and some are even building their own models." (Adams: 1992). This extraordinary diffusion of econometric models and their forecasts is in large part due to the persistent and pioneering modeling efforts of Klein.

Klein's contribution to the construction and dissemination of econometric models of business fluctuation and forecasting is unrivaled by any of his contemporaries. In 1950, he published *Economic Fluctuations in the United States 1921-1941*. With this major piece of work, he was soon recognized as a leading authority on the art and science of econometric modeling of macroeconomics. A streamlined version of this model which he put together jointly with his student, Arthur Goldberger, came to be called the Klein-Goldberger model. Klein used the model to successfully refute the prediction of other leading economists of the day, which claimed that the winding down of the Korean war would cause a large-scale recession in the United States.

Encouraged by the early successes and the breakthroughs in computer technology, Klein exploited new datasets and broadened the scope of his models in new directions. He pioneered the development of a new generation of macroeconometric models that paid close attention to the supply (cost) side of the economy. He achieved this by integrating the earlier macromodels based on national income accounts (NIAs) data, with Leontief's input-output tables, a matrix layout showing how outputs are shipped from the producing to the using sectors of the economy. The new models were complex and versatile, and they could be used to answer many more questions of economic interest and, most importantly, they could be used as instruments for economic policy making. Thus were born the famous Brookings Quarterly Model (1965) and the successive generations of the

Wharton Econometric Models of the United States economy. The Wharton Econometric Forecasting Associates, an organization that stemmed directly from the work of Lawrence Klein, now serves a large clientele of users from the mass media, independent consultants and decision makers of corporations and government agencies. Its detailed quarterly forecasts of the trends of the U.S. economy are a rich addition to the treasure of our knowledge.

Klein then extended his modeling efforts, again in a pioneering way, to the development of an integrated world economic model. As a first step toward the achievement of this daunting task, Klein helped build national macroeconometric models for individual countries around the world, including many countries in Western Europe, Eastern Europe, Asia, Russia and the other members of the Commonwealth of Independent States, as well as the Americas. Having helped to build the individual pieces, paying careful attention to the specific institutional characteristics of each country, Klein turned to the next stage of his modeling career. This was to combine the individual country models into a fully integrated world macroeconometric model, with the aim of increasing our understanding of international economic relationships, to improve the forecasts of world trade and capital movements among nations and to track and perhaps even tame the world business cycle. In a landmark recognition of the fact that "the U.S. economy is no longer closed," Klein, with the able assistance of Professors Bert Hickman and Aaron Gordon, brought together modelbuilders and researchers from the individual countries. Out of this massive group endeavor, unparalleled in the history of economic modeling, was spawned project LINK (The International Linkage of National Economic Models). Almost three decades after its conception, project LINK is still functioning today and "trying to break new grounds." From the beginning, there have been many skeptics and critics of econometric models and their forecasts. Jan Tinbergen's pioneering 1937 attempt to build the first econometric model of the U.S. economy was not wellreceived by the leading economists of the day, including Milton Friedman and John Maynard Keynes. Lawrence Klein, who carried on the work Tinbergen, faced daunting challenges from various sources, including the lack of reliable data, an underdeveloped computer technology and a skeptical economics profession that was still mostly uneducated in statistical methods. Although Professor Klein was neither the first nor the only modelbuilder of his time, his work is important because it was he who first successfully championed the practical and beneficial use of econometric models both in and out of the economics profession. He achieved this feat through his persistent modeling effort, unrivaled by his contemporaries, and by demonstrating to the world the accuracy of forecasts from his own models (Johannes: 1987).

CONCLUSION

The works of Lawrence Klein have touched the lives of people around the world, regardless of their political, racial or religious affiliations. Economists, either Keynesian or non-Keynesian, from developed or underdeveloped countries, from capitalist or communist countries, praise and admire Lawrence Klein, the man and his work. Edmund Phelps, who is an arch enemy of Keynesian economics, can still call him "the most thoughtful and judicious of American Keynesians." Paul Samuelson declared him to be "precocious," and the Chinese characterize him as a "friend of China." Few economists have claim to such warm admiration and deep respect from so wide an audience. Even as an undergraduate student in his teens, Klein knew that economic theory, in order to make a difference to society, must not just explain behavior but more importantly, must also be useful as a practical tool for day-to-day business decisions and for guiding public policies. As a youth during the depression era, Klein was deeply moved by the human suffering caused by mass unemployment and was convinced, as he is to this day, that unemployment is the greatest of all social evils. He has dedicated his life's work to the search for a theory of policy stabilization, which, while firmly grounded in individual's rational behavior, can be both refuted by the data, and passed from one generation to another.

RECOMMENDED READINGS

Adams, F.G., and B.G. Hickman, (eds.) (1983). *Global Econometrics: Essays in Honor of Lawrence Klein*. Cambridge: MIT Press.

——— . (1992). *Lawrence Klein's The Keynesian Revolution: 50 Years After*. Philadelphia: University of Pennsylvania.

Ball, R.J. (1981). "On Lawrence Klein's Contribution to Economics," *Scandinavian Journal of Economics*.

Cairncross, F. (1983). "The Economics of Supply and Demand: Book Review," *The Times Literary Supplement*. pp 13-68.

Datta, M. (ed.) (1995). *Economics, Econometrics and The Link: Essays in Honor of Lawrence R. Klein*. Amsterdam: Elsevier.

Fair, R. C. (1992, February). *The Cowles Commission Approach, Real Business Cycle Theories, and New Keynesian Economics*. NBER Working Paper.

Johannes, J.M. (1987). "A Commentary on Lawrence Klein's Contribution to Economics," *Thinker's of the Twentieth Century*. (ed.) Ronald Turner, Chicago.

Klein, Lawrence (1947). *The Keynesian Revolution*. New York: Macmillan.

Morley, S.A. (June 1984), "The Economics of Supply and Demand: Book Review," *Journal of Economic Literature*. Vol. 26.

Samuelson, Paul. (1991). "Abstracts of Lectures at the Statistics Seminar, MIT, 1942-3," *Statistical Science*. Vol. 6, No. 4.

20

James Tobin (1918-):
An Architect of the Portfolio Selection
Theory and the Laureate of 1981

Abdur R. Chowdhury

BIOGRAPHICAL PROFILE

James Tobin was born in Champaign, Illinois, in 1918. His father, Louis Tobin, was the publicity director of the athletics department of the University of Illinois at Urbana-Champaign. His mother, Margaret Edgerton, was a social worker. Tobin graduated from University High School in Urbana. In addition to him, this high school produced two other Nobel laureates, Philip Anderson (physics) and Hamilton Smith (medicine/physiology). For his undergraduate studies, he entered Harvard University in 1935 with a full scholarship. The idea to apply for a Harvard scholarship came from his father. He graduated in 1939 and then he started his graduate studies in economics, also at Harvard. There, he had the opportunity to learn from such great economists as Joseph Schumpeter, Alvin Hansen, Edward Chamberlin, Gottfried Haberler, Wassily Leontief and many more. At Harvard, he was in the midst of fellow students such as Paul Samuelson, Paul Sweezy, Lloyd Metzler, John Galbraith, Abram Bergson, Richard Musgrave and others. Later on, all of them became well-established economists. Tobin received his M.S. in economics in 1941 and worked for the federal government in Washington, D.C., for some time. When the United States was drawn into the Second World War, Tobin joined the Navy on the destroyer USS Kearny. In 1946, he returned to Harvard as a teaching fellow and, in the following year, earned his Ph.D. in economics. In 1947, he became a member of the Society of Fellows at Harvard. The following three years, he worked extensively and made several remarkable publications primarily in the field of macroeconomics. In 1950, Tobin joined Yale University as an associate professor of economics. At that time, he became a believer of Keynesian tradition and developed his famous "portfolio selection theory." When the Cowles Commission moved to Yale from Chicago and changed its name to the Cowles Foundation, Tobin took over as its new director. A couple of years later, he became Sterling Professor of Economics at Yale. Meanwhile, Tobin got deeply involved in public policy debate that left some impact on the policy of the Kennedy administration. In 1970, he was elected president of the American Economic Association. Since then he has been continuously writing on various aspects of macroeconomic policy controversy. Tobin served as a consultant for various public and private agencies and is a member of many professional societies, including the American Academy of Arts and Sciences and the American Philosophical Society. He holds honorary degrees from several institutions, such as Syracuse University, University of Illinois and Dartmouth College. He married Elizabeth Ringo in 1946. They have one daughter and three sons.

INTRODUCTION

James Tobin won the economics Nobel Prize in 1981 for his "analysis of financial markets and their relations to expenditure decisions, employment and production prices." Since the introduction of the Nobel Memorial Prize in Economics in 1969, a number of prominent economists have been awarded the prize for their lifelong dedication and contribution to the science of economics. Although The Royal Swedish Academy of Sciences cites the most important contribution of the recipient in awarding the prize, in reality, the contributions of a Nobel laureate cannot be confined to a single issue or topic in economics. Their achievements cover a broad spectrum of economic research. James Tobin is no exception. The Royal Swedish Academy of Sciences noted the significance of Tobin's contribution to economic policy making, praising Tobin for laying a solid foundation for studies on the working of the monetary and financial markets and demonstrating how changes in these markets influence economic variables such as employment, output, consumption, investment, and so on.

THE PORTFOLIO SELECTION
THEORY AND THE TOBIN'S 'Q'

Tobin's portfolio selection theory analyzes how individual households and firms determine the composition of their real and financial assets. Economic agents weigh risk and expected return in their decision-making process. In developing the theory, Tobin doesn't confine himself to only monetary assets but considers a broad range of assets and debts. This helps him in extending the channels in the transmission mechanism between the financial market and real expenditure decisions. A policy implication of his finding has been the extensive analysis of economic conditions and stabilization policy in recent years.

He argued that investors do not tend to maximize the rate of return on their investment in exclusion of all other factors. He believed that investors tend to achieve a portfolio balance by comparing high-risk investments with less speculative ones. He developed the mechanism by which changes in the financial sectors of the economy are transmitted to the real sector. He combined the notion of stock-flow relationships with asset equilibrium models in order to develop the q factor–defined as the ratio of the market valuations of capital assets to their replacement costs. He substituted the relative price of capital goods (Tobin's 'q') for Keynes' rate of return (the supply price of capital). The use of the 'q' variable in an asset-equilibrium framework helped him in analyzing the effect of monetary policy changes as well as different methods of financing a budget deficit.

IN SUPPORT OF KEYNES

In a classical theory, the price level adjusts to eliminate excess demand or supply in the market. Similarly, the wage rates adjust to remove any excess demand or supply in the labor market. Hence, any unemployment must be voluntary, and the economy should always be at the full employment level. Keynes, on the other hand, argued that money wages are rigid in a downward direction and are, therefore, not immediately subject to market forces. As a result, they do not adjust to restore full employment as suggested by the classical theory. Hence, an equilibrium with involuntary unemployment is possible. Tobin pointed out that Keynes' conclusion would hold even if money wages are simply slow to adjust in order to restore equilibrium. In this case, the output will adjust to restore equilibrium. The slower the change in money wages, the larger the change will be in output.

Tobin wrote his senior thesis on this difference between the Keynesian and the classical position on the labor market. His first professional publication was a 1941 article published in the *Quarterly Journal of Economics*. Based on his senior thesis, the conclusions of this paper started an intense debate among the economists of that period over the relative speeds of adjustment of prices, wages, and output to shocks in an economic system. Over the years, Tobin and his followers have envisioned a sluggish economy with sticky wages and prices, an economy where output gives way before prices in response to economic downturns. He has repeatedly turned back attempts by the classical economists to reestablish the notion of flexible market adjustments. He developed the concept of sticky money wages by speculating on the workers' decision to supply labor. This provides an understanding of the micro foundation of most of his macro theories.

A New Interpretation of Keynes

Tobin gave a new interpretation of Keynes' speculative motive of the demand for money. Keynes developed the liquidity preference theory, where he showed that the demand for money for the aggregate economy is an inverse function of the interest rate. Although economic agents have different expectations about changes in the interest rate, Keynes suggested that these different expectations are held in such a way that a smooth downward-sloping function is generated. During periods of high interest rates, economic agents would expect that interest rates would eventually decline and that bond prices would increase, so they would tend to hold more bonds and less money. During periods of low interest rates, economic agents would likewise hold less bonds and more money. The downward-sloping demand for money function critically depended on Keynes' assumption about how expectations are formed. Many economists failed to agree with Keynes' argument in this regard.

Tobin addressed this question by assuming that an economic agent faces a trade-off between the degree of risk and the expected return on his portfolio. In his words, "People may prefer liquidity, and prefer it more the lower the interest rate on noncash assets, not because they expect capital losses on average but because they fear them more than they value the equally probable capital gains." The economic agent is able to derive a probability distribution about the capital gain or loss associated with his portfolio. This distribution is assumed to have an expected value of zero, meaning that on average capital gains balance capital losses. The probability distribution for the portfolio's return is described by the expected value and standard deviation of the distribution. However, this mean - variance approach to portfolio analysis has been subsequently criticized by several other economists.

THE ROLE OF MONEY
IN LONG-TERM GROWTH

Another innovation of Tobin was to put money into the theory of long-run growth. He also wanted to develop an appropriate measure of the effect of monetary policy on investment decisions. He wrote several papers over the years showing a positive relationship between the stock of capital in a growing economy and the rates of monetary growth and inflation. He also contributed, along with several of his colleagues at Yale, to the development of a general model of asset markets and then integrated it into a macroeconomic growth model. He differed with Keynes' treatment of the rate of interest as the sole determinant of investment decision and instead related the desired capital stock to the market rate of interest.

While Tobin differed with Keynes on certain issues, he never failed to defend Keynes against what he termed as "distortions in the profession." According to this distorted view of the Keynesian theory, fluctuations in real output and employment are caused by innovations to nominal aggregate demand, which become real innovations only because of rigid prices. Tobin clearly pointed out that the Keynesian theory of business fluctuations stresses shocks to real aggregate demand–investment, consumption, or government purchases. Although some shocks may indeed arise from the monetary side, such monetary policy actions that change nominal interest rates also change the real rates and affect investment decisions. Similarly, a shift in the production function that raises the marginal productivity of capital may simultaneously stimulate investment while lowering the demand for money. He argued that aggregate demand in the Keynesian theory is constrained by amounts actually sold in the marketplace, which in some cases may be different from the amounts that economic agents would like to sell at the existing prices.

PUBLIC POLICY

During his entire professional career, Tobin has demonstrated an intense interest in public policy. He formally entered the arena of public debate on government economic policy by criticizing the tight monetary policy of the Federal Reserve Bank in an article published in early 1961. He suggested that the Federal Reserve's policy would hinder attempts by the Kennedy administration to raise the levels of employment, output, and income. He then started writing articles on current economic issues for various newspapers and periodicals. In early 1961, he was invited by President Kennedy to serve as a member of his Council of Economic Advisors. He served in the council for almost two years before returning to Yale University to take up his teaching position. Given his name recognition, he continued to write and speak more frequently on various policy issues.

Tobin was convinced of the economic cost of unemployment and was unwilling to accept deep recessions as a means of fighting inflation. He compared the gains from expanding employment against the costs of inflation. He argued for expansionary policies in order to reduce unemployment, even below its natural level. Over the last four decades, Tobin has served as a consultant for both government and private agencies, including the Federal Reserve Bank, the Congressional Budget Office, and the Ford Foundation.

CONCLUSION

Tobin is rare among recent economists in the originality and simplicity of his theoretical and empirical works. His clear and concise explanation of quite complex and sophisticated economic issues is almost unique among the leading economists. His participation in policy debates has also enriched the thinking of all economists–friends and critics alike. His years in Washington, D.C., introduced him to the inadequacies and inefficiencies of the federal and state welfare programs. He wrote several papers in the late 1960s highlighting these issues. His interest in this area can still be seen in his various writings. He has been an active participant in the policy discussions on various economic issues. In particular, he has defended the Keynesian position in various debates with the Monetarists, especially with Milton Friedman. He has written extensively on stabilization policies and has been involved in debates regarding the conduct of monetary policy. He has been a strong advocate of an activist policy by the government.

A challenge of orthodox theories and ideas has been common in the works of all reformists. James Tobin is no exception. In questioning ideas that he thought were unconfirmed by empirical evidence, he wrote eloquently expressing his alternative views. He has raised many questions that have been asked in subsequent literature and also has provided the framework within which these questions can be raised. The statistical techniques and simulation methods developed and applied by him are still used by economists in their research endeavor.

The Royal Swedish Academy of Science cited his work on financial market analysis and its relationship with expenditure decisions, employment, output, and prices. He is perhaps most widely known for his contributions on monetary theory, macroeconomics, and stabilization policies. However, he has published path-breaking works in the areas of econometric methods, risk theory, consumer behavior, and economic policy. He has developed statistical techniques for use in several different areas. These include, but are not limited to, analyzing survey data in order to gather information and using them for forecasting purposes and using pooled cross-section-time series data, and techniques for discrete and limited dependent variables. He is also known for his works on poverty and his contribution in the popular press on various economic issues. In addition, he has served the government in various capacities, including the Council of Economic Advisors to the president. Tobin has conducted a thorough analysis of financial markets and the transmission mechanisms between the financial and the real sector of the economy. His study can be described as a major breakthrough in the integration of the various sectors in the economy. His work on the portfolio selection model opened the door for further research in related areas in the 1970s. Few economists have exerted such influence on contemporary economic thinking.

RECOMMENDED READINGS

Blecha, Betty. (1989). "James Tobin," in Bernard Katz, ed. *Nobel Laureates in Economic Sciences: A Biographical Dictionary*. New York: Garland.

Myhrman, Johan. (1982). "James Tobin's Contributions to Economics," *Scandinavian Journal of Economics*. Vol. 84, No. 1, pp. 89-99.

Purvis, Douglas. (1991). "Introduction: James Tobin's Contributions to Economics," in William Brainard, William Nordhaus, and Harold Watts, eds. *Money, Macroeconomics, and Economic Policy: Essays in Honor of James Tobin*. Cambridge: MIT Press.

Solow, Robert. (1991). "Tobin on Money Wages and Employment," in William Brainard, William Nordhaus, and Harold Watts, (eds.) *Money, Macroeconomics, and Economic Policy: Essays in Honor of James Tobin*, Cambridge: MIT Press.

Tobin, James. (1986). "James Tobin," in William Breit and Roger Spencer, (eds.) *Lives of the Laureates: Seven Nobel Economists*. Cambridge: MIT Press.

———. (1989). In Werner Sichel (ed.) (1989). "James Tobin," in *The State of Economic Sciences: Views of Six Nobel Laureates*. Kalamazoo: W.E. Upjohn Institute for Employment Research.

21

George Stigler (1911-1991):
An Authority on the Economics of Regulations and Industrial Organization and the Laureate of 1982

Mahbub Ullah

BIOGRAPHICAL PROFILE

George Stigler was born in Seattle, Washington, in 1911. He was the only child of his parents. His father, Joseph Stigler, came to the United States from Europe toward the end of the nineteenth century. So was the case with his mother, Elizabeth Stigler. Stigler started his education in the Seattle public school system and received his high school graduation in 1931. For higher education, he moved to the Midwest and spent a year at Northwestern University. Then he entered the University of Chicago and completed his Ph. D. in economics in 1938. At Chicago, he was greatly influenced by his teachers—Frank Knight, Jacob Viner, and Henry Simons. Among them, Frank Knight was his thesis supervisor. There he was also inspired by his fellow students Allen Wallis and Milton Friedman. In 1936, he joined Iowa State College, where Theodore Schultz was the department head. In 1938, he moved to the University of Minnesota, from where he took leave for several years to serve the Statistical Research Group at Columbia University. In the mid-1940s, he returned to Minnesota, then moved to Brown University and later joined Columbia University, where he stayed from 1947 to 1958. At Columbia, he had the opportunity to work closely with Kenneth Arrow, Milton Friedman, Melvin Reder, and Robert Solow. From the late 1930s, Stigler started to make his major publications. He worked on price and cost theories and various topics of industrial organization. In the 1960s, he became deeply involved in the study of public regulations. He also had a good deal of interest in the history of economic thought. In 1981, although he resigned as the Walgreen Professor of Economics, he maintained some association with the University of Chicago. Stigler was a president of the American Economic Association and the History of Economics Society. He received honorary degrees from Carnegie Mellon, Rochester, and Brown universities as well as the Helsinki School of Economics. Stigler married Margaret Mack in 1936. She died in 1970, leaving her husband and three sons. Stigler passed away in 1991.

INTRODUCTION

George Stigler won the economics Nobel Prize in 1982 for his "seminal studies of international structures, functioning of markets and causes and effects of public regulation." Very few economists in a developing world are familiar with the works of Stigler because of the novelty of the issues and themes he chose, but most of the undergraduate students around the world in the sixties read his book, *The Theory of Price*. This made them familiar with his style of presentation and economic logic. However, his major contributions remained unknown to many for some time. Galbraith has quoted Stigler, saying on more than one occasion that it is a tragedy of our time that so many had read Galbraith and so few had read Adam Smith. Galbraith replied that the deeper tragedy is that no one read much Stigler at all. This is probably because Stigler abhorred the journalistic type of writing and was committed to serious academic exercise.

What is pervasive through and through his works is Stigler's deep devotion to understanding the economic process. The citation for Stigler's Nobel Prize in economics highlighted his work on regulation, but what Stigler himself felt, and Gary Becker tended to agree with him, was that his most important contribution was to the economics of information. At the White House reception for Stigler's prize, the press was interested in his comments on President Reagan's new initiatives in the areas of tax cuts and government spending rather than on his erudite deliberations. This was the time for supply-side economics and the presidential aides expected that the venerable conservative economist would shower praises for the president's program. Stigler's reaction was however, critical. He termed supply side economics as "a gimmick or a slogan," and he opined that the economy was "bumping along" at the bottom of a full-blown "depression." The fame of Nobel Prize gave him opportunities to provide his views on many occasions. In an interview with the *U. S. News and World Report*, Stigler argued that "economic stability would be reached if large swings in the money supply, such as those occurring in 1982, could be eliminated." But Stigler remained firm in his insistence of government noninterference: "Equally important, the government should stop tinkering with the tax law, price controls, business regulations, and things like that. Less of that would contribute greatly to a stable investment climate. When I say 'government' I really mean people, including the media. I don't blame the politicians as much as I do the public and the press for making unrealistic demands on government to 'do something' about every problem that comes along. Next the government would be expected to prevent natural calamities such as earthquakes and meteoric showers. There is really no limit to the pretended competence of the state.

STIGLER'S WORLD-OUTLOOK

An appropriate approach to understanding a social thinker is first to locate where he is placed in the spectrum of ideas. McCann and Perlman, in their *Economic Journal* article, termed Stigler as "the quintessential 'conservative' if perhaps mordant, professional economic scholar. In the continental European sense, Stigler is considered to have been a classical liberal. "The corpus of economic analysis, " said Stigler, " can be turned to a thousand contradictory ends. But by and large it is not: my thesis is that the professional study of economics makes one politically conservative." He means, "by a conservative in economic matters a person who wishes most economic activity to be conducted by private enterprise, and who believes that abuses of private power will usually be checked, by the forces of competition. He traced the conservatism of the economists to "the effect of the scientific training the economist receives. He is drilled in the problem of all economic systems and in the method by which a price system solves these problems. It becomes impossible for the trained economist to believe that a small group of selfish capitalists dictates the main outline of the allocation of resources and the determination of outputs.

In the broader sense, Stigler was in favor of conserving the existing ideas and institutions. But what was the time frame for those existing ideas and institutions? Stigler was an ardent supporter of Adam Smith's views. Interestingly enough, at the bicentennial celebration of the *Wealth of Nations*, held at Glasgow University, he declared that Adam Smith was alive and well at the University of Chicago. He never felt shy in admitting that he supported what Smith supported and opposed what Smith opposed while not being oblivious of Smith's errors in analysis. Like Smith, Stigler favored free markets and disdained regulation, which in Smith's time got into effect through mercantilist policies. Very often economists are classed as conservatives or radicals with respect to their stand on the question of equality. Stigler had a very precise position on this score. He felt, "The liberal goal is unattainable in the presence of great and permanent inequalities, and it is also unattainable in the presence of permanent equality. On the liberal philosophy, it is necessary that all contestants begin the race at the same point, but it is fatal to require that they reach the finish line simultaneously. There is only one resource in reconciling these desiderata: time. And society should use time lavishly, for it is one thing of which it possesses more than its individual members." He advocated the elimination of inequalities of resources rather than inequalities of income. His prescriptions were to make labor incomes more equal by enlarged educational systems, improvement of labor mobility, elimination of labor monopolies, provision of medical care for poor children and the like. His suggestions for reducing property income inequality included elimination of monopoly and extremely heavy taxation of inheritances. Natural law institutions that emanate from the play of long-term market forces, in Stigler's mind, had the potential for being most efficient and productive. Sometimes governments are forced to adopt populist measures like price and rent controls. But these policies, according to Stigler, tend to be "faddish at best, and truly counterproductive at worst." These policies play devil with the efficiency of the market.

THE ECONOMICS OF REGULATION

Stigler's collaborative article with Claire Friedland on electricity rates and another that he wrote alone marked a sharp departure from the tradition of economists' analysis of regulation. The novelty of the contributions lay in the penetrating insights that they generated rather than in their technical sophistication or their rigor in conclusion. Before Stigler (along with Friedland) gave a jolt to the existing traditions of analysis of regulation, economists believed that the appropriate role of the government was to rectify private market failures observed in departures from marginal cost pricing and that regulatory institutions were capable of restraining those departures.

Monopolies in general and natural monopolies in particular were areas that drew such regulations. Since natural monopoly cost conditions created conditions of private exploitation of market power, the role of the regulators would be to restrict such market power. The reigning orthodoxy was that political and legal constraints on subsidization of the difference between marginal and average cost discouraged the forcing of prices down to marginal cost, that the regulators had to set something approximating average cost prices, and that this was substantially lower than it would have been without regulation. Stigler and Friedland's 1962 paper was basically an empirical study that demonstrated that the difference between prices in regulated and unregulated electricity utilities was not significant. However, a recent study after correcting the errors of Stigler and Friedland's regression exercise showed that the original study results produced incorrect and understated magnitudes of differences of prices and outputs and not much statistical significance while using the original data set. The implication is that regulation lowered price by about a fourth and thereby caused output to rise by over half. Notwithstanding the lacunae in the Stigler-Friedland study, it provoked a series of studies on regulation and made economists curious about theoretical questions.

Many of these studies, however, found regulation effective in a way opposite to that which the traditional models of regulation implied. There occurred a shift from the "public interest" model of regulation to "producer protection hypothesis." In the producer protection hypothesis, ex-regulation market structure is a very crucial datum. If the character of ex-regulation market structure is monopolistic, as in the case of electricity, regulation would be ineffective. But in an ex-regulation market structure characterized by competition, as in the case of transport, the effect of regulation would be to lower output, raise prices, and generate monopoly rents. The emerging image of regulation was of regulators being captured by the regulated. There were a good number of studies that provided evidence in favor of capture hypothesis. The large body of evidence provoked the question of why regulation should happen to work in the perverse manner that it did. The answer provided in Stigler's 1971 article (published in the *Bell Journal of Economic and Management Sciences*) was a landmark in the economic theory of regulation. This is indeed a theory, as it was constructed within a broad frame of supply and demand. Stigler made an attempt to integrate the economics of regulation with the economics of politics.

We all know that transactions in market are costly. Stigler's ingenuity lay in his charming ability to unravel the costs of articulating politically effective demand before the regulators. This brought to the fore the importance of organized interest groups that is an integral part of modern analysis of regulation. The suppliers in Stigler's theory are a homogeneous bunch of political actors like legislators, executives, and their regulator agents. They have one commodity to sell–power–power of prices and entry. This power ultimately determines the wealth of regulated industry buyers and sellers. The buyers and sellers in the regulated industry market compete for access to this power. In the bargain the higher bidders win. The demanders offer heterogeneous currencies, such as votes delivered in support of the politicians, campaign services and jobs in the political afterlife, in their bid. In this market for power, the cohesive groups of producers have an edge over the noncohesive groups of consumers.

The outcome is reflected in the regulatory decisions on prices and entry that transfers rent from the consumers to the producers. In the political equilibrium of Stigler's analysis, "the cohesive minorities tax the diffuse majorities." Stigler's 1971 article, "The Theory of Economic Regulation," published in the *Bell Journal of Economics and Management Science* inspired an in-depth reexamination of the origins and effects of regulatory institutions in the United States. Scholars feel that Stigler's basic model of the economics of political process needs revamping, his approach to the problem still endures. Economists today are not content with examining regulatory government policies or a host of other government policies alone, but would go beyond those. This is the lasting impact of Stigler's theory of economics of regulation.

MICROECONOMICS AND INDUSTRIAL ORGANIZATION

George Stigler revised and improved microeconomic theory to enable it to handle a wide range of real-life phenomena. He was equally concerned with analyzing the implications of theory as with developing new theoretical models. His economic insights and ingenuity speak of his extraordinary power to pose theoretical questions. In the arena of pure theory, Stigler introduced the notion that firms could decide how much flexibility to build into short-run cost functions. In Stigler's view, by permitting the fixed service to undergo variations of form, entrepreneurs can achieve maximum output from various proportions between fixed and variable services in the short run. The incentive of entrepreneurs lies in the fact that it increases marginal product without any additional investment in the fixed services. Stigler, in his book *The theory of Price* wrote, "Their power to do so is also often clear, for very few productive services come only in a few sizes or forms. The entrepreneur can sometimes sell the inappropriate form of equipment and replace it with an appropriate form, and he can almost always wear out the inappropriate form and replace it with an appropriate form. The full adaptability of the fixed service often can be achieved only in the long run. ...Even in the short run, however, there will usually be some adaptability." Stigler was a forerunner of the application of the linear programming technique for minimizing the cost of obtaining a balanced diet. Even as early as in 1943, Stigler wrote a short and important paper on how to satisfy the minimum requirements for a healthy diet at least cost. Since the problem involved maximization subject to inequalities, he solved a linear programming problem before the simplex method was developed. He used strong common sense and an iterative method to arrive at the solution, which was quite close to the best possible one.

Stigler's contribution to the economics of information is epochal. Before the 1950s, there was hardly any analysis of the gathering of information by the economic actors, but the importance of information in market exchanges can be appreciated from the facts of day-to-day life. For example, consumers have very imperfect information about the prices charged by different retail shops and, the quality of the products and services made available by them. In the same manner, information about wages offered to the workers by the employers in the job market is never perfectly known. Employers also do not have perfect knowledge about the prices of raw materials and the skill of the workers. All these are obvious, but economists did not know how to analyze the ways in which actors in different markets gather information. Stigler, with his usual depth of insight, developed a systematic theory of rational search of information in the market by the imperfectly informed agents. Because information is costly to search, a rational economic agent will search for information till the value of additional information is equal to its cost. Stigler tested his theory by analyzing the distribution of prices of durable goods and labor markets. He also put this theory to use to understand the use and effects of advertisement. His works in this area provoked others to undertake large number of studies in this area.

Stigler made significant contributions to improve upon the analysis of monopoly. In the beginning of his professional career, Stigler was a firm believer in antitrust policies such as restrictions on mergers, which were considered to reduce competition, and breaking up companies having significant monopoly power. But he made a shift from this stand, convinced partly by the findings of Aaron Director's analysis of actual cases of antitrust measures, that government officials and political appointees in the antitrust bodies had a very different objective in mind. Bad economics in combination with political pressures to attack or defend "big" business, to protect small companies, or to come to the rescue of companies in the constituency of powerful congress members often distorted the enforcement of antitrust measures. Stigler thought that the best measure would be to have a minimalist anti-trust policy that would help all honest business practices and discourage conspiracies to raise prices and divide up the market. This, Stigler thought, could be achieved by encouraging domestic and foreign competition and not by regulating business.

Stigler made a successful critique of the theoretical inadequacy and predictive failures of the kinky-shaped oligopoly demand curve model in his 1947 paper, "The Kinky Oligopoly Demand Curve And Rigid Prices," (published in the *Journal of Political Economy*.) He stressed the frequency of price changes in oligopolistic markets. In his 1951 essay, "The Division of Labor is Limited by the Extent of Market," (published in the *Journal of Political Economy*,) Stigler analyzed the determinants of the structure and boundaries of the firms. He proposed the use of the survival principle for understanding the economies of scale in his 1958 essay on "The Economies of Scale." In simple terms, the principle says that scale economies can be assessed by observing the survival and prosperity of firms in the marketplace. This is still an important instrument in the tool box of the industrial economists. Stigler's 1964 paper, "A Theory of Oligopoly" (published in the *Journal of Political Economy*), produced a very valuable insight to the effect that the stability of collusive behavior in a market with few sellers, like oligopoly, depends on the possibility of detecting and punishing deviations from overt or covert deals to restrict output. This is an example of the application of classic cartel theory in an oligopolistic market structure. Stigler's detection problem can be viewed to be under the broad umbrella of information economics. This paper gave a big jolt to the received understanding of the economists about the pervasiveness of collusive practices in oligopoly markets and provided effective tools for analyzing individual markets.

POLICY ANALYSIS

Stigler exploded some major myths prevailing in the arena of policy formulation. In his 1946 National Bureau of Economic Research employment studies, "The Economics of Minimum Wage Legislation," Stigler analyzed the distorting effect on resource allocation, the restrictionist effect on employment, and the failure of the federal minimum wage legislation to alleviate poverty. At a much later stage in his life, during President Johnson's "great society" era, when a great deal of social legislation was taking place, Stigler linked minimum wages to civil rights in a way that was quite contradictory to the ruling orthodoxy. He found that the government's effort to create employment opportunities for black youths hinged primarily on legislative measures. Despite the best of intentions of the lawmakers, unemployment persisted. Stigler's prescription was to enhance the skill of the black youths through a program of educational grants. Stigler's point was that market forces would enhance their level of employment due to enhanced skills. Recognizing that minimum wage legislation led to the unemployment of the unskilled youths, Stigler opted for a policy of facilitation rather than intervention into the forces of the market.

He forcefully argued that working below a minimum wage was preferable to not working at all. In his book, *Roofs or Ceilings*, co-authored with Milton Friedman, Stigler made the point that government rent controls were of no avail. Such interventions led to decreased housing construction and housing shortage. He also pointed out the difference between the short run when the tenants got the benefit and the long run, when the property values decline through owner neglect. The liberals did not like the idea when the book was published, because the book advanced arguments counter to the popular sentiments.

ECONOMIC THOUGHT

Stigler made a very painstaking and incisive analysis of the thought process of great thinkers in economics. From his point of view, the scope and subject matter of the history of economic thought is very restrictive indeed. He defined " the subject matter of history of economics to be economics which is not read to master present-day economics." However, while making his own theoretical point he did not refrain from "referencing historical episodes and invoking historical analogies." His first published article, "The Economics of Carl Menger," a piece that reappraised the economic theories of Menger and the Austrian School, is an example of his interest in the history of economic thought from the early days of his professional career. His doctoral dissertation, written under the guidance of Frank Knight and published *Production and Distribution Theories*, is a historical analysis of price and value theory covering giants like Jevons, Wicksteed, Marshall, Edgeworth, Menger, Wieser, Böhm-Bawerk, Walras, Wicksell, and Clark. He wrote in the introduction of the book: The present work is a critical study of the theories of distribution which rose out of the theory of subjective value, and which were finally systematized into general marginal productivity theory. The period covered, therefore, lies between 1870 and 1895. It was in this quarter century that economic theory was transformed from an art, in many respects literary, to a science of growing rigor. The support for this generalization will be suggested by the most general comparison between Mill's Principles, the apogee of theoretical English economics at the beginning of the period and Marshall's Principles, near the end of the period.

Stigler was not only engaged in analyzing the thoughts of great minds in economics; he also inquired into the history of particular concepts of economics like perfect competition or the Giffen Paradox. In his article, "Perfect Competition, Historically Contemplated," Stigler made a very brilliant survey of the concept of perfect competition, covering thinkers of the classical school like Smith and Cairnes, critics of private enterprise like Marx and the early Fabian school, members of the mathematical school like Cournot, Jevons, and Marshall and reaching ultimately to the complete formulation by Clark and Knight. In his concluding reflections, Stigler suggested that the appropriate name of the concept should be "competition," meaning absence of monopoly. But since this would restrict the meaning of a concept that had so long been used in a wide sense, it would be expedient to denote this narrow concept with the suggestive phrase *market competition.* Stigler, in his *Journal of Political Economy* article published in 1957 said, "Perfect market competition will prevail when there are indefinitely many traders (no one of which controls an appreciable share of demand and supply) acting independently in a perfect market. A perfect market is one in which the traders have full knowledge of all offer and bid prices." Stigler thought it was unwarranted to treat a perfect market as a subsidiary feature of competition, because, perfect market was also compatible with monopoly, since in realistic cases a perfect market might be more likely to exist under monopoly and with monopoly complete knowledge is easier to achieve. Here again, Stigler displayed his intuition about the economics of information. After applying his keen logical mind, Stigler arrived at the broad concept of perfect competition that fulfills the condition that the rate of return of each resource would be equal in all uses.

Stigler, while dealing with the history of economic thought, analyzed trends in the economic profession such as the appearance of professional journals and their changing contents. He dealt with this aspect of the history of economic thought in his article, "Statistical Studies in the History of Economic Thought." Stigler strongly challenged the view that economic thinking had been influenced by immediate events, and immediate events by economic thinking. While providing the force of example to his argument, he said that even at the height of the industrial revolution, the classical economists treated the state of technology as a given, the opposing camps of the wage fund theory did not acknowledge the surrounding conditions, and the marginal utility revolution reflected no discernible environmental change. On the other hand, he said, "A war may ravage a continent or destroy a generation without posing new theoretical question." A new theoretical question is likely to lead to the development of original ideas. Stigler argued that the question of originality was not a simple, naive question of who first stated a particular proposition, but rather who made the idea intellectually important. Judging from this perspective, Stigler himself has found a place in the arena of contemporary economic thought for his brilliant ideas on economics of information, industrial regulation, and microeconomics.

CONCLUSION

Stigler was a great professional economist who made wide-ranging contributions. He was a prolific writer. He did not use mathematics like Arrow, Debreu, or Samuelson in exposition. The descriptive approach of his writings was appreciated widely for "clarity, elegance and erudition." His works over a fifty-year period consisted of no less than thirty books and pamphlets, 130 articles, and seventy book reviews, which really touched the frontiers of knowledge. Stigler also led a very active professional life in the sense that he served on numerous government boards, was elected to many learned societies, served as the Director of the Chicago Board of Trade, and also served as president of the American Economic Association in 1964. He was the editor of the *Journal of Political Economy* from 1972 till his death. He was awarded numerous honorary degrees. Stigler was also a very competent book reviewer. He wrote a number of pieces on the problems of higher education and its pedagogy. Stigler made mathematics serve economics without turning into its servant. The success of his works lay in their originality, rigor, and the vigor with which he persisted with them.

RECOMMENDED READINGS

Blaug, Mark. (1985). *Great Economists Since Keynes: An Introduction to the Lives and Works of One Hundred Economists*. Sussex: Whitesheaf Books, pp. 239-41.

Bruggink, Thomas H.(1989). "George J. Stigler 1982," in Bernerd S. Katz, (ed.) *Nobel Laureates in Economic Sciences*. New York: Garland.

Friedman, Milton. (1993). "George Stigler: A Personal Reminiscence," *Journal of Political Economy*. Vol. 101, No. 5, pp. 768-73.

McCan, C.R. Jr., and Mark Perlman. (1993, July). "On Thinking About George Stigler," *The Economic Journal*. Vol. 103.

Peltzman, Sam. (1993). "George Stigler's Contribution to the Economic Analysis of Regulation," *Journal of Political Economy*. Vol. 101, No. 5.

Stigler, George J. (1939). "Production and Distribution in the Short Run," *Journal of Political Economy*. Vol. 47, pp. 305-27.

Stigler, George J., and Claire Friedland. (1962). "What Can Regulators Regulate? The Case of Electricity," *Journal of Law and Economics*. Vol. 5, pp. 1-16.

Stigler, George J., and Milton Friedman. (1946). "Roofs or Ceilings?" Irving -on-Hudson: Foundation for Economic Education.

———. (1941). *Production and Distribution Theories*. New York: Macmillan.

———. (1945, May). "The Cost of Subsistence ," *Journal of Farm Economics*. Vol. 2, pp. 303-14.

———. (1946). "The Economics of Minimum Wage Legislation," *American Economic Review*. Vol. 36, pp. 358-65.

———. (1947). "The Kinky Oligopoly Demand Curve and Rigid Prices," *Journal of Political Economy*. Vol. 55, No. 5, pp. 432-39.

———. (1949). *Five Lectures On Economic Problems* . London: Longmans, Green and Co.

———. (1951, June). "The Division of Labour is Limited by the Extent of Market," *Journal of Political Economy*. Vol. 59, pp. 185-93.

———. (1952). *The Theory of Price*. New York: Macmillan Company.

———. (1955, November). "The Nature and Role of Originality in Scientific Progress," *Economica*. Vol. 22.

———. (1957, February). "Perfect Competition Historically Contemplated," *The Journal of Political Economy*. Vol. 65.

———. (1958, October). "Economies of Scale," *Journal of Law and Economics*. pp. 54-71.

———. (1961, June). "The Economics of Information," *Journal of Political Economy*. Vol. 69, No. 3, pp. 213-25.

———. (1964, February). "A Theory of Oligopoly," *Journal of Political Economy*. Vol. 77, pp. 44-61.

———. (1965). "Statistical Studies in the History of Economic Thought," *Essays in the History of Economics*. Chicago: The University of Chicago Press.

———. (1965). *Essays in the History of Economics*. Chicago: The University of Chicago Press.

———. (1971, Spring). "The Theory of Economic Regulation," *Bell Journal of Economics and Management Science*. Vol. 2, pp. 3-21.

22

Gerard Debreu (1921-):
A Brilliant Mathematician and a Frontiersman of the Theory of the Existence of Equilibrium and the Laureate of 1983

Masudul A. Choudhury

BIOGRAPHICAL PROFILE

Gerard Debreu was born in Calais, France, in 1921. His parents were Fernande and Camille Debreu. His father was in the lace manufacturing business that was quite common in Calais at that time. His grandfather was in the printing business. Debreu's early education started in the College of the City of Calais. In the Second World War, under German occupation, France was divided into several zones, and he moved from Ambert to Grenoble, both in the free zone. From 1941 until 1944, he studied at Ecole Normale Superieure. In that institution, Debreu developed a profound interest in mathematics under the influence of his teachers, Henri Cartan and N. Bourbaki. He joined the French army in the Second World War and was stationed at the Algerian Front. On return from army, he took his last formal examination, called *Agregation de Mathematiques*, toward the end of 1945 and the beginning of 1946. Meanwhile, he was introduced to the Walrasian general equilibrium theory by the writings of Maurice Allais. In 1948, he attended the Salzburg seminar in American studies, where he met Wassily Leontief. In 1949, he visited Harvard University, the University of California-Berkeley, the University of Chicago, and Columbia University as a Rockefeller Fellow. His visits to these American institutions gave him first-hand knowledge about the latest developments in economics. In 1950 he joined the Cowles Commission at Chicago as a research associate and stayed there for eleven years with a small break of six months that he spent in Paris to work for the French Electrical Service. In 1955, he moved to Yale along with the Cowles Commission. He spent 1960-1961 at Stanford University and worked on the proof of the existence of general economic equilibrium. In the fall of 1961, he returned to the Cowles at Yale. In the late 1960s and early 1970s, he visited the University of Louvain, Belgium; Churchill College, Cambridge; the University of Bonn; the CEPREMAP, Paris; and the University of Canterbury, New Zealand. He also worked at the University of California at Berkeley, where he studied concave utility functions in collaboration with Tjalling Koopmans. Debreu has been a fellow at the University of Louvain, Churchill College, and the University of Canterbury. He became a U.S. citizen in 1975. He is a member of many academic societies, including the American Economic Association. He received honorary degrees from the Universities of Bonn and Lausanne, Northwestern University, and others. Debreu married Francoise Bled in 1945. They have two daughters.

INTRODUCTION

Gerard Debreu won the economics Nobel Prize in 1983 for "having incorporated new analytical methods into economic theory and for his rigorous reformulation of the theory of general equilibrium." Debreu has been one of the successful products of the Cowles Foundation housed at Yale University–formerly known as the Cowles Commission and affiliated with the University of Chicago. Debreu has an extremely strong mathematical bent of mind. At Cowles, he undertook rigorous axiomatic analysis of the theory of general economic equilibrium. He also studied several problems in the theory of cardinal utility, notably, the additive decomposition of a utility function defined on a Cartesian product of sets. Debreu is the center of attraction at the University of California-Berkeley, Gifted students and colleagues from all over the world have been drawn to Berkeley because of his [Debreu's] work, and his well-attended lectures have been described as exceptional for their mathematical rigor and virtual lack of verbal explanation.

CONCEPTION OF MARKET EQUILIBRIUM
AS A PURE MATHEMATICAL STATE

In his *Theory of Value*, Debreu laid down the groundwork of a comprehensive theory on the existence of general equilibrium in microeconomic perspectives. By general equilibrium, Debreu meant the mathematical state acquired by relations describing market clearance with prescribed consumer preferences, a given regime of prices, wealth, and endowments and with a prescribed production vector of commodities. Equilibrium is then defined by Debreu as a mathematical state of consumer demand and producer supply that reduces the excess demand to zero. It is important to note here that Debreu is interested in the mathematical nature of consumer preferences and producer supply vector. His interest is not in defining what constitutes a demand function or a production function in terms of their attributes, such as gross commodity and factor substitutions or complementarities, relative prices, taste, and technology, all of which are known to characterize preference functions and production functions in microeconomic theory. Thus marginal utility and marginal productivity, diminishing marginal utility, and diminishing marginal return are not used by Debreu in describing the mathematical state that is market equilibrium.

Contrarily, one finds that such attributes were invoked earlier by the foundational economic theorists, such as Hicks and Walras. This is not to mention Marshall and the marginalist school of Jevons and Menger, who invoked utility theory and marginal rates of substitution to explain the state of market equilibrium, the very state that becomes a mathematical structure in the hands of Debreu. In Hicks, we find the consumer demand relation to be formulated by behavioral attributes. Hicks defines the state of consumer equilibrium in the following words: "If an individual is to be in equilibrium with respect to a system of market prices, it is directly evident that his marginal rate of substitution between any two goods must equal the ratio of their prices. Otherwise he would clearly find an advantage in substituting some quantity of one for an equal value (at the market rate) of the other. This is therefore the form in which we must now write the condition of equilibrium on the market."

In Walras, we find the equations of general equilibrium to constitute a large number of markets for commodities, resources, and factors of production. Some of these equations are nonlinear in form because Walras, unlike Hicks and now Debreu, was deeply concerned with social behavior that remain nonlinear. Walras would like to see his general equilibrium explain not simply the state of market equilibrium but also a grand social equilibrium within which is premised the market order. Yet as a great methodologist of the mathematical school in economics, Walras saw an interplay taking place among the domains of the pure natural sciences, the pure moral sciences, and the pure applied sciences. Within the pure applied sciences, Walras also considered the pure natural applied sciences and the pure moral applied sciences.

Returning to Debreu, we find that the concept of market equilibrium meant to Debreu not a reality of actual human transactions but a purely mathematical existence provided by an optimization state assumed by functions defined by quantities, utilities, and profits under given exogenous regimes of preferences and prices for both consumers and producers. This mathematical state is configured by the particular assumptions and topological characters of the consumer and producer spaces that Debreu axiomatizes in mathematical language. Such an approach is indeed a methodological novelty. For even though many of the founding fathers of economic theory had not thought out such an approach, Debreu provided an independent outlook of a purely scientific nature to embrace the meaning of market equilibrium.

AXIOMATIZATION OF
ECONOMIC THEORY

The results of such a methodology are two fold. First, Debreu was able to introduce in modern mathematical language an axiomatization of economic theory on purely scientific grounds bereft of value judgments. Debreu was thus inculcating, albeit in much more rigorous topological concepts, the same scientific legacy in economics bequeathed to posterity by Edgeworth, Pareto, Cournot, Walras and recently by von Neumann, Arrow, and Samuelson. Each of these personalities and others saw in the mathematization of economic theory a pursuit in rigor over empty conundrums. This is also a manifestation of the scientific spirit of our age that calls for dire facts and logical precision, shorn of all extraneous factors. Clower refers to this spirit as "a change in conceptual perspectives (that) marked both the Copernican and the Einsteinian revolutions, and both mind-shifts rid science of countless analytical conundrums." Yet Debreu's approach in the axiomatization of economic theory was in many ways distinct from the other approaches. Debreu was not concerned with human behavior as such, as was the case of others on matters of economic exchange among competitive partners or duopolistic ones, on the topics of inefficient and efficient resource allocations, on the institution of social welfare and social choice, and on the nature of cost of production. This reduced nature of Debreu's approach to the study of economic theory comes out in various ways in his writings.

The axiomatization of economic theory in the hands of Debreu meant introducing a sophisticated language using the epistemology, symbols, logic, and analysis that treated the role of mathematics in economics not as a tool. Rather, by such a design, mathematics is found to assume the character of economic structure. Mathematics is, therefore, seen to be capable of unraveling those hidden economic meanings that cannot be precisely expressed in the language of the textual theorists. McCloskey's writing presents an example of the support for the rhetorical theorists. The truth of Debreu's statement is discovered in McCloskey's writing by the latter's irresolution of the unguided detour that rhetoric in economic theorizing creates.

TOPOLOGY OF MARKET EQUILIBRIUM

Where textual economists would wander in the woods of language to define the uniqueness of equilibrium, Debreu uses differential topology and global analysis in economic theory. In this approach, the local equilibrium of a Euclidean space of consumer goods, producer goods, resources, and wealth, is made to describe a space of linear functionals of the primitive vectors. The space of functionals, called a Euclidean manifold, is then shown to generate a mathematically compact topology that corresponds one-to-one (isomorphism) with the primitive Euclidean space of vectors (commodities). Debreu goes on to prove that by means of the standard result of fixed theorem in topology, the two Euclidean spaces–primtive and manifold–correspond with each other uniquely via the fixed point mapping. This proves the existence of an equilibrium in the local neighborhoods of the points in the primitive and manifold Euclidean spaces. The concept of local equilibrium as opposed to global equilibrium, enables Debreu to develop several related concepts as well. The Edgeworth-Bowley concept of the core of the economy was further developed by Debreu as the neighborhood where competitive equilibrium remains undisturbed. The elaborate conditions for the existence of market equilibrium for Debreu requires stringent adherence to the core of the economy, as the same conditions cannot be explained in the global sense. In the parlance of locally and globally stable equilibria, a local stability means for Debreu the maintenance of equilibrium in the neighborhood of the core. On the other hand, global stability means maintenance of equilibrium outside the neighborhood. Morishima defines this relevant global space to comprise the entire non-negative orthant of commodity, price, and resource vectors.

By using the concept of the core of an economy, it was possible for Debreu to provide a topological definition of a private ownership economy. An economy is then defined as a system that obeys all the assumptions underlying consumer and producer commodity spaces under the assumption of preassigned prices and preferences. These relations connecting consumer and producer commodities, resources and wealth, are then invisibly interacted together to establish a market equilibrium. An economy in Debreu's concept is essentially made up of such final states of Pareto-optimal allocations in the core of the economy. Equilibrium is, thereby, a mathematical state that is both prescribed by and then perpetually maintained in that core. The ability to realize this state is due to the critical assumptions underlying such a mathematical solution.

The limitation of the definition of competitive equilibrium as a Pareto-optimal allocation of resources and commodities, constrained to the core, is recognized by Debreu. He writes on this matter: A partial explanation of the observed state of an economic system had been provided by proofs of existence of equilibrium based on fixed point theorems. A more complete explanation would have followed from persuasive assumptions on a mathematical model of the economy ensuring uniqueness of equilibrium. Unfortunately the assumptions proposed to that end were excessively stringent, and the requirement of global uniqueness had to be relaxed to that of local uniqueness. Even then an economy composed of agents on their best mathematical behavior (for instance each having a concave utility function and a demand function both indefinitely differentiable) may be ill-behaved and fail to have locally unique equilibria. If one considers the question from the generic viewpoint, however, one sees that the set of those ill-behaved economies is negligible. In order to define his competitive equilibrium, Debreu must therefore ascribe a stringent set of primitive assumptions for laying down a mathematical state. Such a mathematical state may not conform with real agent-specific behavior at large. Yet, Debreu's goal being rigorous axiomatization of economic theory, the underlying assumptions of his mathematical constructs, remain simply a scientific nicety par excellence.

The assumptions for the existence of competitive equilibria are as follows: convexity of commodity spaces for the consumer and producer, which implies rational choices and optimality; separable utility and production functions, which imply independence and competition among optimally acting self-interested agents; the absence of public good, implying a purely private ownership economy as the sole focus of the axiomatization program; all prices and preferences are preassigned, which implies exogeneity of all other events apart from those that define the end state of an optimal private exchange at the core of the economy. Debreu does not define utility by reference to marginalist assumption on commodities, as is always in vogue. Rather, utility is seen as a monotonically increasing mathematical value that assigns a real number to every assignment of commodities, once prices are set and consumer preferences are manifested. This kind of assignment of preferences, given the pricing regime and the mathematical properties of commodity spaces, is termed preordering. The mathematical properties are termed by Debreu as upper and lower semicontinuities, and in the event that both of these exist, the preference function is said to be continuous everywhere, or in the measure-theoretic parlance, as being continuous almost everywhere. The idea of utility as a mathematical association between preordered commodity choices of consumers and the real number system is similar to Arrows's method of defining the social welfare function. A social welfare function is defined as an association of particular social choices–given preordering in the set of such social choices–with the real number system. The separability assumption of preferences in Debreu enables him to mathematically aggregate utilities. Hence, the market equilibrium determined by such preordering remains unique for each agent. In social welfare and social choice methodology, however, the social market equilibrium is not unique, as the social welfare function is not uniquely defined, although it satisfies monotonicity assumption like the utility functions. On a deeper argument, Debreu's preordering is strictly restricted by a transitivity or rationality (hence convexity) assumption, whereas social choices may not satisfy this assumption.

ARROW-DEBREU CONTRIBUTION TO THE EXISTENCE OF ECONOMIC EQUILIBRIUM

Arrow and Debreu extend the concept of market equilibrium to economic equilibrium in the Arrow-Debreu version of the theorem on the existence of a general economic equilibrium. An individually consumed commodity is now determined in relation to the total consumption plan. Hence, an individual good is socially determined and is also a social determinant. Social welfare functions then assume all the properties of individual utility functions. Arrow-Debreu assumptions for the existence of economic equilibrium in the case of such socially determined and socially determining commodities in the consumer and producer sets once again maintain all the precepts of economic rationality (convexity), given exogenously set appropriate prices and preference preordering. The Arrow-Debreu theorem on the existence of general equilibrium assumes that in the economy as a whole with a given number of consumers, producers, and commodities, full information always exists. This stringent condition enables two things to occur at once. First, prices are well determined and, on this basis, consumers and producers can decide and implement plans for attaining optimal ends. Second, as the result of full information, commodities can be finely distinguished by their attributes in response to their prices.

EXTENSION OF EXISTENCE THEOREMS
ON ECONOMIC EQUILIBRIUM

Beyond competitive market and economic equilibrium defined in terms of upper and lower semicontinuity of preferences defined over commodity spaces, Debreu has also contributed richly to the field of less than globally continuous functions. Here he develops the concept of quasiequilibrium and differentiable preferences. These enable an extension of the methodology of competitive equilibrium in the core of an economy to a larger domain around local neighborhood. Quasiequilibrium concepts are associated with those of partial nonconvexity of preference functions and the resulting utility functions of consumers. It is shown by Shubik, that if it is not possible to define uniformly convex preferences, then it is equally not possible to define the associated concave utility functions, even within a small neighborhood. However, the class of functions that falls under such a quasiconvexity condition, is found to be small. Hence, as Debreu then proves, a quasiequilibrium can lead to the existence of market equilibrium. That is, in a state of quasiequilibrium with the limiting condition of the excluded cases, consumption spending of all consumers can be satisfied by a minimal wealth endowment by freely disposing of some of the demanded commodities.

Debreu also examines the case of differentiable preferences by using measure-theoretic methodology. This means that it is possible to extend a class of preference functions into higher classes by maintaining the generic transitive and reflexive relations of assigned preferences. While highly sophisticated methodologies of measure theory, abstract algebra (Borel sets, sigma-rings, and fields) and topology (Hahn-Banach extension theorem, global analysis, and manifolds) are used, at the end of all these, the globally invariant properties of Debreu's fundamental assumptions characterizing consumer preferences remain unchanged. The use of quasiconvexity, quasiequilibrium and differentiable preferences as extensions of the fundamental analytical works of Debreu opens up possibilities for incorporating factors other than those strictly characterizing the core of an economy. Thus it would appear that by using such extension results of advanced mathematics, treatment of public goods, institutional forces, and ethical questions beyond simple depiction of private goods with given observed prices and perfect information can be afforded. Such questions, which must go together with any axiomatization of economic theory, bring us again to the kind of general economic equilibrium concept that was upheld by Walras. The social economy was the goal of study in such a Walrasian system and not simply a restricted domain of private ownership economy that finds its mathematical nicety within the core of an economy. The latter is equivalent to the permanence of Pareto-optimality, nonexplanation of the actual processes of deriving rules from prescriptions, and noninteraction in the agent-economy domain and is devoid of the real-world implications of society-institution-economy interface.

CONCLUSION

In conclusion, one must say, that the most important contribution of Gerard Debreu to the field of economic theorizing was precisely this positive awakening of the discipline toward the demand for axiomatization. The new and extensive idea of axiomatization must now be embraced in the broad sense of ethical endogeneity to be found in the study of political economy, beyond the narrow limits of convex analysis and economic theory. Debreu, too, wrote in this regard: "an axiomatic theorist succeeds in communicating the meaning he intends to give to a primitive concept because of the completely specified formal context in which he operates. The more developed this context is, the richer it is in theorems and in other primitive concepts, the smaller will be the margin of ambiguity in the intended interpretation."

RECOMMENDED READINGS

Choudhury, M.A. (1990, spring). "Price, Value and Social Equilibrium in Ethico-Economics," *The Journal of Social Sciences*. Vol. 18, No. 1, pp. 268-79.

———. (1991). "A Critique of Developments in Social Economics and the Alternative," *International Journal of Social Economics*. Vol. 18, Nos. 11-12, pp. 36-61.

———. (1995a). "Ethics and Economics: A View From Ecological Economics," *International Journal of Social Economics*. Vol. 22, No. 2, pp. 40-60.

———. (1995b). "A Mathematical Formulation of the Principle of Ethical Endogeneity," *Kybernetes: International Journal of Systems and Cybernetics*. Vol. 24, No. 5, pp. 11-30.

Debreu, G. (1958). "Stochastic Choice and Cardinal Utility," *Econometrica*. Vol. 26, pp. 440-44.

———. (1962, September) "New Concepts and Techniques for Equilibrium Analysis," *International Economic Review*. Vol. 3, No. 3, pp. 257-73.

———. (1963). "A Limit Theorem on the Core of an Economy," *International Economic Review*. Vol. 4, No. 3, pp. 235-46.

———. (1965). *Theory of Value, An Axiomatic Analysis of Economic Equilibrium*. New York: John Wiley & Sons, Inc.

———. (1967, January). "Preference Functions on Measure Spaces of Economic Agents," *Econometrica*. Vol. 35, No. 1, pp. 111-22.

———. (1970, May). "Economies with a Finite Set of Equilibria," *Econometrica*. Vol. 38, No. 3, pp. 387-92.

———. (1976). "The Application to Economics of Differential Topology and Global Analysis, Regular Differential Economies," *American Economic Review*. Vol. 66, No. 2, pp. 280-86.

———. (1984, June). "Economic Theory in the Mathematical Mode," *American Economic Review*. Vol. 74, No. 3, pp. 267-78.

———. (1986). "Theoretic Models: Mathematical Form and Economic Content," *Econometrica*. Vol. 54, No. 6, pp. 1259-70.

23

Richard Stone (1913-1991):
A Specialist of the Consumer Demand Theories and Empirical Modeling and the Laureate of 1984

Salah Uddin Ahmed

BIOGRAPHICAL PROFILE

Richard Stone–the only child of Gilbert and Elsie Stone–was born in London in 1913. His father was an attorney who wanted him to be the same. In his early life, unlike other Nobel laureates, Stone did not have much interest in mathematics, nor did he learn much about this subject. In 1930, his father went to Madras, India, to become a High Court judge. Stone spent one year with his father in India and then began his undergraduate studies at the University of Cambridge in 1931. He started with law and then switched to economics. His father did not like it, but Stone thought economics would help him understand the Great Depression better. His college (Gonville and Caius) did not have economist, so he had to attend King's College to learn economics from Richard Kahn. There, he came in close contact with two great economists, Colin Clark and John Maynard Keynes. Stone did pretty well in college and graduated in 1935. Upon graduation, he took a light job with an insurance company–Lloyd's of London. In 1937, he started to edit an economics and business monthly with Colin Clark. In this magazine, Stone published articles about all types of current economic and business issues. After the beginning of the Second World War, Stone joined the British government in the Ministry of Economic Warfare, where he was responsible for the statistics on shipping and oil. Within a year, he was relocated to the War Cabinet Secretariat, where he worked with John Keynes and James Meade. Along with Meade, Stone estimated the British national income and products. His method was different from earlier attempts in the sense that he explicitly integrated national income into a double-entry bookkeeping framework. In 1945, he left the government service and became the director of the newly established department of applied economics at Cambridge. The same year, he visited Princeton University and wrote a position paper for the League of Nations to make an international guideline for national income accounts. It was published in 1947. In 1955, he became P.D. Leake Professor of Finance and Accounting at Cambridge. Stone's system of national income accounts was adopted by many industrialized countries of the world. He was knighted in 1974, and he retired from Cambridge in 1980. Stone was a member of Econometric Society and the International Statistical Institute. He received honorary degrees from the universities of Oslo, Brussels, Geneva, Warwick, Paris, and Bristol. He married his first wife, Winifred Mary, in 1936. After the dissolution of the marriage, he married Feodora Leontinoff in 1941. She died in 1956. Stone's third marriage was to a woman named Giovanna Crift-Murray. Stone died in 1991

INTRODUCTION

Richard Stone won the economics Nobel Prize in 1984 for "having made fundamental contributions to the development of systems of national accounts and hence greatly improved the basis for empirical economic analysis." Stone made towering contributions   to the field of national income accounting in macroeconomics. He is not the first to estimate national income and products. However, his method is unique, original, and distinct. He used a double-entry bookkeeping framework requiring that all outputs must be consumed and that all consumption must be produced. This provides an empirical counterpart of the Keynesian theory in macroeconomics. Stone also made valuable contributions to popularize his method internationally. He worked in collaboration with the League of Nations and the United Nations to develop guidelines for a globally uniform system of national income accounting. Apart from his role in the development of national accounts, which is generally considered to be his main contribution to economics, Stone had also been a major contributor to other areas of applied economics. Principal among these are the analysis of consumer demand and the Cambridge Growth Project.

NATIONAL INCOME ACCOUNTING

Stone's work on national accounting problems began in 1940, when he and James Meade began the task of collecting, processing, and making systematic the vast amount of data needed by John Maynard Keynes in his attempts to plan the British war effort. They worked under the stimulus of Keynes' ideas for running the war economy and Colin Clark's earlier work, which established the basis on which national accounting was to develop. Their objective was to produce a complete account of the nation's resources to assist in the war effort, and they set out to do this by obtaining a full integration of the United Kingdom's accounts for different subsectors. These subsectors included the household sector, businesses, the public sector, national savings and investments, and transactions with the outside world. The basic approach was to apply and modify the ideas of double-entry bookkeeping, in which each item was to appear as an item of revenue on one side of the account and an item of expenditure on the other. The fact that the same item appeared on both sides of the ledger meant figures had to agree with each other, and while this specification involved a massive amount of work, it also provided an important check on the reliability and consistency of the data. When completed, this exercise was to produce an overview of the interplay and interdependence of the entire economy, and a full account of its resources.

Stone's starting point was the notion of transactions between different sectors. Apart from the relatively obvious problems of collecting data and ensuring that they were reliable, Stone had to face the problems of how the immense number of transactions within the economy should be consolidated and aggregated in a meaningful way in sectoral accounts, and how these accounts should be presented. Stone's approach to the problem went far beyond the routine application of bookkeeping rules, and he insisted that economic theory had a major role to play. As the Royal Swedish Academy of Sciences put it, he saw the "theoretical analysis of national economic balance problems as the starting point and justification for national accounts." One might add that while this analysis was motivated by Keynesian ideas of economic imbalance and the need for appropriate policies to counteract it, national accounts are in fact neutral in a policy sense and imply support for no one particular philosophy of economic policy over another.

Stone had to deal with three major problems in order to arrive at a system of national income accounting. The first problem was to develop a set of definitions and practical conventions to measure the main types of economic activity in the economy. These are production (or output), accumulation, and consumption. (Note also that these factors are related by the identity that states that all output is either accumulated or consumed, so that output is the sum of accumulation and consumption.) Let us consider first the problem of developing a suitable measure of output. The essential problem is to "collapse" the outputs of heterogeneous goods into a single measure of "output." To do that requires assigning appropriate price "weight" to each particular good produced to arrive at a figure for the value of aggregate output. The obvious procedure, and the one Stone adopted, was to value the output of different goods at market prices, although this still leaves problems where market prices have been distorted (for example, by rationing or by taxes). A more basic problem, however, was what to do with output that is not sold on a market. Stone's approach to this problem was essentially pragmatic. Where data were available, as with government expenditures, for instance, his approach was to assess the value of output by the value of the inputs that produced it. If data were not available (for example, with household production), his approach was to ignore it. The essence of Stone's approach was that one did the best one could with the data one had. Household production was ignored and government "output" measured at cost, not for any theoretical reason, but because at the time there was little else that could be done. If data on household production or government input-output indices became available, however, then one would usually want to use them.

We now consider the issue of measuring accumulation. Again, the approach was fundamentally a practical one. Where the only data available were on private-sector asset accumulation, one had little alternative but to do with that. However, if one had data on "infrastructure" accumulation (for example, roads, schools, and bridges), one ought to include that as well. A lot of work went into trying to get such data, but one encounters similar problems here as with the valuation of output. Much infrastructure output is not sold on a market–although there are exceptions (for example, toll bridges)–so one is often forced to value such accumulation by the expenditure on them. An additional problem, however, is how to deal with depreciation. Ideally, one would infer the depreciation of an asset from the price of similar assets on second-hand markets, but such markets frequently do not exist, and one is often forced to rely on relatively ad hoc procedures instead. The usual procedure is to assume that a commodity has a given expected life and depreciates in a given way, but this sort of procedure is obviously fraught with problems. Estimates of depreciation tend to be very sensitive to the precise assumptions one makes, and in any case, they tend to correspond more to "physical" estimates of depreciation rather than to "economic" estimates of it that take into account relevant changes in relative prices. One also has to deal with the related problem of valuing stocks. In principle, one might want to value stocks at their replacement value, but much of the data one is likely to get would refer only to their initial cost. Where prices are relatively stable, of course, this might only cause minor problems, but one is likely to encounter more severe problems in periods of inflation.

Furthermore, there is the problem of measuring consumption. The problem here is that one typically has data on consumer expenditures, and one has to figure out some way of extracting estimates of actual consumption from them. Consumption expenditures and actual consumption differ, of course, because of current and past consumer expenditures on durable goods. A proper estimate of consumption would therefore subtract from consumer expenditures the amount spent on durable goods but add in the value of the services consumers currently enjoy from past and present expenditures on durable goods. It is then necessary to derive implicit estimates of the stock of consumer durable and to be able to estimate the flow of services they yield. This problem is particularly acute when dealing with housing services: In that case, it is necessary to estimate not only the stock of housing (which is difficult enough) but also the service flow it yields.

Once settled on suitable conventions to measure the basic categories of activity in which one is interested, one then has to put one's data set together. This is a massive undertaking and involves solving a number of specific problems, such as the collection of data, filling in the gaps, resolving inconsistencies, and standardizing the data to make figures comparable. Stone put much effort into trying to find reliable ways to resolve these types of problems. A way to handle gaps in the data is to fill them "residually" (that is, by using accounting identities in which all terms except one are measured and inferring the missing one). This is frequently done, for example, to obtain estimates of savings, which are not generally observed directly. Unfortunately, obtaining data residually has the disadvantage of using up an identity that could otherwise have been used to check on the consistency of one's data. Another practice sometimes used is to add in all the discrepancies to one side and arrive at some "balancing item" that can be considered as "measurement error," but this procedure is often unsatisfactory, since it presupposes that the errors all take place on that side of the balance sheet. One can also "adjust" data in line with prior assessments of their reliability and thereby assign putative "errors" to them. Stone wrote several papers indicating how this might be done. Finally, once the data are sorted, one has to find a way to represent them. This is where Stone's work went far beyond a routine bookkeeping approach. As Leif Johansen put it, "Stone's early work on national accounting problems [illustrates] the fact that his perspectives and advanced analytical ideas aimed far beyond a systematic, although rather conventional bookkeeping approach to describing the economic conditions and development in a country. Even if he did invest considerable effort in working out practical details and a seemingly conventional means of presenting national accounts, it was because this was a prerequisite for initiating the practical work involved and ensuring the reliability of data at an early stage. Concurrently, he worked on more advanced theoretical ideas which pointed towards the subsequent development we have witnessed in the national accounts literature and the use of national accounts data for analytical purposes. Stone's intention was to use accounting conventions to develop a representation of national accounts in the form of "transaction matrices," which provide a more or less aggregated account of all the transactions taking place within an economy. His attitude towards aggregation was a flexible one: The appropriate level of aggregation depends on the kind of data one has and the purpose for which one wants to use it. Consequently, a system of national accounts needs to be flexible enough to accommodate most potential users of it. This means that a system of national accounts should be organized in large matrices and aggregated as needed. However, to aggregate two sets of transactions into a larger set raises some difficult issues. Each of the two smaller aggregates would need to be weighted by a "convertibility multiplier" to construct the overall aggregate. In principle, problems like this are index-number problems of a conventional sort, and Stone put a considerable effort into solving them. His approach to solving them was typically pragmatic, however, and relied at least as much on ensuring those data were consistent as on the economic theory of index numbers.

Stone's work during the war consisted of laying out the groundwork of what later evolved into national accounting and in compiling preliminary national accounts for the United Kingdom and the United States. After the war, his work expanded to cover other countries as well. Immediately after the war, Stone headed a group of experts working first under League of Nations and then under United Nations auspices to prepare standardized forms of national accounts for general international use. The work of Stone and his team was widely accepted and forms the basis of many other countries' national accounts and international comparisons between them. The methodology was still relatively rudimentary in 1945, of course, and it was constantly revised and updated in the following years. Problems were gradually ironed out as time went on, however, and it eventually reached a reasonably mature form in the 1968 United Nations handbook, *A System of National Accounts*. Regular revisions continue to be made as more data become available and more problems are sorted out, but the essential methodology remains as it was set out then, and it is generally agreed that the U.N. definitions of production, consumption, and accumulation and the many subsidiary conventions that go along with them are sufficiently flexible to be useful in most practical situations. As the Royal Swedish Academy of Sciences puts it, "National accounts have created a systematic data base for a number of levels of economic analysis, including the analysis of different types of economic activity, inflation analysis, the analysis of economic structures, growth analysis and, particularly, international comparisons between countries."

Much of Stone's later work on national accounting was devoted to extending the basic methodology to provide accounts for new and less conventional areas. Among these sectors are the financial sector, the education system, and the population. In each case, the objective was to provide a complete representation of available resources with a view to the possible use of such information for public policy purposes. This extension of the scope of national accounting reflected Stone's view that a system of accounts was much more than a mere inventory of the number and type of goods traded in markets and should take into account all forms of economic activity, nonmarketed as well as marketed. Indeed, the scope of national accounting went well beyond the purely economic to embrace sociodemographic and environmental factors as well. As Stone put it in his Nobel Lecture: The three pillars on which an analysis of society ought to rest are studies of economic, sociodemographic, and environmental phenomena. Naturally enough, accounting ideas are most developed in the economic context but they are equally applicable in the other two fields. By organizing our data in the form of accounts we can obtain a coherent picture of the stocks and flows, incomings and outgoings of whatever variables we are interested in, whether these be goods and services, human beings, or natural resources, and thence proceed to analyze the system of which they form part. He then elaborated on the role of accounting systems in that analysis of society. Such an analysis should begin with "our facts, organized as far as possible into a coherent set of accounts. Given this quantitative framework, we can formulate some hypotheses, or theories, about the technical and behavioral relationships that connect them. By combining facts and theories we can construct a model which when translated into quantitative terms will give us an idea of how the system under investigation actually works."

THE ANALYSIS OF CONSUMER DEMAND

Stone also carried out a considerable amount of work on consumer-demand analysis while he was working on the development of national accounting. Apart from a handful of papers published in the late 1930s, his work on consumer demand really began during the war, when he and his coworkers put together the most comprehensive and detailed data set yet assembled for the U.K. consumers' expenditures and the price, income, and other data needed for an empirical analysis. The data set covered the period 1920-1938 and was to be used extensively in Stone's later work. While Stone was well aware even at an early stage that demand functions for different commodities form a coherent system and ought in principle to be treated as such, such treatment was effectively precluded by practical considerations at the time, and so equations for each commodity or group of commodities were estimated separately. A typical equation had demand for the good or goods in question depending on total consumption expenditures, the price of the commodity or a price index for the commodity group, other relevant prices, a time trend, and occasionally other variables. Elasticities were taken to be constant. Economic theory was used in a relatively loose way to suggest what other prices or miscellaneous variables might be relevant in any particular equation. Stone went to enormous efforts to ensure that his data were as accurate possible and to correct for sources of error in his empirical work.

This work produced some papers in the 1940s and early 1950s, but the main result was the monumental study, *The Measurement of Consumers' Expenditure and Behavior in the United Kingdom, 1920-1938*, which was published in two volumes in 1954 and 1966. More effort went into collecting and revising data for this study than went into the empirical estimates that it presented. It was characterized by a careful treatment of data problems, a loose but insightful use of economic theory, and a practical approach to methodological problems, and it was the first major comprehensive empirical analysis of the U.K. consumer demand. The methodology used was similar to that used in earlier studies but provided a much more thorough treatment of the dynamic problems caused by serially correlated residuals. It was one of the first studies to make use of the Durbin-Watson test that later became so widespread. Stone's results indicated that equations estimated with data in levels tended to exhibit high residual serial correlation, but the serial correlation was reduced considerably when equations were estimated in first-difference form. This study also broke new ground in combining time-series data and data from cross-section household budgets, which take account of family size, social class, and other such sociodemographic variables, and this combination helped to reduce the errors in time-series estimates.

Also in 1954, Stone began to publish estimates of simultaneous systems of demand equations instead of relying only on equations estimated separately Stone was a pioneer in this field. The advantage of estimating systems of equations simultaneously was that it allowed one to make full use of economic theory that imposes restrictions on the system as a whole as well as on individual equations. (For instance, theory tells us that the matrix of Slutsky substitution effects should be negative semidefinite, and this requires simultaneous estimates of demand equations. The prediction that a consumer-demand equation should exhibit no "money illusion," on the other hand, can be tested with single-equation estimates.) One can use such restrictions either to test the theory by investigating whether they are refuted or else one can use them to derive more efficient estimates.

In this paper, Stone worked with the linear expenditure system (LES), in which expenditure (that is, price times quantity) is a linear function of income and relevant prices. He showed that the LES could be interpreted as a system in which each household needed to buy certain minimum "subsistence" levels of each good and then choose additional amounts of goods to maximize utility once "subsistence" has been assured. He made a major contribution in deriving the restrictions imposed on the linear expenditure system by the hypothesis that the consumer maximizes utility, and he showed that the LES that satisfies these conditions has far fewer parameters than an unrestricted LES and that these "over identified parameters" can be used to test the theory or improve one's parameter estimates. The system had to be estimated simultaneously, however, because some of the parameters of the LES were common to each equation. Stone developed an iteration procedure to estimate the system and estimated it using his U.K. data set for 1920-1938 to obtain quite reasonable estimates. The paper also presented some results of experiments that attempted to determine consumption for 1920 and 1952.

We might also mention two other issues in consumer analysis to which Stone made useful contributions. One was in the handling of the dynamic problems caused by durable goods. In his work with D.A. Rowe, Stone developed a framework that emphasized the distinction between the flow of consumption services derived from a durable good and the "capital stock" of the good itself. This framework allowed researchers to handle both durable and nondurable goods and led to a distinction between the long-run and short-run elasticities of demand for durable goods, the difference being that stocks of durable goods are at their "desired" levels in the long run but not necessarily in the short run. However, the framework did not explain how "desired" stocks of durable goods were themselves determined. The other area was in the econometric analysis of saving behavior. In the early 1960s, Stone developed models that improved on simple Keynesian explanations of saving behavior by incorporating wealth as well as income as explanatory variables and by distinguishing between their temporary and permanent values. His models also investigated the differential effects of labor and nonlabor income on consumption, the effects of government policy on saving, and the distinction between the saving of consumers and that of firms.

THE CAMBRIDGE GROWTH PROJECT

In the 1960s, Stone's main efforts were devoted to a project intended to shed some light on the prospects for more rapid British economic growth. This was the "Program for Growth" carried out at the Department of Applied Economics at Cambridge under Stone's leadership. The motivation behind the project was the concern aroused by Britain's relatively slow growth rate in the postwar period and the sense of economic failure which that inadequate growth rate aroused. The project worked on the basis of a mixed economy with a competitive private sector and various forms of state intervention or control. The underlying philosophy behind the project was expressed as follows: We should approach the economic system as an engineer approaches a complicated piece of machinery or as a doctor approaches his patient. Any adjustment or treatment depends on a sound diagnosis. Only in this way can we meet the arguments of the reactionary who can say with some plausibility that things might be worse and that tampering with them will probably make them more so, and those of the revolutionary who can say with equal plausibility that things might be better and invites us to follow his particular nostrum. The common link between these very different types is their utter disregard for the economic facts of life, a disregard they would never think of showing if their car broke down or if they contracted pneumonia. By exaggerating differences in political and social objectives, they obscure the fact that the main reason why we do not have a more successful economic policy is that we do not understand the economic system sufficiently well, and that what we should be doing is to study anatomy and physiology instead of endlessly debating quack prescriptions. So, let us follow the normal course of action: analysis, diagnosis, prescription, treatment. We shall get nowhere if we continue to short-circuit the first two stages. The objective of the Growth Project was not to give specific policy advice or to give detailed scenarios of the consequences of different policies. It was rather to look more generally at ways in which economic policy affected British economic growth. It was hoped that it might be able to identify potential growth sectors and give a rough idea of the effects that different policies might have on them. The Growth Project examined both explicit "policy instruments" (for example, changes in the tax regime, and changes in the exchange rate) and ways in which the government might indirectly be able to influence the private sectors. The latter would include, for instance, the effects of government policies on private-sector expectations and the effects, if any, of "indicative planning," in which the government tries to encourage the private sector to achieve its targets but does not coerce it.

The project consisted of two models that coexisted in an uneasy kind of way. One was a model of the economy in a steady state, and the other was a transient model that tried to explain how the economy could reach its steady-state path, taking into account the problems of capital adjustment and capacity constraints on available labor and capital. A considerable amount of work went into developing algorithms to carry out the very extensive computations involved, but much of Stone's earlier work was used as "building blocks" as well. Consumers' expenditures were modeled using the LES, for instance, and the model of saving behavior borrowed much from his earlier work in that area. The project also saw an extension of the scope of national accounting and some new uses made of it. Work was done to add to existing national accounts a more sophisticated treatment of financial transactions and a more sophisticated treatment of labor issues that included health, education, and demography. Stone also extended his earlier work linking national accounting to input-output tables by developing a methodology to allow limited changes in input-output coefficients. This methodology helped to overcome the main drawback of input-output work and marked a notable advance in the field. As Johansen says, "The overall method has been used to a large extent in subsequent input-output analyses. Indications of this type of changes in the coefficients may be found in some of Leontief's early work and a parallel method has been used in earlier statistical contexts. But Stone and his colleagues have carried out the most fundamental and thorough work on this method with respect to input-output analysis and have thus provided support for a means of treating changes in input-output coefficients which has been applied in many countries. The Growth Project also broke new ground in modeling the economy sector by sector rather than by the fashionable procedure of modeling by broad output categories such as consumption, investment, and saving. This method was considerably more difficult–especially when one recalls the primitive computing facilities the Cambridge group would have used–but perhaps more sensible. It was always difficult providing even remotely "robust" microtheoretic foundations to highly aggregated models, and such models do not appear to have shown much stability in face of the various "shocks" that have hit Western economies since the mid-

1970s. Stone's disaggregated approach may therefore prove to be the more fruitful one in the end.

CONCLUSION

We have seen that Stone's principal contribution to economics was the development of national accounting and that he has also made valuable contributions to the empirical analysis of consumer demand and to large-scale empirical modeling. In all these areas the contribution has been quite fundamental in nature. A great deal of modern empirical work, such as macroeconometric modeling, is based on national accounting. Stone's national accounting methodology may yet set the groundwork for further developments in fields like demography and the study of the environment. In fact we have already seen the beginning of the development of green accounting, which takes environmental impact into account while evaluating the performance of the economy.

RECOMMENDED READINGS

Deaton, Angus, (ed.) (1981). *Essays in the Theory and Measurement of Consumer Behaviour in Honour of Sir Richard Stone.* London and New York: Cambridge University Press.

Stone, Richard (1985). "Bibliography of Richard Stone's Works, 1936-1984," *Scandinavian Journal of Economics.* Vol. 87, No. 1, pp. 33-43.

———. (1986, January). "Nobel Memorial Lecture 1984: The Accounts of Society," *Journal of Applied Econometrics.* Vol. 11, No. 1, pp. 5-28.

———. (1986). "Social Accounting: The State of Play," *Scandinavian Journal of Economics.* Vol. 88, No. 3, pp. 453-72.

———. (1986). "Special Issue on the Review of the United Nations System of National Accounts: Comments on the Overall Programme," *Review of Income and Wealth.* Vol. 32, No. 2, pp. 117-27.

24

Franco Modigliani (1918-):
A Founder of the Life Cycle
Hypothesis and the Laureate of 1985

Moazzem Hossain

BIOGRAPHICAL PROFILE

Franco Modigliani was born in Rome in 1918. His father, Enrico Modigliani, was a leading pediatrician and his mother, Olga, was a social worker in Rome. Enrico died when Franco was only thirteen. His schooling during the next three years was disturbed due to the death of his father. However, he made good progress afterwards and entered the University of Rome at the age of seventeen. He studied medicine first but was unable to continue due to his intolerance toward the sufferings of sick people. Instead, he decided to study law. The University of Rome awarded him a doctorate of jurisprudence degree in 1939. Eventually, his interest shifted to economics due to the Great Depression in the early 1930s and to a nationwide essay competition on the effects of price controls. He was awarded the first prize in that competition. Modigliani married Serena Calabi, a well-known antifascist activist, in 1939. His family immigrated to the United States immediately before the start of World War II in 1939. He pursued economics further with a free tuition fellowship awarded by New York's New School. For the next three years, he worked and studied between six and ten at night. Franco Modigliani received his PhD in social science in 1944 and became an assistant professor of mathematical economics and econometrics at the New School in 1946. He moved first to the University of Chicago in 1949, as an associate professor in economics and then to the University of Illinois as a full professor in 1950. Between 1952 and 1960, he worked for the Carnegie Institute, Harvard University, and Northwestern

University. His association with the Carnegie Institute was a very productive and fruitful one. According to Modigliani, the foundations for his two major works, the "Life Cycle Hypothesis" and the "Theory of Rational Expectations," were laid in this institute. Modigliani joined MIT in 1960 and has been working there ever since.

INTRODUCTION

Franco Modigliani received the economics Nobel Prize in 1985 for his pioneering analyses of saving and financial markets. Modigliani's works on macroeconomic issues and their role in the economic development of a nation have been regarded in the economics literature as a leading contribution that brought Keynesian economics into the center of economic debate in the post-World War II period. His major contribution in this regard was to show clearly the relation between the Keynesian economics, classical economics and monetary economics. His vision was to make a clear link between these schools of thought and to demonstrate to the policymakers how to objectively assess the macroeconomic problems and accordingly work out the implications for monetary and fiscal stabilization policies. Modigliani's recent work in the area of financial markets has been regarded in the literature as an eye opener for the present day international investors. In particular, the Nobel Prize was awarded in recognition of his formulation and development of the life cycle hypothesis of household saving and his contribution to the Modigliani-Miller theorems of the valuation of firms and of capital costs.

MACROECONOMIC POLICY ISSUES

As mentioned earlier, Modigliani began his career in economics in 1939, also the time when John Maynard Keynes' *General Theory* was revolutionizing the field of economics. The contribution of Keynes not only has covered the new theoretical analysis but also has been popular in economic policymaking following the Keynesian approach. The Keynesian revolution, however, came under attack even before it had celebrated its twentieth birthday. Milton Friedman, along with few other colleagues, began a counterrevolution in the mid-1950s by advocating the monetarist approach in macroeconomic management of a nation. Since this period the monetarists' approach has put Keynesian economics on the defensive side until the oil crises in the 1970s. These two schools of thought brought huge macroeconomic policy debate worldwide in the last half of the twentieth century. There is no doubt that both of these approaches have good and bad sides, and Modigliani has contributed the most to picking the good and bad sides of these thoughts. In his works in this area of economics have demonstrated the basic differences that divide the monetarists from the Keynesians.

In his presidential address to the American Economic Association in September 1976, Modigliani suggested that "the basic difference is that non-Monetarists accept what I regard as the fundamental practical message of the *General Theory,* that a market economy is subject to fluctuations in aggregate output, unemployment and prices, which need to be corrected, can be corrected and therefore, should be corrected. Monetarists on the other hand hold that there is no real need to stabilize the economy as long as the growth of the money supply follows a simple predictable rule, that even if there were a need we do not have the ability to stabilize it, and that even if we could stabilize it we should not trust the authorities with the necessary discretionary power."

Macroeconomic stabilization policies have been the major focus of Modigliani's works in macroeconomic problems. He sees the differences of non-monetarist and monetarist views on stabilization from two angles: first, differences in empirical assessment; and second, differences in social philosophy and attitudes. As far as the empirical differences are concerned, he made it clear that monetarist attitudes toward correcting any disturbances in the economy need short- term measures that can be measured in quarters or in months, whereas the non-monetarists measure it in terms of years. With regard to the differences in social philosophy, he suggested that the monetarists believe that the economic disturbances cannot be corrected by governments because the governments cannot be trusted with any discretionary power due to their shortsightedness and self-serving motives. In some circumstances the governments even tend to be dishonest. The non-monetarists, on the other hand, strongly advocate for governments to make adjustments for correcting any economic imbalances.

With these fundamental differences between monetarists and non-monetarists, Modigliani concluded from his work that it is necessary the government to take steps to correct economic imbalances through stabilization policies. To do so, however, care must be taken at least in two fronts: first, timing and the parameter selection of the stabilization policies; second, honesty by the government toward adopting discretionary power to implement the stabilization policies. The second front, by all means, is not a matter of economic analysis but a value judgment only. By mentioning timing and parameter selection, Modigliani refers to the short-and long-term policy interventions with selected macroeconomic variables in a given country. His research in this area concentrated on clarifying the role of monetary and fiscal policy in the determination of aggregate output (GDP/GNP), the price level (inflation/wages), and interest rates. With these information in hand it is possible to assess the extent to which monetary and fiscal policies can be relied upon to stabilize the economy. During the last thirty years, almost all nations have adopted Modigliani's prescriptions to stabilize the economy to avoid economic cycles.

SAVING BEHAVIOR HYPOTHESIS

Modigliani and Brumberg demonstrated the basis for modem consumption theory. This theory of consumption simply argues that a rational person bases his/her decisions on consumption using expected lifetime income instead of current income. For example, a fresh graduate with his/her first job would probably go into debt to buy a car, furniture, and even a home. The decision to go into such a debt is backed by an anticipation that the person will earn so much money in the future that it will be easy for him/her to repay the loans. In economic terms, this is regarded as utility maximization by smoothing consumption over time. This, however, needs for the consumer to have a good idea of their life time income stream. They use these information to make rational consumption choices in early years. The diagram below demonstrates such a life time condition.

Figure 24.1 Modigliani's Life Cycle Hypothesis

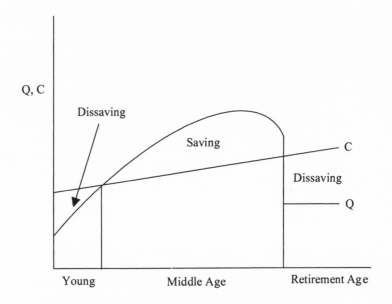

The Q line in the graph represents the typical pattern of income likely to be received by consumers. The whole life span of a consumer could be divided into three portions: low income age (young), high income age (middle age), and retirement age (old age). Since the income is low in the young age, typically the consumers go into debt with a dissaving. In middle age, not only do high wages in jobs produce high income, but there is also some income generated by return on wealth. This period of high income is also a period of saying for a typical consumer. In old age, after retirement, the income of typical consumers drops suddenly and the income is generally sourced from past savings, social security, or from other retirement plans. Once again the typical consumer fails into a period of dissaving. The C line in the graph shows a typical consumer's consumption trend. The slope of the line shows a linear growth over the whole period of the life cycle. It is, however, possible that in the retirement age the consumption line could be horizontal or even nonlinear. In the graph, the distance between Q and C represents saving and dissaving in various stages of life. The life cycle hypothesis (LCH) has contributed over the last three decades to explain why in some developed countries the saving rate is lower than the rate in relatively less developed nations or why the current rate of saving in a given country is lower than the rate in a century ago, even though the current per capita income is several times higher than the past.

CORPORATE FINANCE

Modigliani began working in the corporate finance area in the late 1950s. Two articles, "The Cost of Capital, Corporation Finance and the Theory of Investment," published in *The American Economic Review* in 1958, and "Dividend Policy, Growth and the Valuation of Shares," published in the *Journal of Business* in 1961, were the most important works to contribute towards redirecting the whole theory of finance. These two articles pioneered the application of economic analysis in finance and also put forward some views that were contrary to the conventional views widely accepted in the literature in those days.

Modigliani's contribution to the theory of corporate finance addressed two main issues that had been central to the theory of corporate finance since the pre-Keynesian period: (i) the extent to which it is advantageous for a corporate firm to finance its assets by debt rather than by equity; and (ii) whether the value of corporate stock is determined primarily by dividends, earnings or by something else. With Merton Miller, Modigliani demonstrated that in a competitive market with rational investors (and as long as the effects of taxes are ignored): (i) the way in which firms are financed is irrelevant in the sense that the total market value of firms will be independent of their financial structure; and (ii) the market value of shares will be independent of dividend policy.

Modigliani's work in the corporate finance area in the last forty years brought huge changes in the world's financial markets and institutions. These changes are prominent at least in three major areas: financial innovation, financial globalization, and financial deregulation Since the 1960s, there has been a revolution taking place in the area of financial innovations. These innovations can be classified into three categories: market-broadening instruments (these instruments increase the liquidity of markets and the availability of funds by attracting new investors and offering new opportunities for borrowers), risk-management instruments (which reallocate financial risks to those who are less averse to them), and arbitraging instruments and processes (which enable investors and borrowers to take advantage of differences in costs and returns between markets).

The global integration of financial markets and institutions in the last two decades has revolutionized the international transfer of funds, be it by government or private businesses. For example, exchanges in different countries, firms, and governments issue securities in their home markets as well as in foreign markets, and investors move funds across international boundaries with ease. Financial deregulation has been a major economic policy reform in most developed and developing countries in the 1970s and 1980s under the guidance of the International Monetary Fund (IMF). The proponents of deregulation argue that the financial deregulation makes the economy competitive against its trading partners and competitors. It is needed to make the market forces to work, to make the market more efficient, to increase access to market information, and to run the economy with as little intervention as possible. All these achievements in the corporate finance area were made possible by the works of Modigliani and his colleagues in the 1970s and 1980s. If not for these studies, the corporate finance area would not have seen the light of the modern financial dealings and the way financial institutions have developed in recent years.

CONCLUSION

In conclusion, it can be said that it is Franco Modigliani's lifetime contribution that made managing a modern economy, which has so many complexities and uncertainties, easier for policy makers and governments around the world. Modigliani's works in three areas, macroeconomic management, national and household saving behavior, and corporate finance, are the most important areas through which progress has been achieved for the ordinary public of a nation. Modigliani's prescriptions in these areas have been put in practice by the nations of East Asia. All these countries have used effectively Modigliani's theories on macroeconomic management, saving behavior (household and nation), and corporate finance. It is hoped that in the future the developing countries and the developed countries alike will benefit from Modigliani's works further and will bring progress for the ordinary masses.

RECOMMENDED READINGS

Ando, A.K., and R. Brumberg. (1954). "Utility Analysis and the Consumption Function: An Introduction of Cross-Section Data," in K. Kurihara (ed.) *Post Keynesian Economics.* New Brunswick: Rutgers University Press.

Ando, A.K., and R. Cohn. (1979, March-April). "Inflation, Rational Valuation and the Market," *Financial Analysts Journal.* Vol. 33, No. 2.

Ando, A.K., and D. Lessard. (1975). *New Mortgage Designs for Stable Housing in Inflationary Environment.* Boston: Federal Reserve Bank of Boston.

Ando, A.K., and M.H. Miller. (1958, June). "The Cost of Capital, Corporation Finance and Theory of Investment," *American Economic Review.* Vol. 48, No. 3.

Ando, A.K., and F. Modigliani. (1963). "The Life Cycle Hypothesis of Saving: Aggregate," *American Economic Review,* Vol. 53, No. 1.

Ando, A.K., and H. Neisser. (1953). *National Incomes and International Trade.* Urbana: University of Illinois Press.

Ando, A.K., and G.A. Pogue. (1974, March-April). "An Introduction to Risk and Return: Concepts and Evidence," *Financial Analysts Journal.* Vol. 30, No. 2.

Modigliani, F. (1944, January). "Liquidity Preference and the Theory of Interest and Money," *Econometrica.* Vol. 12, No. 1.

——. (1976). "The Monetarist Controversy or, Should We Forsake Stabilization Policies?" Presidential Address delivered at the American Economic Association, 17 September.

——. (1980). *The Life Cycle Hypothesis of Saving.* Cambridge: MIT Press.

———. (1980). *Collected Papers of Franco Modigliani.* Vol. 1. Cambridge: MIT Press.

———. (1980). *Essays in Macroeconomics.* Vol. 2. Cambridge: MIT Press.

———. (1980). *Theory of Finance and Other Essays.* Cambridge: MIT Press.

———. (1986). *The Debate Over Stabilization Policy.* Cambridge: Cambridge University Press.

25

James Buchanan (1919-):
A Pioneer of Public Economics
and the Laureate of 1986

Minh Q. Dao

BIOGRAPHICAL PROFILE

James Buchanan was born in 1919 in Murfreesboro, Tennessee, and grew up on a farm. He obtained his B.A. from Middle Tennessee State College in 1940 and his M.S. from the University of Tennessee a year later. His mentor, noted economist Frank Knight, had a tremendous influence on him when he taught him to challenge and criticize all orthodoxy in economics. After serving in the armed forces during World War II, Buchanan resumed graduate education at the University of Chicago, where he earned his Ph.D. in economics in 1948. The works of Swedish economist Knut Wicksell influenced his public choice theory of economics. James Buchanan also spent a year in Italy (1955-1956) where he picked up the influence of Italian economists on the model of politics and began to realize that American economists at that time still had a rather romantic notion of politics, holding the naive view that politicians always acted in the public interest. While at his first teaching job at the University of Virginia, which he began in 1956, James Buchanan met Gordon Tullock, who was there on a postdoctoral fellowship after having spent nine years with the U.S. Department of State. Their collaboration led to *The Calculus of Consent*, which was first published in 1962. A year later, they, together with political scientists such as William Riker and economists such as Mancur Olson, Vince Ostrom, Anthony Downs, Duncan Black, Roland McKean, and Jerry Rothenberg, started a journal called *Papers on Non-market Decision Making*, which became *Public Choice* in 1967. James Buchanan then moved to UCLA in 1968, after having set up the Thomas Jefferson Center for Political Economy at the University of Virginia. The riotous events of the 1960s in California having greatly upset him, he and Tullock, who had gone to Rice, returned to Virginia and in 1969 went to Virginia Polytechnic Institute and set up the Center for Study of Public Choice. He remained there until 1983. Since then, he has been with George Mason University, where he founded the James Buchanan Center for Political Economy. He was awarded the Nobel Prize in economics in 1986 for his work in developing public choice theory. In addition to *The Calculus of Consent*, Buchanan's many influential books include *Cost and Choice* (1969), *The Limits of Liberty* (1975), *Liberty, Market, and State* (1985), and his autobiography, *Better Plowing and Other Personal Essays* (1992). His most recent publication is *Politics by Principle, Not Interest*, co-authored with Roger Congleton. James M. Buchanan is currently Advisory General Director of the Center for Political Economy and Holbert L. Harris University Professor at George Mason University in Fairfax, Virginia.

INTRODUCTION

James Buchanan won the economics Nobel Prize in 1986 for his "development of the contractual and constitutional bases for the theory of economic and political decision-making." His most important contribution to the field of economics in general and to the sub-field of public finance in particular is public choice theory, which in a nutshell is the extension of the theory of markets to explain the way political markets function.

THE ROLE OF GOVERNMENT

The economic philosophy of James Buchanan was molded when he was enrolled in Frank Knight's course in price theory at Chicago. Before that he had a brief flirt with libertarian socialism. One might say that James Buchanan is a strong believer in individualism, arguing that only the individual knows what is best for him or her. He holds a mechanistic view of government, according to which the individual interest should be placed above that of the state and the latter exists only to serve the former. This view calls for giving as much freedom of choice to the citizen as possible and, thus, for a minimal role for government. It is also consistent with the capitalist or laissez-faire form of economic system, in which the government intervenes very little in the economic functioning of a nation. This view is rooted in the classic book, *The Wealth of Nations,* written in 1776 by Adam Smith, whom many consider as the founding father of economics. In this type of system, individuals should be left alone in their pursuit of happiness and will reap the highest of benefits if they can freely enter into legally enforceable contracts. Some of the limited functions of government, hence, are to provide for law and order and to see to it that contracts made among individuals be carried out in a peaceful manner. Buchanan then goes on to argue that the success of a political system also follows the same principle. He advocates constructive social cooperation–for this is the only way in which everybody can gain–and thus the necessity for a constitution.

THE NEED FOR
CONSTITUTIONAL RULES

Buchanan argues that even at the constitution-making stage, individuals who act in their self-interest will come up with a set of rules that will benefit society simply because there is no way that any individual can know a priori know to which group he or she will belong in the course of his or her life. In coming up with these rules, a rational voter will opt for those that exert the minimum amount of expected pain. And if the current rules are nonoptimal, then reforms may be brought about so as to make at least some members of society better off without anyone being made worse off.

There are three important considerations that need to be taken into account when constitutional rules are made up. First, these rules must be powerful enough to put constraints on both the government and its citizens. Elected politicians, Buchanan argues, must be given sufficient leeway so that they will be able to stand up to the ever increasing demands of the citizenry. Second, constitutional rules must be changed in the same way that they were brought about. Here, Buchanan sees very little difficulty in improving existing rules by extending the very same process that was used to create them. Finally, those who alter constitutional rules must do so while watching the three criteria of overall improvement, the nonzero sum game, and Pareto optimality or economic efficiency, which is described as a state in which any movement away from it in an effort to improve the lot of someone will result in someone else being made worse off. Buchanan observes that over time piecemeal policymaking has resulted in the "cumulation of distortions" produced by a politics of compromise.

Insofar as public expenditures are concerned, Buchanan advocates that the constitution should make a restriction that only those proposals that will generate general benefits to the community as a whole be considered. He would go so far as to say that unanimity is the only efficient voting rule in the sense that it guarantees that no one would be made worse off as a result of collective change. The power of the government to tax should be limited by the constitution because there is always the temptation on the part of government at some juncture to act not in accordance with the public interest.

CRITICISMS OF KEYNES' ACTIVISM

A strong believer in the working of the markets, Buchanan the political economist sees John Keynes' prescription of government activism in order to fine tune the economy as a major blow to the survival of the democratic order. He himself proclaims that there is no place for macroeconomics, either as a part of our positive science or as a realm for policy action. He sees four dimensions of the deadly problem brought about by the combination of Keynesianism and democracy. The first one has to do with the fact that the Keynesian prescription often results in government budget deficits, which are usually financed by government borrowing from the private sector. Buchanan argues that this method of financing imposes a burden on future generations when future taxes have to be levied in order to monetize the government debt. This is what he refers to as taxation without representation. Buchanan is completely against the practice of borrowing against the future for he argues that it is impossible for the people of the present generation to know ahead of time what future generations desire to do. The second dimension of the problem has to do with asymmetry over the business cycle. Buchanan observes that while budget deficits are used in getting the economy out of a recession, surpluses are not set aside but somehow are justified even in periods of high inflation brought about by an overheated economy. As a result, deficits are never made up, and the government will be in debt on a perpetual basis.

Another dimension of the problem is related to inflation. Buchanan notes that the government has also resorted to money financing when raising taxes is a politically unpopular action, particularly in election years. This type of financing leads to an increase in the price level, the consequences of which will be a redistribution of income from the creditors to the debtors (if the inflation is unanticipated), an erosion of the purchasing power of those on fixed incomes, and an increase in uncertainty in the economy with respect to investment decisions. That is not to mention the problem of spiraling inflation when people formulate expectations about future inflation and act as if it were a fact of life–a phenomenon that occurred in the mid- to late seventies. A final dimension of the problem is the frustration that people feel when they perceive that their government has not delivered what they had demanded. In light of these dimensions, Buchanan strongly believes that the only way an economic system can secure its long-run growth path is by removing all sources of macroeconomic instability, such as an unbalanced government budget, an ever increasing public debt, and unchecked monetary expansion.

PROPOSAL FOR CHANGE

Buchanan proposes three changes to the structure of government. First, he advocates the decentralization of political authority along geographic lines. He identifies certain government functions, decisions for which can be more logically made at the local rather than the state or federal level. Second, he suggests that taxes should be earmarked to finance projects that yield specific benefits. Taxpayers should be able to clearly see how their tax money is being used by government. Without this provision, Buchanan argues, it will become relatively easy for government to exploit taxpayers in the sense that it will fail to deliver them the goods and services they want. In fact, one of the theories of the growth of the relative size of the public debt referred to as "fiscal illusion hypothesis" dwells on the government's ability to increase its size by designing complex taxing schemes in an effort to hide the true costs of government expenditure programs. Finally, for certain publicly provided private goods, Buchanan proposes the use of direct user charges rather than tax revenues as a means of financing. He cites inconsistencies in the British National Health Service as an example, in which he points out that individuals behave differently when it comes to whether they are playing the role of potential users or demanders of health services versus that of voter taxpayers making decisions on how much to tax themselves in order to provide for the financing of these same services.

A COMPARISON WITH RAWLS

It is interesting to note the similarities between Buchanan and another philosopher who also believes in contractual arrangements, John Rawls, whose ideas may be found in his well-known book, *A Theory of Justice*. First, they both believe that the concept of justice is more of a process governed by rules than one having anything to do with outcomes or results. Second, both assume that everyone, in reaching a contractual agreement, does so behind a veil of ignorance, and it is this lack of knowledge and this randomness which give birth to justice. Third, both strongly believe that citizens if given a choice, will prefer individual freedom to paternalism. Fourth, both view the average individual in society more as a risk-averter than as a risk-plunger.

CONCLUSION

A prolific writer, James Buchanan has published more than 20 books and 300 articles in scholarly journals. In 1962, he published his most renowned work, *The Calculus of Consent*, which he co-authored with Gordon Tullock. From 1956 to 1969, he taught at the University of Virginia and also directed the Thomas Jefferson Center for Studies in Political Economy and Social Philosophy. In 1963, he and Tullock founded the Public Choice Society, with 1,500 members strong today, and started the journal *Public Choice*. From 1969 to 1983, he taught at Virginia Polytechnic Institute, where he and Gordon Tullock, along with Charles Goetz, founded the Center for Study of Public Choice. Since 1983, he has been the Holbert Harris University Professor at George Mason University, where he continues to be general director of the center. Interestingly enough, the man who co-authored *The Calculus of Consent* believes that mathematics should only be used as a tool in economics and not as an end in itself. In his Nobel Lecture, he condemns economists who have gotten too preoccupied with the mathematics and in the process lost sight of what economics is all about. Buchanan may be considered as one of the forerunners in applying economic theory to explaining real-world issues.

RECOMMENDED READINGS

Buchanan, J. M. (1965). *The Inconsistencies of the National Health Service*. London: Institute of Economic Affairs.

——. (1969). *Cost and Choice*. Chicago: Markham Publishing.

——. (1992). *Better than Plowing, and other Personal Essays*. Chicago: University of Chicago Press.

Buchanan, J.M., and R.D. Congleton (1998). *Politics by Principles, Not Interests*. New York: Cambridge University Press.

212   James Buchanan

Buchanan, J. M., and G. Tullock. (1962). *The Calculus of Consent*. Ann Arbor: University of Michigan Press.

Buchanan, J. M., and R.E. Wagner. (1977). *Democracy in Deficit*. New York: Academic Press.

Katz, Bernard S. (1989). *Nobel Laureates in Economic Sciences: A Biographical Dictionary*. New York: Garland.

Rawls, John (1972). *A Theory of Justice*. Oxford: Clarendon Press.

Sichel, Werner. (1989). *The State of Economic Science: Views of Six Nobel Laureates*. Kalamazoo: W.E. Upjohn Institute for Employment Research.

Smith, Adam (1776). *The Wealth of Nations*. London: Methuen.

———. (1968). *The Demand and Supply of Public Goods*. Chicago: Rand McNally.

———. (1970). *The Public Finances: An Introductory Textbook*. Third edition. Homewood: Richard D. Irwin.

———. (1975). *The Limits of Liberty*. Chicago: University of Chicago Press.

———. (1977). *Freedom in Constitutional Contract*. College Station and London: Texas A & M Press.

———. (1986). *Liberty, Market and State*. Brighton: Wheatsheaf.

26

Robert Solow (1924-   ):
A Founder of the Modern Growth
Theories and the Laureate of 1987

B. Mak Arvin
Marisa A. Scigliano

BIOGRAPHICAL PROFILE

Robert Solow, the oldest of three children, was born in Brooklyn, New York, in 1924. His parents, Milton and Hannah Solow, were children of immigrants. Solow began his university education with a scholarship to Harvard at the age of sixteen. At age eighteen, he left Harvard and joined the U.S. Army serving in the Signal Corps in North Africa and Italy. Upon return from war in 1945, he married Barbara Lewis and continued his studies at Harvard, choosing to major in economics. After completing his B.A., Solow continued his education at Harvard, winning the David Wells prize for the best Ph.D. thesis in 1951. Shortly before the completion of his thesis at Harvard, Solow began teaching at MIT, rising to the rank of full professor at the age of thirty-four. He was made Institute Professor in 1973. While on leave from MIT, Solow served as a senior economist on the Council of Economic Advisers during the Kennedy administration. During the 1970s, he spent a few years as a member and later as chairman of the board of directors of the Federal Reserve Bank of Boston. Solow was also appointed by presidents Johnson and Nixon to serve on various commissions. A revered economist, he was awarded the John Bates Clark Medal by the American Economic Association in 1961 and was named President of the Econometric Society in 1964 and of the American Economic Association in 1979. Solow holds several honorary degrees form universities on both sides of the Atlantic. A publisher of several books and more than 100 articles in scholarly journals, he once commented that had he neglected his students, he could have written 25 percent more scientific papers. For Solow the choice was easy to make, and he has no regrets. He and his wife, who is also an economist, live in a converted wharf in Boston's waterfront, spending their summers in Martha's Vineyard, where he sails avidly.

INTRODUCTION

Robert Solow won the economics Nobel Prize in 1987 for his "contributions to the theory of economic growth." Although Solow was popularly known as a growth theorist, he was quite strong in mathematics as well. When he was a graduate student, acquiring proficiency in mathematics was uncommon and unnecessary, and it was possible to obtain Ph.D. from Harvard without knowing the basics of calculus. In this sense, Solow was different from his fellow classmates and colleagues. His mathematical skills helped him recognize the loopholes of economics. Once he confessed that "he does not feel that he understands something completely until he has a model of it–usually a mathematical one."

THE THEORY OF
ECONOMIC GROWTH

It is commonly agreed that the modern growth theory began with the independent contributions of Harrod and Domar, who, assuming fixed capital-output and fixed labor-output ratios, concluded that the capitalist system is intrinsically unstable. The unstable growth path of the Harrod-Domar model was not plausible, so interest in their model faded away. The next wave of interest in growth theory was sparked by the development of the neoclassical model by Solow, which focussed on the factors affecting the long-term growth of an economy. In the decade that followed, his model was the most important catalyst for the tremendous outpouring of research toward constructing a more realistic model of growth. The model took its name from the neoclassical form of its production function, which allowed for capital and labor to be substitutes for one another. This was a much more reasonable representation of technology than the earlier model's constant capital-output and constant labor-output ratios. Together with the assumption of a constant saving rate, this characterized general equilibrium for an economy, yielding a path that was more closely aligned with the observed historical time series. The main contribution of Solow's work, however, was that it challenged earlier work that had focussed on capital accumulation as the main engine for economic growth. He demonstrated the importance of technical change (broadly interpreted) in the process of growth. More specifically, Solow established that improvements in the quality of factor inputs is a more significant regulator of economic growth than a mere stockpiling of them, thereby bringing to the forefront of the discussion the significance of research and development (R & D) and improvements in labor productivity in accounting for growth. A colleague at Harvard, Hendrik Houthakker, recalls that while serving on the National Commission on Employment, Solow was instrumental in persuading labor unions to accept technical change–rather than to resist it.

Solow's work also provided an answer to other important questions, among them, why some countries and regions may have higher growth rates than others. He explained that all other things (including technical change) being equal, the lower a country's initial real per capita income is, relative to its long-run or steady-state position, the faster is that country's growth rate. This followed from a key characteristic of his production function, namely that of diminishing return to capital meaning that additional capital injections (increasing capital intensity) make smaller contributions to production. Solow's later work provided solutions to problems surrounding the environmental consequences of growth and whether continued economic growth is possible where resources are finite. Later work on the neoclassical growth model by other economists allowed for the endogenous determination of the saving rate and other extensions, which led to a refinement of the model. However, the next major phase of development on growth theory did not begin until the 1980s, when endogenous growth models began to make an appearance beginning with the independent work of Romer and Lucas. The endogenous growth models abandoned the notion of earlier models, where the exogenous rate of technical progress determined the long-term growth rate and allowed the latter to be determined within the model. Hence, the main contribution of this wave was to rekindle interest in the determinants of long-term growth. One recent strand of this literature has assessed the role of R & D activity and diffusion of technology for endogenous growth. Another has focussed on empirically testing the new models as well as the earlier neoclassical ones. In a recent review article, Solow regards this revival of interest in growth theory as having "an air of promise and excitement about it." As well as talking about the achievements of growth theory, Solow, in a number of articles including his Nobel lecture, draws our attention to some of the shortcomings of the developments and the gaps that remain to be filled. In the Nobel lecture delivered in Stockholm, Solow hopes that growth theory can serve as "a framework for simple, strong, loosely quantitative propositions about cause and effect in macroeconomics." Solow's latest book, *Learning from "Learning by Doing": Lessons for Economic Growth,* is indicative of the fact that he continues to take an active interest in the topic. He demonstrates how learning by doing, together with random innovations, fits into the modern theory of economic growth. There can be no doubt that Solow established the modern growth theory as it is known. As research on this subject continues, future developments and debates undoubtedly will bear the imprint of his pioneering work.

GENERAL MACROECONOMIC THEORY

Solow admits that growth theory played an integral part in his learning of macroeconomics. He credits Keynes with having invented macroeconomics as a subject, even though he cites Wicksell, one of his favourite nineteenth-century economists, as coming close to the spirit of macroeconomics. He is critical of those economists who, while claiming expertise in microeconomics, shy away from macroeconomics because they find it puzzling or incomprehensible. According to him, if one does not understand principal macro issues, one cannot claim to understand economics at all. In Solow's mind, the role of macro theory is "not necessarily to make a single all-purpose model to represent the world [but] rather the uncovering of mechanisms that cause the economic system to malfunction in significant ways, and then the analysis of policy measures that are potentially therapeutic." Perhaps it is in this mind set that one can understand Solow's opposition to the macroeconomics of the new classical school, which he criticizes as being too monolithic by providing one model that is supposed to fit all (or as Solow puts it, a "System of the World.") As one of his generation's foremost Keynesian economists, Solow also lashed out at Reaganomics, stating that the best thing that one could say about it was that it probably happened in a fit of inattention. In several articles, Solow rejects the Walrasian equilibrium concept as a foundation for modern macroeconomic analysis, maintaining that it assumes away all the issues that make macroeconomics interesting. Walrasian theory envisages a frictionless economy where markets clear by perfectly flexible prices leading to a Walrasian equilibrium. According to Solow, once one is freed from the notion that the only equilibrium concept worth discussing is the Walrasian one, then a multiplicity of equilibria can be observed in the real world, which is vulnerable to market failure. In the same vein, Solow does not believe the notion of a stable natural rate, labelling its underlying theoretical and empirical foundations as flimsy. In his view, if there are many possible equilibria for the economy, there are probably many possible natural rates, with the rates depending, among other things, on the economy's history, institutions, and beliefs.

Solow finds little merit in the work of monetarists and their new classical descendants. The latter build models assuming Walrasian market clearing as a norm for the economy. It is not difficult to understand how growing up in the 1930s would make Solow sceptical of the work of the new classical economists (for example, Lucas and Sargent), who never experienced the Depression and regard short-term fluctuations as optimal supply-side adjustments to unforeseeable shocks and the business cycle as a stochastic process taking place around a generally satisfactory long-run equilibrium or trend. Fundamentally, Solow's views on the economy set him apart from the new classicals, who have very different assumptions about the economy. In his published contributions to macro theory, Solow set out to explain why the economy diverges from a satisfactory equilibrium following a disturbance and what policies are required under these circumstances. Over the past few decades, Solow has devoted much of his effort to answering or clarifying many questions involving macroeconomic theory, emphasizing the need for managed capitalism. These can be seen in a series of works on the status of macroeconomics and macro policies, perhaps the most notable beginning with the text of the W.A. Mackintosh lecture delivered at Queen's University and published in 1979, and following with others. Solow's earlier contributions included making the Phillips curve known in North America, following its introduction in England, and in opposing the views of the Cambridge (England) economists, both with Samuelson. However, most economists will recall Solow's specific theoretical contributions, which have partly shaped macroeconomics through a series of articles written mostly between the 1960s and the early 1980s. Three examples of the most widely read and cited are Solow and Stiglitz, Blinder and Solow, and

McDonald and Solow. Each article begs a brief introduction. Solow and Stiglitz present a theory of short-run macroeconomic behavior where the real wage is not flexible enough to clear the labor market instantly. The paper explains why the economy might get trapped in a situation of unemployment equilibrium–a notion that Keynes had in mind but, like many economists of his generation, lacked the analytical tools to express properly himself. To date, Solow claims that Keynes' instincts were correct, namely that an economy may be in aggregative equilibrium with widespread unemployment–a markedly different scenario than that of a Walrasian equilibrium–but still an equilibrium in the sense that there would be no pressure for the situation to change. This paper was important and came well before the fixed-price temporary equilibrium models of the French school, most notably Malinvaud, and others.

Solow's call for stabilization policy is evident in the 1973 article with former student Alan Blinder. In this they refute the monetarist position that fiscal policy is powerless. In particular, monetarists, notably Friedman, had long argued that if government financed its spending through issuing bonds, the multiplier could be zero or even negative due to crowding out. Blinder and Solow used a conventional IS-LM model with wealth effects to demonstrate that this may not be the case and how bond-financed government spending or deficits may have a net expansionary effect on the level of economic activity. Indeed, fiscal policy may be more expansionary under bond financing than it is under money financing. This theme is further explored in their 1976 article. In another important contribution reprinted in standard graduate texts such as Mankiw and Romer's edited work, entitled, new Keynesian macroeconomics, McDonald and Solow show that efficient wage bargains lie on the contract curve, an idea due originally to Solow's Harvard tutor, Leontief, which the latter published in a 1946 article. Most significantly, the paper provides an alternative explanation for wage rigidity, which many earlier articles, including Solow's own, had taken for granted. Among many things, one of Solow's more recent books (with Hahn, 1995) provides yet another explanation for wage rigidity. Based on a game-theoretic analysis, Hahn and Solow provide an explanation of real-wage resistance anchored on social sanctions against wage undercutting that builds on workers' refusal to undercut one another even in the face of open unemployment. This further discredits new classical economists' central arbitrary modeling device of market clearing with flexible prices.

Finally, in spite of Solow's lampooning of new classical models, which combine rational expectations (RE) with the market clearing assumption, it would be erroneous to think he rejects RE outright. He believes RE is like a primitive religion that has an explanation for just about everything, but he nonetheless sees a role for RE in some setting. It is regrettable that Solow never bothered to publish some of his graduate lecture notes, in which he incorporated the RE hypothesis in non market clearing settings with rigid prices. His lectures demonstrated that, in fact, RE can enhance the effectiveness of both fiscal and monetary policies–a result in sharp contrast to the new classical position. Fundamentally, however, Solow believes expectations in the short run are best handled in an ad hoc common-sense manner.

CONCLUSION

Solow's technical contributions range from the practical 1958 textbook with Dorfman and Samuelson, which made the mathematical techniques of linear and non linear programming as well as game theory accessible to future economists, to a highly complex abstract model examining optimal land use in a long, narrow city (with Vickrey, 1971). Besides contributions to growth theory and macroeconomics, Solow has written extensively on many areas, including intergenerational equity and exhaustible resources, congestion costs, and economic development. Solow is a delightful commentator on the developments and achievements of mainstream economics and shares his concept of the nature of economics as a discipline. In a series of articles, he traces its evolution over a span of over fifty years–about the length of time he has been a professional economist. Curiously, although he despises society's current fascination with the cult of the personality, he is thoughtful enough to share with the audience his own coping strategies and is not averse to making light of his own shortcomings.

RECOMMENDED READINGS

Blinder Alan S. and Robert M. Solow (1973). "Does Fiscal Policy Matter?" *Journal of Public Economics*. Vol. 2, pp. 319-37.

McDonald, Ian M. and Robert M. Solow (1981). "Wage Bargaining and Employment," *American Economic Review*. Vol. 71, pp. 896-908.

Solow, Robert M. (1956)."A Contribution to the Theory of Economic Growth," *Quarterly Journal of Economics*. Vol. 70, pp. 65-94.

——. (1957). "Technical Change and the Aggregate Production Function," *Review of Economics and Statistics*. Vol. 39, pp. 312-20.

——. (1973). "Congestion Cost and the Use of Land for Streets," *Bell Journal of Economics and Management Science*. Vol. 4, pp. 602-18.

——. (1974a). "Intergenerational Equity and Exhaustible Resources," *Review of Economic Studies*. (Symposium),Vol. 4, pp. 29-45.

——. (1974b). "The Economics of Resources or the Resources of Economics," *American Economic Review*. Vol. 64, pp. 1-14.

——. (1979). "Alternative Approaches to Macroeconomic Theory: A Partial View," *Canadian Journal of Economics*. Vol. 12, pp. 339-54.

——. (1980). "On Theories of Unemployment," *American Economic Review*. Vol. 70, pp. 1-11.

——. (1983). "Economic Development and the Development of Economics: Discussion," *World Development*. Vol. 11, pp. 891-93.

——. (1986). "What is a Nice Girl Like You Doing in a Place Like This? Macroeconomics After Fifty Years," *Eastern Economic Journal*. Vol. 12, pp. 191-98.

——. (1988). "Growth Theory and After," *American Economic Review*. Vol. 78, pp. 307-17.

———. (1989). "Dr. Robert M. Solow," *The State of Economic Science: Views of Six Nobel Laureates.* (ed.) Werner Sichel. Kalamazoo: W.E. Upjohn Institute for Employment Research.

———. (1992). "Notes on Coping," *Eminent Economists: Their Life Philosophies.* (ed.) Michael Szenberg. Cambridge: Cambridge University Press.

———. (1994). "Perspectives on Growth Theory," *Journal of Economic perspectives.* Vol. 8, pp. 45-54.

———. (1995). "Robert M. Solow," *Lives of the Laureates: Thirteen Nobel Economists*, Eds. William Breit and Roger W. Spencer. 3rd ed. Cambridge: MIT Press.

———. (1997a). "Is There a Core of Practical Macroeconomics That We Should all Believe?" *American Economic Review.* Vol. 87, pp. 230-32.

———. (1997b), "It Ain't the Things you Don't Know That Hurt You, It's the Things You Know That Ain't So," *American Economic Review.* Vol. 87, pp. 107-8.

———. (1997c). "How Did Economics Get That Way and What Way Did They Get?" *Daedalus.* Vol. 126, pp. 39-58.

———. (1997d). *Learning from "Learning by Doing:" Lessons for Economic Growth.* Stanford: Stanford University Press.

Solow, Robert M., and Joseph E. Stiglitz. (1968). "Output, Employment and Wages in the Short Run," *Quarterly Journal of Economics.* Vol. 82, pp. 537-60.

Solow, Robert M., and William S. Vickrey. (1971). "Land Use in a Long Narrow City," *Journal of Economic Theory.* Vol. 3, pp. 430-47.

27

Maurice Allais (1911-):
An Applied Microtheorist and
the Laureate of 1988

Bruce Cater
A. Eric Kam

BIOGRAPHICAL PROFILE

Maurice Allais was born in 1911 in Paris, France. His grandfather was a carpenter. His father fought in the First World War and died in 1915 in Germany as a prisoner of war. His father's death had a long-lasting effect on his life. Allais received his high school diploma in Latin and science in 1928 and in mathematics and philosophy in 1929. Throughout his college life, Allais was the best student in his class. He studied at the prestigious Ecole Polytechnique and graduated from there in 1933. After that he served in the artillery division of the French army for a year and joined a government service, Corps National des Mines as an engineer. Within a short period of time, when he was only twenty-six, he was in charge of Nantes Mines and Quarries Service–five of eighty-nine government departments including a local railway system. As the Second World War broke out, he was called again for the military service and performed duties in the Briancon front. After being released from the army, he joined his old government service in 1940. In 1941, he became director of the Bureau of Mines Documentation and Statistics in Paris. Along with his administrative job, during the early 1940s, he carried out fundamental research in economics and made his noted publications, such as *A la Recherche d'une Discipline Economique* (*In Quest of an Economic Discipline*); *Economie et Intérêt* (*Economy and Interest*); *Economique Pure et Rendement Social* (*Pure Economics and Social Efficiency*); *Prolégomenes à la Reconstruction Economique du Monde* (*Prolegomena for the World Economic Reconstruction*), *and Abondance où Misère* (*Abundance or Misery*). This was one of the most productive times of his life, when he used to work eighty hours a week. In 1948, he left the government service and became a professor of economic analysis at the Ecole Nationale Superieure des Mines. He later held teaching positions at other institutions, including the Institute of Statistics at the University of Paris, the Thomas Jefferson Center of the University of Virginia as a distinguished visiting scholar, the Graduate Institute of International Studies in Geneva, and the University of Paris-X. Allais was not only an illustrious economist but also a well-known physicist and historian. In 1980, although Allais retired from active service, he continued his research and writings on various topics of economics, physics, and history. During his long professional career, Allais received more than a dozen scientific prizes. In 1978, Maurice Allais became the first, and still the only, economist to be awarded the Gold Medal of the National Center for Scientific Research, the highest honor in French science.

INTRODUCTION

Maurice Allais won the economics Nobel Prize in 1988 for his "pioneering contributions to the theory of markets and efficient utilization of resources." The original works of Allais were largely published in French. As such, he is relatively unknown to the English-speaking world. Allais' talent is indeed very rare. Beyond economics, he has significantly contributed to several branches of knowledge, including history of civilizations, politics, theoretical and experimental physics. Allais is the first French economist to win the Nobel Prize. The influence of his research, if only indirect, has been far-reaching.

MARKETS AND EFFICIENCY

One of the fundamental missions of basic research in economics "is to formulate a rigorous model of equilibrium in markets and examine the efficiency of this equilibrium." In the late eighteenth century, Adam Smith's theory of the "invisible hand"–the notion that the self-serving, independent decisions of the many, as if coordinated by some unseen force, result in the efficient allocation of resources–represented the earliest attempt at such a formulation, albeit only in descriptive terms. A century later, the work of French economist Leon Walras, Italian economist Vilfredo Pareto, and Swedish economist Gustav Cassel presented the ideas of Smith in more rigorous, mathematical terms. One of Maurice Allais' most significant contributions–the monumental *In Quest of an Economic Discipline.* (A la Recherche d'une Discipline Economique)–expanded on the earlier work of Walras and Pareto. Allais' work presented, among other things, very general proofs of the two basic propositions of welfare theory: (1) Any market equilibrium is socially efficient in the sense that no one can be made better off without making someone else worse off, and (2) under certain conditions, any state of social efficiency is a state of market equilibrium. These contributions were, of course, theoretical in nature. Yet Allais' theoretical work was not theory for theory's sake. Indeed, while the above results were necessarily presented in a very technical manner, rendering them impenetrable to many readers, they were, and continue to be, very important as guidelines for planning. In particular, the results show that any economic system, be it characterized by collective or private property ownership, should be organized on a decentralized basis. Indeed, Allais has consistently been opposed to any government intervention that would tend to undermine the efficient operation of free markets.

Because *In Quest of an Economic Discipline* was completed in French and went untranslated (into English) for almost fifty years, its influence was largely indirect beyond the French-speaking world, and its profound importance was not fully understood for decades. Despite his results, Allais, ever cognizant of his earlier observations of the Great Depression, was not of the view that free markets were capable of solving every economic problem. For example, as early as 1943, Allais advocated government ownership, or at least the strict regulation, of natural monopolies. Indeed, his 1943 book also developed necessary and sufficient conditions that, for the management of plants in sectors such as electricity and railway transportation, would result in the competitive prices required for efficiency. In addition, Allais has consistently been of the view that the issuing of money should be strictly under the control of a country's central bank; no private bank should be allowed to create money. Allais was also of the view that, under certain conditions, the equilibrium toward which free competition drives markets should be discarded. While such a free market equilibrium will be efficient in that resources will tend to be allocated in a manner reflective of society's current preferences, it will not properly reflect the preferences of the current generation during subsequent periods or the preferences of future generations.

DECISION-MAKING
UNDER UNCERTAINTY

Despite his many significant contributions, Maurice Allais is perhaps best known for his research in the field of decision theory. In particular, his examination of how people behave when choosing between various risks has, in the view of fellow Nobel laureate Kenneth Arrow, kept Allais at the forefront of technical economics. Over two centuries ago, Daniel Bernoulli solved the famous St. Petersburg paradox by suggesting that a rational individual, when choosing between uncertain alternatives, will select that which, on average, gives greater utility (or satisfaction). John von Neumann and Morgenstern formalized Bernoulli's notion with their theory of expected utility maximization by demonstrating that, if an individual behaves in a manner consistent with a few axioms of rationality, then there exists a "utility function" for that individual and his/her choices when faced with uncertainty can be understood as an attempt to maximize the value of the function. On an intuitive level, however, this theory did not jibe with Allais' sense of the psychology of risk. To test this intuition, he devised four hypothetical "lotteries" or "gambles": A, B, C, and D. Each had associated with it three possible monetary prizes. As shown in Table 27.1, the lotteries differed in terms of the probability of each prize being won.

Table 27.1 Allais' Four Hypothetical Lotteries

Payoffs	Lotteries			
	A	B	C	D
$500 million	0%	10%	0%	10%
$100 million	100%	89%	11%	0%
$00	0%	1%	89%	90%

With lottery B, for example, there is a 10% probability (or chance) of winning a $500 million prize, an 89% probability of winning a $100 million prize, and a 1% probability of receiving no monetary–that is a $00 prize.

Allais then carried out a survey of a number of individuals at the 1952 Paris Conference on Mathematical Economics and Risk. Each respondent was well trained in probability theory, and many were themselves supporters of the von Neumann-Morgenstern theory. When asked to choose between A and B, the majority of respondents preferred A. When asked to choose between C and D, the majority chose D. These survey results were important in that they conflicted with the expected utility hypothesis of von Neumann and Morgenstern. That is, there exists no utility function that would predict that an individual would make the choices that the majority were observed to make. Indeed, if a decisionmaker derives greater expected utility from A than from B, then the expected utility from C must exceed D. The choices made, therefore, suggested that the surveyed scholars did not, in fact, behave in a manner consistent with their own axioms. This result came to be known as the Allais paradox, although it is not paradoxical at all. Rather, "it merely corresponds to a very profound psychological reality, the preference for security in the neighborhood of certainty."

CAPITAL AND GROWTH THEORY

Maurice Allais' contributions to capital and growth theory included, and indeed predated, many of the results of the neoclassical theory of growth. In particular, his 1947 book, *Economy and Interest* (*Economie et Interet*), showed that in a stationary state–that is, an economy in which output and prices remain constant over time–a zero rate of interest maximizes real national income. This insight is the first version of the so-called "golden rule" of accumulation, presented fourteen years later by Edmund Phelps. The intuition underlying Allais' "golden rule" can be conveyed through the following example. Suppose labor can contribute to the production of wheat in one of two ways: either directly through its use in planting and harvesting wheat this year, or indirectly through its use in building equipment that, in turn, can be used in the planting and harvesting of next year's crop. There exists, of course, some allocation of labor between its two potential uses that will maximize total wheat production. The question, is how can the labor market achieve such an optimal allocation? If labor were more productive in one use than the other, total wheat production could be increased by reallocating labor toward the more productive use. Logically, then, maximization of wheat production is achieved only when the marginal productivity of labor is equal across its two uses. Yet, because equilibrium in the labor market requires that wages for the two uses be proportional to the marginal productivities at any point in time, it follows that the wages paid in each of the two uses must be equal. With a one-year lag between the respective outputs of direct and indirect-use labor, the described equilibrium conditions can only hold if interest rates are zero. Allais then extended the above rule for the case of a growing rather than stationary economy, showing that the optimal rate of interest should equal the rate of growth.

MONETARY DYNAMICS

The observation that economies characterized by monetary instability achieve neither economic efficiency nor an equitable distribution of income motivated a consideration of the role of monetary dynamics. Using what he called the Fundamental Equation of Monetary Dynamics, Allais developed a dynamic theory of global expenditure or business cycles based on the gap between the supply of and demand for money, where the demand for money was itself influenced by previous expenditure variations. The theory proved capable of describing cycles similar in duration and amplitude to those observed.

CONCLUSION

In awarding the 1998 Nobel Prize for economics to Maurice Allais, the Royal Academy of Sciences of Sweden specifically noted the significance of the contributions contained in Allais' *In Quest of an Economic Discipline* and *Economy and Interest*. Despite being less widely read because of their publication in French, these works compare favorably with Sir John Hicks' *Value and Capital* and Paul Samuelson's *Foundations of Economic Analysis*. Allais' contributions to economic science, however, extend far beyond those two volumes. In addition, he has consistently devoted a portion of his efforts to research in the fields of history and theoretical and experimental physics. The significance, relevance, and clarity of his work arise from his own passion for research and the pursuit of scientific truth. To quote Allias, "Research is a sort of adventure full of risks, but a fascinating adventure. When a researcher undertakes some research, he is never sure of success. Very often he fails: reality is contrary to his expectations; and if he carries out an analysis and discovers some new regularity, what he finds is generally not exactly what he was looking for. Sometimes the results may even be more or less disappointing, but also, sometimes, at the end of an often painstaking effort, he discovers under the extreme complexity of the facts new regularities whose reality cannot be doubted. Sometimes, too, his findings can surpass his expectations. Such moments are rare, but they exist, and they compensate for the rest."

RECOMMENDED READINGS

Allais, Maurice. (1943). *A la Recherche d'une Discipline Economique–Premiere Partie– L'Economie Pure*. Paris: Ateliers Industria.

——. (1947). *Economie et Interet*. Paris: Imprimerie Nationale.

——. (1962). "The Influence of the Capital Output Ratio on Real National Income," *Econometrica.*. Vol. 30, pp. 700-28.

——. (1992). "The Passion for Research," *Eminent Economists: Their Life Philosophies*. (eds.) M. Szenberg. Cambridge: Cambridge University Press.

——. (1997). "An Outline of My Main Contributions to Economic Science," *American Economic Review*. Vol. 87, pp. 3-12.

Hicks, John. (1939). *Value and Capital*. Oxford: Clarendon.

Phelps, Edmund. (1961). "The Golden Rule of Accumulation: A Fable for Growth Men," *American Economic Review*. Vol. 51, pp. 638-43.

(1989). Royal Swedish Academy of Sciences Press Release. *Scandinavian Journal of Economics*. Vol. 91.

Samuelson, Paul A. (1947). *Foundations of Economic Analysis*. Cambridge: Harvard University Press.

von Neumann, J., and O. Morgenstern. (1944). *Theory of Games and Economic Behavior*. Princeton: Princeton University Press.

28

Trygve Haavelmo (1911-1999):
A Founder of the Simultaneous
Equations System and the Laureate of 1989

Abu N.M. Wahid
Baker A. Siddiquee

BIOGRAPHICAL PROFILE

Trygve Haavelmo was born in Skedsmo, Norway, in 1911. After finishing secondary education in 1930, he entered the University of Oslo Law School's program in political economy. He completed his undergraduate degree in 1933. After graduation, Haavelmo became Ragnar Frisch's research assistant, a position he held until 1938, when he took a one-year lectureship in statistics at the University of Aarhus in Denmark. It was during these years that Frisch restructured the economics education at the University of Oslo. Commenting on this change, Haavelmo later said that "the economics curriculum shook in its foundations." In 1939, Haavelmo came to the United States on a Rockefeller fellowship. Thus when Hitler's army entered Norway on April 8, 1940, Haavelmo was a Rockefeller fellow. During the next two years, he worked on his doctoral thesis, *The Probability Approach in Econometrics*, at Harvard. This work was completed in 1941. After the war, this path-breaking work was submitted to the University of Oslo, in 1944, and Haavelmo was awarded the doctoral degree by the University of Oslo in 1946. At that time, the thesis had already changed econometrics forever, particularly after it was published as a supplement to *Econometrica* in July 1944. In that year, at the age of thirty-two, Haavelmo became a fellow of the Econometric Society. By 1941, the exiled Norwegian government had been installed in both England and in the United States. After his Rockefeller fellowship ended, Haavelmo was offered a position in the Norwegian government's Maritime Fleet Administration (Notraship) in New York. Here he worked as a statistician for two years until he was appointed to the Norwegian embassy in Washington, D.C., as a commercial attaché, a position he held until the war ended. After the war, Haavelmo continued his academic and scientific work at the University of Chicago, where he became a researcher for the Cowles Commission, led by Alfred Cowles. Upon his return to Norway in 1947, Haavelmo entered into government service as the section chief of national economic planning in the Ministry of Commerce and Industry and the Ministry of Finance. This office was charged with preparing the national economic plans for the reconstruction of the war-torn Norwegian economy. This started a lifelong involvement with the Norwegian Labor Party, although Haavelmo did not publicly become a party member until 1965. His research and writing directions were, however, very much influenced by his long-term party affiliations. In 1948, Haavelmo was appointed as a full professor at the University of Oslo, a position he held until he became a professor emeritus in 1979. Although one can easily visualize Trygve Haavelmo as a scientist and university professor, it is difficult to see him as a politician. In the classrooms and lecture halls, he was forceful but still withdrawn, almost shy. It is symptomatic for Haavelmo that on the day of the Nobel Prize announcement, he went hiking in the woods north of Oslo, rather than giving interviews to the international press that besieged his home. The outdoors was an important part of Haavelmo's life, so such a reaction to a stressful situation should have been expected from a man who loved fishing and skiing in addition to riding his Harley-Davidson motorcycle.

INTRODUCTION

Trygve Haavelmo won the economics Nobel Prize in 1989 for his "clarification of the probability theory foundations of econometrics and his analyses of simultaneous economic structures." Haavelmo presented a new and path-breaking approach to the estimation of economic relations by applying methods used in mathematical statistics. His work established the foundations for a new field of research that came to dominate the study of estimating complex economic relations. In his review of Haavelmo's doctoral thesis, the British Nobel laureate Richard Stone wrote that it was a brilliant contribution to econometrics that would have a revolutionary effect on the degree of success in estimating economic relations.

ECONOMIC THEORY

After he became a professor at the University of Oslo, Haavelmo's research interests turned to economic theory. His book entitled *A Study in the Theory of Economic Evolution*, published in 1954, was a pioneering study of the possible reasons for economic underdevelopment of a country in relation to other countries, long before other economists became seriously engaged in development research. As early as in his dissertation, he stressed the relationship between "Abstract Models and Reality." A year later he published "Multiplier Effects of a Balanced Budget," in *Econometrica* where his conclusions, the "Haavelmo Theorem," was proven. The theorem stated that an increase in government spending paid for by an equal increase in taxes would result in an increase in GNP by an amount equal to the increased government spending. In "A Study in the Theory of Economic Evolution," Haavelmo (1954) clearly indicated that he was not satisfied by merely modeling and analyzing the national economic unit but that he also included the global view. Later, Haavelmo moved away from econometrics and concentrated more on economic theory. Here again, the global view became much more important, although a large part of his work was directed toward the perceived needs of the Norwegian economy and the needs of his Labor Party taskmasters.

Both in his writings and in his lectures, Haavelmo always stressed the theoretical and philosophical foundations of economics. In his quest for generality and autonomy in his model specifications, Haavelmo could sometimes confuse readers and listeners. In his strive to keep the conceptual relationships at the highest degree of autonomy, he sometimes became inaccessible. Haavelmo's concern, however mathematically inaccessible the discussion might end up, was that behavior, institutions, and policy changes should explicitly be incorporated in a model. In this way, the models were not outdated the moment they were estimated. This is normally the case if the coefficient set of a model does not include explicit institutional and policy parameters. A simple example might clarify this issue. Increasing concentration and monopoly power in an industry will gradually eliminate the supply function of that industry. If this aspect is not explicitly included in the model specifications, the model will be useless as a forecasting or policy evaluation tool.

Moene and Rodseth go as far as saying, "If Haavelmo's prescriptions had been followed, the now famous Lucas critique that a Phillips Curve estimated under one policy regime would break down if the government changed to another policy rule might not have been necessary. The Lucas Critique is a special case of Haavelmo's criticism of making policy simulations with relations that do not possess the required degree of autonomy." As most social scientists know, unintended consequences are the results of bad analysis. This was the case of the Phillips Curve, as pointed out by Lucas. What Moene and Rodseth do not point out is that a model's degree of autonomy is dependent on the state of economic theory at any point in time, thus making their argument moot indeed. Haavelmo had earlier pointed out that economic theory was relatively primitive compared to econometrics. In this article, which actually was his presidential address to the Econometric Society in Philadelphia in 1957, Haavelmo discussed the frequent discrepancies that were discovered when economic theories were confronted with data. He did not blame econometrics for these shortcomings but, rather, indicated that it was the result of inadequate economic theories. He asserted that economists had been "living in a dream-world of large but somewhat superficial and spurious correlations." According to Haavelmo, these discrepancies were due mainly to a lack of consistent and profound economic theories, in other words, theories that contain the "true" parameter set.

In his doctoral dissertation, Haavelmo had introduced probability models into econometric research. In these models, it was frequently assumed that the stochastic residuals were somehow a measure of our theoretical ignorance. Thus the "large but somewhat superficial and spurious correlations" reflect our ignorance of the phenomenon at hand. But the classical Ordinary Least Square (OLS) technique of coefficient estimations, then as now, requires clear assumptions on both the explanatory variables and the residuals to hold before the procedure is valid, that is, existing and constant first and second order moments. Thus it is difficult to completely understand how Haavelmo could lay the blame solely on the doorstep of economic theory, as these assumptions were almost never explored and were, in reality, almost never correct. With 20/20 hindsight, it is always easy to criticize previous economic philosophers and thinkers like Haavelmo for oversights and omissions. It is, however, difficult to understand how a deep and profound thinker like Haavelmo could constantly use OLS and its various modifications and variants and never explore the issue of the stationarity of the variables seriously and definitely.

In Haavelmo's view, the econometric science had progressed far ahead of economic theory and it was futile to proceed in applied economics without significant improvement in economic theory. Haavelmo heralded a change in his scientific endeavors. True to his convictions, his writings from then onward had mainly dealt with economic theory, as the bibliography below shows. Haavelmo's change in scientific direction may have been a genuine philosophical determination. Knowing the politically inflamed environment that was emerging in Norway and in the Norwegian academic circles and the prevailing attitude at the University of Oslo's department of economics, and particularly Haavelmo's strong affiliation with the socialistic Norwegian Labor Party, it is difficult to believe that it was solely a philosophically based decision. More likely, however, is that the change was caused by: (1) the changed mathematical direction of econometrics (2) political expediency, and (3) political correctness. From the 1950s onward, econometrics changed into a very stringent subdiscipline of mathematical statistics by economists with superior mathematical skills. Particularly, British, French, and the U.S. economists were in the forefront developing econometrics. The lead had been taken away from the University of Oslo department of economics. Ragnar Frisch, the department head and research director, who relinquished his position as editor in chief of *Econometrica* in 1955, was not a supporter of the way econometrics was developing. In fact, his annoyance came to the surface in 1970, when he referred to modern econometrics as "playometrics."

The political master in Norway at that time was the socialist-leaning Norwegian Labor Party, whose political/economical agenda centered around macroeconomic planning. Haavelmo was a passive party member until 1965, when he became a member of the Labor Party's Committee for Economic Policy. Econometrics is a science neutral of politics. There are no political points to be gained from developing econometrics. Economic theory, on the other hand, has a long and sordid history of serving political masters even before Karl Marx. Thus it should come as no surprise that a Labor Party member would be inclined to develop thoughts and ideas that could serve the aim and purpose of the party. The issues covered by Haavelmo from then onward were clearly of the "politically correct" kind. Furthermore, the Labor Party needed more solid foundations for the planning models in the "Norwegian reality (den norske virkelighet)," in other words a highly regulated and planned economy where general economic theory is of very limited use. The list of Haavelmo's later publications can be categorized as: (1) development economics, (2) environmental economics, (3) macro economic planning and control, and (4) investment theory.

DEVELOPMENT ECONOMICS

Based on lecture notes from the University of Oslo on economic long-term development tendencies, Haavelmo published *A Study in the Theory of Economic Evolution*. In this analysis, the attention was on explaining the apparent differences in economic developments that exist between regions and people across the globe. Based on macrodynamic models where the behavioral patterns are equal across countries, he analyzed many possible development paths. His conclusion was that small differences in initial conditions can have significant accumulative effects over the years. He also concluded that countries with poor initial conditions remain at a lower level of economic development than countries with better initial conditions even if all other economic aspects are the same. Additionally, when he introduced stochastic shocks as proxies for recurring natural disasters in these models, the development paths were, not surprisingly, devastating. In his effort to increase the degree of autonomy in his model, he rejected the idea of superior institutions as a reason for advanced economic development. Institutions are endogenous and should be explained by the model.

In his article "On the Dynamics of Global Economic Inequality," published by the Institute of Economics, Oslo University, he started with the following programmatic statement: "Economic progress for everybody, more equal distribution of goods and services and a more careful exploitation of world resources; these are some of the keynotes in current plans for global economic development." This "motherhood and apple pie" statement was then put to a test using one of his global dynamic macroeconomic models. Although no clear conclusions were drawn, various scenarios were offered. One scenario opened the possibility of population growth choking off per capita economic income and of a maximum number of people all living near the starvation level. At this level it is the groups that are used to very little that survive.

ENVIRONMENTAL ECONOMICS

Haavelmo's work in environmental economics consists of only one small article. In this article, however, he developed an economic model, solidly founded on economic theory, that are able to handle explicitly many of the pollution problems that were emerging. In this model, the individual consumer's utility is compared with the increased environmental costs that this consumption entails. He pointed to the now so familiar marginal inconvenience of one's own consumption versus the cumulative social costs of all consumption. Here Haavelmo pointed to the fact that a free market organization of the economy would lead to too much consumption of the polluting good. Whereas Haavelmo made a case for other economic instrumentation to take care of the pollution problem, he did not foresee the possibility that the market mechanism, given a new set of institutions, would be able to achieve the same results as direct governmental interventions.

MACRO ECONOMIC
PLANNING AND CONTROL

As indicated earlier, both by natural inclination and by political affiliation, Haavelmo was at an early stage in his economic career keenly interested in economic policies and the central authority's ability to guide or force the economy in one direction or the other. Haavelmo's theorem, mentioned earlier, is just one early manifestation of this fascination. When he returned from the United States of America in 1947, he became the head of a government office outlining the national economic plan for the reconstruction of the Norwegian economy. In 1965, Haavelmo was invited to a Vatican symposium on the role of economic analysis on the formulation of development planning. His contribution had the title "Some Observations on Counter-cyclical Fiscal policy and Its Effects on Economic Growth." It should be noted that this was the year he became a member of the Norwegian Labor Party's Committee for Economic Policy. In the 1965 paper, Haavelmo concentrated his analysis on the effects of private investments and their tendencies to fluctuate widely over time. The remedies for dampening these fluctuations were tight government-controlled investments, particularly direct government investment in the economy. Later, as it became more obvious that the Labor-Party induced and directed investments in the Norwegian economy did not guarantee a fluctuation-free economic environment. Haavelmo directed his attention toward the more philosophical aspects of society, governance, and welfare. In this paper, he discussed the optimal use of economic inequalities and the advantages of the Platonic state versus the modern Western Democratic ideals. In the wake of the 1973 "oil shock" and the Club of Rome's "Limits to Growth," Haavelmo came out with his views in "Welfare Policies for Future Generations in a General Welfare Theoretical Framework. " In these endeavors, Haavelmo necessarily had to cross over into other social sciences, such as sociology, political science and even history. In Haavelmo's "Variations on a theme by Gossen," he advocated for the analytical apparatus built up by economists over the years. The tools of economic analysis were particularly suitable for keeping track of many different aspects simultaneously. These approaches and methodologies could be applied to a range of phenomena confronting the scientists in other social science disciplines. A case in point was Gossen's utility maximization conditions. Here the utility of the last dollar spent on any good should be equal to the sacrifice necessary to earn that extra dollar. This defines rational behavior patterns for an individual. Thus, the daily choices are based on easily understood compromises.

Another interesting aspect of this study is that Haavelmo here deliberately touched the "third rail" of classical consumer theory. Instead of assuming consumer preference structures as given or constant, he opens up the possibility that preferences are endogenous. Thus, through advertisements and indoctrination, one could "align people's consumption patterns, thus creating a basis for more effective production and scale economics and through such efforts create the foundation for higher incomes and profits" (author's translation). No wonder Haavelmo was popular with the socialist Labor Party. This was exactly what the party had been striving for since it was formed. Aligning people's opinions (ensretting) along party lines at all levels of the educational system was a central theme the Labor Party's cultural and educational programs from the time they came to power after World War II. Now this apparatus could be used to change consumer habits along party lines.

INVESTMENT THEORY

Haavelmo also made a valuable contribution to the theory that determines the development of investments in a country. His book, entitled, *A Study in the Theory of Investment*, introduced theories on the demand for real capital and on the sluggishness in the adjustment of real capital, which have been of fundamental importance in subsequent research. Numerous theoretical and empirical studies of investment behavior have been inspired by his work. Many of Haavelmo's other studies, such as a monograph on environmental economics that appeared long before such research came into existence, have been an inspiration to other researchers. The first major theoretical work, after his 1957-1958 change in research direction, was the 1960 monograph, *A Study in the Theory of Investment*. In this book, Haavelmo gives a critical review of earlier investment theories and develops his own. He agrees with Keynes that the interest rate can influence the demand for capital goods, but that the time element in this demand is important basically due to the increasing marginal cost of production as a function of time. The shorter the period of investments is for a certain amount of investment, the higher the costs. This, of course, leads to an evaluation of the capital goods industry and its capacity for shipments. This capacity adjustment cost, as Haavelmo calls it, makes the interest rate a much more complex economic instrument variable than what is normally accepted. This is not the only area of macroeconomic policy on which Haavelmo differed from Keynes.

CONCLUSION

Haavelmo had a decisive influence on economics in Norway–not only as a researcher, but also as a teacher. During his active years at the Institute of Economics at the University of Oslo, he was the leading teacher in the field. He covered numerous areas of economic theory, and many of his students and assistants received their first instruction in authorship by writing expositions based on his lectures–under stimulating guidance. No less inspiration was given to the many research recruits for whom Haavelmo served as advisor.

RECOMMENDED READINGS

Haavelmo, Trygve. (1409, October). "The Inadequacy of Testing Dynamic *Theory* by Comparing Theoretical Solution and Observed Cycles," *Econometrica.* Vol. 8.

——. (1943a). "The Statistical Implications of a System of Simultaneous Equations," *Econometrica.* Vol. 11.

——. (1943b). "Statistical Testing of Business Cycle Theories, *Review of Economic Statistics.* Vol. 25.

——. (1944, July). "The Probability Approach in Econometrics," *Econometrica.* Vol. 12, supplement .

——. (1945, October). "Multiplier Effects of a Balanced Budget," *Econometrica.* Vol. 13.

——. (1947a). "Statistical Analysis of the Demand for Food: Examples of Simultaneous Estimation of Structural Equation," (with M.A. Girschick), Econometrica. Vol. 15.

——. (1947b). "Methods for Measuring the Marginal Propensity to Consume," *Journal of the American Statistical Association.* Vol. 42.

——. (1950, January). "The Notion of Involuntary Economic Decisions," *Econometrica.* Vol. 18, No. 1.

——. (1954). *A Study in the Theory of Economic Evolution.* In the series, (Contributions to Economic Analysis Series). Amsterdam: North-Holland Publishing Company.

——. (1958, July). "The Role of the Econometrician in the Advancement of Economic Theory," *Econometrica.* Vol. 26.

——. (1960). *A Study in the Theory of Investment.* Chicago: University of Chicago Press.

——. (1965). "Some Observations on Countercyclical Fiscal Policy and its Effects on Economic Growth," *Semaine d'Etude sur le Rôle de l'Analyse économique dans la Formulation de Plans de Dévelopment, Pontificia Academiae Scientiarum Scripta Varia.* Vol. 28.

——. (1968). "Business Cycles II: Mathematical Models," *International Encyclopedia of Social Sciences.* New York: Macmillan and the Free Press.

——. (1971). "Forurensningsproblemet fra samfunnsvitenskaplig synspunkt" (The Pollution Problem from a Social Science Point of View), *Sosialøkonomen.* Vol. 25, No. 4, årgang.

——. (1972, May 19). "Variasjoner over et tema av Gossen" (Variations on a theme by Gossen). *Memorandum from The Institute of Economics.* Oslo: University of Oslo.

——. (1974)."What Can Static Equilibrium Models Tell Us?"*Economic Inquiry.* Vol. 12.

——. (1976, February 13). "Samfunn, styring og velferd" (Society, governance and welfare). *Memorandum from The Institute of Economics.* Oslo: University of Oslo.

——. (1977). "Velferdspolitikk for fremtidige generasjoner" (Welfare policies for future generations), *Sosialokonomen.* Vol. 31, No. 1, årgang.

——. (1982, May 7). "On the Dynamics of Global Economic Inequality," Economic Essays in Honour of Jorgen Gelting, Supplement to Nationalokonomisk Tidskrift. Previously published in Memorandum from the Institute of Economics. Oslo: University of Oslo.

——. (1987). "Om a treffe upoulaere okonomiske tiltak" (On making unpopular economic policy decisions), *Festskrift til Eivind Erichsen* (Essays in honor of Eivind Erichsen). Oslo: Tano.

——. (1990). "Econometrics and the Welfare State," *Les Prix Nobel*. Stockholm: The Nobel Foundation.

29

Harry Markowitz (1927-   ):
A Founding Father of the Modern
Portfolio Theory and a Laureate of 1990

John M. Hasty

BIOGRAPHICAL PROFILE

Harry Markowitz was born in Chicago in 1927. He was the only child of his parents, Morris and Mildred Markowitz, who had a small grocery store. In his early life, Markowitz used to enjoy reading and playing baseball and the violin. In high school, he found accounting, astronomy, and physics pretty interesting. His undergraduate education began at the University of Chicago, where he took a two-year bachelor's program. At the upper division level, he took economics courses and was intrigued with the von Neumann-Morgenstern utility maximization under uncertainty. At Chicago, Harry Markowitz got the opportunity to learn from Friedman, Marschak, Savage, and Koopmans. He was a student member of the Cowles Commission. He continued his Ph.D. at the University of Chicago and chose "the application of mathematical methods to the stock market" to be his dissertation topic. The basic idea of the portfolio theory that Markowitz developed came to his mind when he was reading John William's theory of investment value in the library one afternoon. After finishing his Ph.D., Markowitz joined the RAND Corporation in 1952. At RAND, he worked out the details of his portfolio selection theory. At the invitation of James Tobin, Markowitz spent 1955-1956 at Yale University. In 1989, he received the von Neumann award from the Operations Research Society of America and the Institute of Management Studies. In the early 1960s, he returned to the RAND Corporation and devoted himself to developing the computer programming language SIMSCRIPT. Markowitz is still very active in computer and financial economics research.

INTRODUCTION

Harry Markowitz, along with Merton Miller and William Sharpe, won the economics Nobel Prize in 1990 for his "pioneering work in the theory of financial economics." Markowitz has applied computer and mathematical techniques to various practical decision-making areas. He is often referred to as the father of modern portfolio theory (MPT). This is based on his contributions to portfolio theory first in the article "Portfolio Selection," published in the *Journal of Finance* in 1952, and then in his book, *Portfolio Selection: Efficient Diversification of Investments,* first published in 1959. Between these two publications and since the publication of the book, Markowitz has made many other contributions using mathematical programming and computer modeling techniques to address real-world problems to aid in decisionmaking. He got the Nobel Prize for the development of the theory of portfolio choice and contributions to the theory of price formation for financial assets, the so-called Capital Asset Pricing Model (CAMP).

EMERGENCE OF THE ECONOMIST

Becoming an economist was not a childhood dream of Harry Markowitz. His first two years at the University of Chicago were spent emphasizing the reading of original material where possible. Here again, he was especially interested in the philosophers. When it was time to choose his upper-division major at the University of Chicago, after some consideration. He first went through the basics of macroeconomics, which is the big picture of the economy of a country and its governance. Then he went through microeconomics, which is the economics of individual economic units of business. After going through these basics, he found his true love, the economics of uncertainty. The concepts of expected utility, personal probability, efficiency, and efficient sets, as taught by the outstanding faculty at Chicago, inspired him to pursue his later works.

Harry Markowitz tells the story of how he stumbled up on his dissertation topic in the Personal Notes section of the third printing of his first book, *The Portfolio Selection: Efficient Diversification of Investments*. He was a student in the economics department of the University of Chicago and a research fellow of the Cowles Commission. He was sitting outside Jacob Marschak's office waiting for the opportunity to discuss suggestions for his Ph.D. dissertation topic. An older man also was waiting outside the Marschak's office and they began talking. The other man identified himself as a stockbroker and suggested that Markowitz should consider doing a dissertation on the stock market. When he later spoke to Marschak about the idea, he agreed that it was reasonable. Markowitz recalled that Alfred Cowles, the founder of the Cowles Commission, had done work in that area. Markowitz was sent to Marshall Ketchum in the Business School to get a reading list so that he could understand the theories on stock investments as revealed in the literature. The basic concepts of portfolio theory came to him one afternoon in the library while reading John Burr Williams' *The Theory of Investment Value*.

MARKOWITZ AND THE
FINANCIAL ECONOMICS

The dissertation that resulted provided the underpinnings of Modern Portfolio Theory (MPT). In reviewing Williams' work, as referred to above, Markowitz noted that he recommended that a stock be valued by finding the present value of its future dividends. His treatment of risk involved finding a large number of securities with maximum present value and divide funds among them. This treatment provided no measure of individual securities nor of the resulting portfolio. Markowitz provided the methodology for eliminating that shortcoming. His approach was to use expected return as the positive attribute of a security and the variability of the possible returns around its expected return as a measure of risk or uncertainty, the negative attribute of the security. This provided the missing risk measure for individual securities. However, the problem of the portfolio of securities also needed to be addressed. The question was, when securities are mixed into a portfolio, how will the expected return and the risk measure of the portfolio be determined? This is the next contribution that Markowitz provided in his portfolio theory.

The third ingredient needed to put the securities together in a portfolio was a methodology for handling the interaction of the respective variabilities of individual securities when mixed together in a portfolio. Quantification of this key element had been missing in investment theory up to this point. A couple of simple examples to help understand this problem follow. First, visualize taking two securities that have identical variability of returns over time. If we mix these together in a portfolio, the portfolio will look just like the two individual securities looked separately. The result is that we have not diversified away any rise by building that portfolio. Now, think about taking two securities that move in opposite directions in their variability of returns over time. As time passes, the portfolio variability of return will be less than the individual securities variability of returns because of the canceling out of the variability of one security's deviations by an opposite deviation from the other security. These are two extreme examples to illustrate the concept of diversification. In the real world, we usually have something in between these two extreme examples, but some risk reduction can be achieved by diversification. Accordingly, the portfolio's risk could be less than any of the individual securities included in the portfolio. A measure of this interaction between securities' variability is called the correlation of returns variability.

INDIVIDUAL SECURITIES AND
THEIR EXPECTED RETURNS

The next large contribution provided by Markowitz was that he was able to demonstrate mathematically that given a group of individual securities with their measures of expected returns, individual variabilities, and the correlations of their variability with the variability of each of the other securities, one could determine an efficient set of portfolios of those securities. This efficient set is the set of portfolios that have the highest expected return for any level of portfolio risk. Alternatively, it can be said that this efficient set is the set of portfolios that have the lowest portfolio risk for any level of expected return feasible with those securities. This is the cornerstone of Modern Portfolio Theory. Every textbook on investments used by colleges and universities all over the world includes the Markowitz MPT concepts. In his book, *Portfolio Selection: Efficient Diversification of Investments,* he also introduced the concept of a one-factor model. This model would reduce greatly the number of measures of correlations needed to determine portfolio risk.

According to Markowitz in the Personal Notes, By mid 1960, I had returned to the RAND Corporation. Later that year a young man named Bill Sharpe, also employed at RAND and working on his Ph.D. degree at UCLA, dropped by my office and said Professor Fred Weston thought I might have some suggestions for a dissertation topic. I pointed out the need to evaluate the one-factor model. This event may be taken as the end of the beginning of portfolio theory. Soon Sharpe, Lintner, Mossin, Treynor, Baumol, Fama, Jensen, K.V. Smith, Samuelson, Merton and others would be spearheading a surge of interest in portfolio theory and CAPMs. Having written out in Markowitz what I had to say about portfolio theory, my own interests had wandered elsewhere, namely, at that time, to the design and development of the SIMSCRIPT programming language to facilitate the building of discrete event simulators. The reference above of the CAPM is referring to the Capital Asset Pricing Model developed by Sharpe, *Capital Asset Prices: A Theory of Market Equilibrium under Conditions of Risk,* and others referred to above. Markowitz's work on SIMSCRIPT as referred to above resulted in two books on the subject. The first, in 1963, was *SIMSCRIPT: A Simulation Programming Language.* The second, in 1969, was *The SIMSCRIPT II Programming Language.*

During the 1950s, Markowitz, along with others, decided that many practical business problems were beyond analytic solution. This implied that simulation techniques were required. One of the problems with simulation models is the amount of time required to program a detailed simulator. This is the problem that he attacked in his work on SIMSCRIPT. It allowed the programmer to describe the system to be simulated rather than describing the detailed steps the computer must take to accomplish the simulation. SIMSCRIPT, would then take the system description provided by the programmer and translate it into detailed computer actions necessary. This provided a very large time savings in putting together simulation models for many kinds of business situations. Between the two books on SIMSCRIPT Markowitz, with others, published another book on economy-wide production capabilities in 1963. This book is *Studies in Process Analysis: Economy-wide Production Capabilities.* Later, in 1967, this book was published in Russian.

CONCLUSION

Two books were published in 1981 in conjunction with other authors. One introduced another computer programming language, *The EAS-E Programming Language.* The other, *Adverse Deviation,* published by the Society of Actuaries, relates to risk management. Another book on portfolio theory, *Mean Variance Analysis in Portfolio Choice and Capital Markets,* was published as a paperback in 1987 and was subsequently reprinted in 1989 and 1990. In addition to the books described above, Dr. Markowitz had chapters published in eight books prior to the Nobel Prize and has had two since then. As of the time of the Nobel Prize, he had twenty-three articles published in professional journals, and since1990, he has had seventeen more articles published in professional journals. Markowitz's contributions is one of the most difficult areas of economics and finance. He deals with the application of mathematical or computer techniques to practical problems of business decisions under uncertainty. Sometimes they applied existing techniques; other times they developed new techniques. Some of these techniques have been more successful than others, success being measured here by acceptance in practice. In his works, he leaves clear signs of originality and brilliance. The profession demands more, much more from him in the coming years.

RECOMMENDED READINGS

Markowitz, H. M. (1952, March). "Portfolio Selection," *Journal of Finance.* Vol. 7, No. l, pp. 77-91.

———. (1959). *Portfolio Selection: Efficient Diversification of Investments.* New York: Wiley.

Sharpe, W. (1964, September). "Capital Asset Prices: A Theory of Market Equilibrium Under Conditions of Risk," *Journal of Finance.* Vol. 19, pp. 425-509.

———. (1987). *Mean-Variance Analysis in Portfolio Choice and Capital Markets.* New York: Basil Blackwell.

Sharpe, W., B. Hausner and H. Karr. (1963). SIMSCRIPT: *A Simulation Programming Language.* New York: Prentice Hall.

Sharpe, W., P. Kiviat and R. Villanueva. (1969). *The Simscript II Programming Language.* New York: Prentice Hall.

Sharpe, W., A. S. Manne, et al. (1963). *Studies in Process Analysis: Economy-wide Production Capabilities.* New York: John Wiley and Sons. (Published in Russian, 1967).

Williams, J. B. (1938). *The Theory of Investment Value.* Cambridge: Harvard University Press, pp. 55-75.

30

Merton Miller (1923-2000):
A Guru of Corporate Finance
and a Laureate of 1990

Syed M. Harun
M. Kabir Hassan

BIOGRAPHICAL PROFILE

Merton Miller was born in Boston, Massachusetts, in 1923. His father was a graduate of Harvard University (B.A, 1916). Following his father's footsteps, he entered Harvard in 1940 and graduated in 1943 (B.A., magna cum laude, class of 1944). During the war years, he worked as an economist, first in the Division of Tax Research of the U.S. Treasury Department and then in the Division of Research and Statistics of the Board of Governors of the Federal Reserve System. In 1949, he decided to return to graduate school and chose Johns Hopkins University in Baltimore. His first academic appointment after receiving his doctorate from Hopkins in 1952 as a was visiting assistant lecturer at the London School of Economics for 1952-1953. From there he went to the Carnegie Institute of Technology (now Carnegie-Mellon University). In 1958, he and Franco Modigliani published the first of their joint "M&M" papers on corporation finance. In 1961, he left Carnegie for the Graduate School of Business at the University of Chicago. He was a one-year visiting professor at the University of Louvain in Belgium. In the early 1980s, he became a public director of the Chicago board of trade and his research interests shifted from corporate finance to economic and regulatory problems of the financial services industry, especially of the securities and options exchanges. He was public director of the Chicago Mercantile Exchange, where he had served earlier as chairman of its special academic panel to conduct the postmortem on the crash of October 19-20, 1987. Merton Miller died in 2000.

INTRODUCTION

Merton Miller, along with Harry Markowitz and William Sharpe, the economics Nobel Prize in 1990 for his "pioneering work in the theory of financial economics." Miller made a fundamental contribution to the theory of corporate finance and the evaluation of firms on markets. The contribution of Miller represents a decisive breakthrough for the theory of corporate finance and has had a great impact on later research in capital structure and dividend policy. Merton Miller is the guru of modern corporate finance. He, along with Franco Modigliani, revolutionized the way economists think about how corporate capital structure and dividend policy affect the value of firms. Miller and Modigliani showed, in the absence of taxes, transactions costs, and other market frictions, the choice of a firm's capital structure and dividend policy should not affect its market valuation, because investors could replicate any strategy followed by firms with regards to capital structure and dividend policy.

Since the publication of the Miller-Modigliani (MM) paper in 1958, this theory has been investigated extensively both theoretically and empirically. Theoretical papers dealt with how robust the model is to more realistic assumptions regarding market imperfections and information sets available to both stakeholders and managers of corporations. Agency cost theory developed in the 1980s just elaborated the basic propositions of capital structure theory and dividend policy.

THE MILLER-MODIGLIANI (MM) THEOREM

The Miller-Modigliani (MM) theorem states that the value of the firm can be calculated by the discounted value of its expected future returns, before interest, provided that the return on investment in shares of firms in the same risk class is used as the discount factor. This implies that the value of the firm is completely determined by this discount factor and by the return on existing assets and is independent of how these assets have been financed. It further implies that the average cost of capital is independent of the volume and structure of the debts and equal to the expected return on investment in shares of firms in the same risk class. The theorem also states that the cost of equity capital increases linearly with the leverage ratio of the firm.

The original Miller-Modigliani analysis rested on the assumptions that (1) firms could be sorted into different "risk class," (2) individual borrowing can substitute for firm borrowing (homemade leverage), (3) all market participants have full and equal information concerning the returns to the firm (there is no information asymmetry), and (4) the capital market is perfect (there are no taxes, transaction costs or bankruptcy costs). All these assumptions were crucial in proving the Miller Modigliani proposition. Miller and Modigliani showed that if two firms belong to the same risk class but differ only in their leverage, then arbitrage argument requires that the market value of the firms must be the same.

Arbitrage proofs are now common throughout finance, but Miller and Modigliani was first to apply them rigorously Two assets with identical attributes should sell for the same price, and so should an identical asset trading in two different markets. If the prices of such an asset differ, a profitable opportunity will arise to sell the asset where it is overpriced and to buy it back where it is underpriced. More formally, an arbitrage opportunity exists if it is possible to make infinite return with certainty without any investment. Using the arbitrage argument, Miller and Modigliani further showed that arbitrage will tend to equalize the market value of the firm's with equivalent earning power and riskiness regardless of how they are financed. The assumption that agents have equal access to the capital market plays a crucial role in the capital structure irrelevance proposition. In the presence of equal access, investors can create "homemade leverage" to suit their risk preference. Therefore, firms do not have to package their debt-equity ratio to make the shares of the firms more desirable to a certain class of investors.

The second Miller-Modigliani theorem states that for a given investment policy, the value of a firm is also independent of its dividend policy. A dividend increase, for instance, certainly increases shareholder's incomes, but this is neutralized by a corresponding reduction in shareholder's income. The two Miller-Modigliani theorems hold well, irrespective of individual differences between shareholders' valuation of risk, leverage effects, durability of loans, and so on. The Miller-Modigliani theorems have had important implications for the theory of investment decisions. One important implication is that investment decisions can be completely separated from corresponding financing decision. Another implication is that the rational criterion for investment decisions is a maximization of the market value of the firm. Finally, the rational concept of the cost of capital refers to total cost and should be measured as the rate of return on capital invested in shares of firms in the same risk class. The main message of the MM theorems may be expressed as follows: If there is an optimal capital structure and dividend policy for firms, in other words if the capital structure and dividend policy affect a firm's market value, then this reflects the consequences of taxes or other explicitly identified market imperfections. The MM theorems have become the natural basis or norm of comparison for theoretical and empirical analysis in corporate finance. Miller-Modigliani propositions have long been accepted in economic theory. The propositions have been extended even to areas beyond corporate finance. It has found wide application in the fields of money and banking, fiscal policy, and international finance. Interestingly, the classical economist David Ricardo first observed the irrelevance proposition in a different context. Ricardo observed that whether the government deficit is financed by issuing debt or tax finance has the same effect. This observation is known as the Ricardian equivalence. The Miller-Modigliani propositions are the logical extensions of the Ricardian Equivalence in corporate finance.

CAPITAL STRUCTURE

The Theory

Miller and Modigliani totally reshaped the research agenda in corporate finance. The earlier research in this area tried to identify the conditions under which the irrelevance propositions does not hold. As Miller has said, "Looking back now, perhaps we should have put more emphasis on the other, upbeat side of the 'nothing matters' coin: showing what *doesn't* matter can also show, by implication, what does." Both of the Miller and Modigliani theorems were originally derived under highly simplified assumptions. The conclusion that capital structure and dividend policy does not have any effect on the market value of the firm seemed to have resulted from the "unrealistic" assumptions of the model. A lot of research has been done in this respect, and researchers have identified the conditions under which the irrelevance propositions hold. Stiglitz provided a general equilibrium proof of the financial structure irrelevance. He showed that the risk class assumption could be dispensed with. In a general equilibrium context, Stiglitz proved that if there exists a positive probability of bankruptcy, then a firm's debt-equity ratio does not matter. More specifically, Stiglitz showed that if there is an equilibrium with a firm having a particular debt-equity ratio and market value, there exists another equilibrium with the firm having any other debt-equity ratio, and in the new equilibrium the firm has the same market value as it did in the original equilibrium. Extending the analysis, Stiglitz also showed that the dividend payout ratio, the maturity structure of debt, or any other aspect of its financial policy has no effect on the market value of the firm.

Another important assumption, which seems to have received little attention compared to the other assumptions, is that investors have equal access to the capital market. In the real world, investors are sometimes credit constrained, and the cost of borrowing is higher for individual investors compared to that of firms. Corporate finance generally ignored the possibility of having a credit constraint in the model, because in the perfect capital market, credit constraints cannot exist. But if firms could borrow at a lower rate than the individual investors' could, then the individual investors own net worth would be dependent on the amount of debt issued by the firm. The individual investor would not be able to costlessly undo a change in the firm's portfolio composition if it involved borrowing on his own account. In this case, the investor would prefer the firm to borrow at a preferred rate. Therefore, if individuals are credit constrained, then they will prefer a firm to have a higher debt-equity ratio.

The existence of asymmetric information also may invalidate the irrelevance propositions. In the early models with full information, debt and equity differed only in the type of risk they involved. In an imperfect information scenario, debt and equity differ in other respects, too. With asymmetric information, an agency problem arises between the debtholders and equity holders, between managers and shareholders. Because of the adverse selection and moral hazard problem related to debt issue, models have been developed that see the firm's financial structure as a solution to these problems. Firms might want to signal information through its capital structure (or dividend policy) about the true quality (riskiness, future growth prospects) of the firm. In a survey of 150 articles on non-tax based capital structure theory written after 1980, Harris and Raviv concluded, "the asymmetric information approach has reached the point of diminishing returns." This signifies the amount of work that has been done in this area regarding Miller-Modigliani propositions. The importance of the no-tax assumption was immediately evident to Miller and Modigliani in deriving the irrelevance propositions. If taxes exist, then financial structures may matter. Debt and equity are taxed differently, and according to the current tax code, debt seems to have a tax advantage over equity at both the corporate and the individual levels. Miller's paper discusses the issue. Miller showed that, in the presence of corporate taxes, the market value of a firm rises linearly with the amount of debt issued. This implies that in the presence of corporate taxes, firms should be totally debt financed.

The original Miller-Modigliani proposition about capital structure concludes that there does not exist any optimal capital structure at the individual firm level. But this does not imply that an aggregate optimal leverage ratio does not exist. In fact, in the appendix of their original version of the 1958 paper, they developed a general equilibrium macroeconomic model of the determination of aggregate real investment and aggregate debt equity ratio, which reflected the risk preferences of households for holding wealth. This appendix was later removed from the published paper because they found some irregularities in some of its equations. The foregoing discussion can be summarized by saying that the research in the last forty years in capital structure policy was aimed at formulating a theory, that would lead to an optimal capital structure at the individual firm level. Miller has actively taken a leading part in the research.

Empirical Evidence

The leverage ratio has been steadily rising for the U.S. manufacturing industry in the postwar period. Retained earnings have been the dominant funding source for the U.S. nonfinancial corporations and is steadily declining and debt-dominated equity as an external funding source. A similar trend has been observed in other developed countries. Harris and Raviv and Eckbo and Masulis summarized the empirical observations regarding capital structure. They observed that the announcement effect of secondary offering is nonpositive and negatively related to the offer size. The announcement effect is most negative for common stock and least negative (or statistically insignificant) for debt or preferred stock. The announcement effect is positive for common for debt/preferred stock exchange offer and negative for debt/preferred stock for common stock exchange offer. The announcement effect is positive for share repurchase. The empirical observations are broadly consistent with the models of capital structure policy. The conflict remains in which type of model explains the capital structure policy best.

The observed capital structures observed around the world show the following empirical regularities: (1) observed capital structures show distinct national patterns; (2) capital structures have pronounced industry patterns, and these are the same around t he world; (3) within industry, leverage is inversely related to profitability; (4) taxes clearly influence capital structures, but are not decisive alone; (5) leverage ratios appear to be inversely related to the perceived costs of financial distress; (6) existing shareholders invariably consider leverage-increasing events to be "good news" and leverage-decreasing events to be "bad news"; (7) changes in the transactions costs of issuing new securities have little apparent impact on observed capital structures; (8) ownership structure clearly seems to influence capital structures, though the true relationship is ambiguous; (9) corporations that are forced away from a preferred capital structure tend to return to the same preferred structure over time.

The first theory based on an MM theorem, called the Agency Theory/Tax Shield Trade-off Model, assumes that observed capital structures are the results of firms trading off the tax benefits of increased debt usage against increasing bankruptcy-related costs as firms approach to critical debt levels. The second theory, called the Pecking Order Hypothesis, concludes, on the basis of two assumptions, that (1). managers are better informed than outside investors and (2) managers act in the best interest of existing shareholders, that a firm may sometime forgo positive Net Present Value projects. The third model, the Signaling Model of Financial Structure, assumes information asymmetry between corporate managers and stakeholders (bondholder and stockholder) and concludes managers use costly signals to convey their firms' strength to outsiders.

DIVIDEND POLICY

The Theory

Prior to the Miller and Modigliani paper, the market value of a firm was thought to be positively related to the amount of dividend paid: The more dividend a firm pays, the more valuable the firm is. This idea was derived from the basic discounted dividend valuation approach to the firm. Miller and Modigliani showed that in a perfect capital market, the firm's dividend policy is irrelevant: dividend policy has no effect on firm value. Miller and Modigliani argued that firm value is determined by the investment policy of the firm, not by the financing or dividend policy. From investors' perspective, dividend policy is irrelevant, because an investor can obtain the desired amount of payment by the appropriate sale/purchase of the equity they own. From the firm's perspective, dividend policy is irrelevant because a firm can pay out any amount of dividend by an appropriate share issue/repurchase. Miller and Modigliani developed a dividend policy framework, which is consistent with firms maximizing profit and investors maximizing utility. The basic insight gained from the Miller-Modigliani model is that firm value is maximized by an optimal investment policy; dividend policy has no effect on firm value.

The Miller-Modigliani model of dividend policy was developed under the assumption of a perfect and complete capital market with no taxes, no transaction costs, symmetric information, and complete contracts. As in the case of capital structure policy, the situations, that lead to dividend relevancy are the situations when any or some of these crucial assumptions are violated. A large body of literature has focused on the issue of taxes and dividend policy. The tax-related literature tried to see if any tax effect exists: If dividends are taxed at a higher rate than capital gains from repurchases, then the optimal payout policy for corporations is to pay out through share repurchases. In the presence of asymmetric information between insiders and outsiders, dividends can play a role in signaling the insider's valuation of the firm to the market: Dividend has an information content. Again Miller played a significant role in developing a model of dividend signaling. Miller and Rock showed that under asymmetric information, a firm will pay a higher dividend to signal high future earnings even if they have to reduce investment. Increasing the dividend is good news for a firm because it reflects the positive earning potential of the firm.

In the absence of complete contracting possibilities, dividend policy may reflect the agency conflict between the shareholders and bondholders. Shareholders can increase dividend payments by reducing investment or by raising more debt. In either case, shareholder is trying to expropriate bondholder's wealth. Therefore, increasing dividends are good news for the shareholders but bad news for the bondholders. Another potential agency conflict is between managers and shareholders in the presence of free cash flow. Higher dividend is good because, by paying out dividends, the amount of free cash available to the managers is reduced, and therefore the possibility of overinvestment is reduced.

Empirical Evidence

Allen and Michaely summarized the empirical evidence regarding dividend policy. According to them, dividend has always been the dominant form of corporate payout policy, and a significant portion of corporate earnings are paid out as dividends; corporations seem to try to smooth dividends; individuals pay a huge amount of taxes on dividends: and market reacts favorably to an announcement of dividend increase, while it reacts negatively to a dividend decrease announcement. Unfortunately, the empirical evidence regarding dividend is mixed: It is not known why firms pay dividends when share repurchases are more cost effective in providing signals to the market; we do not know why firms pay dividends when dividends have a tax-disadvantage compared to repurchases. Definitely, much more theoretical and empirical research is needed in this area.

CONCLUSION

Merton Miller will be remembered for his contribution to the way we now think about corporate finance. One striking result is that corporate value comes from a firm's activities, not from reshuffling between debt and equity of financing corporate activities. Miller is an avid promoter of free-market solutions to economic problems, very much in the same tradition of his fellow Chicago laureates, Milton Friedman, Theodore Schultz, and George Stigler. Miller has influenced a generation of finance academics. As Bhattacharya puts it, the key methodological contributions of the three MM seminal papers are (1) introduction of riskless class (set of payoff patterns mutually replicable through trading) idea;

(2) consideration of investor arbitrage (homemade leverage) in pricing securities; (3) initiation of integrated after-tax analyses of dividend and debt supply policies of firms; (4) consideration of empirical evidence and introduction of "respectable" econometric methods in corporate finance; and (5) planning seeds for economic modeling of unexplained phenomenon such as "information content" of dividend and debt policies. Financial economics blends theory and practice, which the rest of the economics profession should emulate. Miller, along with his co-authors, has established a research agenda that will influence economists for decades in the future. A systematic exploration of market "irrationalities" should be the new wave of research in corporate finance.

RECOMMENDED READINGS

Allen, F.B., R. Michaely. (1995). "Divident Policy," in Jarrow, et.al. (Eds.) *Finance Handbooks in Operations Research and Management Science*. Vol. 9, Amsterdam: NorthHolland. pp. 793-838.

Black, Fischer, Merton H. Miller, Richard A. Posner. (1978, July). " An Approach to the Regulation of Bank Holding Companies," *Journal of Business*. Vol. 51, No. 3, pp. 379-412.

——. (1977). "Debt and Taxes," *Journal of Finance*. Vol. 32, No. 2, pp. 261-75.

——. (1977, autumn). "The Wealth Transfers of Bankruptcy: Some Illustrative Examples," *Law and Contemporary Problems*. Vol. 41, No. 4, pp. 39-46.

Miller, Merton H. (1977). "Debt and Taxes,"*Journal of Finance*. Vol. 32, No. 2, pp. 261-75.

——. (1988). "The Modigliani-Miller Propositions After Thirty Years," *Journal of Economic Perspectives*. Vol. 2, No. 4, pp. 99-120.

——. (1991). "Leverage," *Journal of Finance*. Vol. 46, No. 2, pp. 479-88.

Miller, Merton, and Franco Modigliani. (1961). "Dividend Policy, Growth and the Valuation of Shares," *Journal of Business*. Vol. 34, 4, pp. 411-33.

——. (1966). "Some Estimates of the Cost of Capital to the Utility Industry 1954-57," *American Economic Review*. Vol. 56, No. 3, pp. 333-91.

——. (1961). "Dividend Policy, Growth and the Valuation of Shares," *Journal of Business*. Vol. 34, No. 4, pp. 411-33.

Miller, Merton H., Jayaram Muthuswamy and Robert E.Whasley. (1994, June). "Mean Reversion of Standard & Poor's 500 Index Basis Changes: Arbitrage-Induced or Statistical Illusion?" *Journal of Finance*. Vol. 49, No. 2, pp. 479-513.

——. (1993, December). "The Regulation of Financial Markets," *Hitotsubashi Journal of Commerce and Management*. Vol. 28, No. 1, pp. 1-14.

——. (1992). "Volatility, Episodic Volatility and Coordinated Circuit Breakers: The Sequel," in Ghon S. Rhee and Rosita P. Chang, (eds.) *Pacific-Basin Capital Markets Research*. Vol. 3. Amsterdam: North-Holland.

Miller, Merton H, and Daniel Orr. (1990). "A Model of the Demand for Money by Firms," in Thomas Mayer, (ed.) *Monetary Theory*. International Library of Critical Writings in Economics, No. 7, Aldershot, UK and Brookfield, VT: Edward Elgar, pp. 15-37. Originally published in 1966.

————. (1990). "The Crash of 1987: Bubble or Fundamental?" in S. Ghon Rhee and Rosita P. Chang, (eds.) *Pacific-Basin Capital Markets Research*. Amsterdam, Oxford, and Tokyo: North-Holland, pp. 27-40.

————. (1989, December). "Volatility, Price Resolution, and the Effectiveness of Price Limits: Commentary," *Journal of Financial Services Research*. Vol. 3, Nos. 2-3, pp. 201-3.

————. (1988). "The Modigliani-Miller Propositions After Thirty Years," *Journal of Economic Perspectives*. Vol. 2, No. 4, pp. 99-120.

————. (1988). "Explaining the Events of October 1987," in Robert J. MacKay, (ed.) *After the Crash: Linkages between Stocks and Futures*. AEI Studies, No. 477. Washington, D.C.: American Enterprise Institute for Public Policy Research, pp. 17-21.

————. (1987). "The Informational Content of Dividends," in Dornbusch, Fischer, and Bossons, eds. *Macroeconomics and Finance: Essays in Honor of Franco Modigliani*. Cambridge: MIT Press, pp. 37-58.

————. (1986, December). "Financial Innovation: The Last Twenty Years and the Next," *Journal of Financial and Quantitative Analysis*. Vol. 21, No. 4, pp. 459-71.

————. (1986, October). "Behavioral Rationality in Finance: The Case of Dividends," *Journal of Business*. Vol. 59, No. 4 part 2, pp. S451-68.

Modigliani, Franco. (1988). "MM – Past, present and Future," *Journal of Economic Perspectives*. Vol. 2, No. 4, pp. 149-58.

————. (1998). "Asian Financial Crisis," *Japan and the World Economy*. Vol. 10, No. 3, pp. 355-58.

————. (1998). "The Current Southeast Asia Financial Crisis," *Pacific-Basin Finance Journal*. Vol. 6, Nos. 3-4:, pp. 225-33.

————. (1997). "The Future of Futures," *Pacific-Basin Finance Journal*. Vol. 5, No. 2, pp. 131-42.

————. (1995). "The 1987 Crash Five Years Later: What Have We Learned?" in Dilip Ghosh, K. Khaksari Shahriar, (eds.) *New Directions in Finance*. London and New York: Routledge.

————. (1995, June). "Do the M&M Propositions Apply to Banks?" *Journal of Banking and Finance*. Vol. 19, Nos. 3-4, pp. 483-89.

Miller, Merton, and Kevin Rock. (1985). "Dividend Policy under Asymmetric Information," *Journal of Finance*. Vol. 40, pp. 1031-51.

Miller, Merton, and Myron Scholes. (1982). "Dividends and Taxes: Some Empirical Evidence," *Journal of Political Economics*. Vol. 90, No. 6, pp. 1118-41.

————. (1978). "Dividends and Taxes," *Journal of Financial Economics*. Vol. 6, No. 4, pp. 333-64.

Miller, Merton H., and Charles W. Upton. (1985, July). "The Pricing of Oil and Gas: Some Further Results," *Journal of Finance*. Vol. 40, No. 3, pp. 1009-18.

————. (1985). A Test of the Hotelling Valuation Principle, *Journal of Political Economy*. Vol. 93, No. 1, pp. 1-25.

————. (1976, June). "Leasing, Buying, and the Cost of Capital Services," *Journal of Finance*. Vol. 31, No. 3, pp. 761-86.

Modigliani, Franco and Merton Miller. (1958). "The Cost of Capital, Corporation Finance and the Theory of Investment," *American Economic Review.* Vol. 48, No. 3, pp. 261-97.

———.(1991). "The Nobel Memorial Prize in Economics 1990: This Year's Laureates Are Pioneers in the Theory of Financial Economics and Corporate Finance," *Scandinavian Journal of Economics.* Vol. 93, No. 1, pp. 4-6.

———. (1990, December). "International Competitiveness of U.S. Futures Exchanges," *Journal of Financial Services Research.* Vol. 4, No. 4, pp. 387-408.

———. (1972, May). "Money and Stock Prices: The Channels of Influence: Discussion," *Journal of Finance.* Vol. 27, No. 2, pp. 294-98.

———. (1963a). "The Corporate Income Taxes and the Cost of Capital: A Correction," *American Economic Review.* Vol. 53, No. 3, pp. 433-43.

———. (1963b). "The Corporate Income Tax and Corporate Financial Policies," in *Stabilization Policies*, The Commission on Money and Credit. Englewood Cliffs: Prentice Hall, pp. 381-470.

31

William Sharpe (1934-):
A Founder of the Capital Asset Pricing
Model (CAPM) and a Laureate of 1990

Linda L. Carr

BIOGRAPHICAL PROFILE

William Sharpe was born in Boston, Massachusetts, in 1934. Prior to his birth, his parents had completed their undergraduate educations. His mother's degree was in science and his father's degree was in English literature. His father was employed in the placement office of Harvard University. When his father's national guard unit was activated as a result of world events in 1940, the family moved to Texas and, subsequently, to California. Sharpe attended public schools in Riverside, California, which he considered to be excellent. Even as a young student, Sharpe appreciated the stimulating teachers and challenging curricula. Sharpe credits his parents and step-parents with teaching him by example: They all continued their educations in mid-career. His father retired as a college president, his mother as an elementary school principle, and his step-father was a public defender. Sharpe's wife is an accomplished painter and serves as the administrator of William F. Sharpe Associates. Sharpe's original intention upon enrollment at the University of California at Berkeley was to follow in his mother's footsteps and major in science. He planned to pursue subsequently a medical degree. After a year of this plan of courses, he decided to change his major and his environment. He transferred to the University of California at Los Angeles (UCLA) and declared a major in business administration. There he was greatly impressed by the rigor and relevance of economic theory. Eventually, Sharpe was named to Phi Beta Kappa for his accomplishments in pursuit of his bachelor of arts degree in economics in 1955. After earning his master of arts degree in economics in 1956, he served in the army for a short period. Sharpe joined the RAND Corporation as an economist in 1956. He appreciated the atmosphere at RAND and learned computer programming. Work was also being done in the areas of game theory, linear programming, dynamic programming, and applied economics at RAND. While at RAND, Sharpe pursued a Ph.D. degree in economics at UCLA. His dissertation concerned the economics of transfer prices, and Armen Alchian, professor of economics at UCLA and Sharpe's role model, was chairman of his dissertation committee. Following Alchian's suggestion, Sharpe consulted with Harry Markowitz, then a RAND employee, about his dissertation topic. Sharpe and Markowitz subsequently worked closely together on the topic *Portfolio Analysis Based on a Simplified Model of the Relationships Among Securities.* Sharpe gives great credit to Markowitz for his advisement during the dissertation process, although he was not a committee member. Sharpe received his Ph.D. in 1961.

INTRODUCTION

William Sharpe won the economics Nobel Prize in 1990, along with Harry Markowitz and Merton Miller, for his "pioneering work in the theory of financial economics." Sharpe is one of the first financial economists who received the Nobel Prize in economics. He has been known as the founder of the Capital Asset Pricing Model (CAPM). He also made invaluable contributions to the portfolio theories and securities analysis.

MODERN PORTFOLIO THEORY

Sharpe is considered to be one of the main architects of Modern Portfolio Theory. He investigated the relationship between the investment risk and reward in his doctoral thesis. Later on, the main finding of his thesis was published in the *Journal of Finance* and became known as the Capital Asset Pricing Model. Markowitz's original work required that the covariance or the correlation between each stock and every other stock be calculated in order to measure the relevant risk inherent in each stock. This required complicated calculations of covariances among stocks. Sharpe's main contribution in his thesis was to extend Markowitz's argument on the efficient frontier of optimal investment and combine it with James Tobin's separation theorem. In this way, he managed to bypass Markowitz's complicated computer calculations and came up with a practical way to price risky financial assets. The key concept stressed by Sharpe in the CAPM illuminates the mechanism by which financial markets determine the price for both individual securities and investment portfolios. Sharpe argued that for investors in financial markets, risk is the variability of the security's return.

CAPITAL ASSET PRICING
MODEL (CAPM)

Sharpe's main contribution in finance is published in his article, "Capital Asset Prices: A Theory of Market Equilibrium Under Conditions of Risk." In CAPM,

Sharpe suggested that the total variability of return, or variance, could be divided into two parts: a systematic or nondiversifiable component, and an unsystematic or diversifiable component. Financial investors, through diversification of their portfolios, can eliminate the unsystematic component of the variance of their return. The market thus provides a reward to a rational investor only for bearing the systematic component of the risk, known as market risk. In other words, the security's return is actually a compensation or a premium for bearing the nondiversifiable component of the risk of the investment, since the rational investors can eliminate the-firm specific risk through a well-diversified portfolio. A rational investor would expect to be compensated for bearing the market risk, thus the greater the market risk of a security, the higher the required return from that security. Market risk of a stock is measured by the beta coefficient. Beta captures the sensitivity of a stock's return in relation to some market index. The higher the beta, the riskier the stock return, compared to the market index. For example, a beta of two for a stock suggests that the stock's return is two times more volatile than the general market portfolio return. Since the volatility of the stock is two times greater than the market, an investor would expect a rate of return on the stock that is two times greater than the average return on the market.

The relationship between risk and return is efficiently summarized in the Security Market Line (SML) Equation. The SML Equation consists of the risk-free rate, plus beta times the market risk premium. The risk-free rate is generally measured by the one-year treasury rate. The risk premium of the market is the difference between expected market return and the risk-free rate. CAPM, as developed by Sharpe, provided a mechanism for empirically measuring the systematic risk of a security through a simple linear regression equation. Since its inception, CAPM has become one of the most widely used approaches for determining the equilibrium return of various equities.

CONCLUSION

Sharpe is considered, along with Linter, Mossin, and Treynor, to be one of the main architects of Modern Portfolio Theory. Sharpe's CAPM is known as a single-factor asset pricing model because it singles out market return as the main explanatory factor responsible for the fluctuation in share prices. Sharpe's results are an elegant way of capturing the notion that a higher return is the reward for assuming higher risk, and only the type of risk that you cannot eliminate through diversification. This result, as simple as it may seem, is based on rigorous mathematical analyses. Sharpe provided a powerful yet simple analytical tool to solve a very complicated dynamic investment question. Sharpe, among others, tried to expand the number of independent variables that might further help to explain the fluctuation in share price. His efforts in this area continue to this day. He has created a website that helps individual investors to determine the appropriate risk-return combination for their portfolios.

RECOMMENDED READINGS

Lee, Cheng-Few. (1991). "Markowitz, Miller and Sharpe: The First Nobel Laureates in Finance," *Review of Quantitative Finance and Accounting*. Vol. 1, pp. 209-28.

Mac Queen, Jason. (1986). *Beta is Dead. Long Live Beta. The Revolution in Corporate Finance*. (eds.) Joel M. Stern and Donald H. Chew Jr. New York: Basil Blackwell Inc.

Royal Swedish Academy of Sciences. (1990)."This Year's Laureates are Pioneers in the Theory of Financial Economics and Corporate Finance," Press release–The Sveriges.

Riskbank (Bank of Sweden) Prize in Economic Sciences in Memory of Alfred Nobel. Home Page of the Nobel Foundation.–<webmaster@www.nobel.se/>. February 25, 1997.

Sharpe, William. (1961). "A Simplified Model for Portfolio Analysis," *Management Science*. pp. 277-93.

——. (1964, September). "Capital Asset Prices: A Theory of Market Equilibrium Under Conditions of Risk," *The Journal of Finance*. pp. 425-42.

——. (1970). *Portfolio Theory and Capital Markets*. New York: McGraw-Hill Inc.

——. (1985). *Investments*. Third edition. New Jersey: Prentice Hall.

——. (1991, June). "Capital Asset Prices With and Without Negative Holdings," *The Journal of Finance*. pp. 489-509.

——. (1997). William Sharpe's Home Page, <http://www-sharpe.stanford.edu>

Varian, Hal. (1993, winter) "A Portfolio of Nobel Laureates: Markowitz, Miller and Sharpe," *Journal of Economic Perspective*. pp. 159-69.

<http://www.nobel.se/laureates/economy-1990-3-autobio.html>

32

Ronald Coase (1910-   ):
A Pioneer of the Economics of Property Rights
and the Economics of Law and the Laureate of 1991

Saud A. Choudhry

BIOGRAPHICAL PROFILE

Ronald Coase was born in Willesden, a suburb of London, England, in 1910. He passed his matriculation examination (high school graduation) in 1927, with distinction in history and chemistry. At the University of London, his first inclination was to study history. But since history's entrance requirements called for a knowledge of Latin that he did not have, he turned to the other subject in which he had secured distinction–chemistry. However, on discovering that chemistry was not his cup of tea, he switched to commerce. In October 1929, he transferred to the London School of Economics to continue his studies for a bachelor of commerce degree. Coase first visited the United States as a twenty-year-old on a travelling scholarship (the Sir Ernest Cassel Travelling Scholarship). This trip, which was devoted to examining the structure of American industries and studying why industries were organized in different ways, eventually led the way to his becoming an economist. He shared his newly acquired insights in a lecture delivered in Dundee, Scotland in October 1932. Eventually these ideas formed the basis of his article, "The Nature of the Firm," published in 1937 and cited sixty years later by the Royal Swedish Academy of Sciences as his main contribution to economics. Coase migrated to the United States in 1951 and has held positions at the University of Buffalo, the University of Virginia, and since 1964, the Law School at the University of Chicago. At Chicago, he was also appointed editor of the Journal of Law and Economics, a position that he held until 1982. Professor Coase continues his lifelong affiliation with academia. In a recent interview, he advised today's students of economics "to look at the world and find problems they'd like to work on. Start by trying to frame the problem well and then learn along the way what techniques of analysis you will need to know to solve it." These words very succinctly describe Coase's lifelong approach to economic issues and controversies. He started off in his early twenties by taking a stroll in the real world, studying the real problems of the economic system. He relied more on intuition and common sense than on complex mathematical analysis, which he says, is "unable ... to analyse the real economic system" and ends up instead "inventing imaginary ones." Little wonder that the insights and arguments that he developed along life's meandering path continue to receive scholarly attention even half a century later.

INTRODUCTION

Ronald Coase won the economics Nobel Prize in 1991 for his "discovery and clarification of the significance of transaction costs and property rights for the institutional structure and functioning" of the economy .For the connoisseur on a chance visit to the London School of Economics in the 1930s, the reward would be an intellectual feast like no other. With the likes of John Hicks, Roy Allen, Nicholas Kaldor, Friedrich Hayek, and Lionel Robbins on staff, every point of view was represented on the faculty, and the school was the acknowledged front-runner in the development and worldwide expansion of neoclassical economics. But while its students studiously struggled to keep pace with the enormous output of new and interesting ideas, little did they know that they were harboring in their midst two future Nobel laureates–Arthur Lewis and Ronald Coase.

The other similarities between these two great contemporaries are even more striking. Arthur Lewis is on record admitting that he never meant to be an economist. He became one when he really wanted to be an engineer, took up teaching because there was nothing else to do, and became an applied economist because his mentor (Arnold Plant) was one. Likewise, his fellow student at the London School of Economics, Ronald Coase, had no initial desire to be an economist. As an undergraduate, most of his courses were in accounting, statistics, and law and had nothing to do with economics. Then one fateful day in 1931, Ronald Coase attended a seminar by the same Arnold Plant, and a future Nobel laureate was born.

THE NATURE OF THE FIRM

Coase was intrigued by Plant's explanation of Adam Smith's "invisible hand" and how the whole economic system was coordinated by a price mechanism leading producers to produce things that consumers valued most at the lowest possible cost. He was puzzled by Plant's opposition to economic planning and his assertion that the pricing mechanism, acting through competition, would provide all the coordination the economy needed. "If pricing did it," Coase wondered, "why do we have management?" The foundations were thus formed for his first published work, "The Nature of the Firm," which appeared in *Economica* in 1937.

"The Nature of the Firm," which attracted little attention when it first appeared, posed an innocent question: If the price mechanism does it all, why do we have management whose function is to coordinate? In other words, why do business firms exist? Coase's answer pioneered a general approach that is now widely used to determine whether specific production activities will be coordinated inside a multiperson firm or through the marketplace by means of transactions among vertically interrelated firms or by a hybrid of the two. The choice, Coase argued, will depend on the relative costs of the competing options. To simplify his argument, a firm will equate at the margin. That is, it will expand to the point at which the organizational cost of adding another in-house function is just equal to the transaction cost of coordinating that function through the marketplace. Coase's idea was revolutionary because this was the first time that anyone had focussed on the "costs" of using the market mechanism. To illustrate his theory, let us classify inputs entering into the production process into two categories generic and specific, and examine the transaction costs associated with each.

GENERIC INPUTS

Consider a bakery that uses flour as an input. If the flour produced in-house is identical to the flour produced elsewhere, flour becomes a generic input as different sources of it are interchangeable. The flour market will then be composed of many sellers (millers) and many buyers (numerous bakeries both big and small). In such markets, Coase points out, one can distinguish between the activities coordinated in-house from those coordinated through markets by simply comparing their respective costs.

SPECIFIC INPUTS

In some production processes, inputs are not generic but specific. Consider, for instance, a parts manufacturer producing door locks for Toyota Corollas. This specific input is of no use to anyone but the Toyota Motor Company. Hence, there is no other market for this input in the ordinary sense of the word. There may be more than one producer, but there will be only one buyer. Hence, suppliers of firm-specific inputs will not engage in production merely on speculation that the lone demander will buy their products. Likewise, the buyer of a specific input is dependent on his suppliers. His business will be affected adversely if the supplier fails to produce the inputs according to specifications or to make deliveries on time or at prices agreed upon at an earlier date. The consequence of all this is that detailed and legally binding contractual agreements must be entered into whenever a firm acquires a specific input from another. But such agreements are costly. Hence, there is a bias toward in-house production whenever specific inputs are involved.

The full impact of Coase's revolutionary idea became evident years later. Today it is used to explain, for instance, how Nabisco decides whether to buy raw wheat and process its own flour or to buy flour from another farmer and how the Campbell Soup Company decides whether to produce and process its own fried eggs or to buy them from another firm. Coase's explanation is that when the transaction costs of coordinating these activities through markets becomes too high, businesses find that it pays to replace the market by opting for more in-house production. The firm size thus increases, and this in turn adds to costs. Since these costs increase as the firm expands in size, there is a limit on how large a firm can grow. Beyond that optimal size, the firm finds that it pays to farm out additional transactions to outside firms.

RELEVANCE OF HIS THEOREM

The relevance of Coase's theory is all too transparent. In today's economy, transactions and coordination costs sometimes outweigh the production costs of many goods and services. By economizing on the former, a new firm can easily find a niche for itself, thereby threatening the market shares of older, established rivals. A favorite example in this category is the seasonal painting firm College Pro. By locating customers in the spring and hiring students during the summer vacation, College Pro has effectively reduced transaction costs for both students and homeowners. Little wonder therefore, that it has made such great inroads into the business of professional home painters.

Ronald Coase has written only one book and approximately eighteen articles over a long academic career. Astonishingly, only two papers from this short list–"The Nature of the Firm" and "The Problem of Social Cost" (published in the *Journal of Law and Economics*, 1960)–form the foundations of his formidable reputation. The second paper (on social costs) is notable as the first systematic discussion of how well-defined property rights can allocate resources efficiently in situations involving externalities. It is also one of the most widely read papers in the history of economics.

INTERNALIZATION OF
EXTERNALITIES

In Coase's view, the cause's of resource misallocations are various "technological externalities" –the situations where market activities generate harmful or beneficial side-effects (externalities) on people who are not directly involved in these market exchanges. Externalities thus represent costs and benefits that are not incorporated into the private supply and demand curves that guide economic activity. For instance, if your neighbour sprays chemical fertilizers on his lawn and the rain washes most of it onto your lawn, an externality occurs. If the chemicals burn your grass, a negative externality occurs; if they enhance your lawn you will receive a positive externality. Life is full of such externalities, ranging from the trivial (your next-door neighbour owns the ugliest house on the block) to the more momentous (a chemical company dumps its waste into the river, killing fish and increasing the incidence of cancer in communities living downstream). If the polluting firm is not charged for these damages, the wastes are effectively being removed at zero charge to the polluter. The polluter is then induced to pollute a great deal resulting in the over-production of a "bad" and hence a gross mis-allocation of societal resources. Clearly the reason that pollution issues such as this are so difficult to resolve is that they are rife with problems of externality, which in turn stems from the fact that clear property rights do not exist. Who owns the air or the rivers: the general public or the owners of the firms that discharge the waste? Ronald Coase attempted to resolve the dilemma by demonstrating that with well-defined property rights in externalities, bargaining can achieve an efficient pattern of resource use. This has now been generalized into what is known as the Coase Theorem, which may be stated as follows:

THE "INVISIBLE HAND"

"Regardless of the specific initial assignment of property rights, in market equilibrium the final outcome will be efficient–provided that the initial legal assignment is well-defined and that transactions involving exchange of rights are costless." The appeal of Coase's Theorem is that it assigns a minimal role to government. The government simply assigns property rights and then leaves the efficient outcomes to markets. The theorem's basic thrust is that Adam Smith's "Invisible Hand" is much more effective than the argument about externalities at first suggests. There are natural market forces that tend to bring externalities into the calculations of the parties involved. If a producer initially owns the right to generate a negative externality, parties adversely affected can offer him financial compensation for not exercising that right. Conversely, if the affected parties are initially entitled to protection from the negative externality, it is up to the producer to offer terms of compensation at which they will accept a measure of harm. (The argument applies in reverse in the event of a positive externality.) As long as the legal rights are well-defined and marketable, market forces will lead the parties to an efficient outcome, in other words, to a result that exhausts all possibilities for further mutual gain. The following court case will provide a real-life illustration of the essence of the Coase Theorem.

The case–Spur Industries vs. Del Webb–involved a housing developer, Del Webb, and a cattle feedlot owned by Spur Industries. The developer had built a retirement community advertised as offering fine homes, quality air, spectacular views, community recreational facilities, and so on. The feedlot on the other hand, was a profitable business allowing cattle to complete the growing cycle under professional inspection before being herded off to the market. Initially, the feedlot was located at some distance from the residential community. But as the latter expanded, the feedlot began to impose negative externalities on the retiree population in the form of pungent odors and a large fly population–both of which increased the potential for other illnesses. As the complaints became common knowledge, Del Webb discovered that it was affecting the sale of its new homes. Finally, the developer decided to take action by seeking a court injunction to force Spur to cease its feedlot operations.

The court's solution turned out to be an ingenious application of the Coase Theorem. The judge recognized that although Webb's development of the retirement community fulfilled a very real need for housing, the feedlot was also a very profitable operation and one that had been there first. By seeking an injunction, the developer was attempting to recruit the court's help in eliminating the feedlot at no cost to himself. The judge's solution was to issue a purchased injunction. This meant that the court issued injunction against the operation of the feedlot would become effective only after Webb had made a payment to Spur, adequate enough to pay for Spur's exit. In other words, the payment would have to equal a reasonable estimate of Spur's lost profit due to the exit plus all moving costs. The end result was that the feedlot exited after receiving a monetary compensation from Webb. The purchased injunction order had forced Webb to reveal (by monetary payment) that the benefit to him of halting the feedlot externalities exceeded the benefit to Spur of continuing operations in that location. In the negotiations that transpired, Webb would find it self-defeating to overstate the value of Spur's exit; Spur was also prevented from overstating its expected lost profit in order to hold out for an inefficient combination of housing and feedlots. The purchased injunction thus solved an important information problem by creating a forum in which bargaining between the parties forced them to reveal their respective benefits and, in the process to internalize the feedlot externality. This was Coasian bargaining at its best, demonstrating the invisible hand's ability to facilitate value-increasing exchange and guiding resources to their most useful uses.

THE COASE THEOREM
AND THE GOVERNMENTS

The Coase Theorem applies not only to people but to governments as well. This was evident in the September 1987 agreement between feuding city officials of New York and New Jersey, over garbage spills. The problem, which had been brewing for many years, involved garbage leaking from New York's waterfront trash facilities and, thus, affecting the quality of water along the New Jersey shore. The worst incident occurred when more than 200 tons of garbage formed a fifty-mile-long slick off New Jersey's shores. Under the circumstances, New Jersey could sue New York City for damages associated with garbage spills. It could also approach the courts asking for an injunction prohibiting New York City from using its trash facilities. But what New Jersey really wanted was cleaner beaches, not simply monetary compensation for damages suffered. New York, on the other hand, wanted to be able to operate its trash facility. Since there was room for mutually beneficial exchange, two weeks of intense negotiations finally resulted in a settlement. New Jersey agreed not to bring a lawsuit against New York City. The city, on its part, agreed to adopt special measures to contain future spills. It also agreed to create a monitoring team to survey all trash facilities and shut down those that failed to comply. Simultaneously, New Jersey officials were granted unlimited access to New York's trash facilities to monitor the effectiveness of the program.

When problems are fairly localized, agreements such as the above are feasible, even if more than one country is involved. A case in point is the acid rain controversy, created by emissions of sulphur dioxide and nitrogen oxides from the fossilfuel-burning smokestacks of industry in Ontario, Canada, and the northern

United States. These oxides mix with water vapour in the air to form weak sulphuric acid and nitric acid, which later falls as acid rain. It was alleged that 50 percent of the acid rain that falls in Canada comes from American sources and that about 10 percent of the acid rain that falls in the eastern United States comes from Canada. It is the latter that convinced the Americans about the potential for mutually beneficial exchange, and eventually led them to agree to discuss the issue. Unless both the United States and Canada were affected, it would not pay the American (or Canadian) owner of a smelter for processing nickel ore, for instance, to construct a costly smokestack that reduces sulphur dioxide emissions just so that the lakes and forests across the border would be protected. Not surprisingly, therefore, in the negotiations to limit acid rain, the governments of Ontario, New York State, Canada, and the United States all agreed to limit this pollution by 50 percent by 1996. However, when even more jurisdictions are involved, agreements become harder to reach. For instance, Germany and Austria routinely complain about acid rain and river contaminations originating in the Czech Republic and Slovakia, yet nothing has been done to resolve the problem.

In the final analysis, these examples go to demonstrate, as the Coase Theorem suggests, that if the polluter and the victim can bargain easily and effectively, even private negotiations should result in an efficient outcome regardless of who has the initial right to pollute or prevent pollution. Some people have even interpreted the Coase Theorem to imply that it does not matter from an efficiency perspective who has to pay for pollution–victims or polluters. Either way, one arrives at an efficient solution. In fact, however, efficiency will be better served under a "polluter pays principle," because if firms are given the right to pollute (or are subsidised to reduce pollution), this lowers their costs. In the long run this encourages entry into the industry, thereby creating even higher levels of pollution. The situation is similar to the one where taxpayers at large pay for the construction of landfills, leaving individual households and firms with little long-run incentive to minimise their production of waste.

CONCLUSION

Though he was a far less prolific producer than most of his fellow Nobel laureates, economics owes the birth of two rapidly growing subdisciplines–the economics of property rights and the economics of law–to Ronald Coase. The origins of both can be traced directly to his 1960 paper, "The Problem of Social Cost." This is an extraordinary accomplishment, considering that it is only rarely that a single article generates an entire branch of economics, much less two branches. Perhaps even more striking is the fact that in an age that increasingly stresses the hard quantitative nature of economic science, Coase's path-breaking paper contains no diagrams or equations. Instead, it is full of quotes from lawyers and judges, proving once again that most of the important questions in economics remain questions of interpretation, advocacy, and plain common sense.

RECOMMENDED READINGS

Blaug, M.. (1978). *Economic Theory in Retrospect*. Cambridge: Cambridge: University Press.

——. (1985). *Great Economists Since Keynes*. Sussex: Wheatsheaf Books.

Coase, R.H. (1937). "The Nature of the Firm," *Economica*. Vol. 4, pp. 386-05.

——. (1960). "The Problem of Social Cost," *Journal of Law and Economics*. Sussex, England. Vol. 3, pp. 1-44.

33

Gary Becker (1930-):
A Champion of the Economics of Household, Marriage, and Divorce and the Laureate of 1992

Mobinul Huq

BIOGRAPHICAL PROFILE

Gary Becker was born in Pottsville, a small coal-mining town in eastern Pennsylvania in 1930. His father left school after eighth grade and moved to the United States from Montreal to run his own small business. His mother, an emigrant from Eastern Europe, also left school after the eighth grade. The Becker family moved to Brooklyn, New York, when Gary was about five years old. He started his university education at Princeton University and in three years completed his BA in economics in 1951. For his graduate studies in economics, Becker went to the University of Chicago and obtained his MA in 1952 and his Ph.D. in 1955. Becker wrote his doctoral dissertation on the economics of discrimination under the supervision of Milton Friedman. After his third year of graduate studies, Becker became an assistant professor at the University of Chicago, where he stayed for three years. In 1957, Becker accepted a position at Columbia University and moved to New York. During the period between 1957 and 1968 Becker divided his time between teaching at Columbia and doing research at the National Bureau of Economic Research. In 1970, he returned to the University of Chicago as a professor in economics and in 1983 accepted a joint appointment in the sociology department. Becker was the president of the American Economic Association in 1987. He holds honorary degrees from a number of universities, including Hebrew University, Princeton University, and Columbia University. In the year 2000, Becker received the United States National Medal of Science for his work in social policy. Gary Becker is currently the Rose-Marie and Jack R. Anderson Senior Fellow at the Hoover Institute, and

University Professor of Economics and Sociology at the University of Chicago. He writes a monthly column for Business Week magazine. Becker's first wife died in 1970, and in 1980 he married Guity Nashat, a historian with similar professional interests in the areas of role of the women and economic growth.

INTRODUCTION

Gary Becker won the economics Nobel Prize in 1992 for "having extended the domain of microeconomic analysis to a wide range of human behaviour and interaction, including nonmarket behaviour." In announcing the Nobel award for Becker, the Swedish Academy stated that they honoured Becker for "extending the sphere of economic analysis to new areas of human behavior and relations." Becker's application of economic tools to social issues, traditionally considered beyond the domain of economists, allowed us to better understand a wide range of individual behavior as well as the aggregate social implications of such issues. As Ramon Febrero and Pedro Schwartz put it, "Gary Becker's contributions to economics are anything but conventional. Becker is without doubt a leading figure in nonconventional economics." Becker's contributions extend over a large number of areas, including labor market discrimination, education, crime, and different aspects of family formation, such as marriage, divorce, and fertility. One important characteristic of Becker's work is a multidisciplinary approach that helps bring together the areas of economics, sociology, psychology, and biology. His original research contributed significantly toward development of a unified theory of social sciences. Becker's diverse application of economic principles to such an array of social issues helps explain why he is a professor of both economics and sociology at the University of Chicago.

THE ECONOMICS OF
HOUSEHOLD PRODUCTION

One of the major contributions made by Becker very early in his life was the incorporation of production theory in standard consumer theory. The conventional economic analysis separates consumer theory completely from production theory. Consumers are assumed to derive satisfaction from goods and services purchased in the market, and they face income constraints. In Becker's approach consumers derive satisfaction from consumption of *commodities* that are produced in a household but cannot be purchased in the market. A commodity is something produced by combining some market goods and one's own time. An example of a commodity is reading, which is produced by an individual by combining his or her own time with a book. The incorporation of the time element in choice theory allows one to distinguish between market goods and commodities, where the latter is something that is produced at a household level. Thus, in Becker's approach, each household is considered a little factory that makes choices not just about standard consumption but also about production. Specifically, in this framework, individuals make two different types of choices: first, the consumption decision regarding which commodities to consume (for example, whether to go to a play or read a book); second, the production decision regarding how to produce a commodity (for example, to buy or borrow the book he/she wants to read).

Since commodities are not purchased in the market, there is no observed market price for different commodities. However, in Becker's formulation it is possible to derive implicit prices of different commodities by valuing all inputs, including one's own time used in production. This full price of a commodity includes monetary components paid for market goods as well as the time cost based on alternative uses of time (the price of time). One important implication of explicitly including time in the full price is that different individuals pay different full prices for the same commodity, although they pay the same for the market goods component of the cost. In a full price sense, a high-wage earner pays a higher full price for a slower but cheaper mode of transportation than the amount paid by a low-wage earner. This is also true for any single individual on different days of the week, such as lower earning opportunities during the weekends. The choices made by individuals reflect these differences in the full prices they face. Many observations regarding allocation of time have been studied by Becker within this richer household production framework.

DIVISION OF LABOR
IN A HOUSEHOLD

Becker's approach to rationality allows an individual to derive satisfaction from material gains to other individuals. This solves the decision-making problem in a multiperson household by examining the choice made by the head of the household for the family. In a multiperson household production choice framework, one additional problem the household needs to solve is the best allocation of time between market production and household production for each member of the household. For each member, there is a benefit from allocation of time in market work (wage earned) and from nonmarket work (household production). An efficient allocation of time dictates division of labor according to relative benefits; that is, a member with relatively more benefits in the market (household) work should allocate more time in the market (household). In other words, the theory of comparative advantage is applied at the household level. Thus, in Becker's approach, the observed division of labor is a result of differences in market opportunities (wages) and/or differences in level of skills in household production. In a long-run framework, with opportunities to invest in skills development, Becker showed that even small biological differences or a little difference in relative market wages can lead to a sharp division of labor within a household.

VALUATION OF
HOUSEHOLD WORK

Becker's formulation, incorporation of time in economic decisionmaking, explicitly shows that household production is an important component in the welfare of an individual, a family, and the society as a whole. The traditional economic measure of well-being at the aggregate level is a nation's gross domestic product (GDP). The GDP is a market-based measure in the sense that when transactions are taking place in the market it is accounted for at market price. Becker's household production model shows that a significant part of our most scarce resource, time, is allocated in productive activities (household production) outside the market. These include a wide range of activities, such as growing vegetables, cleaning, and childcare, to name a few. Since these activities do not involve market transactions, they are not counted as part of GDP, which results in an underestimate of real well-being. When household-produced commodities (for example, care for one's own children) are replaced by market goods (day-care services), the exclusion of housework from GDP leads to an overestimate of economic growth. Becker included household production in measures of aggregate production, both in order to have a correct measure of welfare and growth as well as to help us in formulation of better public policies.

DEMAND FOR CHILDREN

Analysis of fertility is another area where Becker contributed significantly by applying his approach to understand the issues. In Becker's view, the decision to have children is associated with having a flow of pecuniary and nonpecuniary services, as well as a flow of time and monetary costs. He applies the economic principles of standard cost benefit analysis in explaining fertility. By explicitly including the time cost in this formulation, he was able to isolate some key determinants of family size. An increase in the female participation rate and/or an increase in the female wage rate, by increasing the time cost, increases the full cost of raising children and reduces the number of children per family. Thus, wealthier families having fewer children does not imply that children are inferior goods, but is rather a result of the higher full price of children. Becker also argues that parents not only want to have more children (quantity) but also desire to spend more on each child (better quality). This implies a quantity-quality trade-off in parents' choice, and higher parental income generates a substitution effect away from quantity toward quality, toward more expenditure per child. Becker's analysis of fertility also helps in understanding why in developing countries the fertility rate is high (low full price) and the educational investment per child is lower (less quality).

ECONOMICS OF
MARRIAGE AND DIVORCE

Becker viewed family formation and desolation as a result of a rational economic decision made by self-interested individuals' choices rather than an irrational decision. He argues that individuals decide to marry or divorce when the benefits from doing so outweigh the costs. One implication of Becker's economic analysis of family formation is that the net gains from marriage increase with income and with more complementarity between the two spouses' time. Several predictions follow from his analysis, such as wealthier individuals being likely to marry earlier and likely to have lower divorce rates, and households with different sexes being more efficient than same-sex ones.

Concerning the characteristics of matching outcomes, Becker argues that when the level of household commodity production is maximized through marriage we should expect a positive assortative matching with respect to complementary characteristics (such as education, age, height) and a negative assortative matching with respect to substitutes in commodity production (such as market wages). Becker also introduced uncertainty in his theory of family formation by assuming imperfect information regarding potential gains from a marriage. His application of search theory in the marriage market predicts more uncertainty in a marriage at a younger age and, therefore, a higher divorce rate.

HUMAN CAPITAL INVESTMENT

Integration of investment theory into households' choices is another contribution of Becker. Although Adam Smith and others considered the possibility of productivity enhancing education and training, economists until the 1950s considered labor power as given. In the 1960s, Becker started to apply the economic principles in understanding the determinants of individual choices regarding human capital investment, such as schooling, job training, and health care. Again, it is the cost-benefit analysis that results in the choice, where, on the benefit side, the most important one is an increase is future earning while the most important component on the cost side is the time spent in learning, valued by income sacrificed while undertaking the venture. Like any other investments, human capital formation also requires paying the costs in one period and receiving benefits in the future. Becker's analysis predicts that forward-looking and younger individuals are more likely to invest heavily in schooling.

In his work on job training Becker made a distinction between general training and firm-specific training. The latter type of training helps explain a variety of observations like differences in quit rates, lay-off rates, and within-firm promotion. Becker argues that since human capital determines the productivity of an economy, expenditures on education and job training should be counted as part of national savings and investment, and the stock of human capital as a part of national wealth. When all forms of human capital are accounted for and forgone earnings are included as a part of the total cost of human capital investment, he showed that the United States invests more on human capital than on physical capital. One implication of this exercise is that the prevailing income tax code in an economy may encourage or discourage investment in human capital and affects output. Becker's work on human capital also enables economists to better understand the process of economic growth. In recent years, studies show that human capital formation plays a significant role in determination of the economic growth rate, and Becker's analysis helps us in identifying the potential role of government in enhancing growth.

ECONOMICS OF CRIME

Criminal behavior is another area where Becker has expanded the domain of economic analysis. Crime was traditionally considered a result of mental or social problems that lead to irrational choices. Becker, in his work on crime, considers criminal activities as a choice made by rational individuals, a choice made regarding the best allocation of one's time. Like any other choices, individuals are assumed to be rational and capable of evaluating expected gains and expected costs of being engaged in an illegal activity. The expected cost may include nonmaterial components such as giving up moral and ethical values. Individuals are likely to be engaged in criminal activities when the expected benefits exceed the expected costs. Becker's analysis predicts that a higher punishment for a crime will reduce the level of crime by raising its cost.

The expected cost depends on the prevailing public policies that determine the possibility of apprehension and the level of punishment if convicted. Thus, there is a trade-off between probability of conviction and the severity of punishment. From the social benefit point of view, Becker argued that fines, if possible, are better than any other form of punishment, since they also generate revenue for the government. Although criminal activities lead to a redistribution of wealth among society's members, Becker considers such redistribution to be a social cost, since real resources are used by criminals in the process. He also argues that resources spent on protection against crime should be considered a part of the social cost of crime.

DISCRIMINATION IN
THE LABOR MARKET

Discrimination in the labor market is the area of research that Gary Becker studied for his doctoral dissertation and later expanded into *The Economics of Discrimination*. He developed a theory of discrimination based on prejudice, where employers, employees, and customers derive satisfaction/dissatisfaction from the personal attributes/ characteristics of the people with whom they interact in the marketplace. He argues that some employers are willing to pay more to avoid hiring members of a group they dislike. The same holds for workers as well as for customers. In his model, employers make rational choices, but rather than maximizing profits, they maximize their own satisfaction, which includes their psychic benefit or cost. The market level of discrimination is a complex outcome determined by the distribution of the level of prejudice, the level of market competition, the production structure, the relative size of different groups, and the existing legal framework. Becker showed that under certain conditions, discrimination will not be effective if a minority (discriminated against) group is large enough to provide a parallel economy of its own. His theory of discrimination predicts that discrimination by a majority also lowers its own net income, and the decrease is more when the minority (discriminated against) group is a large proportion of the market. This can explain why the apartheid policy broke down in South Africa.

CONCLUSION

Becker also worked on pubic policies and modeled the competitive outcome in a process where different interest groups try to influence government decisions. Another area of his research is explaining addictive behavior. In his view, addiction is an outcome of rational choices, and it has long-term effects through accumulation of addiction capital. Gary Becker's most recent book, *Accounting for Tastes*, examines the process of preference formation that in conventional economics is considered given. In this work, past experiences, social interactions, and norms created by a certain class are assumed to influence present preferences. Gary Becker continues to take up wide-ranging everyday problems in his regular monthly column in *Business Week* and applies economic reasoning to suggest solutions that are often controversial, such as legalization of drugs and reform of welfare and public pensions.

Becker does not restrict himself only to analyzing market behavior; rather he expanded the domain of economics by applying an economic approach in understanding problems beyond those characterized by market transactions. The economist's way of thinking about behavior is one where economic agents, both as individuals as well as parts of a larger community, face resource limitations that force them to make choices. At an individual level they make rational choices that are coordinated through the market or some other mechanism. In other words, economists apply an optimization principle subject to resource constraint and use equilibrium conditions for coordination of individuals' actions.

RECOMMENDED READINGS

Becker, Gary S. (1957). *The Economics of Discrimination*. Chicago: University of Chicago Press. 2nd edition, 1971.

———. (1960). "An Economic Analysis of Fertility," *Demographic and Economic Changes in Developing Countries*. Princeton: Princeton University Press.

———. (1964). *Human Capital*. Chicago: University of Chicago Press. Second edition, 1975. 3rd edition, 1993.

———. (1965, September). A Theory of Allocation of Time,"*Economic Journal*. Vol. 75, pp. 493-617.

———. (1968, August). "Crime and Punishment: An Economic Approach," *Journal of Political Economy*. Vol. 76, pp. 169-217.

———. (1971*)*. *Economic Theory*. New York: A. Knopf.

———. (1976). *The Economic Approach to Human Behaviour*. Chicago: University of Chicago Press.

———. (1981). *A Treatise on the Family*. Cambridge: Harvard University Press, Second edition, 1991.

———. (1993, June). "Nobel Lecture: The Economic Way of Looking at Behavior," *Journal of Political Economy*. Vol. 101, pp. 385-409.

———. (1996). *Accounting for Tastes*. Cambridge, MA, and London: Harvard University Press.

Becker, Gary S. and Guity Becker. (1997). *The Economics of Life*. New York: McGraw-Hill Inc.

Febrero, Ramon, and Pedro Schwartz. (1995). *The Essence of Becker*. Stanford: Hoover Institution Press.

Time. (1992, October 26).

34

Robert Fogel (1926-   ):
An Originator of "Cliometrics"
and a Laureate of 1993

Abu N.M. Wahid

BIOGRAPHICAL PROFILE

Robert Fogel was born in New York City in 1926. Only a few years earlier his parents had immigrated to the United States from Russia. Immediately after Fogel was born, his parents started a small business. Because of this business, they went through the Great Depression without much difficulty. His schooling was done in a New York public school from 1932 to 1944. The school prepared him quite well for higher education in science. He got his B.A. from Cornell, his M.A. from Columbia, and his Ph.D. from Johns Hopkins University in 1948, 1960, and 1963 respectively. At Cornell, his interest shifted from science to economics and history. As an undergraduate student, Fogel was able to connect the institutional and technological changes of the past to the present economic instability. In order to explain and establish his hypothesis, he started to learn mathematical and statistical tools. At Columbia, he was immensely influenced by two of his professors, George Stigler and Carter Goodrich. There he also learned the process of American economic growth. In doing so, his approach was largely mathematical and quantitative. At Johns Hopkins, his Ph.D. thesis dealt with quantitative interpretation of economic history. It was supervised by Simon Kuznets. From Kuznets, Fogel learned "that the central statistical problem in economics was not random error but systematic biases in the data." After leaving Johns Hopkins, he did extensive research on the impact of government policies, technological innovation, and institutional changes on economic growth. He also studied economic history from mathematical and statistical perspective. When Martin Feldstein was the president of the National Bureau of Economic Research (NBER) in 1977, Fogel joined NBER as program director of the Development of American Economy Project. There he worked in consultation with Simon Kuznets, Douglass North, Richard A. Easterlin, Moses Abramovitz, and others. In 1981, Fogel succeeded Stigler at the University of Chicago and became the Walgreen Professor of American Institutions. Fogel's wife was Enid Cassandra Morgan. They have two sons–Michael and Steven. Fogel's wife and children have been very supportive of his intellectual works.

INTRODUCTION

Robert Fogel won the economics Nobel Prize in 1994 along with Douglass North for "having renewed research in economic history by applying economic theory and quantitative methods in order to explain economic and institutional change." Fogel has been one of the greatest historians and economists. He disproved the hypotheses of Joseph Schumpeter and Walter W. Rostow that economic growth was due to certain important discoveries. Fogel established that " The sum of many specific technical changes, rather than a few great innovations, determined economic development." Fogel and North, along with a rather extraordinary group of scholars who came of age in the late 1950s and early 1960s, were pioneers and leaders in developing a branch of the discipline that focuses on the systematic application of economic theory and methods to the study of history–a field of work that has come to be known as cliometrics. These "new economic historians" were part of a generation of economists who were intensely concerned with the sources and underlying processes of economic growth, reflecting the concerns of society at large in the aftermath of World War II and at the height of the Cold War. Fears that industrial economies might be prone to secular stagnation or recurrent severe business downturns like the Great Depression of the 1930s, as well as concern about the agonizingly slow diffusion of industrialization across the world, had fostered a general awareness that effective policies to resolve real-world problems required an improved understanding of economic growth. With creativity and hard work, systematic and quantitative methods could be applied usefully to the study of virtually all subjects.

THE RAILROADS

This confidence that even highly complex phenomena could be explored systematically was strikingly evident in Fogel's doctoral dissertation, later published as *Railroads and American Economic Growth*. In this work, he sought to empirically evaluate what was at the time the dominant vie–especially among policymakers–about the onset and processes of economic growth in early industrial economies. According to Walter Rostow, this perspective's most prominent advocate, industrialization typically began discontinuously in a takeoff, and was rooted in the expansion of so-called leading sectors, which benefitted from dramatic technological breakthroughs or infusions of capital investment and in turn stimulated major changes in other industries. Small-scale producers of agriculture and manufacture were not capable of significant progress on their own, and the achievement of sustained growth depended on drawing resources out of such activities and into more modern production facilities, where higher capital intensity could yield major gains in productivity. Rostow relied on railroads in the United States during the nineteenth century as his chief example of how a single industry could have such pervasive linkages to others that it could pull an entire economy into sustained growth. Fogel's study of the railroads was designed to subject this hypothesis of the centrality of one industry in the growth process to a test of consistency with the evidence. Assessing the contribution of such a large and important industry was and remains a truly mind-boggling project. But as has been characteristic of his work, Fogel boldly set out a framework to reduce the complex problem into essential subcomponents, each of which could be addressed empirically by bringing massive amounts of data to bear in ingenious ways. The key analytic concept of his approach was the social saving of railroads, or the amount of resources that were saved through the use of the railroad technology over the best available alternatives in providing the freight transportation services that were actually consumed, or their equivalent, in a single year, 1890. He estimated a conservative upper bound for the social saving, and concluded that it was no more, and likely much less, then 5 percent of the GNP–a figure that did not seem consistent with the idea that the extent of the U.S. economic growth over the nineteenth century had depended crucially on the railroad technology or industry. Most of these social savings came from the use of railroads in intraregional, as opposed to interregional, transportation. Waterways were rather good substitutes for railroads over long distances, but there were no good substitutes over short distances until the automobile.

It is not possible to provide here a comprehensive exposition of what was involved in carrying out this tour de force. Briefly, the effort focused on estimating the actual costs in 1890 of transporting a core set of agricultural commodities, which constituted the bulk of all railroad freight, and then estimating what would have been the costs without the railroads–that is, relying exclusively on a combination of water and horse-drawn wagon transport. Data on the precise quantitative flows of these commodities between various points, as well as engineering and rate data for all forms of transport, were employed in extraordinarily detailed calculations and simulations of the differences between the costs of alternative modes of transporting the same set of commodities from points of origin to points of destination. The estimated social savings for the core set of commodities studied was then used as a basis for inferring the figure for all freight traffic.

In computing his estimates of transportation costs in a hypothetical 1890 economy without railroads, Fogel constructed an elaborate counterfactual world, with great amounts of thought and work behind every significant detail. Especially creative were his approaches to estimating the costs of slower and more seasonal forms of transportation than railroads and to valuing the cost of land far from waterways going out of, or never having come into, cultivation. In addition to preparing his estimate of the social savings, he also examined the extent of linkages between railroads and other important industries, such as iron and steel, and demonstrated that the expansion of railroads was not indispensable to their growth and development. Moreover, as has been his practice throughout his career, he took the criticisms addressed at his work seriously and reexamined the data to consider their significance. Some years later, in his presidential address to the Economic History Association, he explained what additional insight had been gained from the further work inspired by the criticisms and why the qualitative results still held. Fogel has always recognized the role of controversy in producing further advances in knowledge by inducing scholars to dig deeper and work harder.

There remain a few caveats or questions that still can be leveled, and there will always be a few individuals to repeat them–if not actually to do the work to resolve them. Nevertheless, Fogel's work on railroads dramatically changed our understanding of the process of early economic growth in the United States and in the world more generally. His work established clearly that the record in the United States was of much more balanced progress than many had thought and cast doubt on conjectures that a single industry or technology defined with reasonable narrowness could be so important as to dominate the process of growth. When growth occurs, it encompasses a broad range of industries. This principle or finding is of crucial intellectual significance, as well as of relevance for policymakers concerned with both developed and less-developed countries. The result can be understood as following from the fact that no single industry is all that large relative to an entire economy experiencing growth, and that the processes of economic growth generates progress throughout the economy. Moreover, reasonably good substitutes for products or technologies are generally available. And where they are not, increased investments in inventive activity directed at satisfying the demand or need will produce them.

Today, after the failures of heavy industry development plans in Eastern European countries and a number of other economies, the successes of building up from traditional labor-intensive industries in East Asia, as well as much scholarly work, the Fogel result that American growth did not turn on the availability of railroads may not seem all that surprising. He must be amused and pleased when people wonder what all the fuss was about, for the work was highly controversial and important in the intellectual and policy context of the time. His project on railroads in the United States was not the only investigation to undermine the "leading sector," or unbalanced, theory of growth, but it was a pioneering study in the demonstration that the consistency of this view with the evidence could be examined systematically on a ground of its own choosing and be found wanting.

As is suggested here, the contribution of Fogel's work on railroads to the study of economic growth went beyond the substantive results to methodology. He demonstrated that the power provided by even simple economic models was sufficient to tackle some rather grand counterfactual questions and, in doing so, made clear that in studying the sources and processes of a phenomenon as complex as economic growth, it was necessary to think hard and be specific about the essential mechanisms at work. Fogel, for example, focused on the direct effect of railroads on the amount of resources needed for transportation services as essential and labored mightily to prepare estimates of the magnitude of that effect. Implicitly, he left it to others to identify other mechanisms or effects that they might see as more important and to prepare estimates of their magnitudes. In other words, much of the measurement problem that bedevils economists perhaps could be overcome if we devoted more attention to distinguishing or specifying the different mechanisms at work, and then confronted the empirical issues with each of them individually in turn. This methodological orientation has been evident throughout his professional life. Reflection on this aspect of Fogel's work might be particularly appropriate now, in an era when the mere expression of a mathematical function is confused with analytical rigor and when there has been a recent revival of interest in, if not careful empirical work on, economic growth.

SLAVERY AND THE DEVELOPMENT OF THE SOUTHERN ECONOMY

Fogel's interest in the impact of slavery on the long-run growth of the southern economy was first aroused when he was a graduate student at Johns Hopkins University. In an article appearing in the *Journal of Political Economy,* Alfred Conrad and John Meyer reported their finding that slaves had been profitable investments right up to the Civil War. The work generated much controversy throughout the profession, and Fogel and his classmate Stanley Engerman were in the thick of the discussion amongst the Hopkins economics community. The debate over what the result meant was still going on in the late 1960s, when Fogel and Engerman were again colleagues at the University of Rochester. They decided then to embark on a major study of slavery. In the years since, individually or together, they and their students have made vast additions to our knowledge of this institution by systematically exploring an enormous number and range of sources of evidence, including census materials, probate records, plantation records, shipping manifests, auction records, and transcripts of interviews carried out after the Civil War with ex-slaves. The two volumes of *Time on the Cross*, the four volumes of *Without Consent or Contract*, and many of the hundreds of published articles from, or stimulated by, the project will likely still be read a century or more from now.

Embedded in the rich tapestry of Fogel's work on the institution of slavery and its impact on the southern economy and population, are several fundamental contributions to our understanding of American economic growth and economic growth in general. First, his demonstration with Engerman that slave agriculture, as compared to free, was extremely productive indicated that it is unlikely that the direct effect of slavery on the American South was to retard its economic development. This was a spectacularly important finding. It suggests that the economic backwardness of the South that haunted that region and the entire nation for 100 years after the Civil War cannot be attributed in a simple way to a long exposure to an inefficient mode of agricultural production. The result has challenged scholars to explore other possible sources of, or mechanisms for, regional backwardness, such as the economic consequences of unequal provision of public goods like education and legal protection in the postbellum south. It also reminds economists that although institutions may have substantial effects on economic growth, they are often determined by factors other than pure economic considerations. Slavery yielded high output per unit of input in southern agriculture but was ultimately put to an end–with the expected consequences on agricultural productivity–by a political movement fueled by a sense of morality. Another central contribution was to identify the major source of the higher productivity of slave agriculture. Fogel and Engerman demonstrated persuasively that most of the advantage was accounted for by gang labor–a system of organizing slave labor that required a minimum of roughly fifteen slaves before it could be employed and that yielded substantial improvements in total factor productivity–but only in the production of certain crops, like cotton or sugar. Those plantations that were large enough to employ the gang-labor system averaged about 35-50 percent higher total factor productivity. The gains in productivity due to gang-labor appear to have been realized effectively through the achievement of greater labor intensity or more units of directed work per unit of time. The system relied on an intricate division of labor, along with methods of maintaining an intense pace of work, such as having the field workers perform their specified tasks in an interdependent fashion or having teams of workers matched against each other. Unlike another famous case of intensified labor going hand in hand with higher productivity–the continuous moving assembly line introduced by Henry Ford in 1914 along with a near tripling of the wage within six months–the gang labor system was not quite productive enough to fully compensate workers for the unpleasant nature of the more intense work. The gang labor system was never effectively employed with free labor; it worked with slaves, because of the additional instruments slave owners had to elicit labor from them.

The finding about gang labor was especially interesting because it documented clearly that changes in the organization of work or labor could be a quantitatively important source of productivity advance in early or preindustrial economies. Indeed, considerable work since by other scholars has shown that systematic alterations in the organization of labor yielded substantial increases in productivity–even without changes in the amount or types of capital utilized–in a wide range of early nineteenth-century manufacturing industries in early industrial Britain and the United States. These studies have provided further evidence against the unbalanced growth model, which held that the onset of early economic growth was discontinuous and based on major breakthroughs in a small number of leading sectors. What accounted in these two first industrial nations for the discovery and diffusion of methods to increase productivity through changes in the organization of labor, and how much of the gains were due to greater labor intensity, are fascinating problems that may be relevant to our understanding of how and why sustained economic growth gets under way in less-developed economies more generally.

NUTRITION AND HEALTH

Fogel's preeminent skills include the ability to inspire and orchestrate ambitious projects involving large numbers of researchers working in cooperation–what might be called "big social science." His current study of changes in health over the last several centuries, and their economic consequences, is his biggest yet and has employed hundreds of personnel and been carried on now for more than twenty years. It has been a massive undertaking. Among the data sets he and associated scholars have been constructing are one that traces families for three centuries, linking information on vital events and other socioeconomic variables to randomly selected individuals from each generation over their lives, and another that follows the Civil War veterans over their lives, obtaining detailed information on their health status from reports of medical examinations contained in pension records. The data sets ultimately will encompass material on several million individuals in total.

Fogel is concerned with health as both an output and an input. On the output side, given the valuation people put on their health and additional years of life, he contends that conventional economic measures of standard of living and economic growth miss an enormous amount if they do not take the health of populations into account. To provide a more specific example, economists vastly understate the extent of progress over the last several centuries in the United States if they do not factor in the dramatic increase in life expectancy that has been realized. Moreover, if economists want to understand all of the processes by which human welfare is raised, they need to pay more attention to the question of what conditions or changes brought about these improvements in health, as well as the myriad economic effects of changes in the length of life and in health generally. Thus far, Fogel has focused on the former. Employing a variety of databases, including those described above, and relying primarily on anthropometric measures as indicators of nutritional status, he has argued that the contributions of increasing levels of nutrition have been underestimated and that those of advances in medical knowledge have been overestimated, in explaining the long-run decline in mortality rates. As always with Fogel, the work has aroused controversy for both its conclusions and for some startling findings, such as the attainment of the World War II levels of stature by the time of the American Revolution and a decrease in heights over most of the last two-thirds of the nineteenth century. But also as usual, Fogel takes his critics seriously and remains committed to doing the further work required to resolve the issues they have raised, and to produce new knowledge.

Fogel is also investigating the extent to which improvements in health, encompassing nutrition, may have contributed to the rates of economic growth that we have observed historically in the United States and in other industrialized countries. He has already made a strong case that many Europeans were so malnourished into the eighteenth century, if not beyond, that they were effectively constrained in how much work they could perform or how productive they could be. This energy or health constraint was eased as food supply conditions improved from the seventeenth through the nineteenth centuries with technological progress, institutional changes that boosted agricultural productivity, and the expansion of international trade. A better nourished population led in turn to further gains in productivity–through increases in the intensity of labor and in the number of hours worked and perhaps through technical advances that would not have been possible without the enhanced physical vigor of workers. Overall, the evidence Fogel has compiled suggests that improvements in nutrition and health did play a significant role in raising productivity and in the processes of early industrialization, particularly in Europe. He and his associates plan eventually to use the material on the Civil War veterans to study this health-productivity nexus in the late nineteenth- and the early twentieth-century United States as well. Although their relative importance in accounting for productivity or economic growth in industrialized economies may be less in the modern era, major advances in health and nutrition continue to be made, and there is no reason to believe that their effects necessarily have been exhausted. Moreover, it is clear that this source of higher labor productivity and economic growth remains quite relevant for many underdeveloped countries, whose populations still suffer from poor nutrition and health.

CONCLUSION

Throughout his career, Robert Fogel has exemplified the best traits of economists together with the best traits of historians. With historians he shares an appreciation of the significance of processes that operate over long periods of time, like those involved in economic growth or institutional change, and a broad perspective that helps in identifying what is truly important. As an economist, he is adept at applying the analytical frameworks of the discipline to reduce even highly complex problems to the fundamental issues, breaking them down into hypotheses that are formulated so as to be clear, precise, and subject to empirical tests. Moreover, he is enormously creative in seeing what all of the empirical implications of various theories are, and of how to make systematic use of data to examine their consistency with the evidence. His is a powerful combination of qualities, allowing him to expand knowledge substantially on each of the frontiers he has worked at and to have a major influence on the research agendas of critics, students, and cliometricians overall. For forty years now, Robert Fogel has maintained an intense pace of intellectual discovery that has inspired economists and historians alike. The award of the Nobel Prize in 1993 was a fitting tribute to a great scholar.

RECOMMENDED READINGS

Robert W. Fogel. (1960). *The Union Pacific Railroad: A Case in Premature Enterprise*. Baltimore: Johns Hopkins University Press.

———. (1986). "Nutrition and the Decline in Mortality Since 1700: Some Preliminary Findings," in Stanley L. Engerman and Robert E. Gallman, eds., *Long-Term Factors in American Economic Growth, Studies in Income and Wealth*. Vol. 51. Chicago: University of Chicago Press, pp. 439-527.

———. (1992). "Second Thoughts on the European Escape from Hunger: Famines, Chronic Malnutrition, and Mortality," in S.R., (ed.) *Nutrition and Poverty*. Oxford: Clarendon, pp. 243-86.

———. (1994, February). "Robert William Fogel," University of Chicago. Unpublished Autobiographical Statement.

———. (1994, June). "Economic Growth, Population Theory, and Physiology: The Bearing of Long-Term Processes on the Making of Economic Policy," *American Economic Review*. Vol. 84, pp. 369-95.

Fogel, Robert W., and Stanley L. Engerman. (1974). *Time on the Cross: The Economics of American Negro Slavery*. Vols. 1 and 2. New York: Little Brown.

——. (1980), "Explaining the Relative Efficiency of Slave Agriculture in the Antebellum South: Reply."*American Economic Review*. September, Vol. 70, pp. 672-90.

——. (1989). *Without Consent or Contract: The Rise and Fall of American Slavery*. New York: W.W. Norton.

Fogel, Robert W., Ralph A. Galantine, Richard L. Manning , et al. (1989a). *Without Consent or Contract: The Rise and Fall of American Slavery-Evidence and Methods*. New York: W.W. Norton.

——. (1989b). *Without Consent or Contract: The Rise and Fall of American Slavery-Technical Papers*. Vols. 1 and 2. New York: W.W. Norton.

Rostow, Walt W. (1960). *The Stages of Economic Growth*, Cambridge: Cambridge University Press.

——. (1979, March). "Notes on the Social Saving Controversy," *Journal of Economic History*. Vol. 39, pp. 1-54.

Sokoloff, Kenneth L., (1984, October). "Was the Transition from the Artisanal Shop to the Nonmechanized Factory Associated With Gains in Efficiency?: Evidence form the U.S. Manufacturing Censuses," *Explorations in Economic History*. Vol. 21, pp. 351-82.

35

Douglass North (1920-   ):
A Pioneer of the Economics of Institutions and a Laureate of 1993

Norman Schofield

BIOGRAPHICAL PROFILE

Douglass North was born in Cambridge, Massachusetts, in 1920. His father used to work for the Metropolitan Life Insurance Company. In connection with his father's job, North moved to various places, including Canada and Europe. He attended elementary school in Ottawa, Canada, and during 1929-1930, he studied at a school in Lausanne Switzerland. He returned to the United States in 1933, entered a private school in New York City, and then finished his high school in Wallingford, Connecticut. At that time, he was deeply engrossed in photography. He won several awards in photography competitions. North did not grow up in an intellectual environment. Although his father had a good job, he was not even a high school graduate. Neither was his mother. For his college education, he was accepted at Harvard but his father was transferred to San Francisco, and to stay near the family, he decided to attend the University of California at Berkeley instead of Harvard. At Berkeley, he became a convinced Marxist and opposed the Second World War. When Hitler invaded the Soviet Union, he was the only one among his close friends who favored peace. He graduated from Berkeley with slightly better than a 'C' average but with a triple major in politics, philosophy and economics. On graduation, he joined the Merchant Marine and made several voyages to Australia, New Guinea, and the Solomon Islands. During World War II, he read extensively and also learned navigation. He was thinking seriously about whether to become an economist or to pursue a photography career. Finally, he tilted toward economics. He entered the Berkeley graduate school of economics. At Berkeley, he was most influenced by his thesis advisor, M.M. Knight (Frank

Knight's brother), who was a great teacher with a clear understanding of the history of economic theory. While doing his dissertation research, he visited Columbia University and Harvard University. At Harvard, he came in contact with Joseph Schumpeter, who exerted a strong influence on North's intellectual development. His first job was at the University of Washington, Seattle, where he learned economic theory and economic reasoning from colleague Don Gordon. He spent a year in 1956-1957 at the National Bureau of Economic Research as a research associate. That was a very rewarding year in his professional life. There he not only had the opportunity to know many great economists, but he also had a chance to work with Simon Kuznets for one day a week, the outcome of which was his major quantitative study of the balance of payments of the United States. Between his year at the National Bureau and his visit to Geneva in 1966-1967 with a Ford Foundation Fellowship, he did his seminal work on the economic growth of the United States from 1790 to 1860. During his time in Geneva, he developed interest in the economic history of Europe. At the University of Washington, Seattle, he developed the graduate program and attracted some of the best graduate students for research in economic history. In 1983, North joined Washington University, St. Louis. There he founded the Center in Political Economy. Since 1990, North's research has focused on how individuals make decisions under uncertainty and ambiguity. North's first wife, whom he married in 1944, was first a teacher, then a mother to their three children, and later a successful politician in the Washington State Legislature. In 1972 he married Elizabeth Case, who continues to be his wife, companion, critic and editor: a partner in the projects and programs that the two undertake together.

ECONOMIC HISTORY AND THEORY

Douglass North, along with Robert Fogel, won the economics Nobel Prize in 1993 for "having renewed research in economic history by applying economic theory and quantitative methods in order to explain economic and institutional change." North is famous for studying and examining some nonconventional economic issues. He rigorously dealt with the explanation and rationality of why people make the choices they do. He has also attempted to explain how peoples' beliefs and ideologies shape their choices and decision-making processes and the resulting economic and social implications. He believes that the way people make choices under uncertainty and ambiguity is one of the most fundamental and challenging issues of the present time. The science of economics must address this issue appropriately to ensure further progress in social sciences. In North's early work on economic growth, the role of institutions was somewhat less emphasized, while in his later work, he has focused increasingly on how the systems of beliefs held by individuals in a society sustain the institutions that are used. It may be useful to divide North's work over the last four decades so as to bring out the change of viewpoint that has occurred.

NORTH AND THE HISTORY OF
GROWTH IN THE UNITED STATES

In the research up to his book on *The Economic Growth of the United States 1790-1860* (1961), North's emphasis on the evolution of the market economy, where the behavior of prices of goods, services, and productive factors was the major element. While "institutional and political policies have certainly been influential, they have modified rather than replaced the underlying forces of a market economy." One of his studies during this period was of the effect of a decline in ocean freight rates on economic development in the period 1750-1910. However, his work in the next few years suggested that the decline in freight rates was due less to technological change prior to 1850 than to the elimination of piracy. This, in turn, was a consequence of an institutional transformation– namely the dominance of the British Navy and its ability to "police the seas."

NORTH AND THE HISTORY
OF GROWTH IN EUROPE

From 1968 to 1975, North increasingly studied the way in which economic growth and the "capture of the gains from exchange" often required changes in property rights and institutional arrangements. In an early article and a later book with Robert Thomas, *The Rise of the Western World* (1973), North began to explore further the relationship between growth and individual incentives. As North and Thomas say, "Individuals must be lured by incentives to undertake... socially desirable activities. Some mechanism must be devised to bring social and private rates of return into closer parity." From this "public choice" perspective, justice and the enforcement of property rights are simply other examples of public goods publicly funded.

The origins of this book lay in their earlier work on the manorial system in the high Middle Ages in Europe. There, they argued that this system was a self-enforcing "contract" that allowed an exchange between lord and serf and made possible population expansion into unsettled land. In particular, the manorial contract, with its implicit conventions, or norms, partially solved a situation of high transaction costs and created a context within which protection was provided by the lord while goods and services were provided by the serf. Population growth and increasing specialization brought about the "inception of the market economy," and this in turn induced transformation in the manorial system. In the later chapters of the book, North and Thomas began an examination of constitutional power in the European polities. The key to their analysis is the capacity of the Crown to tax or borrow. In England, Parliament has been able to wrest control over taxing power from the monarch. This imposed restraint on the Crown doubtless contributed to the increasing level of real wages in the seventeenth century. In France, on the other hand, "the chaos of the fifteenth century, in which all property rights were insecure, had led the Estates General to give up power over taxes to Charles VII. The French King eliminated his close rivals, placing the Crown in a better position to demand a larger share of the social savings generated by government."

According to their figures, real wages fell by approximately 50 percent between 1450 and 1600 in France and were effectively flat throughout the seventeenth century.

In this work with Thomas, North had begun to discuss the origins of economic growth in Europe in the Middle Ages and the reasons why economic growth was particularly pronounced in England from 1600 but not in France or Spain. After 1975, the work with Thomas broadened in scope to encompass a discussion of the first economic revolution, namely the transition between hunter/gatherer economies and agriculture, as well as the second (industrial) revolution. His book *Structure and Change in Economic History* (1981) attempted to set up a unified "public choice" theory based on property rights and transaction costs to account for these economic revolutions. Thus the transition from hunting to agriculture was seen in terms of the problem of common property rights in hunting, as contrasted with exclusive communal rights in agriculture. To elaborate briefly, common property rights may result in overexploitation. This can occur in fishing today, where not all fishing fleets can take from the common pool up to their capacity without damaging (possibly irreparably) the renewable resource. In primitive agriculture, on the other hand, some sort of cooperation is required and enforced by conventions or norms. As long as land is available, overexploitation is unlikely. North's argument as regards hunting is derived from a famous paper by Vernon Smith on Pleistocene extinctions. North's discussion of this first economic revolution will be elucidated further in the following section. To set up the foundations of a theory to account for economic growth over the last six hundred years, North essentially posed a neoclassical theory of the state. That is the state–Leviathan–contracts to set up a system of property rights and taxes. However a wealth-maximizing Leviathan may maintain an inefficient set of property rights and fail to stimulate economic growth.

NORTH ON ECONOMIC DECLINE

Secondly the inherent instability of states leads ultimately to economic decline. To some degree North's discussion predates the work of the historian Paul Kennedy in his book, *The Rise and Fall of the Great Powers* (1987). There, Kennedy argues that imperial powers, such as France, Spain and the United States, have faced the dilemma of increasingly costly military adventures overwhelming their ability to cover the cost by taxes. North's particular interest is more theoretical than Kennedy's in that he sought to uncover those conditions under which efficient property rights could be instituted. As North observes, "the twelfth and thirteenth centuries were a period of flowering of international commerce....The Champagne Fairs, the burgeoning Mediterranean trade of Venice, Genoa, and other Italian cities, the urbanization of metal and cloth dealers were only a few of the major manifestations of commercial expansion of the era." Later work was to explore further one facet of institutional innovation fostering growth in the high Middle Ages. In his book, North goes on to say: "There can be little doubt that there was substantial productivity increase in the non-agricultural sector as a result of reducing transaction costs; nonetheless, this sector still accounted for only a tiny fraction of total economic activity. Population growth was causing the prices of agricultural goods to rise relative to other goods, and real wages were falling.... Western Europe was experiencing a Malthusian crisis."

THE CYCLES OF ECONOMIC EXPANSION AND CONTRACTION

The European cycle first of expansion from 1475 to 1600 and then of contraction in the seventeenth century presents a puzzle to Marxian analysis, since feudalism had effectively died by 1500, but capitalism, the next stage, does not fully emerge until three hundred years later. North suggests that the gap was associated with a structural crisis over control of the state that was resolved eventually by the implementation of a set of property rights encouraging modern economic growth. As in the earlier book with Thomas, North emphasizes that there may be great difficulty in the implementation of appropriate property rights. As he notes in the case of France, "The system of trading property rights for revenue provided a solution [to the problem of raising taxes] but required an elaborate agency structure to monitor the system. The resultant bureaucracy not only siphoned off part of the resultant income but became an entrenched force in the French political system." As Schama has recently noted in *Citizens* (1989), after the War of Austrian Succession (1740-1748) and the Seven Years War (1756-1763), the French deficit was over 2 billion livres (over 100 livres per subject, or two-thirds the annual income of a master carpenter). The debt problem caused Louis XVI to call the Estates General in 1789 (the first time since 1614), and this probably precipitated the French Revolution. In later work, North and Weingast examined the implementation of a state structure conducive to economic growth by focusing on the formation of the Bank of England and new Parliament-Crown relations after the "Glorious Revolution" of 1688 in England.

PERENNIAL HISTORICAL QUESTIONS

North's book also discusses two other perennial historical questions, namely the cause of the disintegration of the Roman Empire around 400 A.D. and the effects of the conquest of Constantinople by the Turks in 1453. On the second question, North is correct to observe that Mediterranean trade became more insecure relative to other trade after 1453 and that this may be seen as an extension of Pirenne's thesis that Islam ultimately reoriented Europe away from the Mediterranean toward the Atlantic. However, both the cases of Rome and Constantinople suggest that contingency (or happenstance) is more important than suggested by North's account. Some aspects of contingency will be discussed below.

INSTITUTIONAL AND
COGNITIVE FACTORS

From 1984 onward North has attempted to develop a theoretical account of economic growth grounded in a set of inferences about institutional change. In essence, institutions are seen as mechanisms to facilitate cooperation in a situation of uncertainty. More particularly, institutions can be used to structure individual beliefs. As has been written in a related context, "The fundamental theoretical problem underlying the question of cooperation is the manner by which individuals attain knowledge of each others' preferences and likely behavior." More recently, North suggests that the following propositions govern institutional change: (1) interactions between institutions in a context of scarcity induce institutional change; (2) competition forces institutions to invest in knowledge, which shapes perceptions; (3) institutions generate incentives, which dictate the nature of sought-after knowledge; (4) perceptions derive from mental constructs (beliefs); (5) institutional change is overwhelmingly path-dependent.

It is evident from the way these propositions are framed that North is increasingly concerned with two issues: the formation of beliefs and ideologies within institutions and the process of transformation of both beliefs and institutions. For example, he has argued that the institutional developments in the West were based in socioreligious beliefs prevalent in early modern Europe. For clues about the origin of beliefs, he has increasingly turned to cognitive psychology. A second theme in his writing is that development is path-dependent. Implicit in this argument is the proposition that the dynamic of economic or social development might possibly be chaotic, or highly sensitive to small changes in conditions. When we look back on Western economic development from our current position, continuing growth might very well seem inevitable. In the same way, looking back at biological evolution, there well might be a tendency to assume a progression in the complexity of form. However, Steven Jay Gould, in *Full House* (1996), has warned of the likely "contingency" of evolution. It is entirely possible, for example, that the dinosaurs died out only because of a contingent accident (namely an impact with an asteroid or large meteor). Gould's arguments on the importance of contingent (or punctuated) evolution have been adapted recently to suggest that the evolution of homo sapiens from Austalopithecus over the last 2 million years or so was highly contingent on geomorphological accidents that governed the onset of the Ice Age. To generalize from Gould's arguments that rapid evolutionary change might separate long periods of evolutionary status, it seems quite probable that economic or cultural development also might occur in spurts as a result of highly contingent causes.

With regard to path dependence, it is important to recognize the way contingency is relevant for triggering economic or social transformations. Furthermore, it is worthwhile to emphasize that economic theorists (and game theorists in particular) have been forced to grapple with the notion of beliefs. Their insights may prove useful in understanding how human institutions are based on common beliefs. North is an economic historian (cliometrician) turned economic theorist whose work has increasingly emphasized the importance of *institutions* for the study of economic growth. In his Nobel lecture, North defined institutions as formal constraints, for example, rules, laws, constitutions, and informal constraints e.g., norms of behavior, conventions, self-imposed codes of conduct and their enforcement characteristics. In North's view, neoclassical economic theory is simply an inappropriate tool to analyze and prescribe policies that will induce development, since neoclassical theory is concerned with the operation of markets, not with how they develop.

While North retains the fundamental assumption of scarcity and, hence, competition, he adds "the dimension of time." One of North's preoccupations as far back as the late 1950s was with the relationship between economic growth and institutions such as property rights created by the state. For North, as with Ronald Coase, all exchange involves transaction costs; when these are high, economic activity is limited. Human institutions can help reduce such transaction costs and engender growth. Thus economic growth is dependent not just on technological innovation but on human ingenuity at devising institutional procedures to facilitate trust and confidence, so overcoming transaction costs. In a sense, North's work has gone beyond human capital to emphasize social capital, or the social technology that permits the implementation of material technology.

CONCLUSION

Douglass North has been one of the greatest economic historians of the present time. He thoroughly examined the long-term process economic growth of America as well as Europe. He also did pioneering work on institutions and explained how institutions play a pivotal role in economic decision making. He maintains that when society cannot maximize its overall benefits under the existing institutional setup, it gives rise to a new institutional order. North proved his hypothesis using the nineteenth-century developments of the agricultural, banking, transport, and other policies that evolved in the United States. North also cited examples from the economic history of Europe in support of his proposition and elucidated how people make economic decisions under uncertainty and ambiguity. North's findings not only revolutionized the way economic historians think but has also left a lasting impact on how general economists and politicians interpret the world.

NOTE

Some of the ideas discussed in the essay arose out of conversations with Douglass North, and in part are based on work supported by NSF Grant SAR-94-22548.

RECOMMENDED READINGS

North, D.C. (1958). "Ocean Freight Rates and Economic Development," *The Journal of Economic History*.

——. (1961). *The Economic Growth of the United States, 1790-1860*. New York: Prentice-Hall.

——. (1968). "Sources of Productivity Change in Ocean Shipping, 1600-1850," *The Journal of Political Economy*.

——. (1981). *Structure and Change in Economic History*. New York: W. W. Norton.

——. (1983). "The Second Economic Revolution in the United States," *Proceedings on the Industrial Revolution and Technological Change*.

——. (1990). *Institutions, Institutional Change and Economic Performance*. Cambridge: Cambridge University Press.

——. (1993). "Institutions and Credible Commitment," *Journal of Institutional and Theoretical Economics*.

——. (1994). "Economic Performance through Time," *American Economic Review*.

——. (1995). "The Paradox of the West," in *Origins of Modern Freedom in the West* (ed.) R. M Davis. Stanford: Stanford University Press.

North, D.C., and R.P.M. Thomas. (1970). "An Economic Theory of the Growth of the Western World," *The Economic History Review*.

——. (1971). "The Rise and Fall of the Manorial System: A Theoretical Model," *Journal of Economic History*.

——. (1973). *The Rise of the Western World: A New Economic History*. Cambridge: Cambridge University Press.

——. (1977). "The First Economic Revolution," *The Economic History Review*.

North, D.C., and B. W. Weingast. (1989). "Constitutions and Commitment: The Evolution of Institutions Governing Public Choice in 17th Century England," *Journal of Economic History*.

Schama, S. (1989). *Citizens: A Chronicle of the French Revolution*. New York: Knopf Publishing.

36

John Harsanyi (1920-2000):
A Master of Rational Behavior and Bargaining in Games and a Laureate of 1994

Irwin Lipnowski

BIOGRAPHICAL PROFILE

John Harsanyi was born in Budapest, Hungary, in 1920, the only son of a middle-class Jewish pharmacist. Harsanyi received a superb education at the Lutheran Gymnasium in Budapest, an institution described by Harsanyi in an autobiographical sketch as "one of the best schools in Hungary." (Harsanyi 1994). Coincidentally, the distinguished alumnae of this school included John von Neumann, the inventor of game theory as a formal mathematical discipline. In 1937, Harsanyi won first prize in mathematics in a Hungary-wide annual competition for high school students. Although Harsanyi intimated that he would have preferred to study philosophy and mathematics in university, he acceded to parental pressure and began the study of pharmacy in 1937. His decision was also influenced by the fact that pharmacy would allow him to defer his military service. He could thereby, avoid serving in the forced labor unit of the Hungarian army, to which Jewish conscripts were routinely assigned. Shortly after the German army invaded Hungary in March 1944, Harsanyi was sent to a forced labor camp and in November 1944, he narrowly escaped the cruel fate encountered by his less fortunate comrades who were shipped by train to a concentration camp in Austria. On the way to the concentration camp, Harsanyi managed to escape from the railway station and was given refuge, by a Jesuit father he had known, in the cellar of a monastery. Had John Harsanyi shared the tragic fate of his comrades and perished in that Austrian concentration camp, the world would have been denied many important advances in the realms of philosophy, sociology, and economics. In 1946, Harsanyi resumed his academic studies at the University of Budapest, and having been granted credit for his prewar studies in pharmacy, he received his Ph.D. in June 1947, after only one more year of course work. Because Hungary was becoming "a completely Stalinist country," in April 1950, at considerable physical risk, Harsanyi and his future wife fled Hungary and landed in Australia. Harsanyi completed an M.A. degree in economics in 1953 at the University of Sydney, and in 1956, under the supervision of Kenneth Arrow, he completed a Ph.D. at Stanford University. After a brief stint at Australian National University, Harsanyi was appointed as a professor at Wayne State University, and in 1964, he was appointed visiting professor and then Professor at the Business School of the University of California in Berkeley. His appointment was later extended to the department of economics. Harsanyi remained at Berkeley until his retirement. He died in August 2000 at the age of 80.

INTRODUCTION

John Harsanyi, along with John Nash and Reinhard Selten, got the economics Nobel Prize in 1994 for his "pioneering analysis of equilibria in the theory of non-cooperative games." The Royal Swedish Academy expressed the universally accepted view that "game theory has become a dominant tool for analyzing economic issues" and that games serve "as the foundation for understanding complex economic issues." The contributions made by these three co-recipients in 1994 have been deeply intertwined. The contribution of John Nash was the foundation upon which Harsanyi and Selten developed their significant extensions and generalizations of the core theory of noncooperative games.

HARSANYI AND THE THEORY
OF BARGAINING

Harsanyi brilliantly synthesized two disparate streams in the literature on the theory of bargaining. The pioneering informal analyses of the bargaining problem resulted in either an indeterminate solution, as in Edgeworth (1981) or Pigou (1905), or in the introduction of unsatisfactory ad hoc assumptions to effect a determinate solution. In their analysis of two-party bargaining, Edgeworth and Pigou assumed individual rationality, in other words, that no party would accept a payoff that is lower than the conflict payoff, and joint rationality (or more commonly referred to as the assumption of Pareto optimality), in other words, that the players will not agree to an outcome that would allow one party to become better off without harming the other party, or would allow both parties to improve their respective outcomes. They delimited a set of possible outcomes that satisfied individual and group rationality, but the actual outcome was considered to be indeterminate, depending on the relative "bargaining skills" of the protagonists.

Harsanyi's research on the bargaining problem was inspired by the magnificent contribution of John Nash (1950, 1953). Postulating four plausible axioms, Nash proved that the classical two-player bargaining problem had a unique solution (subsequently called the "Nash solution"). Harsanyi's extensive research in the theory of bargaining began with his 1956 paper that reexamined the contributions of Frederick Zeuthen and John Hicks. After recasting Zeuthen's work in game-theoretic terms, Harsanyi demonstrates the mathematical equivalence between the bargaining solution in Nash's axiomatic model and the outcome in Zeuthen's model. The latter assumed that either a rival's last offer would be accepted or a counteroffer would be made. The latter course entails a risk of conflict if the rival rejects the counteroffer without making some concession beyond the previous offer. The bargaining process in Zeuthen's model is based upon the "Zeuthen principle"–so named by Harsanyi. By endowing Zeuthen's bargaining agents with von Neumann-Morgenstern utility functions, Harsanyi (1989) noted that "the next concession must always come from the player with the smaller risk limit" where risk limit is defined as "the highest probability of conflict that player 1 and player 2, respectively, would face rather than accept the last offer of the other player." Harsanyi thus explicitly introduced a player's attitude to risk as the key determinant of the outcome of the bargaining process.

Over the course of the next two decades, Harsanyi produced successive generalizations of bargaining models, extending the framework from fixed to variable threat points in the event of disagreement (which the threatening party would be bound to implement) and from two-player to n-player bargaining. Harsanyi's successive extensions and generalizations of bargaining theory culminated in the publication of *Rational Behavior and Bargaining Equilibrium in Games and Social Situations* (1977).

A RE-INTERPRETATION OF MIX ED STRATEGY AND NASH EQUILIBRIUM

The existence of a mixed strategy Nash equilibrium in well-defined noncooperative games has been the cornerstone of game theory. However, a satisfactory interpretation of a mixed strategy equilibrium was absent prior to the important contribution of Harsanyi (1973). One problem plaguing mixed strategy equilibria is that each party's mixed strategy yields the same payoff as any other mixed or pure strategy. While this implies that no player can gain by deviating from the equilibrium strategy, neither would an agent suffer any loss by deviating. Indeed, Harsanyi constructed a very interesting example, cited in Robert Aumann and M. Maschler's "Some Thoughts on the Minimax Principle" (1972), of a two-player normal form game in which the unique mixed Nash equilibrium strategy, yields the same payoff as that of a maximin strategy yet the latter is arguably more attractive. The reason is that a player who adopts a mixed Nash equilibrium strategy does so in the hope that the other player will do so as well but is vulnerable to receiving a lower payoff should the other player (without penalty) deviate. In contrast, the maximin strategy secures the mixed Nash equilibrium payoff without risk.

A problem in interpretation of mixed strategy equilibrium was associated with the earlier view that this entailed the private use by each player of a random device (say a roulette wheel) that assigned the appropriate weight to each strategy in an agent's strategy set. It was imagined that a player would select the pure strategy prescribed by the realization of the single experiment with the random device.

While *ex-ante* the player adopting the mixed strategy would maximize expected utility, the *ex-post* implementation of the prescribed strategy might well be inferior to an alternative pure strategy.

Harsanyi provided a far more plausible interpretation of the concept of a mixed strategy Nash equilibrium, viewing the probability weights attached to the strategies in player i's strategy set as j's uncertainty about i's choice of pure strategy. A player's actual type will determine which pure strategy he or she will adopt. However, the mixed strategy Nash equilibrium depicts the expected utility incorporating the mutual uncertainty by all players about the others' type. This interpretation will be further described in the following section.

GAMES OF INCOMPLETE INFORMATION

Prior to the publication by Harsanyi (1967, 1968a, 1968b) of his three companion papers in *Management Science*, the tools of game theory were incapable of analyzing and solving any games in which any player had private information, also known as games of asymmetric information. By limiting game theory to games of complete information, where one assumes that all players are fully aware of the rules of the game as well as of all players' utility functions, the analytical apparatus of game theory was largely irrelevant for addressing social situations that pervade the real world.

To deal with games of incomplete information, Harsanyi's starting point is that players are Bayesian rational and as such, they must have *common prior beliefs*. In other words, they hold the same beliefs "before anything happens" (Binmore 1992, p. 476). The argument supporting this claim is that the only way to account for rational individuals holding *differing* beliefs is that they must have had different data or information to begin with, since they process information in the same way in arriving at their beliefs. After beginning a game with a common prior belief, their posterior beliefs may, of course, differ if one or more of them subsequently receives private information. From this starting point, it is but a small step to assert that it is "common knowledge" among rational agents that all of them have a common prior. (As formalized by Robert Aumann, to say that an event is "common knowledge" implies that everyone knows it, everyone knows that everyone knows it, everyone knows that everyone knows that everyone knows it, and so on *ad infinitum*.) It has been argued that because "the set W on which players' priors are defined is not even specified in precise terms" the Harsanyi doctrine regarding common knowledge about a common prior should be defended "as a working hypothesis rather than as a philosophical principle" (Binmore 1992).

Armed with the so-called Harsanyi doctrine, any game of incomplete information can be transformed into a game of imperfect information in the following way. It is assumed that a static Bayesian game is played in three stages. First, the players' types are determined by nature drawing for each player from the set of possible types that player might become. Thus, if nature draws from a vector of types $t = (t_1, \ldots t_n)$, this means that a representative player i becomes one of the possible types that he or she might possibly have become, that is, the realization of type after the draw is t_i from set T_i, where $i = 1, \ldots n$. At this point, it is assumed that each player acquires private information about his or her respective type. Player i's pure strategy set would comprise the set of all possible functions from domain T_i of i's possible types to range A_i of i's feasible actions. Although i's realized type would be privately known to i, the other players must specify their strategies for all possible realizations of i's type.

Harsanyi's extension of game theoretic analysis to include games of incomplete information has been of fundamental importance in securing game theory as a *relevant* research tool in the social sciences. From the interaction between a buyer and a seller in the marketplace to the theory of auctions to the vast literature on the economics of asymmetric information to the literature on mechanism design, Harsanyi's generalization of the tools of game theory has been far-reaching and its impact has been profound.

EQUILIBRIUM SELECTION IN GAMES

The general dissatisfaction among game theorists with the multiplicity of equilibrium solutions that commonly occur in games found expression in the ambitious collaborative project between Harsanyi and Reinhard Selten to establish appropriate criteria for determining a unique equilibrium solution for all games played by rational agents. This project began in 1972, and as Harsanyi remarks, "In the end, it took us 16 years of hard work to come up with a theory we felt to be worth presenting to the game-theorist community" (1997). That work culminated with the publication of *A General Theory of Equilibrium Selection in Games* (1988). Harsanyi and Selten describe the basic task of game theory: "to tell us what strategies rational players will follow and what expectations they can rationally entertain about other rational players' strategies" (1988, p. 342)

They then make the following observation, "The problems of rational strategies and rational expectations are strongly interdependent and require simultaneous solutions, since for any player's strategy to be a rational strategy, it must be a best reply to his rational expectations about the other players' strategies. Yet there is an inherent ambiguity in the notion of rational expectations. To the question of what expectations are rational we may get one answer if we assume that these expectations are strictly endogenous and a very different answer if we assume that the players' expectations will depend also on factors external to the game [such as social norms.]"

Harsanyi and Selten prescribe a procedure for eliminating all but one equilibrium solution on the basis of Pareto dominance and risk dominance, combined with a criterion for selecting between two candidate equilibria where one is risk dominant and the other is Pareto dominant.

Harsanyi points out that "Over time we first accepted and then rejected at least three different theories of equilibrium selection, before we adopted our final theory described in our 1988 book" (1997, p. 36). In fact, as Eric van Damme and J. W. Weibull (1995) point out, at a 1993 Nobel symposium on game theory, Harsanyi suggested an alternative theory of equilibrium selection, as did Selten the following year. The quest for a dominant single theory to determine a unique equilibrium will undoubtedly continue for the foreseeable future.

CONCLUSION

If there is one unifying element that is woven into the fabric of Harsanyi's lifetime intellectual achievements in such diverse areas game theory proper, bargaining theory, economics, sociology, and social ethics, it is the principle of Bayesian rationality. This underlying axiom has, in Harsanyi's gifted hands, enabled him to produce contributions of enduring intellectual significance in many diverse fields. Harsanyi's lifelong quest for a coherent theory of rational human conduct is perhaps a search for order and understanding in a chaotic world.

RECOMMENDED READINGS

Aumann, Robert J., and Maschler, M. (1972). "Some Thoughts on the Minimax Principle," *Management Science.* Vol. 18, pp. 54-63.

Binmore, Ken. (1992). *Fun and Games.* Lexington: D.C. Heath and Company.

——. (1956). "Approaches to the Bargaining Problem Before and After the Theory of Games: A Critical Discussion of Zeuthen's, Hicks', and Nash's Theories," *Econometrica.* Vol. 24, pp. 144-57.

——. (1967). "Games with Incomplete Information played by 'Bayesian' Players. Part I: The Basic Mode," *Management Science.* Vol. 14, No. 4, pp. 159-82.

——. (1968a). "Games with Incomplete Information played by 'Bayesian' Players. Part II: Bayesian Equilibrium Points," *Management Science.* Vol. 15, No. 1, pp. 320-34.

——. (1968b). "Games with Incomplete Information played by 'Bayesian' Players. Part III: The Basic Probability Distribution of the Game," *Management Science.* Vol. 15, No. 2, pp. 486-502.

——. (1977). *Rational Behavior and Bargaining Equilibrium in Games and Social Situations.* Cambridge: Cambridge University Press.

——. (1989). "Bargaining" *Game Theory.* Reprinted from *The New Palgrave: A Dictionary of Economics.* (ed.) J. Eatwell, M. Milgate, and P. Newman. New York: W. W. Norton.

——. (1992). *Game Theory for Applied Economists.* Princeton: Princeton University Press.

——. (1994). *Autobiography of John C. Harsanyi–Economic Sciences.* Stockholm: Nobel E-Museum, Official Web Site of the Nobel Foundation.

——. (1997). "Working With Reinhard Selten: Some Recollections on Our Joint Work 1965-1988" in Wulf Albers, et al., (eds.) *Understanding Strategic Interaction: Essays in Honor of Reinhard Selten.* Berlin: Springer-Verlag; pp. 35-39.

Harsanyi, John, and R. Selten. (1988). *A General Theory of Equilibrium Selection in Games.* Cambridge: MIT Press.

Osborne, Martin, and A. Rubinstein. (1994). *A Course in Game Theory.* Cambridge: MIT Press.

Van Damme, Eric, and J.W. Weibull. (1995). "Equilibrium in Strategic Interaction: The Contributions of John C. Harsanyi, John F. Nash and Reinhard Selten," *Scandinavian Journal of Economics*. Vol. 97, No. 1, pp. 15-40.

Zeuthen, Frederik. (1930). *Problems of Monopoly and Economic Warfare*. London: Routledge and Sons.

37

John Nash (1928-):
A Discoverer of the Nash Equilibrium
and a Laureate of 1994

Halima Qureshi
Hasina Mohyuddin

BIOGRAPHICAL PROFILE

John Nash was born in 1928 in Bluefield, West Virginia. He was named after his father, who was an electrical engineer. His mother, Margaret Virginia Martin, was a school teacher. After spending his early life in Bluefield, Nash started his undergraduate study in Carnegie Tech at Pittsburgh (now Carnegie Mellon University) on full scholarship, with chemical engineering as his major. Later on, he switched his major to mathematics. Due to his extraordinary scholastic achievement in mathematics, he was awarded an M.S. in addition to his B.S. when he graduated from Carnegie. While at Carnegie, Nash took one elective course in international economics, which exposed him to the economic ideas and problems that subsequently led him to develop the idea of game theory. He received his Ph.D. in mathematics in 1950 from Princeton University, where his game theory ideas were accepted as his doctoral thesis. After receiving his Ph.D., Nash worked as an instructor at Princeton University for a year. In the summer of 1951, he joined the mathematics faculty at M I.T. During 1956-1957, Nash was awarded an Alfred P. Sloan Grant, and he chose to spend the year as a temporary member of the Institute for Advanced Study at Princeton. During this period, he married Alicia, who graduated from M I.T with physics as her major. From 1950 to 1959, Nash enriched the field of economics, as well as mathematics, with his outstanding scholastic works. In the early months of 1959, when Alicia was pregnant, the brilliant career of Nash came to an unexpected halt. Nash was diagnosed as a schizophrenic. As a consequence, he resigned his position as faculty member at

M I T in the spring of 1959. The next twenty-five years of his life were spent in psychiatric care, which required him to be hospitalized from time to time. In the later part of the 1980s, after a long period of ailment, Nash came back to academic life and started producing respectable research papers. He hopes to contribute something of value through his current studies in the near future.

INTRODUCTION

John Nash, along with John Harsanyi and Reinhard Selten, won the economics Nobel Prize in 1994 for his "pioneering analysis of equilibria in the theory of non-cooperative games." Nash, the brilliant mathematician from Princeton University, is the most well known of the three–with good reason. It was Nash who truly provided the foundation on which the mathematics of game theory was built. As Robert Solow stated, "It wasn't until Nash that game theory came alive for economists." In a series of four scientific papers published between 1950 and 1953, Nash laid down the framework for the development of game theory. Today, game theory can safely be called the most significant recent development in economic analysis, and no well-rounded economics program can be complete without teaching it. As Fisher writes: "Bright, young theorists tend to think of every problem in game theoretic terms, including problems that are easier to deal with in other forms. Every department feels it needs at least one theorist who thinks in game theoretic terms. Oligopoly theory in particular is totally dominated by the game theoretic approach." It is Nash who made the distinction clear between cooperative and noncooperative games. He defined a unique concept of equilibrium in noncooperative games that is known as the Nash equilibrium in economics literature.

A BRIEF HISTORY OF
GAME THEORY

Game theory is the study of the strategic interaction between two (or more) parties, where the actions of one heavily influence the actions of the other. It gives both economists and other social scientists a model of behavior with which to analyze real-world problems in a manner that yields results more powerful than any other economic tool to date. Game theory assumes that people work optimally, rationally and in their own best interests to maximize their welfare, given the conditions of the environment that they are in. The agents in the game become known as the players, and the "payoffs" are modeled after the economic environment in which the players act. However, to fully understand the importance of game theory, it is important to understand what came before it.

Before the advent of game theory, the neoclassical theory of perfect competition dominated economic analysis. In perfect competition, the number of participants is so large that no single buyer or seller has power to influence the market. Therefore, there is no need for any firm to worry about the market actions or responses of others in determining what the equilibrium in the market will be. While perfect competition is a powerful tool to analyze markets such as the wheat market (with thousands of buyers and sellers), it takes game theory to provide an adequate framework with which to analyze how General Motors will change the price of its GeoMetro if Ford marks down the Festiva. With few participants in a market, every participant must take into account the actions of others. The economic logic is that given few players in a market, each player has the ability to change the market with its actions (for example, a firm can alter market price or use advertising to change consumer demand, etc.). Changes in the market obviously affect the competing firms, who must then decide how to respond to the changes made in the market. Thus, every participant must put himself in his competitors' shoes, predict what actions his competitors will choose, and then decide for himself what the best course of action would be, given his predictions. This is the essence of the game theoretic method.

The first application of this type of mutual interdependence was found in Cournot's 1838 book on economic theory. He constructed a theory of oligopolistic firms that explicitly took into account the mutual interdependence of firms. However, Cournot's emphasis was on explaining a single phenomenon (that of oligopoly) rather than on building a general framework with which to analyze economic behavior. The first systematic attempt to analyze strategic interactions in a more general framework was provided by John von Neuman and Oscar Morgenstern in their fundamental book, *Theory of Games and Economic Behavior*. In an earlier paper, von Neuman argued that virtually any competitive game can be modeled in a mathematical framework with the following structure: there is a set of players, each player has a set of strategies, each player has a payoff function that depends upon the strategy, and each player must choose his strategy independently of other players. In the first chapter of their 1947 book, von Neuman and Morgenstern claim that the theory of "games of strategy," as initiated by von Neuman, is the proper instrument with which to develop a theory of economic behavior. Thus they wrote, "We hope to establish satisfactorily that the typical problems of economic behavior become strictly identical with the mathematical notions of suitable games of strategy."

In the formal development of their theory, however, von Neuman and Morgenstern did not develop this idea fully. Two restrictions of their model, the zero-sum game (a game in which one person can gain only if another person loses, so that the sum of gains and losses equals zero) and transferable utility (the ability to exchange gains and losses in terms of utility, a condition of the zero-sum game), severely limited its claim to being a general model of economic behavior. Although the zero-sum game did provide a general framework with which to analyze economic behavior, its real-world applications were limited. In reality, the existence of nonzero-sum games (games in which mutual gains or losses are possible) are far more prevalent. John Nash recognized this fundamental problem with the von Neuman and Morgenstern model and began developing his own version of game theory, which would correct the problem.

John Nash arrived at Princeton University in 1948 as a young doctoral student in mathematics. The result of his doctoral research is reported in his dissertation, *Non-Cooperative Games*. In his dissertation, Nash introduced the distinction between cooperative games, in which binding agreements can be made, and noncooperative games, where binding agreements are not feasible. His most important contribution to the theory of noncooperative games was to formulate a universal solution concept with an arbitrary number of players and arbitrary preferences (i.e., not solely for a two-person zero-sum game). This solution concept later came to be known as the Nash equilibrium, a solution virtually unanticipated in economic literature. The Nash equilibrium is an outcome in which every player is acting optimally, rationally, and in his own self-interest to maximize his welfare. In a Nash equilibrium, no player can unilaterally do better by changing his strategy.

In deriving his equilibrium solution, Nash dropped the zero-sum game and transferable utility restrictions. By getting rid of these two weaknesses in the von Neuman and Morgenstern model, Nash provided economic theory with a general framework that could be applied to any form of game, thereby introducing games in which mutual gains or losses are possible. Thus, Nash ushered in the beginning of a new era of game theory. Despite its usefulness, there are problems associated with the concept of Nash equilibrium. If a game has several Nash equilibria, the equilibrium criterion is not sufficient to immediately predict the outcome of a game. Reinhard Selten, a joint Nobel laureate, enriched the Nash model by offering theories for discriminating between game outcomes that are reasonable and those that are unreasonable. Nash equilibria involving noncredible threats are unreasonable in economic terms and should, therefore, be eliminated as possible solutions to a game. Selten's formalization of the requirement that only credible threats should be taken into account led to the concept of subgame perfection, a refinement of the Nash equilibria concept. Another problem with the Nash equilibrium is its assumption of perfect information. In reality, however, each player rarely has perfect information about the strategic moves and payoffs of others. John Harsanyi showed that games with incomplete information could be remodeled as a game with complete but imperfect information, thereby enabling analysis of this important class of games and providing a theoretical framework for "the economics of information."

REAL WORLD APPLICATION
OF GAME THEORY

In game theory literature, several forms of games are presented to analyze real-world phenomena. The most famous game is perhaps the Prisoner's Dilemma. The story behind the game is that two people are arrested for committing a crime. The district attorney has little evidence in the case and is anxious to extract a confession. She separates the suspects and tells each, "If you confess and your associate does not, I can promise you a reduced sentence of six months, and your associate will get ten years in prison. If you both confess, you will each get a three year sentence." Each suspect also knows that if neither of them confesses, then the lack of evidence will cause them to be tried for a lesser crime for which they will receive two-year sentences. The promised jail sentences for this situation is given in Table 37.1.

In analyzing the Prisoner's Dilemma, we begin by analyzing A's strategies. Player A must decide whether he should confess or not. If A believes that B is going to confess, then by reviewing the first column, A sees that he has a choice between three years in jail if he confesses and ten years in jail if he does not confess. Clearly, confessing is A's best strategy if B confesses. If A believes B will not confess, then reading down the second column shows that A has a choice between six moths in jail if he confesses and two years in jail if he does not. Again, confessing is the better strategy. Thus, no matter what B does, confessing is the optimal strategy for A. Since B is in exactly the same situation as A, B will reach the same conclusion and confess. Thus, a confess/confess strategy constitutes a Nash equilibrium. However, an agreement by both prisoners not to confess would reduce both of their prison terms from three years to two years. Unfortunately, this rational solution of nonconfess/nonconfess is not stable. Each prisoner has an incentive to squeal on his or her partner in crime. This is the dilemma–the outcome that appears to be optimal is not stable. Any game that has a payoff matrix similar to the one given above can be analyzed using the same strategic decisions as the ones made by Players A and B in the Prisoner's Dilemma.

Table 37.1 The Prisoners' Dilemma

Prisoners' Dilemma	B: Confess	B: Nonconfess
A: Confess	A: 3 Years B: 3 Years	A: 6 Months B: 10 Years
A: Nonconfess	A: 10 Years B: 6 Months	A: 2 Years B: 2 Years

Prisoner's Dilemma-type problems may arise in many real-world market situations. Imagine two firms, A and B, producing similar products. Each must decide how much to spend on advertising. The purpose of advertisements is to increase market share and, thereby, increase profits. However, advertising costs money, and thus the budget allocated for advertising can also reduce profits. Given that the products of A and B are similar, any advertising done, regardless of which firm does it, raises the market share for the entire industry. Each firm must decide whether it should adopt a high budget or a low budget for advertising. The table below gives the possible payoffs of this game, which can be measured in terms of dollar profits. The payoffs can be read as (A's payoff, B's payoff):

Table 37.2 The Pay-off Matrix for Advertising Strategies

Advertising Strategy	B: Low Budget	B: High Budget
A: Low Budget	(7,7)	(3,10)
A: High Budget	(10,3)	(5,5)

By applying the same reasoning as seen in the Prisoner's Dilemma, it is seen that the high budget/high budget strategy constitutes the Nash equilibrium. However, if the two firms can cooperate, they will find that a mutual agreement to reduce advertising expenditures (i.e., using a low-budget strategy) would be more profitable for both parties. Such an agreement, however, would again be unstable, as either firm could increase its own profits even further by cheating on the agreement. Similar Prisoner's Dilemma situations arise in the airline industry, as seen in the practice of awarding bonus miles. There would be larger profits for all airlines if, as a group, they stopped offering free trips, but such a situation is unlikely to occur, given the incentive to cheat on such an agreement. Another real-world example of a Prisoner's Dilemma can be seen when a few firms cooperate, either openly (explicit collusion, as seen in OPEC) or implicitly (tacit collusion), to restrict the output of an industry. By restricting output, the firms in an industry can increase price, and thereby increases profits. The dilemma arises after a high price has been established, as each individual firm has the incentive to cheat by increasing its output (which would increase its own profits).

The Prisoner's Dilemma game can also be applied to the analysis of international trade restrictions. A country imposes trade restrictions in order to protect its industries from foreign competition. However, if two countries simultaneously impose trade restrictions against each other, the outcome is worse for both than free trade would have been. Looking at the strategies for each country, it can be seen that the best outcome is to have high tariffs while the other country has low tariffs; the next best solution is for both to have low tariffs; the next best solution is both having high tariffs; and the worst is having a low tariff while the other country has high tariffs—a classic Prisoner's Dilemma. The noncooperative Nash equilibrium—in which each country pursues its own best interests—will lead both countries to impose high tariffs rather than adopt the cooperative equilibrium (both countries imposing low tariffs) from which each country can benefit. This is the Prisoner's Dilemma of international trade; that is, each country will have the incentive to cheat on trade agreements. Therefore, some arrangement must be made to enforce cooperation among trading countries. This can be done with the help of a treaty such as GATT (General Agreement on Tariffs and Trade) or with each country following some trade policy that enables it to retaliate against foreign countries trade restriction policies (an example is Section 301 of the 1974 Trade Act that enables the president of the United States to retaliate against foreign countries' trade restriction policies that reduce the U.S. exports).

Besides the Prisoner's Dilemma, the other most widely used game in economic analysis is the game known as Chicken. This game has two players, A and B, and each player has two strategies–to cooperate or not to cooperate. Payoffs to the players are recorded in the table below, where zero is the least favorable outcome and three is the most favorable outcome for each player. As before, player A's payoffs are listed first.

Table 37. 3 The Chicken Game Pay-off Matrix

Chicken	B: Cooperate	B: Do Not Cooperate
A: Cooperate	(2,2)	(1,3)
A: Do Not Cooperate	(3,1)	(0,0)

This game has two Nash equilibria points–A cooperates, B does not cooperate; and B cooperates, A does not cooperate. Both of these solutions are, however, vulnerable to threats. If A cooperates and B does not, then A will threaten B that he will also choose not to cooperate. Since the noncooperate/noncooperate strategy is disastrous for both players, B will choose to cooperate. Similar reasoning can be applied to the situation where B cooperates and A does not. Thus, the cooperate/cooperate strategy will prevail. Unlike the Prisoner's Dilemma, the noncooperative solution here is unstable–all the entries in the table offer higher payoffs than the disaster solution. Though the cooperative solution will most likely prevail, it is in the best interests of each player to appear to be committed to a noncooperative strategy even if he or she intends to cooperate.

The game of Chicken is often used to explain oligopolistic behavior. The focus is on how firms maintain the stability of an oligopolistic situation, even though one firm could gain a clear advantage by altering its behavior. That is, by using the Chicken analysis, theorists can explain why the "cooperative solutions" appear to be stable despite the fact that they do not meet the Nash criteria for equilibrium. Consider, for example, the decision of the U.S. auto makers to refrain from building small cars in the 1950s and 1960s. Such restraint appeared to many observers to be unstable–a company that went ahead and built small cars could have made a significant profit by cheating on the agreement. However, the threat that its competitors would quickly enter the market (thereby eroding the profits of both small and large cars) kept any one firm from building small cars in that time period.

A related Chicken situation can be seen in the pricing of gasoline on major highways. In the gasoline market, there are relatively many sellers, all of whom seem to charge the same price at the same time, often changing prices on the same day. Presumably, any one seller faces a fairly elastic demand for its gasoline and could gain significant sales by dropping its price a few cents on the gallon. But if it did so, then its competitors would retaliate, and since total demand for gasoline along the highway is relatively inelastic, all firms would be worse off. Thus, "gas wars" arise because of the periodic breakdown of the cooperative solution, and consumers can see prices drop dramatically as a result. Unfortunately for the consumer, the price drops are usually quite short-lived, and discipline quickly returns to the market and reestablishes the cooperative equilibrium.

The game of Chicken also provides the best representation of the strategic nuclear deterrence policies practiced by the United States and the former Soviet Union. In the game-theoretic interpretation, both superpowers refrain from the use of nuclear weapons because of the threat of retaliation. Similar arguments were also made about the use of chemical and biological weapons during World War II. Although this cooperative solution is unstable in that each party could gain by being the first to use such weapons, the threat that the other nation will do the same maintains this unstable solution.

Prisoner's Dilemma and Chicken are two simple examples of games, the solutions of which come from the concept of Nash equilibrium (a pair of strategies in which each player's action is the best response to the other player's action). The immortal contribution of Nash was to provide an elegant and ingenious answer to an apparently intractable problem in simultaneous move games, where players are faced with a logical circle of reasoning ("I think that he thinks that I think....") as they try to see through each other's strategies. Prisoner's Dilemma produced a simple solution, since each player had a dominant strategy (to confess). The algorithm developed in Nash's classic 1950 paper, however, is capable of providing a framework for solutions to much more complex game structures. The paper "The Bargaining Problem," published in *Econometrica,* is inevitably highly mathematical and beyond the understanding of general readers, but the intuition and the significance of his insight is apparent even in the simple game situations discussed here. Given the applicability of the concept, not only in economics but also in a wide range of social phenomenon, it is not surprising that the Nash equilibrium concept has become an indispensable tool for social scientists. In the words of David Kreps, "Nowadays one cannot find a field of economics (or disciplines related to economics, such as finance, accounting, marketing and political science) in which an understanding of a Nash equilibrium is not nearly essential to the consumption of the recent literature."

CONCLUSION

Nash's bargaining research started in 1948, inspired by an undergraduate economics course at Carnegie and culminating in the publication of the article "The Bargaining Problem," widely recognized as a cornerstone of bargaining theory. After the publication of "Non-cooperative Games" in 1953, Nash extended his work by providing an application of his program designed to reduce cooperative game theory into a noncooperative equilibrium framework. In his paper, Nash offers an ingenious perturbational argument for selecting a unique stable equilibrium. These articles must be ranked among the most significant breakthroughs in economic theory. The elegance and rigor of Nash's approach to economic analysis has earned him the admiration and respect of his peers. Ariel Rubenstein, a leading game theorist from Princeton, commenting on Nash's classic paper "Non-cooperative Games," called him "the master of economic modeling."

In short, Nash had an amazingly productive career. Nash transformed games and related economic theory. Sadly, it will never be known how he would have shaped economic thought and what other impact he would have had on the discipline if illness had not tragically and prematurely curtailed his academic career. As a final word on John Nash, one can do no better than to echo Roger B. Mayerson, who stated, "In a room full of Nobel laureates, there is no one with a greater claim to have launched such a fundamental transformation in the scope of the field."

RECOMMENDED READINGS

Fisher, F.(1989). "Games Economists Play: A Non- cooperative View," *RAND Journal of Economics*. Vol. 20, pp. 113-24.

Kreps, D.M.(1990). *Game Theory and Economic Modeling*. Oxford: Oxford University Press,.

Leonard, Robert J. (1994, May). "Reading Cournot, Reading Nash: The Creation and Stabilization of the Nash Equilibrium," *The Economic Journal*. pp. 492-511.

Mayerson, Roger B. (1996, June). "John Nash's Contribution to Economics," *Games and Economic Behavior*. Vol. 14, No. 2, pp. 287-95.

McMillan, John. (1992). *Games, Strategies, and Managers: How Managers Can Use Game Theory to Make Better Business Decisions*. New York: Oxford University Press.

Nasar, S. (1994). "The Last Years of a Nobel Laureate," *New York Times*. November 13, section 3.

Nash, John F.(1950a). "Equilibrium Paints in N-Person's Games," *Proceedings of the National Academy of Sciences*. Vol. 36, pp. 48-49.

———. (1950b). "The Bargaining Problem," *Econometrica*. Vol. 18, pp. 155-62.

———. (1951), "Non-cooperative Games," *Annals of Mathematics*. Vol. 54, pp. 286-95.

———. (1953). "Two-Person Cooperative Games,"*Econometrica*. Vol. 21, pp. 128-40.

Rubinstein, Ariel. (1995). "John Nash: The Master of Economic Modeling," *Scandinavian Journal of Economics*. Vol. 97, No. 1, pp. 9-13.

Van Damme, Eric, and Jögen W. Weibull. (1995). "Equilibrium in Strategic Interaction: The Contribution of John C. Harsanyi, John F. Nash and Reinhard Selten," *Scandinavian Journal of Economics*. pp. 15-40.

von Neuman, John, and Oscar Morgenstern. (1947). *Theory of Games and Economic Behavior*. Princeton: Princeton University Press, Third edition, 1953.

38

Reinhard Selten (1930-   ):
Who Refines the Concept of
Equilibrium and Is a Laureate of 1994

Irwin Lipnowski

BIOGRAPHICAL PROFILE

Reinhard Selten was born in Breslau, Germany in 1930, the son of a Jewish father and Protestant mother. Following World War II, Breslau became part of Poland and was populated by Poles. Selten's father was a businessman, engaged in magazine distribution, who was forced to dispose of his business when the Nazis assumed power in 1933 and imposed restrictions on Jewish economic activities. The family suffered considerably as a result of the virulent anti-Semitism in Germany during this period. When Reinhard was 12, his father died and at age 14, he quit school to support his destitute family by working as an unskilled laborer. The family fled for their lives first to Saxonia, then Austria and finally Hessia where Reinhard found work as a farm boy. In 1947, the family moved to Melsungen where Reinhard attended high school, spending three and half hours daily walking to and from the school. He studied mathematics, economics and psychology, graduating in 1951. His interest in game theory was sparked by an article he read in *Fortune* magazine during his final year in high school. He enrolled in the University of Frankfurt in 1951, studying   physics and mathematical economics and during this period, he deepened his understanding of game theory by reading the monumental work by John von Neumann and Oskar Morgenstern, *The Theory of Games and Economic Behavior*. He graduated in 1957. Following the completion of a Master's degree, Heinz Sauermann hired Selten as his assistant. Selten continued to study decision theory, the theory of the firm and various aspects of experimental research and co-authored his first publication on experimental economics with Sauermann. In 1961 Selten received his Ph.D. in mathematics from the University of Frankfurt. Shortly thereafter, Oskar Morgenstern facilitated his participation at a conference on game theory at Princeton University, enabling Selten to establish professional links with some renowned economists, including Herbert Simon. In the 1960s, Selten carried out research and published on oligopoly and game theory. In 1965, he was invited to a conference on game theory in Israel where he met John Harsanyi. Selten carried out a productive joint research with both John Harsanyi and Thomas Marschak when he was appointed visiting professor at the University of California at Berkeley and this collaboration continued when Selten accepted an appointment at the University of Bielefeld. In 1984, he accepted a position at the University of Bonn, returning to Bielefeld for the 1987-88 academic year to complete a project on game theory and the behavioral sciences. At the University of Bonn, Selten continues his research on game theory and experimental economics. Reinhard Selten has been married to Elisabeth Langreiner since 1959 and she has fully supported him in his academic pursuits throughout their marriage. They have no children. In 1991, both Selten and his wife were diagnosed with diabetes.

INTRODUCTION

Reinhard Selten, along with John Harsanyi and John Nash, got the economics Nobel Prize in 1994 for his "pioneering analysis of equilibria in the theory of non-cooperative games." For more than three decades, Selten has been at the forefront of important developments in the foundations of the theory of noncooperative games, and his contributions have been seminal and profound. The award of the 1994 Nobel Prize in economics to Selten and his co-recipients reflected a recognition by the Royal Swedish Academy of Sciences that "game theory has become a dominant tool for analyzing economic issues" and that games are viewed "as the foundation for understanding complex economic issues."

THE PREMODERN ERA IN THE
DEVELOPMENT OF GAME THEORY

The invention of game theory as a coherent, integrated, and elegant discipline is universally credited to the collaborative efforts of the renowned mathematician John von Neumann and the eminent economist Oskar Morgenstern. Their book, *The Theory of Games and Economic Behavior,* established the focus and direction for most developments in the newly created field for the next twenty years. Von Neumann and Morgenstern analyzed two categories of games: (1) the two-player zero-sum game and (2) coalitional games played among three or more agents. The first category analyzes games that are strictly competitive and offer no scope for cooperation and compromise between opposing agents, since the gains accrued to one agent are only achieved at the expense of the other.. The second category has been characterized as cooperative games, since this type of game involves the formation of coalitions by various agents in pursuit of benefits for the coalition members.

An inescapable weakness of the analytical framework of cooperative games is that the assumption is made that all agreements between members of a coalition are binding. The theory of cooperative games simply assumes that all agents will comply with any agreements, for example, relating to the allocation among the individual members of a coalition of the joint payoff received by the coalition as a whole, without explicitly modeling the background conditions that would enforce agreements. The question of why all agreements would be binding has not been addressed. Following the approach of von Neumann and Morgenstern, this issue has been taken to be beyond the purview of cooperative game theory. In the real world, it is well understood that agents will abide by the terms of an agreement only if they have a sufficiently strong incentive to do so. The incentive could take the form of either a reward for compliance or a penalty for noncompliance. A penalty for noncompliance typically could be triggered by an aggrieved party who suffers damages from another party's failure to honor an agreement and seeks redress and compensation in the courts for breach of contract.

The analysis of the general class of *noncooperative games*, containing elements of *both cooperation and competition,* but without reliance upon the implicit presence of a third party to enforce agreements, began with the formulation by John Nash of the equilibrium concept, now referred to as Nash equilibrium. Dissatisfaction among game theorists with the cooperative game model and its implicit assumption that agreements are enforced by third parties, provided considerable impetus for the development and growing preponderance of noncooperative games in both theory and applications. Indeed, cooperative games are generally regarded at present as being an unduly restrictive special case of the more general class of noncooperative games. Nash noted that when the bargaining process that is implicit in cooperative games is specified and explicitly modeled, cooperative games can be regarded as a special case of noncooperative games.

Although the 1950s and early 1960s witnessed important strides in the development of solution concepts in the theory of cooperative games and in uncovering important relationships between them, the 1960s witnessed three parallel and complementary theoretical developments in the theory of noncooperative games. First, the generalization of the analytic framework of noncooperative games to that of repeated games (Aumann 1959) provided history-based strategies that provided the means to deter undesirable (noncooperative) behavior by enabling agents to retaliate in the future. Second, the highly restrictive assumption that agents know the beliefs and payoffs of all other players was removed by Harsanyi, who succeeded in generalizing the analytical framework of non-cooperative games to that of games of incomplete information. The third breakthrough in the extension of the theory of noncooperative games arose from the work of Selten in refining the concept of Nash equilibrium.

REFINING THE CONCEPT
OF EQUILIBRIUM

One landmark development in the theory of noncooperative games was the formulation of the solution concept of equilibrium by John Nash, Selten's co-recipient of the Nobel Prize. The noncooperative equilibrium was subsequently named the Nash equilibrium in honor of John Nash's achievement in formalizing the equilibrium concept and proving its existence. The concept of a Nash equilibrium embodies the ideas that all agents in the game have adopted their respective strategies (i.e., their complete plans of action) and that each agent's strategy is optimal, given the strategies adopted respectively by all the others. Thus, in a Nash equilibrium, the set of equilibrium strategies–one for each agent–are mutually best-response. This implies that given the strategies adopted by all other agents, no agent would have any incentive to deviate unilaterally from his/her equilibrium strategy, since this would confer no advantage on the deviating agent and might indeed result in some loss. A Nash equilibrium might be viewed as a situation of social stability, since no agent would be tempted to depart from the status quo. All agents would be simultaneously adopting mutually best-response strategies.

Selten exposed and remedied a serious flaw in the concept of the Nash equilibrium. The very definition of the Nash equilibrium implies that, from the perspective of any particular agent, the strategies of all other agents are taken as given, without examining whether the actions they prescribe are rational. To illustrate this, consider the well-known "entry game" played once between monopoly firm M and potential entrant E, depicted in Figure 38.1.

Figure 38.1 The Well-known "Entry Game"

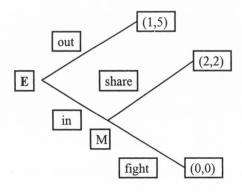

If E stays out of M's market, E's payoff would be 1 and that of M would be 5. If entry occurs, M can "share" the market, with a resulting payoff of 2 to each firm, or "fight" with a payoff to each firm of 0. The entry game has two Nash equilibria: (1) E does not enter the market (out) and M plans to fight if E enters; and (2) E enters (in) and M accommodates this entry (share). However, only Nash

Equilibrium (2) is reasonable. The reason for this is that M's plan to fight if E enters would be irrational, for if M were to actually fight in this situation, this would simply reduce M's payoff from 2 to 0. Selten refined the Nash equilibrium concept in an effort to eliminate all implausible Nash equilibria. There were several sources of such implausibility. First, as in the example above, the equilibrium might have been sustained by an agent lending credence to another player's empty threat—a threat that no reasonable opponent, whose bluff was called, would be prepared to carry out. A second class of implausible Nash equilibria, to be illustrated below, would involve players adopting weakly dominated strategies.

With respect to the first category, Selten introduced a refined subset of the set of Nash equilibria, which he designated subgame perfect Nash equilibria, thereby ushering in a new era in game theory in which only such refined Nash equilibria were incorporated in game theoretic applications. Henceforth, virtually all applications subjected Nash equilibria to an additional test before they were deemed to be sensible, namely that each equilibrium strategy prescribe rational behavior within each sub-game of the original game. Selten's refinement of the Nash equilibrium concept is based upon a compelling idea that has swept the economics profession: that there be a presumption of rationality imputed to one's opponents and that this presumption should be weakened only by evidence to the contrary that might be gleaned in the course of an unfolding game. Whereas Nash blazed the trail in the domain of noncooperative games by formulating the equilibrium concept and proving its existence, Selten focused upon its robustness and stability, in other words, its ability to withstand and survive minor disturbances (perturbations) arising from mistakes (a trembling hand that might inadvertently take an unintended action, albeit with low probability). Selten was concerned about the possibility of a Nash equilibrium that consisted of players adopting weakly dominated strategies. Since a weakly dominated strategy is one in which an agent never fares better and will always fare strictly worse in some circumstances, it would seem to be irrational to ever adopt a dominated strategy. Yet weakly dominated strategies were not inconsistent with Nash equilibrium.

In weeding out from the set of Nash equilibria those that are based upon weakly dominated strategies, Selten focused upon the possibility, however remote, that an intended action might not be taken and that an unintended action might occur. Selten wanted to restrict the set of admissible equilibria to those that were robust in the face of the small possibility of random error, in other words, a perturbation resulting from a trembling hand. If we imagine that the hand of a player who is about to play a pure strategy trembles slightly but uncontrollably, the intended strategy would be played only with probability 1-ε, where ε is positive but very small. In this kind of environment, Selten succeeded in eliminating from the set of Nash equilibria those strategy profiles that contain weakly dominated strategies.

Table 38.1 The Nash Equilibria Strategies and the Pay-off Matrix

	L	R
T	(1,1)	(0,0)
B	(0,0)	(0,0)

To illustrate, consider the normal form game depicted in Table 38.1, played between a Row and a Column player. The first number in each cell denotes the payoff to the Row player, the second number in each cell is the Column player's payoff. The players simultaneously and independently select their respective strategy. The Row player's strategy set is (T,B) while that of the Column player is (L,R.) This game has two Nash equilibria, namely (T,L) and (B,R). Although one might argue that no rational agent would ever play strategy B or R, since these are weakly dominated by T and L respectively, if the Row player expected the Column to play R for sure, the Row player would have no incentive to deviate from playing B. Likewise, if the Column player expected the Row player to play B for sure, the Column player would have no incentive to deviate from strategy R. However, if the Row player is almost certain that his counterpart will play R, or the Column player is almost certain that B will be played, where 'almost certain' means 'with probability 1-ε' where ε is positive but negligibly small, then (B,R) would no longer be a Nash Equilibrium. Thus the unique Nash Equilibrium would become the pair of mixed strategies in which T and L would be each be played with probability 1-ε. By simply adding a dose of realism to the environment and admitting the slight possibility of unintentional actions occurring by mistake, a highly implausible class of Nash equilibria involving weakly dominated strategies is eliminated.

SELTEN AND THE REAL WORLD

Although Selten has a superb mastery of the tools of mathematical economics, the hallmark of his lifetime of contributions is that his ideas are *consistently rooted* in the real world, both in terms of the subject matter and in Selten's interpretation of results. A recurring theme in Selten's papers is that irrationality in the form of mistakes pervades the world. How is a rational agent to come to terms with this fact? Within a few years of Selten's path-breaking theoretical contribution to trembling hand mistakes, he collaborated on a paper that deals with the problem of fear of the irrational in the important arena of arms control. In a paper, written jointly with John Mayberry in 1992, Selton analyzes a simple model of cold-war competition, examining why a blissful status quo of continuing peace, apparently a steady state situation, might be disturbed. The subject matter is of great practical importance. Selten and Mayberry identify the psychological factors of fear and greed as "the two practical obstacles to such a happy state of affairs." One cause of a nation's fear that is associated with weapons in the hands of a potential enemy is that a nation may thereby be left "more exposed to the possibility of an accidental or irrational attack."

Selten's abiding interest in the psychological dimension of conflict situations appears in a seminal paper he wrote in 1978, "The Chain Store Paradox." In it, Selten tackles a theme that was first discussed by D. Luce and H. Raiffa, the finite repetition of the Prisoners' Dilemma game. The "story" Selten tells is as follows: A chain store, also called player A, has branches in twenty towns, numbered 1 to 20. In each of these towns, there is a potential competitor, a small businessman who might establish a second shop of the same kind. Apart from these twenty players, the chain store does not face any other competition, neither now nor in the future. The stage game played sequentially in each town is exactly as described above in the entry game. By a backward induction reasoning process, one is lead inexorably to the conclusion that a rational entrant should enter the market of the chain store at each stage, and that the chain store should accommodate the entry by sharing the market in each town.

The mathematical argument for this is airtight and unassailable. In the final (twentieth) town, the entrant should enter, since the chain store will surely not fight. The reason is that there is no future entrant to deter, and fighting will only lower the chain store's payoff from 2 to 0. A rational entrant should, therefore, enter in the penultimate (nineteenth) town, anticipating that the chain store will share the market, having established that entry and sharing will occur in the last town. Working backward, the conclusion is reached that entry occurs in each town, and the chain store responds always by sharing the market. A corollary of the backward induction argument is that any attempt by the chain store to deter future entry by fighting is futile. Nevertheless, in some revealing remarks about of the relative merits of the backward induction argument and the "deterrence theory" (that prescribes that the chain store react aggressively to entry in the earlier stages of this game in order to enhance its reputation for toughness so as to deter entry in the later stages), Selten demonstrates that he is completely grounded in the real world. In weighing the relative merits of the induction theory and the "deterrence theory," Selten exhibits far greater faith in his intuition than in a blind acceptance of the implications of mathematical logic: "...only the induction theory is game theoretically correct. Logically, the induction argument cannot be restricted to the last periods of the game. There is no way to avoid the conclusion that it applies to all periods of the game. Nevertheless the deterrence theory is much more convincing. If I had to play the game in the role of player A (the chain store), I would follow the deterrence theory. I would be very surprised if it failed to work. From my discussions with friends and colleagues, I get the impression that most people share this inclination. In fact, up to now I met nobody who said that he would behave according to the induction theory. My experience suggests that mathematically trained persons recognize the logical validity of the induction argument, but they refuse to accept it as a guide to practical behavior. "It seems to be safe to conjecture that even in a situation where all players know that all players understand the induction argument very well, player A (the chain store) will adopt a deterrence policy and the other players will expect him to do so. The fact that the logical inescapability of the induction theory fails to destroy the plausibility of the deterrence theory is a serious phenomenon which merits the name of a paradox. We call it the 'chain store paradox.'"

For Selten, intuition and common sense serve as checks upon the behavior prescribed by mathematical logic. Methodologically, Selten's approach is in sharp contrast to the bias of many mathematical social scientists, for whom intuition is deemed to be faulty whenever it conflicts with mathematical logic. Selten's stubborn endorsement of the deterrence theory inspired a host of game theorists, most notably Kreps, Milgrom, Roberts, and Wilson, to rethink the problem of backward induction in a finitely repeated game and to search for a rigorous foundation for a strategy of deterrence. Selten's interest in a rational response to psychological irrationality is again expressed in an interesting paper on kidnaping. A kidnapper (player K) is assumed to demand a ransom $D > 0$ from the family of a hostage in exchange for the latter's release. Assuming that the family pays the kidnapper the sum $C \leq D$, the kidnapper must then decide whether to release or kill the hostage. Selten argues that even though the kidnapper "cannot improve his situation (by killing the hostage) his threat has some credibility." One must fear that under the strain of emotional pressure, the kidnapper may react violently to an unsatisfactory offer in spite of the fact that this is against his long run interests. Therefore, we must expect that with a positive probability α, the kidnapper will perceive an offer $C < D$ as an aggressive act and a strong frustration to which he will react violently by the execution of his threat.

Selten formally incorporates the sequence of "perceived aggression -> frustration -> possible uncontrolled violent reaction" into his model, denoting by $\alpha = a(1 - C/D)$ the probability that the kidnapper will kill the hostage where $0 < a < 1$. Thus, the hostage is released if the kidnapper's demand is fully met, whereas anything less than full compliance with the kidnapper's demand entails some risk that he might irrationally kill the hostage. The key ingredient in rendering the kidnapper's threat credible is the risk of his uncontrolled violence. By setting his applications in a universe characterized by irrationality, where mistakes occur, Selten has significantly increased the realism, relevance, and practical importance of his applied work.

UNIQUE EQUILIBRIUM SELECTION

Perhaps the most ambitious task undertaken by Selten, in collaboration with John Harsanyi, has been the determination of a unique Nash equilibrium in every game. Having initiated the program of eliminating unreasonable Nash equilibria that fail the test of subgame perfection or that include weakly dominated strategies, Selten formed a coalition with Harsanyi in their quest for the ultimate goal in such a winnowing process to eliminate all but a single Nash equilibrium in every type of game played by rational agents. The task has been described by the leading game theorists as "unequaled in its universal scope and fundamental comprehensiveness" (Roger Myerson) and as "a heroic and thorough attempt. No other task may be more significant within game theory" (Ariel Rubinstein). In his foreword to the Harsanyi-Selten book (1988), Aumann describes the book as "a major event in game theory."

The Harsanyi-Selten procedure for equilibrium selection is a complex one, involving many stages of transformation and reductions of the original game. Such procedures are based upon their earlier pivotal contributions and breakthroughs. Cooperative games are transformed into noncooperative games, games of incomplete information are transformed into games of imperfect information, and criteria for choosing between equilibria where they possess different desirable properties are specified. For example, one equilibrium may Pareto-dominate another yet may be "risk-dominated" (as they define the latter concept) by the other. Since Harsanyi and Selten base their equilibrium selection process on the assumption that all agents are rational Bayesian decisionmakers, this entails formulating a theory about the appropriate prior beliefs that agents would hold. To circumvent a succession of hurdles, the authors boldly make a series of reasoned assumptions. In a sense, the jury is still out with respect to the particular equilibrium selection process proposed by Harsanyi and Selten. It is clear that the authors could have made alternative assumptions and developed reasonable alternative theories. Nevertheless, the program initiated by Harsanyi and Selten is a crucial first step in developing a general theory of rationality. Indeed, future researchers may well judge Harsanyi and Selten's heroic efforts in pursuit of this goal to be their crowning achievement.

CONCLUSION

Central to Selten's scientific concerns has been the general objective of building a foundation for rational conduct in a world fraught with irrationality, which takes the form of random events reflecting unintended action or mistakes committed by agents. To place Selten's main contributions to the development of game theory in proper perspective, it is necessary to sketch a very brief overview of developments in the theory of games, beginning with the pioneering work of John von Neumann and Oskar Morgenstern, contained in their monumental book The Theory of Games and Economic Behavior, continuing with the pathbreaking contribution of John Nash; and culminating in Selten's landmark contribution in 1965 (in German) and Selten's further development of the ideas in that paper in 1975 where Selten addressed the problem of refining Nash's concept of equilibrium in noncooperative games.

RECOMMENDED READINGS

Harsanyi, John. (1967). "Games with Incomplete Information played by Bayesian Players. Part I: The Basic Model,"*Management Science*. Vol. 14, No. 4, pp. 159-82.
———. (1968a). "Games with Incomplete Information Played by Bayesian Players. Part II: Bayesian Equilibrium Points," *Management Science*. Vol. 15, No. 1, pp. 320-34.

——. (1968b). "Games with Incomplete Information played by Bayesian Players. Part III: The Basic Probability Distribution of the Game," *Management Science*. Vol. 15, No. 2, pp. 486-502.

Harsanyi, John, and R. Selten, (1988). *A General Theory of Equilibrium Selection in Games*. Cambridge: MIT Press.

Luce, D., and H. Raiffa. (1957), *Games and Decisions*. New York: John Wiley and Sons.

Mayberry, John P., and Reinhard Selten. (1968). "Applications of Bargaining I-Games to Cold-War Competition," in Mathematica, Inc., *The Indirect Measurement of Utility*, Final Report of U.S. Arms Control and Disarmament Agency/ ST-143. Reprinted in J.P. Mayberry, et al., (eds.) (1992). *Game Theoretical Models of Cooperation and Conflict*. Boulder: Westview Press.

Mas-Colell, A., M.D. Whinston, and J. Green. (1995). *Microeconomic Theory*. New York: Oxford University Press.

Nash, John. (1950). "Equilibrium Points in n-Person Games," *Proceedings of the National Academy of Sciences*. Vol. 36, pp. 48-49.

——. (1951). "Non-Cooperative Games," *Annals of Mathematics*. Vol. 54, pp. 286-95.

Osborne, Martin J., and Ariel Rubinstein. (1994). *A Course in Game Theory*. Cambridge: MIT Press.

Royal Swedish Academy of Sciences. (1995). "The Nobel Prize in Economics 1994," *Scandinavian Journal of Economics*. Vol. 97, No. 1, pp. 1-7.

Selten, Reinhard. (1965). "Spieltheoretische Behandlung eines Oligopolmodells mit Nachfragetragheit,' *Zeitschrift für die gesamte Staatswssenschaft*. Vol. 121, pp. 301-24, 667-89.

——. (1975). "Reexamination of the Perfectness Concept for Equilibrium Points in Extensive Games," *International Journal of Game Theory*. Vol. 4, pp. 25-55.

——. (1978). "The Chain Store Paradox," *Theory and Decision*. Vol. 9, pp. 127-59.

Van Damme, Eric, and J.W. Weibull. (1995). "Equilibrium in Strategic Interaction: The Contributions of John C. Harsanyi, John F. Nash and Reinhard Selten," *Scandinavian Journal of Economics*. Vol. 97, No. 1, pp. 15-53.

von Neumann, John, and O. Morgenstern. (1944). *Theory of Games and Economic Behavior*. New York: John Wiley and Sons.

39

Robert Lucas Jr.(1937-   ):
A Pioneer of the New Classical
School of Thought and the Laureate of 1995

Faridul Islam
Norman D. Gardner

BIOGRAPHICAL PROFILE

Robert Lucas Jr. was born in 1937 in Yakima, Washington. During World War II, his family moved to Seattle, Washington. There his father was a steam fitter in the shipyards and his mother was a career fashion artist. Lucas graduated from Roosevelt High School, Seattle, in 1955. During his school years, he was quite strong in mathematics and science. He had a dream to enter MIT to study engineering. His father agreed to it, provided he would get a scholarship, but he did not get a scholarship from MIT. However, the University of Chicago granted him a scholarship. Unfortunately Chicago did not have a school of engineering. Nevertheless, Lucas joined the University of Chicago and took courses in mathematics and physics. Soon he lost interest in both. Then he started studying history and found it quite intriguing. He graduated in 1959 with a major in history. He obtained a Woodrow Wilson Doctoral Fellowship and joined the graduate program in history at the University of California at Berkeley. Without having any knowledge in other European languages, he could not proceed further with his classical interests, so he began taking courses with a rather open mind. At Chicago, the most exciting modern historian he had read was Henri Pirenne. Lucas was impressed with Pirenne's shift of focus from the affairs of the kings and emperors to the struggling daily lives of private citizens. This prompted him to enroll in economic history and economic theory classes at Berkeley. Soon he liked economics and decided to move to the University of Chicago with a generous financial assistance. At Chicago, he had to do some prerequisite courses in economics. For economics, Lucas had to learn a good deal of calculus and mathematics. Lucas obtained his Ph.D. in economics in 1964. As a graduate student at Chicago, he became a good friend of Glen Cain, Neil Wallace, Sherwin Rosen, G.S. Maddala, and many others. Lucas began his professional career by joining Carnegie Mellon University, where he spent a lot of time learning the mathematics of dynamical systems and optimization over time, and trying to see how these methods could best be applied to economic questions. There he came in close contact with John Muth, the originator of rational expectations theory in economics. At Carnegie Mellon, he also got the opportunity to know Edward Prescott, initially as a graduate student and then as a colleague. Soon, they became very good friends, and together they learned modern general equilibrium theory, functional analysis and probability theory and wrote a paper, 'Investment under Uncertainty,' that reformulated Muth's idea of rational expectations in a useful way. During this time, in Lucas' own words, "my whole point of view of economic dynamics took form (along with Ed's), in a way that has served me well ever since." At Carnegie Mellon, being persuaded by David Cass, Edmund Phelps, and from what he learned working with Edward Prescott, Lucas produced perhaps the most influential piece of his works in 1970, entitled, "Expectations and the Neutrality of Money." Published in 1972, the theme of this paper was one of the subjects of his Nobel lecture. In 1974, Lucas returned to the University of Chicago as a faculty member and became the John Dewey Distinguished Service Professor in 1980.

INTRODUCTION

Robert Lucas won the economics Nobel Prize in 1995 for "having developed and applied the hypothesis of rational expectations, and thereby having transformed macroeconomic analysis and deepened our understanding of economic policy." The Royal Swedish Academy of Sciences says in its citation that Robert Lucas is the economist who has had the greatest influence on macroeconomic research since 1970. His work has brought about a rapid and revolutionary development: Application of the rational expectations hypothesis, emergence of an equilibrium theory of business cycles, insights into the difficulties of using economic policy to control the economy, and possibilities of reliably evaluating economic policy with statistical methods. In addition to his work in macroeconomics, Lucas' contributions have had a very significant impact on re search in macroeconometrics. Lucas has been very well known in the economics profession particularly for his research in the field of macroeconomic theory and policy. He has written and published an enormous volume of works by any standard. He has made contributions to macroeconomic literature, particularly in the areas of business cycles, and macroeconomic policy issues based on rational expectations. His work has had profound impact on macroeconomic theory, although its impact on policy aspects has received a mixed reaction in the profession.

Much of Lucas' work is at theoretical level, and there is strong disagreement among economists as to whether his contributions have anything to do with policy issues. It is widely believed that despite the enormous impact of his work on economic research, probably not much has changed as a result. To some economists, he is controversial because he argues against the central banks' fine tuning of economies and intervening in foreign exchange markets. Such actions, Lucas says, are "a mistake," adding that central bankers and treasury officials "haven't learned anything in 200 years." Downplaying the work of Lucas, Oliver Blanchard, the MIT professor, said that it had zero impact on the way government and central bankers perceive their job. Regardless of the impact of Lucas' works on public policy, he is widely recognized as an outstanding economic theorist of the modern time. His contributions may be summarized under several broad categories as below.

THE NEW CLASSICAL SCHOOL OF THOUGHT

As an economist, the views of Lucas belong to the new classical school of thought. This school is built on the foundations provided in the classical postulates. The classical model strongly stresses the existence of full employment of resources as a rule and believes in strict market mechanism in restoring out of equilibrium situations almost instantaneously, without any government intervention of any kind. A brief review of the efforts at restoration of the classical model may be in order. In the wake of the Great Depression, when the very foundation of classical economics was destined to be doomed to failure, John Maynard Keynes came up with what subsequently came to be known as the demand management policy. In that policy, the need for government intervention was explicitly recognized within a free market system. That raised the question about the modalities of intervention. Monetary policy, which is essentially changing the quantity of money, was thought to have no effect on real variables in the economy. Under the classical framework, economy was conceived as having distinctly separated sectors: real and monetary, the former dealing with output, employment, real wage, savings, investment, and so on, while the latter dealt with quantity of money, absolute level of prices, nominal wage, and more. This dichotomization, as it is often referred to, received the theoretical blessings from the quantity of theory of money also known as the Fisherian equation of exchange. This theory suggests a proportional and positive relation between quantity of money and level of absolute prices. Hence changing the quantity of money would not be able to affect the real sector, being determined by the interaction of variables such as technology, resources and others. This dichotomy issue has undergone extensive debate. (Patinkin: 1948)

While the idea of monetary policy as a tool was already there, with the advent of Keynesianism, now came a new concept called the fiscal policy, a regulation of tax, subsidy and the active role of the government. There was not much dispute at the initial stage about the working of the policy, but with the work of Carl Christ, who questioned the separation of monetary policy from fiscal policy, the issue has become a spot of serious debate that is still ongoing. Milton Friedman tried to give another boost to the revivalist strategy, aimed at restoring the classical model being the more realistic picture of the working of the economy and is known as the monetarist school. Under this, only monetary policy was assigned an active role. In the pure classical model, while uncertainty is modeled by perfect foresight, the contribution of Lucas lies in the provision of a behavioral model in which it is hypothesized that the agents are rational in the forming of expectations and that the markets are continuously clearing. This is known as new classical economics in macroeconomic literature. In that sense, his work toward the revival of the classical concept is not something fundamentally different, although it was presented under a different clout. At the heart of the new classical school of thought, there lie two basic principles: first, that individuals, households, and businesses form their expectations rationally based on the same set of information (available to the policy making authorities,) and second, that the markets are believed to be continuously clearing. More simply, these two principles are known as the rational expectations and the continuous market clearing.

Rational Expectations

The concept of rational expectations did not originate in the hands of Robert Lucas; rather it came out of the brilliant mind of John Muth when he was trying to explain why no rule, formula or model has ever been successful in predicting prices in speculative markets and his answer was, in effect, that all available information is already incorporated into current decisions by speculators, whose expectations are 'rational' in this precise sense. Muth's theory did not gain much prominence until the 1970s, when Lucas developed and applied it to the macroeconomic theory and policy. In several ingenious works, Lucas successfully showed the far-reaching impacts of the formation of rational expectations, especially pertaining to effects of economic policy and the evaluation of these effects using advanced econometric techniques.

Lucas is one of the most prominent, vigorous, and outspoken exponents of rational expectations theory. He very persuasively argues that since the expectations of the economic agents are rational, therefore so-called stabilization policies such as monetary and fiscal policies do affect employment and output only very temporarily. He also argues that the rational expectations hypothesis inherently and irreconcilably refutes the Keynesian economics. Rational expectations principle believes that the economic agents are always rational, implying that they are maximizers or optimizers. In other words, the economic agents obtain the best possible outcomes in any given situation. In formulating economic decisions, people always try to get the best results, regardless of whether they are profit maximizers or utility maximizers. In this maximization exercise, the business firms and the households face the present state of technology and the current level of income as their constraints. The implication of rational expectations is that a government's attempt to stabilize the economies by expansionary or contractionary policies is bound to fail, because people form their future expectations rationally. They also have enough information to anticipate the policy effect and thus can change their behavior accordingly, which in turn distorts the intended effects of the policy. The only way governments can succeed is if their policy actions are unanticipated by the public. In that case, according to Lucas, government has to "fool the people" persistently and systematically.

Continuous Market Clearing

The postulate of continuous market clearing implies that equilibrium is restored more or less instantaneously in the financial and commodity markets–markets often referred to as "auction markets." This is what is called efficient market hypothesis that is essentially discerned from Walrisian general equilibrium theory. Efficient markets hypothesis is based on a fundamental relationship between prices and information. A market is said to be efficient when the equilibrium prices determined in that market reflect every bit of information about the commodity being traded. Another feature of the efficient market is that, it not only processes the information in an exhaustive manner but also does it very quickly. Financial markets are found to be efficient in this sense. However, commodity and labor markets are believed to be much less efficient in this sense.

THE PHILLIPS CURVE

After studying nearly 100 years of British data, Arthur Phillips presented an apparently impressive relationship between inflation and employment. That is, the periods of high employment were associated with high inflation and vice versa. Thus employment and inflation seem to be related positively. In other words, unemployment and inflation are inversely related, a relationship that is popularly known as the Phillips curve in the macroeconomic literature. In the late 1960s, the Phillips relation was fairly corroborated by empirical evidence. Since the Phillips curve displays a trade-off between unemployment and inflation, its policy implication was clear–that government can decrease unemployment by adopting expansionary policies resulting in inflation. In response to the Phillips curve and its policy conclusion, Milton Friedman and Edmund Phelps argued that the reduction in unemployment cannot be sustained by expansionary policies because economic agents would adjust their behavior to higher inflation. The Friedman-Phelps argument was not very convincing since they assumed an adaptive scheme of expectations that implies sustained reduction in unemployment provided inflation is allowed to increase persistently.

Lucas' contribution to the interpretation of the Phillips curve has been summarized beautifully in the Nobel website. In a study published in 1972, Lucas used rational expectations hypothesis to provide the first theoretically satisfactory explanation why Phillips curve could be sloping in the short run but vertical in the long run. In other words, regardless of how it is pursued, stabilization policy cannot systematically affect long-run employment. Lucas formulated an ingenious theoretical model which generates time series such that inflation and employment indeed seem to be positively correlated. A statistician who studies these time series might easily conclude that employment could be increased by impending an expansionary economic policy. Nevertheless, Lucas demonstrated that any endeavor, based on such policy, to exploit the Phillips curve and permanently increase employment would be futile and only give rise to higher inflation. This is because agents in the model adjust their expectations and hence price and wage formation to the new, expected policy. Experience during the 1970s and 1980s has shown that higher inflation does not appear to bring about a permanent increase in employment. This insight into the long run effects of stabilization policy has become a commonly accepted view; it is now the foundation for monetary policy in a number of countries in their efforts to achieve and maintain a low and stable inflation rate.

THE LUCAS CRITIQUE

With respect to the definition of appropriate economic policies, there ought to be differences in method to be adopted given the differences in opinion among economists. This, in part, reflects the differing positions on the implementation of both the positive and the normative aspects in economics. The former belongs to the domain of how the economy actually works, while the latter belongs to the differing subjective value judgment. As an example, we might consider an issue from one of the current debates on economic policy, such as those concerning reduction of the federal deficit. The differing views stem from whether budget balancing agenda should begin with concentration on a large tax cut supplemented by a significant cut in entitlement programs, or whether to defer significant tax cuts while reducing the expenditures in phases until debt scenario reveals noticeable reduction. Obviously, these two methods will affect people in different ways through their impact on consumption and investment and, eventually, how they affect the growth of the economy. Such judgments are inherently political. Any discussion at any level of necessity needs to be an informed one so that the positive consequences of pursuing one policy rather than another must be thoroughly investigated by conducting impact studies of such policies. This part of the work, often ascribed as policy evaluation, by all accounts cannot and should not be confined to the theoretical considerations alone. The path an economy follows is determined by the simultaneous interactions of systems of relationships. Therefore, each action will generate a series of benefits and also costs. It is important that benefits be assessed against alternatives lost. Thus quantitative effects of different policy regimes are to be ascertained to make an overall judgment about any policy to be adopted. Also involved is the value judgment about the cost of each alternative that ought to be based on subjective judgment of the policymakers. An in-depth empirical examination of the situations surrounding these environments is necessary for proper assessment of each of the alternatives under review.

The questions not answered are what policy evaluation is and how it works. Any macroeconomic modeling involves a large database. Such models have been tried in many countries using several equations. Using data, these models are estimated. These coefficients of the estimated models are simulated to obtain forecast of future values using the current policies. Based on these, one can then say what are the likely outcomes of applying the current policy without changes. To make things represent reality more closely, an alternative policy regime is formulated and further simulation results are obtained. The differential outcomes under each simulation are then interpreted as rough estimate of the likely consequences of pursuing the alternative policies. With the increasing use of sophisticated modeling approaches and powerful computer hardware and software, simulations are matters of simple everyday exercise. As such, they have earned respectability and an increasing order of importance. Thus they are finding use in a wider scale in the implementation of more and more formal econometric policy evaluation exercises

Lucas, in 1976, was the first author who raised serious doubt about such evaluations. He proposed an explanation that casts serious skepticism on econometric policy evaluations. He argued that the coefficients in the econometric equations might not remain constant in the event of policy changes. He notes: Given that the structure of an econometric model consists of optimal decision rules of economic agents, and that optimal decision rules vary systematically with changes in the structure of series relevant to the decision maker, it follows that any change in policy will systematically alter the structure of the econometric models. Lucas' claim that such evaluations are likely to give rise to seriously misleading conclusions is based on the mechanism as to how parameters of policy rules may enter parametrically into economic agents' optimization rules. Lucas considers examples where agents' "expectations" of policy behavior enter into their optimization problem. Thus the parameters appearing in the policymaker's rules enter into the first order condition of optimization. The question becomes whether an econometric model can effectively isolate the "invariant" of economic process. Such invariance principles have been raised in the lengthy and contentious history that describes the econometric literature. Notable among such writings are those of Haavelmo, Frisch, and Aldrich. The writers of the earlier vintage provide the earlier part of the discussion, while those in the latter vintage provide in an extensive historical perspective.

To motivate readers with his ideas, Lucas refers to four observations: (1) frequent and frequently important refitting of econometric relationships; (2) adjusting the intercept for forecasting purposes; (3) superior forecasts by the use of models with randomly varying coefficients; and (4) excluding the data prior to 1947 for model fitting purposes even if such data could be informative. It is important to note that all of these four observations mentioned by Lucas could very well result from model misspecification of the kind described by Lucas. Even though the fundamental idea on which Lucas' proposition is based derives much of its theoretical foundation from the rational expectations hypothesis (REH), there remains much scope to question the validity of the proposition from the point of view of empirical consideration. REH in its simplest form views rational agents as using all information available at hand in order to make "on an average" an optimum decision. If this is true, individuals forming expectations rationally must be using all the information to model government behavior. So if the estimated coefficients of observable equations contain policy parameters that have entered through their role as predictors of future values, these parameters will change when a new policy is adopted. Hence changes in policy rules will not only affect the parameters of the equation but also parameters in other equations in which these parameters have a role. Hence the Lucas critique suggests that parameter estimates derived under the old policies are not appropriate while one is simulating new policies. Whatever theoretical merit the Lucas critique may offer the question now boils down to its empirical verification. It is true that the Lucas position has shaped how the macroeconomics profession has evolved and developed during the last two decades. For reasons completely unknown, few empirical works have transpired to substantiate the Lucas proposition. It is remarkable that the Lucas policy evaluation critique has triumphed without any indepth and detailed empirical support beyond Lucas' accusation that macroeconometric models in the 1960s all predicted too little inflation for the 1970s. However, the general theoretical point was well-understaood and known before it was so eloquently and forcefully propounded by Lucas. That the point has been important empirically should have been demonstrated rather than asserted.

The focus of recent research, therefore, has been geared more toward the empirical verification of the Lucas critique. The test for the general validity of the Lucas critique is based on how one would like to proceed with the definition and the test criteria for the purpose. The issue of the test being highly technical in nature, the curious reader is referred to an interesting research on this topic given in the bibliography. Of course, the reader might as well supplement his interest using other printed work. As always on the empirical front, there are findings that confirm the Lucas critique. On the other hand, some research results seem strongly to refute the critique. It appears that the question is one of how to interpret the empirical results. This also involves highly technical issues. Without going into them here, a few remarks will be presented that may involve econometric issues, including appropriateness of the specification of the model. Even the modeling of expectation may raise more questions than it answers. Specifically, the modeling itself may not resolve the critique. Even B.T. McCallum observes that "using models based on explicit optimization analysis of individual agents' choices...provide no guarantee of success; explicit optimization models will not help if agents objective function or the constraints are mis-specified. The true message ...is that the analyst must be as careful as possible..." Efforts have been made at constructing databases of articles that cite Lucas during the period 1976-1990. In doing this, a Social Science Citation Index (SSCI) has been used that specifically allows for this kind of check. Ericsson and Irons used the Paradox of the program of Borland to do this. It was found that a total of 590 articles cite Lucas. Of these fifty-six were "bad cites" showing the deficiency of the claim from empirical consideration.

THE LUCAS SUPPLY FUNCTION

An interesting feature among macroeconomists is the strong difference of opinion as to the shape of the aggregate supply function for the economy. As a matter of fact, there is general agreement among the profession that the demand curve for the economy is the regular-shaped downward slope on a price quantity (output) axis. Unfortunately, much less agreement exists on the shape of the supply function. To be more specific, the shape of the aggregate supply curve in the pure classical model is vertical. This is due to the assumption of full employment and price-wage flexibility and an equation of exchange whose role of which is solely to determine the level of prices. In the Keynesian framework, the situation is different due to the underlying depression economy that seems to be the candidate under review. Out of these two extremes, there are the middle-of-the-roaders who would prefer a compromise solution where the supply curve is regularly shaped. Hence the situation seems to be the outcome of specific assumption made about the economy being studied.

Economists try to explain everything in terms of demand and supply. In the context of microeconomic theory, where each market is considered separately covering the specific economic agents, this has posed no problem. But for an aggregate economy, it is a bit hard to imagine demand and supply. Nonetheless, the efforts have never lacked the need for a suitable explanation in the framework economists find very comfortable to deal with. In the tradition of reinterpretation of John Hicks' work, IS-LM framework has provided the foundation for developing a downward sloping demand curve. A supply curve was to be provided in a fashion that meets the challenge of the economists' appetite. It was presented within the framework of production and supply. The contribution of Lucas to the macroeconomic literature is the supply function for the aggregate economy based on work of Richard Lipsey. Lipsey first showed that a positively sloped aggregate supply curve could be derived using the Phillips relation. . What Lucas did was use the correlation between inflation and unemployment, which often is credited to the work of Arthur Phillips, who demostrated an empirical relation using British data. This relationship was originally spotted by Irving Fisher and business cycle analysts at the National Bureau of Economic Research (NBER) much before Phillips. This correlation is paradoxical within the classical framework, since unemployment is a real variable and inflation is a monetary phenomenon, and by postulates of the school the two should not be related. In other words, a monetary variable should not explain movement in any real variable.

Thus such correlation appears to contradict the very spirit of the general equilibrium model, in which agents' decisions about real economic variables are considered to belong to what is known as being homogenous of degree zero. This homogeneity principle states that proportionate change in money and prices leaves real quantity demand unaffected. When the Phillips relation was presented as an empirical fact, it was incorporated within the main framework of macroeconomic literature, even though it lacked any well-developed logical basis. The Phillips curve expressing the relation between the rate of change of wages as a function of rate of unemployment fit very well in the Keynesian model, which allows for endogenizing wage rate over time. This may be seen as a fixed wage over time, with $(1/w)(dw/dt)=f(U)$, so that (dw/dt) is endogenous at each moment. This relation has been seen as a trade-off, that can be exploited by the policymakers, to choose a goal by selecting a point on the space of inflation unemployment, given society's preference between the two evils. The experience of the Western economies in the 1970s did not often produce satisfactory results as expected, due to the lack of the stability in the relation over time. A search for theoretical explanations for this was catalyzed a burgeoning research culminating in a series of articles to address this issue.

Against these backdrops, the Lucas model of business cycles came up with an explanation for a regular-shaped aggregate supply curve using the Phillips curve framework. This was put forward much in the embodiment of the natural rate of hypothesis built on the very essence of the long-run Phillips curve. It may be noted that this long-run relation is based on the idea that, to the agent, only relative prices matter. Within the confines of such a hypothesis, it is necessary to develop a model of "money illusion," which Lucas was successful in providing. In the words of Lucas himself, "all formulations of the natural rate hypothesis postulate rational agents whose decisions depend on relative prices only, placed in an economic setting where they cannot distinguish relative prices from general price movements." The combination of expected inflation with the basic Phillips relation being the hallmark of the standard long-run natural rate of unemployment has been shown to produce the classical type of vertical aggregate supply function for the economy. It is important to stress here that the vertical supply function is obtained in the Lucas framework because of the underlying assumption that agents are rational in the way expectations are formed. This is also known as the Lucas surprise function. As we will see later, the monetary forces by introducing inflationary surprises can indeed create a function that is analogous to the standard supply function but does not admit of any wage-price rigidity.

THE BUSINESS CYCLES THEORY OF LUCAS

Business cycles, also known as fluctuations in economic activity, have been a very unwelcome visitor to the house of growth and economic prosperity. As a matter of fact, they appear to be inseparable entities. While this was an issue of much less concern decades ago, it is becoming a major problem of modern day both advanced and growing economies. As such, there have been increased efforts to develop appropriate theoretical apparatus for explaining its causes. There are many theories, but Lucas' view is worth a serious consideration. Explaining booms and recessions is now a big responsibility for the economists. Time series econometricians are trying hard to explain the problem by using stochastic properties of a series and are becoming schizophrenic about its use. Although there exists absolutely no hope to come up with empirical regularities unless one can feel comfortable assuming that the variables follow a stable stochastic process, over time. It is also well recognized that there have been and will be many more episodes of depression and hyperinflation, when some of the economic variables behave erratically and when many of the time series properties do not remain appropriate. It indeed remains intellectually an uncomfortable situation for a macroeconomist to study the episodes separately and apply time series methods for the periods when some of the assumptions are not obvious. As such, many of the analyses focus on the postwar period, thus implicitly ignoring the period covering the Great Depression.

Facts about the economy that are believed to constitute business cycle fluctuations in the macroeconomic series are accounted for by the presence of significant correlation among the variables. Arthur Burns and W.C. Mitchell, in 1946, mentioned this, which was further noted by Milton Friedman and A. Schwartz, in their monumentally scholarly work, and also by Victor Zarnowitz. The Burns-Mitchell approach has been mostly abandoned due to its inherent judgmental nature coupled with the lack of well-defined statistical properties it generates. Then there were problems in separating trends from cycles, purely based on statistical necessity. However, most economists believe that behind the short-run fluctuation the economy evolves along an underlying growth path. The further analysis involving the issue of series decomposition is technically very challenging and, as such, is not elaborated. The most basic feature in the understanding of the existence of business cycles was discussed in Lucas. In his model, he takes an economy composed of many separate competitive markets, called islands. Demand in each market is affected by two shocks; one is an aggregate shock to the nominal money, while the second one is sector-specific shock. In such an economy, the producers, or suppliers, are assumed to respond differently–not to respond to the first type, while responding to the second one. There is an information gap so that they cannot be distinguished, but they do affect output. No distinction is drawn between workers and firms. Suppliers are assumed to be worker-producers and do not observe the price level directly; hence they must form estimates in each period as to how much to produce and supply.

As noted previously, the aggregate supply of the economy is represented in the Lucas supply function, which positively responds to unanticipated or "surprises in price changes." This feature is also the key to his explanation of the Phillips curve. To be formal, we may add that whereas Phillips' relation was in terms of expression of wage response to labor market disequilibrium, that of Lucas assumes supply demand equilibrium at each period. Thus it portrays a equilibrium relation between unexpected inflation and output. But this also has a simpler and more powerful interpretation of monetary shocks and fluctuation in economic activity via output. In his terminology, cycles are co-movement of output variables as defined in broad sectoral terms. When these co-movements, as measured by correlation among those variables are significantly high, then it is possible to identify them as business cycle fluctuations, as conventionally understood. The specific features may include timing in peaks and troughs for variables that are interrelated either in terms of monetary or real quantitative variables such as output, consumption, investment, and others. Even though some differences are very likely to exist, the overall tendencies should be sufficiently similar among these aggregates. The NBER literature often terms such features in the cyclical fluctuations as being in "conformity" across the sectors being high.

Much of the recent empirical research has examined the correlation analysis to explain the cyclical fluctuations in the economy using annual data where business cycles occur in several years. The results obtained can be considered reasonably good. Recently, some researchers are trying to examine the meaning of cycles in the context of seasonal data, such as quarterly or even monthly data. While the monthly data produce unconvincing results about existence of cycles, the quarterly data are generating much interest, as they seem to exhibit the features of business cycles. Robert Barsky and Jeffrey Miron argue that "seasonal fluctuation [are] worthy of study in their right." They claim, Seasonal fluctuations are an important source of variation in all macroeconomic quantity variables but are small or entirely absent in both real and nominal price levels." The seasonal cycle displays the same characteristics as the business cycle. That is , we find that at seasonal frequencies as well as business cycle frequencies, output movements across broadly defined sectors move together, the timing of production and timing of sales coincide closely, labor productivity is procyclical, nominal money and real output are highly correlated, and prices vary less than quantity. There is a *seasonal business cycle* in the U.S. economy and its characteristics closely mirror those of the conventional business cycle.

This finding is clearly at odds with the Lucas concept of business cycles. Such similarity between the business cycle and the seasonal cycle obviously poses a problem of reconciliation within the framework provided in Lucas, who says that "it suggests the possibility of unified explanation" of both of these cycles. Imposing this requirement immediately presents a challenge to the monetarist model such as that of Lucas. In those models, money can cause changes in the real variables due to misperceptions, and that money output correlation holds only for unanticipated, not anticipated, circumstances. But seasonal co-movements are largely anticipated, and therefore, in the context of money and output, the misperceptions hypothesis is definitely a hard sell.

CONCLUSION

In addition to his work in macroeconomics, Lucas has made outstanding contributions to investment theory, financial economics, monetary theory, dynamic public economics, international finance, and most recently, the theory of economic growth. In each of these fields, Lucas' studies have had a significant impact; they have launched new ideas and generated an extensive new literature. Lucas developed very useful and powerful quantitative techniques to draw conclusions from rational expectations models. These techniques have been applied rapidly to macroeconomic policy analysis and considered as standard tools. Without these, the results of rational expectations models would have been limited to general insights into the importance of expectations instead of clear-cut statements in specific situations. Only Lucas has made rational expectations as the sound and natural basis for further studies of expectation formation with respect to limited rationality, limited computational capacity and gradual learning.

RECOMMENDED READINGS

Barsky, Robert B., and Jeffrey Miron. (1989). "The Seasonal Cycles and Business Cycles," *Journal of Political Economy*. pp. 503-34.

Blaug, Mark. (1985). *One Hundred Great Economists Since Keynes*. Sussex: Wheatsheaf Books.

Burns, Arthur, and W.C. Mitchell. (1946). *Measuring Business Cycles*. New York: Columbia University Press, NBER.

Ericsson, N. Neil, and John S. Irons.(1995). "The Lucas Critique in Practice: Theory without Measurement," *International Finance Discussion Papers*. Vol. 506, Board of Governors: Federal Reserve of USA.

Fisher, Irving. (1930). *Theory of Interest*. New York: Macmillan.

Friedman, Milton. (1968). "The Role of Monetary Policy,"*American Economic Review*.

Friedman M., and A. Schwartz. (1960). *A Monetary History of the United States, 1867-1960.* Princeton: Princeton University Press.

——. (1963). "Money and Business Cycles," *Review of Economics and Statistics.* pp. 32-64.

Lucas, Robert E. Jr. (1973, June). "Some International Evidence on Output Inflation Trade-offs," *American Economic Review.* Vol. 63, pp. 326-34.

——. (1976). "Econometric Policy Evaluation: A Critique," in Karl Brunner and A.H. Meltzer, (eds.), *The Phillips Curve and Labor Markets, Carnegie-Rochester Conference Series on Public Policy.* Vol. 1, pp. 19-46.

——. (1977). "Understanding Business Cycles," in Karl Brunner and Alan Meltzer, eds., *Stabilization of Domestic and International Economy Carnegie-Rochester Conference Series.*

Lucas, Robert E. Jr., and L. Rapping. (1969). "Real Wages, Employment, and Inflation," *Journal of Political Economy.* Vol. 77, pp. 721-54.

——. (1970). "Capacity, Overtime, and Empirical Production Function," *AER, Papers and Proceedings.* Vol. 60, No. 2, pp. 23-27.

McCallum, B.T. (1989) *Monetary Economics: Theory and Policy.* New York: Macmillan.

——. (1980). *The Significance of Rational Expectations Theory,* Challenge, 1-2.

Muth, J.F. (1960). "Optimal Properties of Exponentially Weighted Forecasts," *Journal of American Statistical Association.* Vol. 55, pp. 299-306.

Nobel Website. (1995). Press Release, Bank of Sweden Prize in Economic Sciences in Memory of Alfred Nobel.

Patinkin, Don. (1948). "Price Flexibility and Full Employment." Reprinted in M.G. Mueller, (eds.) *Readings in Macroeconomics.* New York: Holt, Reinehart and Winston.

Peterson, Wallace C. (1984). *Income, Employment and Economic Growth.* Fifth edition . New York: W.W. Norton,.

Phillips, A.H. (1958). "The Relation Between Unemployment and Rate of Change of Money Wage Rates in the United Kingdom, 1861-1957,"*Economica.*

Sargent, Thomas J. (1987). *Macroeconomic Theory.* Second edition, Academic Press.

Sargent, Thomas J. and Neil Wallace. (1976). "Rational Expectation and Theory of Economic Policy," *Journal of Monetary Economics.*

Springfield News Report. (1995, October 10). Springfield, Illinois.

News Gazette. (1995, October 10). Champaign, Illinois.

Sims, Christopher A. (1987). "A Rational Expectations Framework for Short Run Policy Analysis," in W.A. Barnett and K.J. Singleton, (eds.), *New Approaches to Monetary Economics.* Cambridge, Cambridge University Press, pp. 293-308.

Tobin, James A. (1972). "Inflation and Unemployment,"*American Economic Review.*

Zarnowitz, Victor. (1985). "Recent Work on Business Cycles in Historical Perspective: A review of Theory and Evidence," *Journal of Economic Literature.* pp. 523-80.

40

James Mirrlees (1936-):
An Authority on Information
Economics and a Laureate of 1996

Hollis F. Price
A.K. Enamul Haque

BIOGRAPHICAL PROFILE

James Mirrlees was born in the village of Minnigaff in southwest Scotland in 1936. His father was a bank teller. Three years later, they moved to Newton Stewart, and in 1950 they migrated again to a place called Port William. In his early life, Mirrlees, used to wear glasses, so he could not run and play soccer. In what was to portend very well for his future career achievements, Mirrlees developed a strong interest in mathematics by his early teenage years. He found mathematics so interesting that on the school bus, he could finish reading his teacher's college mathematics book. He pursued this interest while matriculating at the University of Edinburgh and completed a degree in mathematics in 1957. Indeed, Mirrlees was admitted to Trinity College, Cambridge, to continue his studies in mathematics; however, his intellectual interest began to change during this period. Although completing the first two stages required to earn the degree in mathematics, the subject matter of economics, particularly poverty conditions in underdeveloped nations, gained his intellectual interests. At Cambridge, he came in close contact with such great economists as Nicholas Kaldor, Richard Kahn, Joan Robinson, Richard Stone, and others, and he benefitted immensely from them. Stone was his thesis advisor. In early 1962, he visited India in connection with a joint Cambridge-MIT research project. In 1962, on his way to India from MIT, he developed t he theory of efficiency wage equilibrium. On return from

India, Mirrlees completed his doctoral requirements in economics and became a father when his wife gave birth to his daughter Carolina. Then he accepted a teaching position at the University of Oxford through the mid-1990s and is presently occupying a distinguished chair at Cambridge University. Mirrlees had profound academic interaction with Kenneth Arrow, Robert Solow, Amartya Sen, and many other noted economic theorists.

INTRODUCTION

James Mirrlees, along with William Vickrey, won the economics Nobel Prize in 1996 for his "fundamental contributions to the economic theory of incentives under asymmetric information." Asymmetry arises whenever one party to a transaction is privy to information ordinarily unavailable to the other parties. Potential difficulties arising from asymmetry are often compounded by the fact that the parties have different–sometimes conflicting–priorities. Mirrlees is best known for his research in the field of economic situations with incomplete information. His pioneering work focused on optimal income taxation and moral hazard and is recognized as the standard in the economics of asymmetrical information. The works of Vickrey and Mirrlees provide pathbreaking and insightful paradigms for analyzing economic uncertainty.

THE "NEW PUBLIC FINANCE"

Standard cases of asymmetric information in the private sector include: (1) bargaining where each of the negotiating parties has access to different information; (2) an auction where the bidders' willingness to pay is unknown (Vickrey's contributions were particularly significant in this area of analysis); (3) credit applications where the lender has limited information regarding the loan applicant's future income; and (4) the corporation in which management has access to information that may not be readily available to the owners. In the public sector, relevant cases would include public good pricing and equitable and efficient taxation policies. In the former example, the public sector provider has no information from the perspective beneficiaries regarding their willingness to pay. In the latter, the tax administrator is unable to ascertain, among other parameters, either (1) the taxpayers ability to pay or (2) any information on the possible disincentive consequences of various tax/transfer alternatives. It was in this complex and controversial area of public finance that Mirrlees made a seminal theoretical contribution to the formulation of tax policy. Conventional wisdom, prior to the "new public finance" pioneered by Mirrlees, was that optimal tax policy from both the equity and efficiency perspectives consisted of lump-sum taxes paid by those with ability to pay and lump-sum transfers to those whose ability to pay was limited. When both tax liability and transfers consisted of fixed amounts, marginal rates for both would be zero. It was presumed, therefore, that there would be no disincentive to alter consumption, work, or investment choices once the tax liability was met and the transfers were completed. The simplicity of this conclusion belies its complexity in terms of implementation. Contrary to what might be expected, the tax administrator does not have any objective measure of ability to pay. The most obvious benchmark is income. Income, however, is the result of the personal interaction of the individual's values and preferences regarding such factors as the utility of income, risk aversion, and work ethic. A high income, for example, might reflect the individual's increasing marginal utility of income. Thus, any tax on income could have substantial disincentive effects. Nor is low income synonymous with low ability to pay. Once again, a variety of subjective factors, for example, low motivation and/or productivity, could be responsible for low earnings, none of which are known to the tax administrator.

Lump-sum tax/transfer systems, therefore, do not eliminate the possibility that people will be motivated to pretend to be less productive than they really are. It should be noted that hiding information, while perhaps unethical, is not irrational. Furthermore, the tax administrator does not have the information at hand to identify the "free riders." A major contribution of Mirrlees' analysis was to articulate an optimal, redistributive tax system, which rationally reconciles the goals of efficiency and equity in the context of informational asymmetry and the potential disincentive effects of any tax system. Mirrlees sought to resolve this problem by first focusing on methods for obtaining accurate information from the most reliable source, the taxpayer, by the most direct means possible. This process was the basis for the Revelation Principle. Prospective taxpayers would be asked to reveal private information regarding their productive efficiency and priorities in such a way that it would not conflict with their self-interest. Tax strategies would then be formulated based on the information received. "All this works as if the government simply asked people to declare their private information and then assigned them appropriate production targets and consumption levels."

MIRRLEES' "SINGLE CROSSING PROPERTY"

The inducement to supply the information would be the assurance that subsequent tax schedules would be what later theorists described as "incentive compatible." Once the tax administrator has addressed the issue of asymmetric information, the next major challenge is the incentive/disincentive problem. That is, as previously noted, individuals factor their tax liability into their work/leisure tradeoffs. To address this case, Mirrlees formulated the Single Crossing Property. The essence of this principle is that indifference curves of individuals with different levels of productive efficiency can intersect only at a single point. The mathematical solution of this condition indicated to Mirrlees that a limited progressive tax structure was necessary to prevent significant disincentives for the most productive workers. In order to place the importance of Mirrlees' tax analysis in full historical perspective, brief reference can be made to the groundbreaking analysis of Francis Edgeworth. Edgeworth was the first theorist to systematically formulate tax theory in the context of social as well as revenue objectives. He concluded, based primarily on speculation regarding the homogeneity of individual preference functions and on normative criteria, that the optimal tax structure would be highly progressive with the specific intent of equalizing income. By highlighting challenges to the formulation of optimal tax policy resulting from both potential disincentive consequences of any tax liability and the fact that productivity of individuals is unknown to the tax administrator, Mirrlees (and Vickrey to a lesser extent) reformulated the debate over the principles of taxation. Incentive problems under conditions of adverse selection are not the only cases of asymmetrical information. Moral hazard also arises from conditions where information is asymmetrical and the need arises to offer incentives that will induce the desired behavior. The two standard cases of moral hazard are the "insurance" and "principal-agent" problems.

MORAL HAZARD AND
ADVERSE SELECTION

In the moral hazard problem, the insurer cannot know, until after the issuance of a policy, what, if any, behaviors people will adopt that would influence the probability of the insured event occurring. For example, people who purchase automobile insurance may drive more recklessly after they are covered, thereby increasing the probability of an accident. Similarly, people with medical insurance may feel less compelled to pursue a healthy lifestyle. Insurance, in other words, may lessen risk aversion. A standard example of the principal-agent problem would be the employer-employee relationship. The worker is the agent employed by the employer, who is the principal. The firms' profitability is dependent on the workers' productivity, but the employer may not be able to accurately ascertain the quantity and/or quality of the worker's efforts. Employees typically have much more complete information regarding these matters than do employers. In extreme cases, this asymmetry has the potential for workers to consistently perform below their capabilities, that is to shirk.

Adverse selection and moral hazard cases are similar in some important respects and dissimilar in other important respects. As previously noted in the discussion of the principles of taxation, adverse selection results from not being able to observe productive efficiencies prior to the formulation of tax policy. Moral hazard, on the other hand, arises from not being able to predict how a person will respond after entering into a contractual agreement. In both cases, however, there is asymmetrical information and the need to use appropriate incentives in order to induce behavior consistent with the self-interest of all parties involved. For example, owners of both the firm and the insurance agency want to select a means of payment that induces the insured or the agent to act in line with the insurer's or the firm's profit-maximizing objectives. The commonalties between the two cases may have been the factor that enabled Mirrlees to bring an insightful perspective to resolving problems posed by moral hazard. "The technical difficulties encountered in analyzing Mirrlees. In the mid-1970s, by means of an apparently simple reformulation of the problem, Mirrlees paved the way for an increasingly powerful analysis." Mirrlees' insight into moral hazard problems was his recognition that both the insured person and the employee (subsequently referred to as agents) made assessments regarding the probability of some range of possible outcomes. Rational agreements would then provide the agents with data regarding the probability of these outcomes, as well as the incentives required to induce the desired outcomes. The challenge becomes how to structure the agents' incentives so that they share some of the costs of unproductive behavior and realize some of the gains from favorable outcomes in light of the probability distribution of the outcomes.

CONCLUSION

Mirrlees' significant contributions to the economics discipline extend beyond his work in analyzing complex information and incentive problems. In the economic development literature, he is recognized as the co-author (with I.M.D. Little) of a manual for industrial project analysis for developing countries. This work has become one of the classic readings in cost-benefit analysis. Mirrlees has shown an enormous breadth of interests as evidenced by his numerous contributions to top-tier journals published on four continents. In these publications, Mirrlees applied the robust theorems of mathematical economics to the analysis of complex theoretical questions with the objective that his answers could provide some direction for the formulation of policies. He brought to each of these projects the rigor and innovation that one would expect of a Nobel laureate. Equally as important, his insights have proven to be a catalyst for subsequent analyses by colleagues and younger generations of scholars whose intellectual curiosity and energies have been stimulated by Mirrlees' pioneering efforts.

RECOMMENDED READINGS

Akerlof, G. (1971). "The Market for Lemons: Qualitative Uncertainty and the Market Mechanism," *Quarterly Journal of Economics*. Vol. 84, pp. 488-500.

Arrow, K.J. (1963). "Uncertainty and the Welfare Economics of Medical Care," *The American Economics Review*. Vol. 53, pp. 941- 69.

Dixit, Avinash, and Timothy Besley. (1997). "James Mirrlees' Contributions to the Theory of Information and Incentives," *Scandinavian Journal of Economics*. Vol. 99, No. 1, pp. 207-35.

Eatwell, John, Murray Milgate, and Peter Newman. (1987). *The New Palgrave: A Dictionary of Economics*. New York: Macmillan.

Little, I.M.D., and Mirrlees, J. (1969), *Manual of Industrial Project Analysis in Developing Countries*. Paris: Organization of Economic Cooperation and Development.

Little, I.M.D., and N. Kaldor. (1962, June). "A New Model of Economic Growth," *Review of Economic Studies*.

Royal Swedish Academy of Sciences. (1996, October 8). "Press Release–The Bank of Sweden Prize in Economics in Memory of Alfred Nobel," October 8.

41

William Vickrey (1914-1996):
An Expert on Moral Hazard
and Adverse Selection and a Laureate of 1996

M. Muin Uddin

BIOGRAPHICAL PROFILE

William Vickrey was born in Victoria, British Columbia, Canada in 1914. His elementary and secondary education was in Europe and the United States, with graduation from Phillips Andover Academy in 1931. He received a B.S. in mathematics from Yale in 1935, followed by graduate work in economics at Columbia University from 1935 to 1937, when he received the M.A. degree. He then worked for the National Resources Planning Board in Washington and the Division of Tax Research in the U.S. Treasury Department. A conscientious objector during World War II, he spent part of his alternate service designing a new inheritance tax for Puerto Rico. Columbia University awarded him the Ph.D. in economics in 1948. His doctoral dissertation, "Agenda for Progressive Taxation," was reprinted as an economic classic in 1972. In 1946, he began his teaching career at Columbia University as a lecturer in economics. He became a full professor in 1958 and was named McVickar Professor of Political Economy in 1971. He was chairman of the department of economics from 1964 to 1967 and retired as McVickar Professor Emeritus in 1982. A long career of research covered a large range of subjects. The first of many involving efficient pricing of public utilities, done in 1939 and 1940 for the Twentieth Century Fund, dealt with electric power. In 1951, he studied transit fares in New York City for the mayor's Committee on Management Survey. He was a member of the 1950 Shoup mission that developed a comprehensive program for revising the tax system of Japan. He lectured widely and served as a consultant in the United States and overseas and to the United Nations. He was elected to the National Academy of Sciences and in 1992 served as president of the American Economic Association. He was a fellow of the Econometric Society and received an honorary degree from the University of Chicago in 1979. He was a founding member of Taxation, Resources, and Economic Development and was a member of many professional and civic organizations and an active supporter of organizations promoting world peace. He belonged to The Religious Society of Friends. A 1994 volume, *Public Economics* (Cambridge University Press), contains a complete bibliography; it lists eight books, 139 articles, twenty-seven reviews, and sixty-one unpublished articles and notes. He was married to Cecile Thompson in 1951. They lived in Hastings-on-Hudson in New York. He died in October 1996.

INTRODUCTION

William Vickrey, along with James Mirrlees, won the economics Nobel Prize in 1996 for his "fundamental contributions to the economic theory of incentives under asymmetric information." Incomplete and asymmetric information on the part of economic actors in a market economy leads to fundamental consequences for decisionmaking and resource allocation, which, in turn, lead to economic inefficiency. Vickrey's goal in dealing with these issues was to generate economic efficiency for a wide range of problems, thereby enriching the field of economics of information–a valuable area of study in modern times. Vickrey's contributions to the economic sciences are extensive. In addition to recognizing his research on asymmetric information, the Royal Swedish Academy noted some of Vickrey's other important work in economics: auction theory, principles of taxation, pricing of public services, and social choice. Additionally, his studies encompass urban economics, economic stabilization, income distribution, welfare economics, and macroeconomic policy, to name a few. Vickrey's research in these varied areas and his solutions to underlying problems were guided by his quest for efficiency and equity, and the academy emphasized his unique talent of following up his theoretical proposal with real-world implementation.

ECONOMICS OF INFORMATION
AND THEORY OF INCENTIVES

The market economy model for resource allocation is based on several key assumptions, one of which is that the economic actors (e.g., buyers and sellers) have complete information about the relevant economic variables necessary to make informed choices. In a world of perfect information, markets operate efficiently, which leads to the optimal allocation of goods and scarce resources among competing ends. However, when there is asymmetric information, in other words, some agents involved in the economic exchange know more than others, the market system fails to generate efficient outcomes, or a market may not exist at all. Such a situation, in which a market is not efficient, is known as market failure.

IMPLICATIONS OF
ASYMMETRIC INFORMATION

Imperfect and asymmetric information can arise in numerous business situations. Ordinarily, a seller of a product knows more about its quality than the buyers. For example, sellers of used cars know more about their cars than the buyers do, while the manager of a firm may know more about the firm's cost conditions, input productivity, overall profitability, and future prospects than a shareholder of the firm. On the other hand, buyers of health insurance know more about their general health than the insurance companies do, and an insurance company does not fully know its insurees' behavior and attitudes toward their insured property. Further, in the market for used cars, prospective buyers are unable to distinguish between low-quality and high-quality cars. Informational asymmetries can create two common classes of problems, known as moral hazard and adverse selection, which give rise to market failure by adversely affecting contracts between parties in business transactions. Contracts between economic agents involve expectations of future behavior and performance for each party. However, all economic agents involved in a contract may not be perfectly moral. Many of them are likely to be opportunistic and to exploit strategically the informational imbalance between the parties of the contract. They may take advantage of the circumstances when their conduct cannot be monitored, thereby violating the implied expectation of future performance.

The problems of moral hazard and adverse selection originated in research on the insurance industry. Moral hazard represents disincentives created by insurance for individuals to lower the probability and/or magnitude of the event that triggers compensation. For example, if my car has complete insurance coverage, I may not take care to prevent it from being damaged or stolen. In another context, if I have a comprehensive health insurance policy, I may seek medical care more frequently than if I had more restricted coverage. An insurance company could assess higher premiums for those who demand more claims only if it could observe policyholders' conduct, but if the company is unable to monitor insurees' behavior, it can incur higher than expected compensation costs. Due to the repercussions of moral hazard, insurance providers may be compelled to raise their fees or even to decline to sell insurance. Moral hazard can arise in private as well as social insurance (e.g., health and disability insurance). Analogous situations of moral hazard can occur when there is asymmetric information in other markets. For example, workers in a given firm may perform below their abilities when managers cannot monitor their performance. In the financial capital market, moral hazard can create the so-called principal/agent problem. Ordinarily, owners or stockholders (principals) of a corporation have less information than the managers (agents) do about the operation and performance of the company. Consequently, a manager may not behave in the best interest of the principals (owners/stockholders) after the investors' funds have been acquired. Rather, managers may be more interested in promoting their own positions by, for example, using corporate funds on unduly expensive business trips, fancy offices, club memberships, and so on, and thereby fail to make sincere efforts to implement efficient and profitable management structures.

Adverse Selection

Another possible result of informational asymmetries, is that market trades may be biased to favor the better informed party, while the less informed agents must choose from the undesirable (or adverse selection) of products or customers. A frequently cited example of the adverse selection problem is the used-car market, in which there are informational asymmetries about the quality of cars offered for sale. Generally, used cars offered for sale are of poorer quality than the used cars that are not available for sale; therefore, buyers must choose from this adverse selection of used cars. Also, not only are buyers less informed than sellers about the quality; they also are unable to differentiate between low-quality and high-quality used cars before making the purchase. In this case, both types of used cars will be traded in a mixed (single) market at the same time. Consequently, too many of the low-quality and too few of the high-quality used cars will be available in the marketplace. Therefore, the implication of this outcome is that asymmetric information gives rise to market failure in which low-quality products (lemons) drive high-quality products (plums) out of market.

Adverse selection is especially significant for the insurance industry because it makes business exchanges problematic. Usually, insurees have better information than the insurance provider does concerning the risks and potential losses involved in the insured property. Since it is difficult for insurance companies to differentiate the levels of risks of the insurees, premiums are likely to reflect the average level of risk for policies in a given category. In the case of medical insurance, unhealthy people, realizing that they are much riskier than the average, find the price of insurance attractive, and more and more unhealthy (riskier) people will buy insurance. As a result, the price of insurance will go up, and many healthy (less risky) individuals will be induced to self-insure. This will necessitate another rise in premiums, inducing still more of the healthy people to drop their policies. This situation, in which people who are unhealthy demand medical insurance while healthy individuals do not, will render the insurance business unprofitable. Corresponding situations of adverse selection will arise in other markets when there is asymmetric information.

ECONOMIC THEORY
OF INCENTIVES

Finding ways to make exchanges and contracts which mitigate the consequences of imperfect and asymmetric information requires proper incentives for economic agents. The economic theory of incentives is concerned with devising schemes to induce economic actors to alter their behavior and course of action in order to achieve efficiency and social optimality. Vickrey's work on the economics of information focused on structuring institutions and contracts to effectively deal with control problems and incentives. He applied his theories to taxation, auctions, and the pricing of public utilities and services.

Income Taxation

An essential part of Vickrey's research concerns the properties of progressive income taxation. Among the various types of levies, income taxation commands special attention because of its significance in the governmental revenue system of the United States and most developed nations. A country's income tax system can be progressive, regressive, or proportional. Under a progressive tax scheme, the average tax rate (expressed as a percent of the tax base) increases with the magnitude of the tax base (i.e., income). The tax is regressive if its rate decreases as income rises. And a proportional tax structure is one in which the average tax rate remains constant at all levels of income. The most well known of Vickrey's works in taxation is his 1947 book, *Agenda for Progressive Taxation*. His interest in income taxation grew out of his concern for economic efficiency and his reaction to a paper published in 1897 by Francis Edgeworth, an Oxford University Professor. Edgeworth developed a model of optimal income taxation, using the utilitarian social welfare principle and considering the dual criteria of social welfare maximization and distributional equality toward optimality. Since Edgeworth sought to neutralize individual income differences to achieve equality, his model implied radically progressive tax schedules.

Speaking out against Edgeworth's optimality model, Vickrey stressed that a progressive tax structure would negatively affect individual incentives (e.g., work effort), thereby leading to a loss in economic efficiency for the economy. A progressive tax schedule causes the marginal tax rate (expressed as the change in taxes paid with respect to change in income) to rise and eventually exceed the average tax rate. This diminishes individual incentive to work more hours because it may move the individual to a higher income bracket and, therefore, to a higher tax rate. Vickrey attempted to correct the underlying problem by taking into account both the incentive problem and the issue of asymmetric information (e.g., individual productivity levels are unknown to the taxing authority). His work includes a model showing how incentive-compatible mechanisms can help achieve an optimal tax scheme, by allowing a balance between the competing goals of efficiency and equity. Vickrey's 1947 book helped him to develop a reputation as a leading scholar in the field of taxation. In 1949, by virtue of a tax mission to Japan, Vickrey, in collaboration with Carl Shoup, laid the foundation for Japan's postwar tax program. Over the years, as part of other tax missions abroad, Vickrey helped shape the tax structures of other countries as well, most notably Puerto Rico, Venezuela (1960), and Liberia (1970). Vickrey's model of optimal taxation was reconsidered by his co-laureate James Mirrlees in the early 1970s. Mirrlees gave this model an explicit characterization and provided a more thorough solution to the problems associated with optimality. Vickrey's incentive-compatible mechanism for dealing with income tax problems also helped Mirrlees devise incentive schemes for analogous situations characterized by moral hazard and adverse selection problems.

AUCTION THEORY

An important area where Vickrey's incentive-compatible mechanisms have played a great role is in auction theory, which has developed into a major research area in recent years. An auction is a mechanism for selling private and public articles based on bids from the buyers. Many types of goods and properties are traded by auction, including agricultural produce, antiques, artwork, second-hand goods, coins and stamps, the underwriting of a security issue (e.g., the U.S. Treasury bills), land, mineral rights, and construction contracts. One special characteristic of goods transacted by auction is a supply that is irregular both in quantity and quality; goods that are traded in the standard marketplace, based on posted, fixed prices, tend to be homogeneous in quality and available on a continuous basis. The auction market is characterized by imperfect and asymmetric information for several reasons. For instance, the price of the good is uncertain, would-be buyers' knowledge about the value of the product is limited, and a bidder's strategy depends upon his/her access to information concerning the perceived value of the article to other bidders. In light of the asymmetric information problem, research on auction theory has focused on forming an explicit price-making model by providing socially efficient incentives to the participants. In two papers, published in 1961 and 1962, Vickrey examined the characteristics and implications of the common, or progressive, type of auction, and the regressive, or Dutch, auction. In the simple progressive auction, the seller asks for ascending prices until one bidder remains. The sellers can either submit their offers or ask for bids from buyers. The bids are openly announced, and the auction concludes when the highest bid is reached. Items like paintings and antiques are examples of goods frequently transacted by progressive auction. Vickrey concludes that, under this scheme, a good will go to the person to whom it has the highest value, at a price approximately equal to the second highest value among the values that the bidders place on the article. Therefore, he contends that this type of auction is likely to generate Pareto-optimal allocation of the good in question.

Vickrey contrasted the progressive auction with the regressive, or Dutch, auction. In the Dutch auction, the seller asks for descending bids; the auctioneer initially calls a relatively high price and then lowers the price at fixed intervals (e.g., $200, $175, $150, etc.). The auction concludes when one bidder accepts the offered price. Wholesale cut flowers in the Netherlands and tobacco in Canada are sold by Dutch auction. In this type of auction, the ultimate buyer of the object is the first bidder, who presumably places the highest value on the object in question. The final price will be the highest bid price rather than a bid price close to the second highest one. Accordingly, Vickrey argues that the Dutch auction does not generally provide Pareto-optimal allocation of resources. Vickrey sought to modify auction mechanisms in order to achieve Pareto-efficient outcomes. He advocated an incentive-compatible, second-price auction, commonly referred to as the "Vickrey auction." Under this auction, buyers submit sealed bids, and the highest bidder wins the object. The winner pays, not his or her own bid price, but the second highest price offered. With this type of auction, according to Vickrey, it is in the prospective buyer's best economic interest to reveal a truthful bid reflecting his true willingness to pay. If a would-be buyer's bid is lower than his willingness to pay, there is a risk that another person will win the item at a price lower than that which the would-be buyer is willing to pay. On the other hand, if his bid is higher than his willingness to pay, there is a risk that another person will bid in the same manner, and he will end up buying the item at a loss. Therein lies the incentive for a would-be buyer to make a truthful bid. Vickrey's second-price auction is thus socially efficient because not only does the good in question go to the buyer with the highest (true) willingness to pay, but the actual price (the second highest bid) reflects marginal social cost. Also, in this type of auction, the seller is able to receive as high a price as with any other type of auction, while in other types of auction, the seller may not get a fair price.

Vickrey's work on auction theory has inspired an animated field of research and has developed such practical applications (in both private and public sectors) as band spectrum licenses, treasury bonds, and oil fields. An example demonstrating the recent application of Vickrey's theory is the auctioning of wavelengths (a pure public good) for personal communication services (e.g., pocket telephones or wireless computer networks). Vickrey's ideas on auctions have enabled game theorists to devise transaction mechanisms to achieve efficient results by securing high prices for the sellers and ensuring that goods go to those buyers who value them most. Following his work in income taxation and auctions, Vickrey moved on to other areas associated with the incentives of pricing, especially the problems of pricing public services (e.g., utilities, transportation, etc.). (His contribution in this field will be discussed in the next section.) Vickrey's seminal work in the area of information and incentives has generated a deeper understanding of such seemingly dissimilar fields as taxation, auctions, pricing mechanisms, private and social insurance, financial capital market, and wage designs, to name a few.

PUBLIC ECONOMICS

Public economics (also known as "public finance" or "public sector economics") is the study of government activities–taxation, spending, borrowing, management of government enterprises, regulation of public utilities, and more–and government's effect on resource allocation, the economy, and the well-being of citizens. The study of this branch of economics is quite complex, because it relies on both normative and positive analyses. Numerous elements of market failure apply to this area of economic study as well, including such unique characteristics as the free-rider problem, externalities, asymmetric information, the nonexistence of competition, nonconvexities of preferences and production sets, and a lack of individual incentives, such as profit motivation. These common characteristics of publicsector activities make the study of an efficient resource allocation mechanism under public economics very challenging indeed. Vickrey is one of the founding fathers of publicsector economics, and his contributions touch all major branches of this field. This section, will discuss a few of his innovative ideas bearing both theoretical and practical importance.

Principles of Taxation

Vickrey sought to perfect the tax base in light of efficiency and equity considerations, and in 1938, he invented the so-called *cumulative averaging* method for assessing income tax. This idea grew out of his consideration of methods of taxing capital gains during his role as an advisor for the United States Treasury. He sought to neutralize incentives for taxpayers, to vary the timing of gain realization on the basis of tax considerations, and to create incentives for reporting all forms of income. The way to achieve these goals, according to Vickrey, is to allow some method of averaging income over a period of years. Vickrey contended that intertemporal tax neutrality can be achieved if tax authorities regard all tax payments, beginning with a given year, as interest bearing deposits with the treasury in the taxpayer's name. The accrued amount on this account would then be counted as a credit against the current assessed tax, based on the cumulated total income (including interest earned on the tax-deposit account) for the entire period to date. The current tax due would be the difference between this assessed cumulative tax and the accumulated balance on the taxpayer's account with the treasury. According to Vickrey, treating taxes paid as an interest-bearing account removes the incentive for taxpayers to vary the timing of realization or reporting of all forms of income.

The cumulative averaging method of tax assessment is a noble innovation in the economics of taxation. Vickrey himself called it his "proudest accomplishment" and a "master stroke of simplification and neutralization." He emphasized that the adoption of cumulative averaging would remove many of the complex rules concerning the timing of income reporting and reduce the income tax code by half. Vickrey's contributions to and influence on the economics of taxation go beyond those ideas presented above. He has considered simplicity, neutrality, and similar principles for other taxes, including ideas on corporate taxation, land value taxation, expenditure taxes, treatment of charitable contributions, and inheritances, to name a few.

Publicsector Pricing

William Vickrey produced more than three dozen articles and papers on the conceptual and practical issues of pricing public services, such as utilities (electricity, telephone, water, etc.) and transportation (bridges, public transit, roads, air travel, etc..) He recognized the prevalence of asymmetric information associated with the mechanics of price determination; therefore, he sought to achieve efficiency and optimality in the structuring of the market and the setting of prices for public services. In view of this goal, Vickrey offered a marginal cost (MC) pricing scheme for public-sector services. He suggested that a flat fee would lead to inefficient use of a given service through a discrepancy in demand between peak and non peak times. A flat fee is also likely to exceed the MC of producing a service; therefore, users willing to pay only the MC would not use the service under flat-fee pricing. Vickrey suggested that an MC pricing scheme would smooth peak and off-peak use by linking the fee schedule to demand. A prominent example of Vickrey's MC pricing scheme is his consulting study of the New York City subway fare structure in the 1950s. Commissioned to find solutions to the problem of fiscal drain of the city's transit system, Vickrey recommended that the prevailing fifteen-cent flat fee be replaced by an alternative efficient set of fees, ranging from five to twenty-five cents according to the time of day (i.e., variation in demand), the origin, and the destination of the riding public. He calculated that such a pricing scheme would recoup $50 million (in 1952 dollars) in deadweight loss and that fees lower than the MC would cause an additional $120 million (also in 1952 dollars) deficit for the city's transit system. With the New York City transit system, Vickrey demonstrated that his MC pricing scheme could be adapted easily. Time-of-day and peak/off-peak pricing is now regularly used by utility and telephone companies, bus and train operators, airlines, and many other public services.

Public Macroeconomics

During the 1980s and 1990s, Vickrey's work focused largely on the macroeconomic stabilization function of the government. He revitalized Keynesian thinking, favoring public policies aimed at attaining full employment. He argued that mass unemployment was one of the main causes of many social problems, such as crime, drug addiction, homelessness, divorce, and domestic violence, and he advocated macroeconomic policy aimed at achieving the full-employment condition. Vickrey discredited programs like affirmative action and enterprise zone for failing to promote total employment and mitigate unemployment. Likewise, he did not favor natural-rate theories of unemployment (e.g., Non-Inflation Accelerating Rate of Unemployment) because of the undesirable tradeoff between mass unemployment and price stability. In 1995, motivated by his devotion to full employment, Vickrey joined the National Jobs for All Coalition–an alliance of progressive social scientists and community activists committed to devising a full-employment agenda. And only few days before the announcement of his Nobel Prize, Vickrey delivered a paper entitled, "Fifteen Fatal Fallacies of Financial Fundamentalism," in which he attacked a governmental budget balancing proposal because of the recessionary effects on output and employment.

URBAN ECONOMICS

The field of urban economics, which Vickrey helped to shape, emerged during the 1970s. It consisted of several important subject areas: location and allocation of land between public and private use, the housing market, financing of transportation services, and local public finance. Vickrey's leading work on transportation services has already been discussed in the section on public-sector pricing. Believing prevailing pricing practices to be irrational, outdated, and wasteful, Vickrey devised a more efficient pricing scheme (MC pricing), which proved quite effective.

Outside the realm of transportation, Vickrey's work in urban economics relates to the strategic issues of firm location and, more notably, to the financing of urban public services. Vickrey considers two different means of levying taxes for financing urban services: general purpose taxes, which would disregard the differences in benefits received and costs of delivering services to individual tax payers, and specific taxes, which would recognize differentials in benefits received and costs incurred. These two types of levies present a conflict between efficiency and equity. Vickrey's goal was to deal with this conflict, and he achieved this through efficiency-equity compromise in such areas as fire protection, water supply, transportation facilities, police and custodial services, recreational facilities, health and hospital services, education, and public utility services.

CONCLUSION

Other noteworthy contributions of Vickrey encompass public policy issues in the fields of welfare economics, public choice theory, educational finance, cost-of-living indices, resource distribution, social justice, philanthropy, and the resolution of international conflicts. Vickrey's analyses range from the philosophical foundation of economics to the technical aspects of economic principles, and all are extraordinary for their logical foundation, methodological and theoretical rigor, originality, and practical significance. Vickrey's intellectual work touches most major branches of economics, and the Royal Swedish Academy of Sciences recognized his outstanding contributions with the 1996 Nobel Prize. Vickrey occupies a special place among noteworthy economists because of his unique talent of following up theoretical ideas with practical applications. His distinctive work is a testimony to the fact that economics is *not*, as Sir John Clapham called it in 1922, an "empty box" of theories lacking user's manuals and, therefore, devoid of practical application.

In terms of contemporary and real-world significance, as well as novelty of perspective, Vickrey's contributions to the economic sciences are justifiably characterized as both "modern" and "classic." He worked actively to make economics and markets work for the general improvement of people's lives, and because of his wide-ranging concern for economic efficiency in the interest of human welfare, he could also be labeled a "humanist." In his intellectual work, he paid a great deal of attention to moral consideration, social justice, and the philosophical basis of economics. Thus he is also a "moral philosopher," an honorable title usually reserved for the father of modern economics, Adam Smith. Vickrey has had a great influence on our understanding and thinking about many important issues of economics, and those engaged in learning, teaching, research, and the application of the economic sciences will continue to benefit from the accomplishments of this outstanding economist.

RECOMMENDED READINGS

Vickrey, William. (1939, June). "Averaging Income for Income Tax Purposes," *Journal of Political Economy*. Vol. 47, pp. 379-97.

——. (1955, February 3). "A Proposal for Revising New York's Subway Fare Structure," *Journal of the Operations Research Society of America*. pp. 38-69.

————. (1955). "The Revision of the Rapid Transit Fare Structure of the City of New York," mimeo, Technical Monograph No. 3, Finance Project, Mayor's Committee for Management Survey of the City of New York.

————. (1961). "Counterspeculation, Auctions, and Competitive Sealed Tenders," *Journal of Finance*. Vol. 16, pp. 8-37.

————. (1962). "Auctions and Bidding Games," *Recent Advances in Games Theory*. Princeton: Princeton University Press. pp. 15-29.

————. (1963). "General and Specific Financing of Urban Services," in Howard G. Shaller, (ed.), *Public Expenditure Decisions in the Urban Community*. Resources For The Future. pp. 62-90.

————. (1972). "Cumulative Averaging After 30 Years," in Richard M. Bird and John G. Head, (eds.), *Modern Fiscal Issues: Essays in Honor of Carl S. Shoup*. Toronto: University of Toronto Press. pp. 117-33.

42

Robert Merton (1944-):
A Solver of the Option Pricing
Model and a Laureate of 1997

Ihsan Isik
M. Kabir Hassan

BIOGRAPHICAL PROFILE

Robert Merton was born in New York, New York, in 1944. His father, born in Philadelphia, the son of the immigrant parents, was a professor of sociology at Columbia University. Merton has been awarded the National Medal of Science for founding the sociology of science and for his fundamental contributions to the sociology of science and sociological concepts such as the self-fulfilling prophecy and the focus group. Just one day after entering Columbia College, he switched to the Engineering School, where he explored mathematics and sciences. After Columbia, he went to pursue a Ph.D. in applied mathematics at the California Institute of Technology. The year spent at California Institute of Technology (1966-1967) added significantly to increase his stock of mathematics. On his decision to leave Cal Tech, Gerald Whitham (the department head) provided him with generous help. He entered MITs program in the fall of 1967. After being rejected as a junior fellow at Harvard, he spent the fall and winter of 1969 interviewing only with departments of economics, but he ended up tacking an appointment to teach finance at MIT's Sloan School of Management. His decision to move from MIT to the Harvard Business School in 1988 was significantly influenced by a turn in his research interests. Shortly after his joining the Harvard faculty, Dean John McArthur resigned from the George Fisher Baker professorship in order to give it to him. In 1972, he was engaged by the options department of Donaldson, Luftkin & Jenrette to develop option pricing and hedging models for the over-the-counter market and later for the new Chicago Board

Options Exchange. In 1975, he was involved in the creation of Money Market/Options Investment, Inc., an open-end mutual fund, which went effective in February 1976. For the rest of the 1970s and much of the 1980s he served on a few mutual fund boards and was elected a trustee of the College Retirement Equities Fund. In 1988, he accepted an offer to become a special consultant to the Office of Chairman of Salomon Brothers. He is also one of the founding principals of LTCM.

INTRODUCTION

Robert Merton, along with Myron Scholes, won the economics Nobel Prize in 1997 for "a new method to determine the value of derivatives." Merton and Scholes, in tandem with the late Fischer Black, developed a new formula for pricing contingent claims in general and stock options in particular, which has revolutionized the practice in both academia and financial markets. The degree of its immediate and combined impact on financial economic theory and practice is without parallel (Merton and Scholes, 1995; Duffie, 1998; and Schaefer, 1998). Their far-reaching formula changed the way investors and others place value on risk, giving rise to the field of risk management, the increased marketing of derivatives, and widespread changes in the valuation of corporate liabilities. Even investors who do not have a clue about contingent claims or options owe a debt to their seminal work.

BACKGROUND OF OPTIONS AND
OPTION PRICING TECHNIQUES

The Black-Merton-Scholes (BMS) masterstroke option pricing model, as well as options did not emerge overnight. The theory of option pricing has undergone rapid advances over time. Simultaneously, organized option markets have developed in the United States and other countries all over the world. Options, which are contingent claims that give the holder the right but not the obligation to conduct a transaction at a future date, have existed for centuries. Ancient Romans, Grecians, and Phoenicians are known to have traded options against outgoing cargoes from their local seaports. A famous example of speculative excesses using options occurred during the tulip bulb mania in Holland during the 1600s. As tulip bulb prices appreciated, a market developed for call options on the bulbs, which gave the buyer the right to obtain the bulbs at a specified price over a specified period.

According to many, even though options trading existed before the Black-Merton-Scholes (BMS) option formula hit the markets and Wall Street, today's volumes would not be possible without their masterpiece. Prior to 1973, options on stocks were thinly traded primarily on the over-the-counter market (OTC), with several dealers in New York City being the principal market participants. However, the OTC market was suffering from numerous trading disadvantages, such as high transaction costs, illiquidity, and individualized contract specifications, which severely limit investor participation. One of the most significant innovations in the securities markets occurred in April 1973, when The Chicago Board Options Exchange (CBOE) began trading standardized call options on sixteen stocks. However, investors were lacking an objective method to rationally put a price on risk. Sellers of options were still pricing them on little more than gut instinct. The BMS formula moved option pricing from a subjective to an objective basis. It provided a benchmark tool for calculating financial risk to a precise degree without having to make a guess about the likely direction of markets. Thanks in large part to such precise pricing of the BMS formula and its subsequent evolutions, investor interest in these contracts grew dramatically, which in turn resulted in explosive growth in stock options and other financial derivatives.

In June of 1977, the Chicago Board Options Exchange filed with Securities and Exchange Commission (SEC) a series of rule changes to enable trading of nonstock options. Although they were proposed with the intention of using the changes to trade options on government securities, the future implications of the eventual acceptance of these recommendations would be felt worldwide and lead to the creation of cash-settled index options. On March 26, 1980, the SEC lifted the moratorium, expressing satisfaction with the improvement of regulatory procedures adopted by various exchanges. Since then, the two largest exchanges, the CBOE and the American Stock Exchange (AMEX), have been leaders in pioneering new products involving options and option-like securities. Listed stock options are also traded on the Philadelphia, Pacific, and New York Stock Exchanges in the United States, and in most European and Pacific Rim countries that have stock and future markets. Aside from the availability of an objective pricing tool, another major reason for the success of the CBOE and other listed options exchanges is that they provide a liquid, secondary market for trading in the options contracts. To make secondary trading possible, the options exchanges established standardized terms for all contracts and the Options Clearing Corporation, which "delinked" individual options buyers and sellers, thus allowing each party to trade independently in a secondary market.

Today, the listed options traded on several exchanges are available on more than 400 stocks, several stock indices, treasury bonds and bills, financial and commodity futures contracts (options on futures), and foreign currencies. None of these markets existed in any active form before the advent of the Black and Scholes option pricing model. Their model provided the public with a benchmark for the valuation of option and option-like financial products as well as a technique for the management of financial risk in a cost efficient way. However, many investors who do not understand options may view them as highly speculative securities suitable only for people seeking a high degree of risk. On the contrary, if properly used, options enable investors to define precisely the level of risk they want to assume. For example, a pension fund could combine the purchase of options with its common stock portfolio to limit its losses in case the market declines, or it could make use of index options to insure the portfolio against these broad market declines while, at the same time, allowing that portfolio to participate in any market advance. Those followed this strategy during the market crash of 1987 and the five-month decline in the last half of 1990 showed no losses over a period in which market averages declined over 20 percent.

OPTION PRICING TECHNIQUES
BEFORE BLACK AND SCHOLES (1973)

There had been a number of endeavors to value contingent claims prior to the publication of the Black and Scholes (BS) paper in 1973. The impetus of modern option pricing techniques dates as far back as 1877, when Charles Castelli wrote a book entitled The Theory of Options in Stocks and Shares. Although his book familiarized people with the hedging and speculation aspects of options, it lacked any sound theoretical base. The earliest analytical valuation for options was offered in a mathematics dissertation submitted by Louis Bachelier to the faculty of sciences of the Academy of Paris at the turn of the century. About fifty years later, Bachelier's study took the attention of the 1970 Nobel laureate, Paul Samuelson of MIT, who wrote an unpublished paper in 1955 entitled "Brownian Motion in the Stock Market." Robert Merton, one of Samuelson's students, writes that The lineage of modern option pricing theory began with the 1900 Sorbonne thesis, Theorie de la speculation, by the French mathematician, Louis Bachelier. This work is remarkable because, in studying the problem of option pricing, Bachelier derives much of the mathematics of probability diffusions, and this, five years before Einstein's famous development of the mathematical theory of Brownian motion. Although, from today's perspective, the economics and mathematics of Bachelier's analysis are flawed, the connection of his research with the subsequent path of attempts to develop a rigorous theory of option pricing is unmistakable.

As was also stated by Merton, although Bachelier was on the right track and came up with the first recognizable option pricing formula, the stochastic process he employed to generate share price permitted not only negative security prices but also option prices that exceeded the price of the underlying asset. A chain of subsequent researchers handled the movements of stock prices and interest rates more successfully. The most notable milestone studies in pursuit of a better pricing technique for options before the BS are due to Sprenkle, Boness, Samuelson, and Samuelson and Merton. These earlier trials to value derivative instruments assumed (incorrectly) that pricing of such contingent claims necessitates calculation of a risk premium, which ultimately depends on the investor's attitude towards risk. Thus, they tried to derive the reservation price of an investor with a particular utility function. They mainly obtained the price by discounting the expected value of the instrument at expiration to the present. However, there are two major problems pertaining to such a pricing method: (1) one must know the expected return of the underlying asset to find the instrument's expected value at expiration, and (2) one must choose the appropriate discount rate. Under this procedure, since the risk of the instrument depends on two factors, the price of the underlying asset and time, the discount rate will also depend on these two factors. Hence, there will be no single discount rate to employ. Moreover, it is hard, if not impossible, to observe the attitude toward risk in the real world, although it can be strictly defined in theory.

DEVELOPMENT OF OTHER OPTION
PRICING MODELS AFTER BMS' MODEL

Since the advent of the BMS in 1973, the model has been the subject of much interest for many researchers. The original Black and Scholes paper, "The Pricing of Options and Corporate Liabilities," is among the most-cited papers ever in finance. No wonder almost all of over 300 references, which are specifically related to options, in Cox and Rubinstein, a leading text book on options, take the BMS model as their starting point. Aside from his role in the origination of the formula, Merton is also credited for his work to extend and improve the BMS model in several dimensions. In 1973, Merton extended the original BS model that was designed to value European options, which can only be exercised on the expiration date, to the case of American options, which can be exercised at any time before the expiration date. He also relaxed the BS's original assumption that underlying stock will not pay dividends. The original BS model also assumed that interest rates are constant. But if interest rates are constant, risk management in the bond market would not be important. In 1976, Merton went one step further and relaxed this original unworldly restriction, which demands that interest rates be nonstochastic. Beside extending the model to the case of discontinuous stock price processes in 1976, in 1977, he also provided an alternative to the original hedging approach, dynamic replication approach, which derives the BMS formula with handier assumptions. The first application of the "self-financing replicating portfolio" approach to option valuation, which was later refined and extended by Harrison and Kreps, is also attributed to Merton.

In 1976, Ingersoll relaxed another major assumption of the original model, which demands that there be no taxes and transaction costs. A number of financial scholars have introduced models that permit alternative processes to the BMS's particular stochastic process (geometric Brownian motion). Cox, Ross, Rubinstein, and Rendleman and Bartter independently derived the option pricing formula using binomial distributions. If the stock price does not follow a continuous path through time, as Black and Scholes assumed, then it follows either a pure jump process or a mixed diffusion-jump model. With a jump process, the stock price will usually move in a smooth deterministic way but will occasionally experience sudden discrete jumps when important new information arrives. Three models relaxed the Black and Scholes assumption that the instantaneous standard deviation is constant through time: the constant elasticity of variance model, the compound option model, and the displaced diffusion model. Most of the research along these lines is very recent, and therefore the conclusions are tentative. However, it has proved that it is difficult to estimate the parameters of these alternative models relative to those of the original model, which implies the robustness of the original model. Once Merton said in an interview that "the important thing to recognize is the specific model, the Black-Scholes model, is still used" in its original form to value options.

Another streamline of research concentrated on the validity of the BMS option pricing technique and its variants. These empirical tests have faced the problem that empirical tests of the techniques are joint tests of market efficiency and the validity of the model. The BMS formula and the volatility estimates always take into account the information at hand. Thus the market might have some kinds of information influencing the pricing of options that the formula does not consider. As Black pointed out, sometimes the values based on the BMS formula will be better than market prices, while at other times the market prices will be better than the formula values. Given this problem, the empirical studies can be categorized under three major categories according to their objectives : (1) those that try to test whether model prices are biased relative to market prices and to investigate the profitability of trading rules based on portfolios of mispriced options, (2) those that are based on violations of option pricing boundary conditions, and (3) those that are based on the performance of hedge portfolios, which contain combinations of options and other assets. Overall, the studies have found that there are no significant economically exploitable biases when transaction costs are deducted from trading rule profits, suggesting that the BMS model fits observed prices well in an economic sense and the results are consistent with market efficiency.

Black and Scholes and Merton independently made a powerful and original observation that the BMS formula could be applied to figure out the values of risky corporate bonds and common stock. Their critical suggestion, which lies now at the core of modern corporate finance, is that the equity in a levered firm is really a call option on the value of the firm. The reasoning is as follows: If, on the maturity date, the value of the firm exceeds the face value of the firm debt, the shareholders will exercise their call option by paying off the debt and keeping the excess. On the other hand, if the value of the firm is less than the face value of the debt, the shareholders will default on the debt by failing to exercise their option. Later studies have shown how the BMS option pricing technique applies to many different corporate finance topics, such as dividend policy, capital structure, mergers and acquisitions, investment policy, spin-offs, divestitures, convertible debt and warrants, and abandonment decisions. As a matter of fact, the BMS formula has applicability so wide that it can be used to value any contract whose worth depends on the uncertain future value of an asset. In particular, the following studies can be given as examples of the application of the option theory to diverse areas: oil leases by Paddock, Siegel, and Smith; corporate debt by Merton; convertible bonds by Brennan and Schwartz and Ingersoll; warrants by Schwartz, Emmanuel, and Constantinides and Rosenthal; deposit insurance by Sharpe and Merton; life insurance policies by Brennan and Schwartz; variable rate loans by Cox, Ingersoll, and Ross; contracts to exchange one asset for another by Margrabe; corporate pension funds by Sharpe; loan guarantees by Sosin; real investment decisions by Dixit and Pindyck; theory of the term structure of the interest rates by Cox, Ingersoll and Ross and Heath, Jarrow, and Morton.

CONCLUSION

Although the BMS formula is the greatest jewel in their crown, as rightly recognized by the Nobel Prize committee, the contributions of Merton and Scholes to the science of economics and finance are not solely limited to that masterstroke formula. Merton devoted himself to developing finance theory in the areas of capital markets and financial institutions with his research on the operation and regulation of financial institutions, including issues of capital budgeting, production, hedging, and risk management. His studies on intertemporal portfolio choice, capital asset pricing, the pricing options, risky corporate debt, loan guarantees, and other complex derivative securities are highly recognized in the finance and economics communities. If necessary to be more specific, Merton found an impressive way to solve the problem of optimal consumption and portfolio choice in a continuous time setting, which is now extended in many different ways by many financial scholars. Merton's method is viewed by mathematicians as the best and most elegant textbook example of a stochastic control problem. Merton presented the first major extension of the CAPM from a static to a multiperiod setting, which constitutes the essence of the dynamic equilibrium problem. As discussed above, Merton, also extended the BS option pricing model in many different ways. Moreover, Merton, together with Mason, provided a variety of option pricing applications to investment and production decisions.

Robert Merton, in conjunction with Scholes and Black, developed the solution technique of the option pricing model, which in turn can be used to value any derivative asset. A derivative asset is an asset whose payoffs are completely determined by the prices or payoffs of other underlying assets. The payoff function of a derivative asset is a mathematical representation of the relation between payoffs of the derivative and the prices or payoffs of the underlying assets. Derivative assets can be used to provide tailor-made patterns of returns constructed from the fabric of their underlying assets to suit the needs of particular investors. The existence of replicating arbitrage has permitted techniques for valuing derivative assets to develop independently, for the most part, from the general theory of equilibrium asset pricing. Given the price and probability distribution of an underlying asset, one can value an option on the underlying asset. The stochastic return generating process of the underlying asset is assumed in option valuation rather than derived from basic hypotheses concerning tastes and technology, as are done in a general equilibrium model. Although derivative asset valuation requires complex tool of economic analysis, it is used widely to make real-life financial decisions. It was possible largely to the concept of no-arbitrage concept and closed form solution technique developed by Merton, Black and Scholes. This breakthrough has created a plethora of research in financial engineering, which involves the design, the development, and the implementation of innovating financial instruments and processes, and the formulation of creative solution in finance.

RECOMMENDED READINGS

Merton, Robert (1992). *Continuous-Time Finance.* Oxford: Basil Blackwell.
——. (1992, winter). "Financial Innovation and Economic Performance," *Journal of Applied Corporate Finance.*

——. (1993). "Pension Benefit Guarantees in the United States: A Functional Analysis," in Z. Bodie, and R. Schmidt, (eds.), *The Future of Pensions in the United States, Pension Research Council.* Philadelphia: University of Pennsylvania Press.

——. (1993). "Operation and Regulation in Financial Intermediation: A Functional Perspective," in P. England, (ed.), *Operation and Regulation of Financial Markets.* Stockholm: The Economic Council.

——. (1994, June). "Influence of Mathematical Models in Finance on Practice: Past, Present, and Future, Philosophical Transactions of the Royal Society of London," series A, Vol. 347. Reprinted in *Financial Practice and Education.*

Merton, Robert, V. Bernard, K. Pelapu. (1995). "Market-to-Market Accounting for Banks and Thrifts: Lessons from the Danish Experience," *Journal of Accounting Research.* Vol. 33. No. 1.

Merton, Robert, Z. Bodie. (1992, Winter). "On Management of Financial Guarantees," *Financial Management,* Vol. 21.

——. (1993, June). "Deposit Insurance Reform: A Functional Approach," in A. Meltzer and C. Plosser, (eds.) *Carnegie-Rochester Conference Series on Public Policy,* Vol. 38.

——. (1993). "Management of Risk Capital in Financial Firms," in S.L. Hayes III (ed.) *Financial Services: Perspectives and Challenges.* Boston: Harvard Business School Press.

43

Myron Scholes (1941-):
An Applied Financial Economist
and a Laureate of 1997

Ihsan Isik
M. Kabir Hassan

BIOGRAPHICAL PROFILE

Myron Scholes was born in Timmins, Ontario, Canada, in 1941. Through his parents and relatives, he became interested in economics and, in particular, finance. Because of his mother's death, he decided to attend McMaster University for undergraduate studies. The summer after his first year at the University of Chicago, he secured a junior computer-programming position at the school, which gave him an opportunity to absorb how professors created and addressed their own research. Following the suggestion of Merton Miller, he entered the Ph.D. Program at the University of Chicago. After he finished his Ph.D. dissertation in the fall of 1968, he became an assistant professor of finance at the Sloan School of Management at MIT. He returned permanently to the Graduate School of Business at the University of Chicago after visiting for the year 1973-1974. During these years in Chicago, he started to work on the effect of taxation on assets pricing and incentives. He became heavily involved with the Center of Research in Security Prices at the University of Chicago between 1973-1980. In 1981, he visited Stanford University and became a permanent faculty member in the business school and the law school in 1983. In 1990, his interests shifted back to the role of derivatives in financial intermediation. He became a special consultant to Salomon Brothers, Inc., and continued on as a managing director and co-head of its fixed-income-derivative sales and trading group while still conducting research and teaching at Stanford University. In 1994, he joined with several colleagues, many from Salomon Brothers, to become a principal and co-founder of Long-Term

Capital Management. He received honorary doctorate degrees from three universities: University of Paris-Dauphine in 1989, McMaster University in 1990, and Katholieke Universiteit Leuven in 1998.

INTRODUCTION

Myron Scholes, along with Robert Merton, won the economics Nobel prize in 1997 for "a new method to determine the value of derivatives." Economists are usually accused of not giving clear-cut practical answers to the economic problems concerning ordinary people. As if challenging this stereotype, the Nobel Prize in Economic Sciences, which is usually given for "dry" academic concepts with mostly theoretical value was rather awarded to Robert Merton and Myron Scholes in 1997 for their path-breaking work with mostly applied value. These two Nobel laureates, in tandem with the late Fischer Black, developed a new formula for pricing contingent claims in general and stock options in particular, which has revolutionized the practice in both academia and financial markets. This is known as BMS. The degree of its immediate and combined impact on financial economic theory and practice is without parallel. Their far-reaching formula changed the way investors and others place value on risk, giving rise to the field of risk management, the increased marketing of derivatives, and widespread changes in the valuation of corporate liabilities. Even investors who do not have a clue about contingent claims or options owe a debt to their seminal work.

It is contended that the BMS formula has done for finance what Einstein's theory of relativity did for physics. Crudely stated, their work enabled investors to price uncertainty and turned risk management from a guessing game into a science. Their formula has such wide applicability that it can be used to value any contract whose worth depends on the uncertain future value of an asset. As a matter of fact, the BMS method is absolutely crucial to the valuation of anything from a company to property rights. Many practitioners use their methods for planning, purchasing, pricing, or accounting purposes. The Economist magazine in 1991 in a series on the "modern classics" of economics stated that "corporate strategists use the theory to evaluate business decisions; bond analysts use it to value risky debt; regulators use it to value deposit insurance; wildcatters use it to value exploration leases." Such a versatile applicability helped build what currently is a $70 trillion global market of derivatives.

Following the announcement of the Nobel Prize in 1997, Paul Stevens, the president of the Options Clearing Corporation in Chicago said, "I can't think of another instance where an academic work has had such a dramatic and immediate impact on an industry." Similarly, Avinash Dixit of Princeton University said that "if you ask what idea in the last 50 or 60 years coming from research has had the biggest impact on the world, this is it." Robert Brusca, chief economist at Nikko Securities International Inc. in New York, said that "people do not recognize it, but their contributions helped make everybody's life a lot better." Because of this wide acceptance, Scholes called the award for their work in option pricing "the people's prize." He said that " it has become the people's prize because the use of options pricing model became ingrained quickly in the practical world."

THE BLACK, MERTON, AND SCHOLES
(BMS) OPTION PRICING MODEL

The pioneer of the endeavor in pursuit of more "correct" pricing technique for contingent claims is Fischer Black, a scientist with a B.A. in physics and a Ph.D. in applied mathematics from Harvard University, whose interest in working on institutional and theoretical problems in finance was sparked by a colleague, Jack Treynor, when he was working for Arthur D. Little, Inc., in Cambridge, Massachusetts. Starting from 1961, Treynor had written a number of unpublished papers in which he independently developed a model for valuing securities and other assets. Treynor's model had focused on stocks, so Black strove to find another niche or loophole of this background that he could use. He worked on methods to price assets other than common stock, such as bonds, cash flows within a company, and even monetary assets. Black later deliberately ignored options and concentrated his work on valuing stock warrants, because the market for options was then an imperfect over-the-counter market. About the same time, like Black, Paul Samuelson and Robert Merton were using the same approach that Treynor had used in his "value equation," an approach that simply suggests definition of the warrant value in terms of stock price and other factors. Although Samuelson and Merton did not come up with the same formula, as Schaefer put it justly, their work was the most significant precursor to the BMS model in many ways. Indeed, under special conditions, their equation is exactly equivalent to the BS option pricing formula.

Black applied the Capital Asset Pricing Model (CAPM) at each instant of time in a warrant's life for all possible stock prices and warrant values. This allowed him to derive a partial differential equation for the warrant price. Although Black struggled so many days to figure out a "closed-form solution" to that equation, he was still unable to find it. Since he was working on other things as well, he put the problem aside for a while. In 1969, Black left Arthur D. Little and founded his own consulting company, Associates in Finance. He had an office near Boston, where he devoted systematically at least one day a week to pure research. It was then that Myron Scholes, who was a 28-year-old assistant professor of finance teaching at MIT, invited Fischer Black, a 31-year-old independent finance contractor, to join him in some of the research activities at MIT. They combined their comparative advantages and formed one of the most productive research teams ever in finance. Black and Scholes (BS) began to work on the option problem together and made rapid progress. It was an ordinary autumn afternoon of 1969 in Belmont, Massachusetts, when this two-person team suddenly hit upon the answer. Unlike the earlier researchers, BS correctly reasoned that risk premium is not a matter of concern and, thus, not necessary to use when valuing a derivative security because the risk premium is already incorporated in the price of the underlying asset. Since the option value relative to that of the underlying asset does not depend in any explicit way on the investor attitude towards risk, BS shrewdly realized that no assumption is required regarding investor's risk preferences. According to their model, the value of an option does not depend on how the risk of the underlying asset is divided between risk that could be diversified away and the risk that could not be diversified away as well as the expected return of the underlying asset or any other asset. Accordingly, the eventual BS option formula does not include the expected return on the underlying asset as well as any utility dependent parameter. The salient difference and beauty of the BS work appears at this point: the correct discount factor is the risk-free interest rate. Using the hedging approach, BS showed that all of the risk of the underlying asset could be diversified away, and thus its beta must be zero. Then it follows that, if all of the asset's risk could be eliminated, so could all of the risk of the option, whose value ultimately depends on the asset. According to the CAPM, if the option position is hedged in this way, so that it becomes locally riskless, then the position should earn an expected return equivalent to the risk-free interest rate. Hence, the risk-free interest rate is the correct discount factor that will take the option's expected future value to its present value. The BS's innocent-looking but vital observation produced a constant single discount rate that would not depend on time or on the price of the underlying asset, as it would if the underlying asset were assumed to earn an expected return other than the interest rate. Unlike the earlier researchers, BS saw this insight, the elimination of the risk through hedging, which made it possible to have a "closed-form solution" to the option value through the relationship between the price of the option and the price of the underlying asset.

Robert Merton was also working on the valuation of derivative products. Thus, as Black put it, there was a close cooperation along with friendly rivalry between them. Merton made a number of recommendations that contributed to the more general derivation of the formula. More specifically, he suggested that if continuous trading were assumed, then the hedged position could be managed over time so that it would become literally riskless, which in turn would imply zero volatility, not solely zero beta, for the position. Merton also suggested that the simple assumption of no arbitrage would be sufficient to derive the formula, and thus there would be no need to rely on market equilibrium under the strong assumptions of the CAPM. Acknowledging Merton's suggestions, Black wrote that "we derived the formula that way, because it seemed to be the most general derivation." As distinct from his later contributions, Merton's original no-arbitrage and continuous trading arguments are perceived by many to be highly critical and surely seminal observations in the derivation of the BS option pricing formula so that it would not be unjust to call it the Black-Merton-Scholes (BMS) formula. The BMS model for pricing call stock options reduces to the following compact theoretical formula:

C = call premium, S = current stock price, E = option exercise price, r = risk-free interest rate, T= time to option expiration, s = standard deviation of stock returns, N = cumulative standard normal distribution, e = exponential function (2.7183), and ln = natural logarithm. According to the BMS formula, the value of the call option is given by the difference between the first term (1), the expected share value (i.e., the expected benefit from acquiring a stock outright), and the second term (2), the expected cost (i.e., the present value of paying the exercise price on the expiration day). The formula suggests that as the call option value, C, becomes higher, so do its following determinants: (1) today's share price, S, (2) the volatility of the share prices, (3) the risk-free interest rate, r, (4) the time to expiration, T, (5) the probability that the option will be exercised, N. In addition, the option value becomes higher, if the exercise price, E, is lower.

THE PRACTICE

According to many, the BMS model is the most widely applied theoretical product in the history of economics. At the time when the model was first invented, options were thinly traded in the over-the-counter (OTC) markets. Even then, Merton could write that options were "specialized and relatively unimportant financial securities." While giving the reason for why they focused more on warrants, Black would write that "at that time, we thought about warrants more than about options, because the over-the-counter options market was such an imperfect market." However, since the time their landmark formula hit the markets, it has provided profound insight into how people think about financial assets and liabilities and has made the public more facile with options and hedging and risk management techniques. Their model helped the development of the derivative-security markets that are at the center of the extraordinary innovations in the global financial system during the last twenty five years. Owing in large part to their precise pricing recipe and its variants, derivatives since have flourished in volume and variety. The outstanding value of derivatives being traded now globally has reached an astonishing $70 trillion worth.

The wide fluctuations in interest and exchange rates, among other factors, created increasing demand for risk management tools. Prior to the advent of the formula, there were two ways to reduce risk. One was to diversify among securities in an asset class, and the other was to allocate among different asset classes. If the stock price and the option price are so intimately related, it should be possible to use options to offset risk inherent in the stock. Options, which are themselves very risky financial instruments, emerged as an alternative hedging vehicle and revolutionized the way to control risk. Options have been used to provide portfolio insurance for a long or short position. For instance, a portfolio comprised of a short position of one option and a long position of a certain number of shares of the stock will have a total value that will not fluctuate as the share price fluctuates, because if the stock price increases, there is an offsetting loss on the option. Likewise, if the stock price falls, there will be an offsetting gain on the option. The BMS model made the application of hedging more economic and precise by more accurately pricing options and other instruments. Although investors could calculate a risk premium to hedge against major financial losses, they lacked the means to predict such a premium accurately.

As pointed out in the previous section, one of the most important side products of the BMS model was the observation that the value of the stock, preferred shares, loans, and other debt instruments in a company depends on the overall value of the firm. Utilizing this insight, the analysts began to use the model to value corporate liabilities. Also, corporations employed the formula to value executive stock compensation plans, warrants, convertible securities, and so forth. Financial controllers, auditors, and regulators employ the BMS model to evaluate the financial condition of the institutions for which they are responsible. Banks and investment banks use it to value deposit insurance and new financial instruments as well as hedge their own and clients' specific financial risks. If the Bank for International Settlement's proposals to determine bank capital requirements are accepted, the BMS model will be the central and indispensable instrument in the tool kit of banks and their regulators. The BMS formula is also used to value guarantees and insurance type contracts because any person who purchases or is given a guarantee holds a type of option. For example, a typical mortgage gives the borrower the option to refinance when rates are low. Another interesting application area is the case of investment decisions, which require a degree of flexibility (option) in their implementation. For example, the owners of a copper mine have the option not to bear the extraction cost when the copper price is low. A power plant that burns oil and coal is more expensive to build than one that burns only oil, but the greater flexibility may be well worth the extra cost. The main theme in these options are flexibility, which gives the right but not the obligation to exploit it under certain cases and thus has value. To determine the best alternative among competing investment projects, one should find a way to value the right of that flexibility in a rational way. Thanks to the BMS formula, it has been possible lately to value such kinds of options under certain circumstances.

CONCLUSION

Merton devoted himself to developing finance theory in the areas of capital markets and financial institutions by his research on the operation and regulation of financial institutions, including issues of capital budgeting, production, hedging, and risk management. His studies on intertemporal portfolio choice, capital asset pricing, the pricing options, risky corporate debt, loan guarantees, and other complex derivative securities are highly recognized in the finance and economics communities. If it is necessary to be more specific, Merton found an impressive way to solve the problem of optimal consumption and portfolio choice in a continuous time setting, which is now extended in many different ways by many financial scholars. Merton's method is viewed by mathematicians as the best and most elegant textbook example of a stochastic control problem. Merton presented the first major extension of the CAPM from a static to a multiperiod setting, which constitutes the essence of the dynamic equilibrium problem. As discussed above, Merton also extended the BS option pricing model in many different ways. Moreover, Merton together with Mason, provided a variety of option pricing applications to investment and production decisions.

Scholes has clarified the impact of dividends on the valuation of common stocks in the works of Black and Scholes and in those of Miller and Scholes. Also, Scholes, together with Williams, made a significant and widely recognized empirical contribution regarding how to estimate the CAPM betas from nonsynchronous data. Furthermore, he is wellknown as one of the leading experts in the area of employee stock compensation plans. Apart from his seminal work in options pricing and the pricing of corporate liabilities, Scholes is also widely recognized for his work on the effects of global tax policies on decision making. The textbook he wrote together with Mark Wolfson, *Taxes and Business Strategy*, is recognized as the first of its kind in one of the least-studied areas of the economics and finance science.

RECOMMENDED READINGS

Dixit, Avinash, R.S. Pyndick. (1994). *Investment Under Uncertainty.* Princeton: Princeton University Press.

Scholes, Myron. (1996, March). "Global Financial Markets, Derivative Securities and Systemic Risks," *Journal of Risk and Uncertainty.* (ed.) Kip Viscuzi.

——. (1996). "Financial Infrastructure and Economic Growth," *The Mosaic of Economic Growth.* (ed.) Ralph Landau. Stanford: Stanford University Press.

Scholes, Myron, and Mark Wolfson. (1992). "Firms' Responses to Anticipated Reductions in Tax Rates: The Tax Reform Act of 1986," *Journal of Accounting Research.* (supplement.)

——. (1989, September). "Decentralized Investment Banking: The Case of Discount Dividend Reinvestment and Stock-Purchase Plans," *Journal of Financial Economics.* Vol. 24, No. 1.

——. (1990, January). "The Effects of Changes in Tax Laws on Corporate Reorganization Activity," *Journal of Business.* Vol. 63, Nos. 1-2.

——. (Spring 1990). "Converting Corporations to Partnerships through Leverage: Theoretical and Practical Impediments," *Debt, Taxes and Corporate Restructuring.* Ed. John B. Shoven and Joel Waldfogel, Washington, D.C.: Brookings Institution.

——. (Spring 1990). "Employee Stock Ownership Plans and Corporate Restructuring: Myths and Realities," *Financial Management.*

——. (1991, July). "Stock and Compensation," *Journal of Finance.*

——. (1991). "Repackaging Ownership Rights and Multinational Taxation: The Case of Withholding Taxes," *Journal of Accounting Auditing and Finance.*

——. (1991). " The Roles of Taxes Rules in the Recent Restructuring of U.S. Corporations," Tax Policy and the Economy, Fifth edition, David F. Bradford. NBER. Cambridge: MIT Press.

——. (1991). "Employee Stock Ownership Plans and Corporate Restructuring: Myths and Realities," *The Battle for Corporate C ontrol.* Ed. By Arnold W. Sametz. Irwin: Business One.

——. (1992). *Taxes and Business Strategy: A Planning Approach.* New York: Prentice Hall.

Scholes, Myron, Pete Wilson, and Mark A. Wolfson. (1990, May). "Tax Planning, Regulatory Capital Planning, and Financial Reporting Strategy for Commercial Banks," *Review of Financial Studies.* Vol. 3, No. 4.

——. (1995). *The Future of Futures*, Risk Management Problems & solutions Solutions. (ed.) William H. Beaver and George Parker. New York: McGraw-Hill.

44

Amartya Sen (1933-   ):
A Champion of Welfare Economics
and Poverty Studies and the Laureate of 1998

Faridul Islam
Ian K. Wilson
Norman D. Gardner

BIOGRAPHICAL PROFILE

Amartya Sen was born in Shantiniketan, India, in 1933. His father Ashutosh Sen's family originated from Bikrampur in Bangladesh. Sen spent his early life in Dhaka, Bangladesh. His father was a professor of chemistry at Dhaka University. Although Sen's early education started in Dhaka, most of his later schooling was done at Tagore's Institution at Shantiniketan. Sen obtained his BA with honors from Presidency College, Calcutta, securing the first position in the first class. He arrived at Trinity College, Cambridge, in 1953 and was enrolled as a second-year student, as he was eligible to do the honors "Tripos" in economics in two years. While culturally and emotionally he is deeply rooted in Bangladesh and West Bengal, his intellectually formative academic life began in the fifties at Cambridge. That gave him a sense of belonging to a great tradition of world-class scholarship. From his early life, he was involved in left politics. In his final year as an undergraduate, he won the Adam Smith Prize for his essay on Choice of Techniques that produced his first published article and subsequently his first book. He was awarded the Wrenbury Scholarship, given to the best performer in the final examination. As a graduate student at Trinity, he had established an honorable reputation as an economist and a scholar of versatile erudition. At Cambridge, he was influenced by such mentors as Joan Robinson, Piero Sraffa, Nicholas Kaldor, and his tutor, Maurice Dobb. In 1957, Sen, then only twenty-four, became the youngest professor and head of the department of economics at

Jadavpur University, India. From Jadavpur, he went to Harvard and MIT in the Fall of 1960 with visiting positions. Having been at Harvard for a while, he returned to Cambridge as a fellow of Trinity College and then returned to the Delhi School of Economics, India, in 1963. Some of Sen's most illuminating theoretical works originated during that period. Between 1971 and 1977, Sen was at the London School of Economics before taking up the most prestigious economics chair in England, Drummond Chair of Political Economy at Oxford, once held by John Hicks. While at Oxford, both Harvard and Stanford offered him their most prestigious chairs to induce him to move there. He was recognized not only with the honor of being president of the World Econometric Society and International Economic Association but he was also the first non-American ever to become the president of the American Economic Association. Beginning early in 1998, after careful consideration and much thought, Sen decided to return to Cambridge as Master of Trinity College, one of the most honorable positions in the academia in England, where the selection is made by the prime minister of England and approved by the queen.

INTRODUCTION

Amartya Sen won the economics Nobel Prize in 1998 for his "contributions in welfare economics." Sen ranks as one of the most brilliant economists after Keynes. His contributions in normative economics have been as impressive as Samuelson's contributions in positive economics. At the time when Sen grew interested in welfare economics, he felt the need to return to the traditional concern of economics with human welfare and social evaluation, raising concerns about the narrowness of the discipline. In departure from most of the modern economists, Sen does not subscribe to the idea of analyzing the trees and ignoring the forest. Sen questions the neoclassical position. He argues that an individual's objective function can include other goals and commitments in addition to maximization, although self-interest must be the major motivating factor. But if people have other goals and motivations, why should they be compelled by economic theory to pursue self-interest? Sen's deep concern for the human side of the problem can be seen in his statement: "When I say I'm an economist, people ask, 'What should I invest in?' But economics also deals with the downtrodden. He has always been concerned with the downside of economics, the miserable guys who end up hungry, unemployed, starving. One of his famous statements is that famine never strikes democracies.

As far as the Nobel Prize, he has been eligible for the recognition for the past twenty years. Some think that the prize eluded him for over two decades because the rhetoric of globalization and market economics happened to be the ruling paradigm of the time, while Sen focused on the issues of distribution, equity, justice, poverty, hunger, and above all, the fundamental issue of human development. This field of research, unfortunately, was not adequately addressed in the mainstay of economics. Much due to our ignorance and inability to deal with rude reality, we often put such matters behind us. Sen, instead, took the hard way to establish what he thought was true. His life's work ultimately paid the dividend. A new branch of knowledge to deal with inequality and poverty was born, which helped the profession continue to search for meaningful solutions and proper understanding of the issues that were otherwise relegated to an order of secondary importance by the profession.

ECONOMICS, ETHICS, AND PHILOSOPHY

The Nobel citation applauded Sen for restoring an ethical dimension to the discussion of vital economic problems. Ironically, the world press hardly cares about anyone from the part of the world called the Indian subcontinent, but whenever there is one news story, this is all about natural calamities or disaster. Amartya Sen has changed that, if only for one day. In testimony to the negative spin, The *Wall Street Journal*, known for its bias in representing the rich, published an article under the caption "The Wrong Economist Won." It is demeaning to professional accomplishment when the criteria of ideology overtakes merit. It is hard to fathom why the journal should be confused in distinguishing between left and right, and right and wrong. We are all proud of the recognition which is a signal to the economics professional and to the policymakers that a world order that does not address the issues, Sen has been working with, adequately may not ultimately be sustainable. Sen has enriched the literature not only of economics but also of philosophy and other areas in social science and humanities. By combining his deep concern for human development with his mastery of technical details, he has virtually changed the course of literature on poverty and welfare economics. Amartya Sen has had a keen interest in economic problems right from his early days. Growing up in Bengal, touched by economic crisis both at the personal and the national level, his views about the surrounding world were influenced drastically. In particular, the 1943 famine in Bengal influenced much of his later work. After starting in natural science, he moved to economics at Presidency College, Calcutta. To him, economics was not only useful and challenging; a large part of it was fun.

Economic science is concerned with society and mankind at large. A decision has to be made in allocation and distribution of scarce resources that have alternative uses with the ultimate objective to attain and enhance welfare in life. The question is, what is welfare and how can it be enhanced? Economics, as we know it, broadly deals with two aspects–positive and normative. While positive economics centers around the laws and rules that govern such decisions, normative economics deals with value judgment issues. As an example, positive economics is concerned with such questions as: what will be the effect of a rise (fall) in price on quantity demanded of goods and services, ceteris paribus? Normative economics, on the other hand, deals with issues such as whether a change in a policy will be good for people. Obviously, choice of good or bad is something that each society has to make using its own judgment. This normative aspect belongs exclusively to the domain of welfare economics. In a free market economy, most welfare augmenting decisions are taken at the individual level. Sen has been preoccupied mainly with the two subdisciplines in economics, as was Kenneth Arrow, a predecessor in the line of Nobel laureates. Arrow's contribution lay in setting up a list of conditions that a good collective decision ought to fulfill in order to be plausible. The axioms presented by Arrow show that if the desire of all the members in a society were to be achieved, not imposed by a dictator, then there does not exist any social preference that is consistent with the choice made by the majority. This conclusion, which came to be known as Arrow's impossibility theorem, dealt a devastating blow to the branch of welfare economics, which was still at its infancy and was in need of nourishment to grow. This indeed cast a dark shadow over the face of welfare economics at that time, dwarfing its growth for almost two decades.

THE THEORY OF SOCIAL CHOICE

Collective decisions are made in every culture and in every society reflecting varying forms and degrees of democracy and equality, with due regard to the question of equity in distribution of welfare. The issue poses a series of questions: Is there a fair and theoretically sound way of aggregating individual preferences into values, still reflecting the preference of the society as a whole? How practical is the majority principle? What criteria must be used to measure, and perhaps, evaluate the results of collective decisions? How can we combine the social decisions with different schools of moral philosophy? The theory raises questions that are of profound importance: How should income inequality be measured in a society? Can the distribution of welfare be compared among different societies? How to judge whether or not poverty has been mitigated?

The branch of knowledge that deals with the systematic analysis of the questions raised above is known as the theory of social choice. It examines the fundamental problems relating to the design of decision rules within democratic norms. This revolves around the question of whether various social decisions are made with due respect to individual preferences and whether different social states can be ranked fairly, or evaluated in some other way. Put differently, social choice theory analyzes the relation between individual preferences and collective decisions. When there is general agreement, the choices made by society are usually uncontroversial. However, the challenge arises when different interests have to be aggregated into decisions that affect everyone. The contribution of Amartya Sen lies in combining his powerful theoretical framework with rigorous empirical application to bring the theory of social choice to its present state of development. He has been working all his life to add something new to economics that has been missing hitherto–an ethical component. Needless to say, his contributions range from the purely axiomatic theory of social choice, over analysis and definition of welfare indexes, to empirical studies of famine. His work has been a source of inspiration to many other researchers who strongly share his view but could not proceed further due to lack of a rigorous scientific methodology. Much of Sen's research and findings have rekindled academic interest in the neglected issue of welfare economics, and in some instances he has extended the established fields of research, giving a new meaning to them.

Despite its inherent limitations, the majority rule has remained the cornerstone for democratic collective decision. One such deficiency is the so-called intransitivity under the "pair-wise voting." Transitivity implies that if X is preferred to Y and Y to Z, then X will be preferred to Z. In the case of a social choice, intransitivity can take place even though the individual preferences are completely transitive. As an example, a majority may prefer X to Y, whereas another majority prefers Y to, say, Z, and yet a third majority prefers Z to X, which is an example clearly showing intransitivity in the social decision. In such events, strategic voting–not always voting for their own best alternative–may be a solution. Such possibilities prompted Kenneth Arrow to develop a framework detailing the problem in aggregating individual preferences into a social one. Based on a set of five axioms, Arrow demonstrated that for a finite set of N individuals, and the finite set X, containing at least three alternatives, there exists no aggregation rule that fulfills the five axioms, the central thesis of Arrow's impossibility theorem.

Arrow's fundamental result surprised the profession. It instantly presented an insurmountable obstacle to progress in the normative branch of economics by setting a limit on the outcomes that can be achieved through collective decision making. This left the profession wondering about methodologies on how to aggregate individual preferences into collective decisions and how to evaluate different social states and compare them in a satisfactory manner? It was not until the late 1960s that Sen's research started addressing these questions, which initiated a new outlook on the social choice theory. He continued to make vital contributions in the 1970s and 1980s. His monograph, *Collective Choice and Social Welfare*, had a far-reaching impact and inspired many researchers to renew their interest in basic welfare issues. The style of the book, interspersing form and philosophy, provided a new dimension for the economic analysis of normative problems.

PROBLEMS OF SOCIAL CHOICE
AND COLLECTIVE DECISIONS

To satisfy Arrow's impossibility theorem one needs to demonstrate that all five conditions must be fulfilled simultaneously. However, there are decision rules that meet four of these five criteria. To achieve consistency, one way is to reduce the domain of the decision rule, that is, by not allowing all transitive and complete individual preference relations. Black argued in favor of so-called single-peaked preferences. Sen, in 1996 (chapter 10 in *Collective Choice and Social Welfare*), introduced a condition on individual preferences, called *value restriction,* which including those with single peaks, encompasses all of the conditions previously proposed. This ensures transitivity of the majority rule under pair-wise voting. In a subsequent work with Prasanta Pattanaik, Sen identified the necessary and sufficient conditions for a majority rule. As an alternative, without a limit on the domain of the aggregation rule, this can be achieved when preferences are complete and transitive.

A SPHERE OF INDIVIDUAL RIGHTS

By replacing one and dropping another (Sen excluded the axioms of independence, required for Arrow's theorem), Sen examined the nondictatorial aggregation principle. Arrow's requirement of individual rights ought to be considered as the minimum to be met for any civilized society. However, in an ethical context, Sen's result demonstrates that it may be difficult in a democratic society to combine individual influence with the decision-making process efficiently within the sphere of individual rights. This argument spearheaded a scientific analysis involving both economists and philosophers over the issue of whether the requirement of an individual sphere of rights can be consistent with a collective decision rule. This analysis relies on the prerequisites of individual rights versus the requirement of compatibility within the Pareto criterion. Sen's analysis has encouraged economic theorists to generate a large amount of literature in the theory of welfare economics and also in philosophical analysis of rights.

INVARIANCE ANALYSIS

One of the most serious limitations of Arrow's impossibility theorem lies with the five axioms themselves, which are bound to create a stalemate in arguing that social preferences are useful ingredients to evaluate the distribution of welfare in society. Sen departs from Arrow's position on a philosophical perspective. He argues that decisions and judgments are sensitive to the information on which they depend. Continuing on the theme, he was able to demonstrate that Arrow's impossibility theorem is not a general result; rather, it is the product of applying a peculiar type of information to economic theory. The Arrow approach entertained information in the tradition of utility, and only of a particular type–the ordinal one. The following example might help to clarify things. Suppose there are two persons and that they both prefer a mango to an apple. It is clear that we have no way of comparing the intensity of their desires, known as cardinality of utility, for mangoes as a basis for allocation and enhancement of the welfare of the two people. The story gets complex when nonutility information is incorporated. Such nonutility character refers to whether one individual has any special "need" for mangoes. The result of not incorporating a broader information base may have far-reaching implication. In a general context, one part of the world having too much and the other, millions not even able to meet the basics for a bare survival, it is not illegitimate to ask if the science of economics can afford to ignore this important ethical dimension–inquiring about the welfare of mankind.

Despite this lapse of adequate methodology to deal with the issues that afflict an overwhelming majority of the population, the standard texts of economics devote little space to addressing the deprivation and misery of mankind. Considering the fact that standard economic reasoning about welfare is exclusively utility-based, which is synonymous with happiness, it is only logical that there will hardly remain any room for discussing poverty. This condition, admittedly, allows for very general individual preferences and avoids the difficult question of whether different individuals' evaluations of social states can really be compared. But the condition also precludes saying anything worthwhile about inequality. Sen argues that in order to make any progress on this issue, the general assumption about individual preferences has to be relaxed in some reasonable way. A possible modification of Arrow's conditions would be to allow for cardinal instead of only ordinal information in individual preferences. Sen showed that this limitation on the domain of the decision rule does not eliminate the inconsistency between conditions (chapter 8 in *Collective Choice and Social Welfare*). While Sen does not explicitly presuppose interpersonal comparability of differences in utility, he does ask whether the possibility of generating more or less complete social preferences depends on the degree of interpersonal comparability. Noncomparability leads to social preferences given by the Pareto criterion, whereas full comparability leads to complete social preferences given by the utilitarian criterion.

Sen gives a new direction for analyzing social choice. He asks whether more information about individual utility scales is compatible with the existence of a collective decision rule and nondictatorial social preferences. This is raised in *Collective Choice and Social Welfare* (chapters 7-8), where he characterizes social preferences and existing ethical principles in terms of both the information contained in individual utility scales and the potential for interpersonal comparisons of utility. Sen's invariance analysis has turned out to be extremely useful in the theory of social choice. The theory now provides many axiomatic characterizations of social preferences, with respect to available information on individual utilities. Some of Arrow's axioms imply that social preferences are identical to those of individuals in the economy. However, by replacing ordinal, interpersonally noncomparable individual preferences with ordinal, interpersonally comparable preferences, the class of possible social preferences is readily extended. It has been shown that Rawls' maxim principle is obtained as a particular instance, in which case the median voter's preferences will determine the outcome. The class of possible social preferences is extended further when more information about, and comparability between, individual utility scales is used.

MEASUREMENT OF WELFARE AND INEQUALITY

Providing measurement for poverty consistent with a sound theoretical framework and constructing indexes to measure differences in income and welfare in a society are formidable and challenging tasks in themselves. They are also important applications of the theory of social choice. There exists a parallel between indexes of inequality and representation of social preferences known as social welfare functions. Formulating axioms is crucial to the process of performing a comparison. Any set of indexes can be evaluated on the basis of those axioms and the invariance axioms. The invariance axioms also characterize the corresponding social preferences. Many welfare indicators are expressed as a comprehensive index, as opposed to a social welfare function. Notable contributors in the development of inequality indexes at a theoretical level include Kolm, Atkinson, and Sen. In fact, poverty indexes are also special class indexes to rank inequality and can be derived from axioms of social preferences. It is no coincidence that the problem of poverty is synonymous with poor countries, which also suffer from data limitations The data problem makes it difficult to determine the degree to which distributions in different countries can be compared.

A poverty index, more commonly used, is constructed by computing the share of the population, H, having an income below a predetermined poverty line. Such measures seem inadequate, as they ignore the distribution of income among the poor. Sen attempted to eliminate this drawback by deriving the poverty index where he combined the Gini coefficient with the H factor just noted above. A Gini coefficient is perhaps the oldest measure for the degree of income inequality in a society. In Sen's index, he refers to informational assumptions and the invariance analysis that enable him to point out the relevance and usefulness of the poverty index in relation to the Gini coefficient. Sen's poverty index has found numerous applications, and it has been applied by those favoring alternative poverty indexes. In his approach to constructing his index, Sen theorized five axioms, three of which have been used widely by other researchers. Subsequently, they have also proposed alternative poverty indexes. In his "Real National Income," Sen extended the axiomatic approach to the concept of national income to provide the foundations of the potential for using them for comparing different countries. This work tries to integrate the distributional indicators with the national income among countries by considering the twin issues of income per capita and the Gini coefficient.

Sen's index for interpersonal comparisons, particularly useful in the context of justice, has received considerable attention. As an example, Rawls' maxim principle is contingent on interpersonal comparability, as is Arrow's impossibility theorem. Sen emphasized that what creates welfare is not goods, per se, but the activity for which they are acquired. This idea is similar to the so-called Lancaster approach, where goods are defined as multidimensional objects in terms of their characteristics. According to Sen, goods create "functional opportunities" for individuals; the set of such functional opportunities can then be used to define an individual's actual opportunities, or "capabilities." Income is significant from this point of view because of the opportunities it creates. Although the actual opportunities depend on a number of these factors, such as health, these factors should also be taken into account when measuring welfare. Alternative welfare indicators, such as the UN's Human Development Index; are constructed precisely in this spirit. Sen's concept of fairness assumes that all individuals should have equal access to actual opportunities in order to achieve the same capability. This resembles the egalitarian view of Rawls, who wanted to maximize the welfare of the worst off in society. Obviously, such a criterion cannot be applied to practice without an interpersonal comparison of the welfare index. Rawls mentions an index of "primary goods" but does not offer any suggestions for solving the index problem. Sen's work, however, provides guidelines for dealing with these matters.

DEVELOPMENT ECONOMICS

Over the last forty years, Amartya Sen has worked persistently to establish what he thought was right. He has been the King Midas of economics. Whatever area he touched became a gold mine for inquisitive researchers. Whatever his mind turned to, he produced a magnum opus, a masterpiece. On exploring the issues of development Sen followed the standard textbook approach wherein students begin with economic development, and distribution of its fruits. In real life, the latter part of the knowledge that deals with distribution disappears. Sen would not let that happen, he embarked on a policy to integrate development with distribution. His work on development, therefore, addresses the fundamental question of poverty. An extreme case of poverty is coincidental with the existence of famine. Sen's approach to examining this issue began more in the nature of an empirical approach. It is a common belief that famine is caused by a lack of food. Sen scrutinized the actual statistical evidence of three famines, two in Bengal and one in Ethiopia. In stark contrast with conventional wisdom, a thorough empirical examination demonstrated that the food grain availability during the famine was not only adequate to meet the demand for food to avoid catastrophe, but the supply of food grain even exceeded the demand compared to normal time. The observed facts seemed to belie the static market theory, which suggests that famine is a market phenomenon–supply demand imbalance. Facts, however, show that famine is not caused by shortage of food supply relative to demand; famine is caused by nonmarket factors. Sen's research is an attempt to answer these fundamental questions.

Sen has demonstrated a deep and lifelong interest in poverty, specifically in the very poorest of the poor. By reorienting the study of poverty from income and utility differences to capabilities, he has helped others to recognize the evils of poverty. Sen's best-known work in the area of poverty is *Poverty and Famines: An Essay on Entitlement and Deprivation,* in which he challenges the common view that a shortage of food as the lone factor explaining famine. Using data from the 1940s to the 1970s and through rigorous empirical examination of the catastrophes in India, Bangladesh, and the Saharan countries, he came to his startling conclusion. He showed that famines have occurred even when the supply of food was not significantly lower than the previous years. He even shows that famine stricken areas have, at times, even exported food. This thesis: People do not die in famines because they do not have enough food, but rather, due to a collapse of what he calls the exchange entitlements, which prevent them from acquiring the possibly plentiful food that is there. As an example, he refers to the inflation-induced 1943 famine in Bengal, where people died in front of shops that had significant stock of food but were protected by the state. They were denied food because of lack of legal entitlement, not because their entitlements were violated. Sen argues that the so-called food availability decline

(FAD), a concept prevailing at the time his book was published, was inadequate to explain the observed phenomena during famines. To summarize, he identifies three factors that cause famine. First, famine has occurred in years when the supply of food per capita was not lower than previous years without famine. Second, food prices increased considerably in some years, although the supply of food was not lower as compared to previous years. Third, in all cases of famine, large groups have not suffered starvation, and fourth, in some cases, food has been exported from famine-stricken areas.

In the context of the 1974 Bangladesh famine, he argues that a flood caused a significant rise in food prices, and opportunities for work in the agricultural sector were not available. The flood destroyed one of the crops totally. Both of these factors caused the real incomes of agricultural labor to fall. As a result, this group was disproportionately stricken by starvation. His point, that democratic society is less prone to famine, assumes political intervention of the constituency in such an event. Autocrats have no compulsion about their constituents. Sen's interest has been simply in famines, rather than in the inequalities of income, and particularly among the poorest of the poor. He is skeptical about measures of poverty that consider only low income and income gap, which is also sensitive to the distribution of income among the poor.

The primary objective of Sen's book was to understand the background and causes of famine and was followed by discussions of ways to prevent famine, or at least to limit its effects once the forces have set in. While there is general agreement as to the quality and outstanding significance of the book, some of its details have been disputed. Some critics questioned the empirical foundations for Sen's results regarding the causes of famine, primarily arguing that data on food supply in a developing country stricken by famine may not be dependable. Given the high quality of the book, such criticisms appear misdirected. The book, nevertheless, remains a masterpiece in the annals of contribution to development economics with emphasis on issues of distribution and poverty. In a subsequent work, Sen carried out empirical studies to substantiate his theoretical results on social choice and welfare measurement that have been widely cited. In particular, Sen's insights into the causes of famine from theoretical considerations are praiseworthy in their own right, regardless of whether some of the empirical results might be unreliable. We need to work with whatever data we have. The book examines very important issues of development economics and is undoubtedly a key contribution in the literature of distributive justice, poverty, and starvation. The book reflects the recurring theme in Amartya Sen's research. It is not too much to say that his work on famine is a masterpiece that aptly summarizes the work of his lifetime. It is perhaps true that what he worked so hard to establish reflects the evolution of his own thinking on various subjects that troubled his mind.

While a vast majority of his work is axiomatic and mathematically sound theory, his theoretical framework is less abstract with the formulations having direct applications to the analysis of poverty. One such application of research deals with development economics. In a sense, most of his works are directed to development economics, just as they deal with the welfare of the poorest of the poor people. His first published work discusses the choice of appropriate production technology in developing countries. *Choices of Techniques* discusses whether a country like India, with scarce capital and huge surplus labor, should adopt labor intensive techniques (hand spinning machine) or modern capital intensive techniques of production. This has been a dominant debate since 1947. Sen came out with an unconventional answer, that these countries should adopt capital-intensive techniques in the modern sector that will increase the rate of capital accumulation. In the long-run, surplus labor will be absorbed in the fast-growing industrial sector. To many, it sounded paradoxical at that time.

CONCLUSION

Rehman Sobhan, Sen's old pal at Cambridge says: "I certainly rate Amartya as the finest intellect of our generation and perhaps the sharpest mind I have ever been privileged to encounter anywhere. Amartya was unknown when he arrived in Cambridge and being a shy young man, no one knew much about him until around June 1954, when his name was posted on the notice board with the grade of first class in the MA (prelim) exam for economics." (Dhaka: Daily Star.) Sen has demonstrated, in the spirit of Aristotle and many of the welfare economists, that human well-being and destitution are not the same as the abundance or lack of income. Much of his reasoning is methodologically abstract and philosophical in nature; however, a significant portion of his enormous literature is accessible to common readers. A central theme reverberating all across his work is a sincere and genuine concern for humankind. Sen successfully integrated three distinct but interrelated disciplines into the spirit of a true economist: welfare economics, social choice, and development economics. However, in the debate over poverty, one should recognize two fallacies. First, the oversimplification of poverty, equating poverty with the lack of income alone and second, economic growth is necessary for economic improvement, but an excessive growth rate may fail to realize and fail to deliver the fundamental question of distribution. It may frustrate the plight for alleviating poverty. The "Asian miracle" may not be replicated everywhere.

RECOMMENDED READINGS

Arrow, K.J. (1951). *Social Choice and Individual Values.* Second edition, 1963. New York: Wiley.

Atkinson, A.B. (1970). "On the Measurement of Inequality," *Journal of Economic Theory*, Vol. 2, pp. 244-263.

Black, D. (1948). "On the Rationale of Group Decision-making," *Journal of Political Economy.* Vol. 56, pp. 23-34.

Blackorby, C. (1975). "Degrees of Cardinality and Aggregate Partial Ordering," *Econometrica.* Vol. 43, pp. 845-52.

Dasgupta, P., A.K. Sen and D. Starrett. (1973). "Note on the Measurementof Inequality," *Journal of Economic Theory.* Vol. 6, pp. 180-87

Deschamps, R. and L. Gevers. (1978). "Leximin and Utilitarian Rules: A Joint Characterization," *Journal of Economic Theory*. Vol. 17, pp. 143-63.

Dreze, J. and A.K. Sen. (1989). *Hunger and Public Action*. Oxford: Clarendon.

Dworkin, R. (1978). *Taking Rights Seriously*. London: Duckworth.

Fine, B. (1975). "A Note on Interpersonal Comparisons and Partial Comprability," *Econometrica*. Vol. 43, pp. 169-72.

Gibbard A. (1974). "A Pareto-consistent Libertarian Claim," *Journal of Economic Theory*. Vol. 7, pp. 338-410.

Hammond, P. J. (1976). "Equity, Arrow's Conditions and Rawls' Difference Principle," *Econometrica*. Vol. 44, pp. 793-804.

Inada, K.I. (1964). "A Note on the Simple Majority Decision Rule," *Econometrica*. Vol. 32, pp. 490-506.

Kolm, S.C. (1969). "The Optimal Production of Social Justice" in *Public Economics*, H. Guitton and I. Margolis (eds.). London: Macmillan.

Maskin, E. (1978). "A Theorem on Utilitarianism," *Review of Economic Studies*. Vol. 45, pp. 93-6.

Pattanaik, P.K. and A.K. Sen. (1969b). "Necessary and Sufficient Conditions for Rational Choice Under Majority Decision," *Journal of Economic Theory*. Vol. 1. pp. 178-202.

Rawls, J. (1971). *A Theory of Justice*. Cambridge : Harvard University Press.

Roberts, K. W. S. (1980a). "Possibility Theorems with Interpersonally Comparable Welfare Levels," *Review of Economic Studies*. Vol. 47, pp. 409-20.

———. (1980b). "Interpersonal Comparability and Social Choice Theory," *Review of Economic Studies*. Vol. 47, pp. 421-39.

Sen, A.K. (1967). "A Possibility Theorem on Majority Decisions," *Econometrica*. Vol. 34, pp. 491-99.

———. (1969). "Quasi Transitivity, Rational Choice and Collective Decisions," *Review of Economic Studies*. Vol. 36, pp. 381-93.

———. (1970a). *Collective Choice and Social Welfare*. San Francisco: Holden Day and London: Oliver and Boyd. (Reprinted Amsterdam: North-Holland.)

———. (1970b). "The Impossibility of a Paretian Liberal," *Journal of Political Economy*. Vol. 78, pp. 152-57.

———. (1970c). "Interpersonal Aggregation and Partial Comparability," *Econometrica*. Vol. 38, pp. 393-409.

———. (1972). "Interpersonal Aggregation and Partial Comparability: A Correction," *Econometrica*. Vol. 40, pp. 959.

———. (1973). *On Economic Inequality*. Oxford: Clarendon.

———. (1974). "Informational Bases of Alternative Welfare Approaches," *Journal of Public Economics*. Vol. 3, pp. 387-403.

———. (1976a). "Liberty, Unanimity and Rights," *Economica*. Vol. 43, pp. 217-35.

———. (1976b). "Poverty: An Ordinal Approach to Measurement," *Econometrica*. Vol. 44, pp. 243-62.

———. (1981). *Poverty and Famines: An Essay on Entitlement and Deprivation*. Oxford: Clarendon.

———. (1981). "Poverty and Famines: An Essay on Entitlement and Deprivation," Oxford: Clarendon Press.

———. (1966). "A Possibility Theorem on Majority Decision," *Econometrica.* Vol. 34, pp. 491-9.

———. (1969). "Quasi transitivity, Rational Choice and Collective Decisions," *Review of Economic Studies.* Vol. 36, pp. 381-393.

———. (1970a). *Collective Choice and Social Welfare.* San Francisco: Holden Day and London: Oliver and Boyd. (reprinted Amsterdam: North-Holland.)

——— (1970b). "The Impossibility of a Paretian Liberal," *Journal of Political Economy.* Vol. 78, pp. 152-57.

———. (1970c). "Interpersonal Aggregation and Partial Comparability," *Econometrica.* Vol. 38, pp. 393-409.

———. (1972). "Interpersonal Aggregation and Partial Comparability: A Correction," *Econometrica.* Vol. 40, p. 959.

———. (1973). *On Economic Inequality.* Oxford: Claredon.

———. (1974). "Informational Bases of alternative Welfare Approaches," *Journal of Public Economics.* Vol. 3, pp. 387-403.

———. (1976a). "Liberty, Unanimity and Rights," *Economica.* Vol. 43, pp. 217-35.

———. (1976b). "Poverty: An Ordinal Approach to Measurement," *Econometrica.* Vol. 44, pp. 243-262

45

Robert Mundell (1932-   ):
Who Offers Consensual Frameworks for Continuing Controversies and Is the Laureate of 1999

James W. Dean

BIOGRAPHICAL PROFILE

Robert Mundell was born in 1932 in Kingston, Ontario, Canada. He attended a one-room schoolhouse in the tiny hamlet of Latimer, ten miles north of Kingston, and then a high school 3,000 miles west, in Maple Ridge, British Columbia. In 1953, he graduated from the University of British Columbia (UBC) in Vancouver with a joint major in economics and Slavonic studies. His doctoral studies presaged his lifelong penchant for intellectual and geographic exploration, starting with a year at the University of Washington in Seattle, followed by a year at MIT in Cambridge, Massachusetts, and then a year at the London School of Economics (LSE). At the LSE he finished his Ph.D. thesis for MIT, entitled *Essays in the Theory of International Capital Movements*. Then in 1956-1957 he migrated to the University of Chicago for a final year of education as a postdoctoral fellow. By 1957, he was back at UBC as an instructor, married Barbara Sheff, and began to publish on international trade, including three articles from his Ph.D. thesis. Also that year at UBC, he presented for the first time his theory of optimum currency areas, one of the ideas that was to make him famous. There followed a string of employments: summer 1958 with a Royal Commission in Ottawa, 1958-1959 at Stanford, 1959-1961 at the Johns Hopkins Bologna Center of Advanced International Studies (which began a long love affair with Italy), 1961-1963 at the International Monetary Fund (IMF), 1963-1964 at McGill, and 1964-1965 at the Brookings Institution. Finally, in the fall of 1965, at the age of thirty-two, he settled in at the prestigious University of Chicago, where he remained until 1971. The late sixties were halcyon years at Chicago, with the Mundell/Johnson seminars on international economics and the Friedman seminars on monetary economics. Mundell quickly acquired a reputation as an *enfant terrible*. One of many apocryphal tales (this one told by Rudiger Dornbusch) has him asking Friedman, during a money seminar, "Milton, what makes you think *money* has anything to do with *inflation*?" But he was more than an *enfant terrible*; he was also charismatic and persuasive, not to mention editor of the *Journal of Political Economy*, by then one of the world's top two or three economics journals. The Chicago period ended with a return to Canada from 1971-1974, as chairman of economics at the University of Waterloo. Mundell then moved to Columbia University in New York, where he has remained ever since. However, he continues to travel the world and, since October 1999, has probably set a record for Nobel Prize winners in any discipline for the number of lectures delivered around the globe. He is a devoted family man with three children, Paul, Bill, and Robyn, from his first marriage to Barbara, and a fourth, Nicholas, who arrived three years ago. He, his wife Valerie, and Nicholas divide time at home between their New York apartment and the Palazzo Mundell (formerly Villa of Santa Colomba), a renaissance palace near Siena, Italy, that he bought in 1969 from the Roman Catholic Church.

INTRODUCTION

Robert Mundell won the economics Nobel Prize in 1999 for "analyzing fiscal and monetary policies under different exchange rate regimes and analysis of optimum currency areas." Mundell is one of the greatest economists who created a legacy of his own in theories of international trade and finance. His theory in support of a single currency is attributable to the unification of Europe and the birth of the Euro. He made substantial contributions to the theory of inflation and interest, fiscal and monetary policy mix, and the growth and balance of payments in an open economy setting. He has been a co-founder of supply-side economics.

THREE CONSENSUAL FRAMEWORKS
FOR THREE CONTINUING CONTROVERSIES

Rather than attempt systematically to survey Robert Mundell's varied, multitudinous, and substantial published work, I will instead focus on three seminal contributions that are also intellectually fascinating because they continue to generate controversy and debate. The first of these is his framework for defining optimal currency areas. Seminal is perhaps too weak a word here, since the framework literally defined a concept. Moreover, the 1961 analysis has inspired generations of economists to advocate particular currency regimes. But it has left the profession as quarrelsome as ever over the merits of common currencies, fixed rates, and flexible rates. And mysteriously to some, Mundell's advocacy of fixed rates and common currencies never wavers, causing many to wonder how they missed his hidden message in the 1961 article. I will devote some space to resolving this mystery. A second seminal contribution is the Mundell-Fleming model. Forty years after its publication, it remains our consensual framework for analyzing open macroeconomies. Like the optimal currency framework, it is not controversial, per se; rather, it serves as a paradigmatic platform for launching controversy. I will not devote space to expositing the model but, instead, will illustrate its application. A third seminal contribution evolved from the application of theoretical principles to a policy problem. The Mundellian principles for assigning policy instruments to their targets, launched from the Mundell-Fleming platform, suggested a controversial assignment of monetary policy to inflation and fiscal policy to real growth. When it was finally applied in the early 1980s, the assignment proved prophetically successful. The fiscal side of that assignment came to be called the "supply-side revolution."

Two years earlier, the American Economics Association was more specific. In 1997, the AEA made Mundell a distinguished fellow because of his seminal contributions to the theory of optimum currency areas, the Mundell-Fleming framework for analyzing open macroeconomies, and the problem of "assigning" policy instruments to policy targets. The AEA also emphasized his contributions to the theory of international trade. In a review of Mundell's work written after the Nobel Prize was awarded, Dominick Salvatore characterized his three enduring contributions as "Three Brilliant Ideas, One Nobel," suggesting that any one of them would have justified the prize (Salvatore, 2000). Salvatore's list is the same as the AEA's except that "supply-side economics" substitutes for "policy assignment." As already suggested, the former can be considered an application of the latter.

Of course Mundell's seminal and lasting contributions are by no means confined to these three. His earliest enduring contributions were to the pure theory of international trade, beginning in 1957 and carrying through to 1993. Much of his early thinking on both trade and finance is consolidated in International Economics (1968), which became the leading textbook for graduate students of its time, and several of his early contributions to monetary theory are captured in a second book, Monetary Theory: Interest, Inflation and Growth in the World Economy (1971). There is a continuous flow of important papers on the balance of payments between 1968 and 1997, on the international monetary system (1972-1995), and on monetary theory and the history of money (1960-1999). And throughout his career, there are dozens of policy papers and depositions to governments. But the "Three Brilliant Ideas" were not only seminal; they are as topical today as they were forty years ago–and not just topical but also frameworks for controversy. I will start with optimum currency areas.

OPTIMUM CURRENCY AREAS

Mundell (1961a) coined the phrase "optimum currency areas" and laid out a framework that has been used ever since to analyze choices between currency regimes. But like the Bible or the Koran, it has been used by particular acolytes to justify just about every regime available to the modern world. Its policy implications are, to put it mildly, controversial. Mundell himself holds firm convictions about appropriate exchange rate regimes, with a strong preference for hard fixes or common currencies. Yet, ironically, many other eminent economists, typically drawing from the 1961 framework, hold preferences just as strong for flexible rates. A third, smaller, but similarly convinced subset of economists argues for adjustable pegs and similar intermediate arrangements.

One key to the continuing controversy is the differing emphases placed on short-and long-run mechanisms for adjusting a country's balance of trade. Since prices and wages are slow to adjust, many economists advocate flexible exchange rates as an alternative mechanism. Nominal exchange rate adjustment promises to by-pass the painful unemployment and real income adjustment that substitutes for price and wage adjustment in the short run. But as proponents of fixed rates point out, in the long run prices and wages will adjust, and furthermore they should be encouraged to adjust via the discipline of a fixed external standard. This argument for "endogenizing" the long run was strengthened in the late 1960s by the evolution of a professional consensus around a theory of the long-run Phillips curve, which suggests that nominal, or "monetary," shocks are inevitably neutral in the long run.

It is important to understand Mundell's advocacy of hard fixes and common currencies in the larger context of the profession's resurrection of classical long-run analysis and corresponding rejection of the ad hoc, short-term aspects of Keynesianism. Part of the by-pass of painful real adjustment promised by advocates of flexible exchange rates relies on money illusion-the illusion that after exchange rate depreciation, real wages have been maintained despite rising prices for imports and, ultimately, other goods as well. Hence, the argument for relying on nominal exchange rate adjustment could be termed Keynesian. In fact, Mundell, in a typically wry twist of the knife, sometimes points out that even Milton Friedman's advocacy of flexible rates rests on an assumption that economic actors (like wage-earners) indulge in recidivist, Keynesian behavior. This would suggest that, in general, advocates of flexible rates are caught in a Keynesian time warp, out of sync with both modern macroeconomic theory and the modern world's practical ability to adjust quickly, prompted by "rational expectations."

A second key to Mundell's position is the role of capital flows. Proponents of flexible rates draw succor from his 1961 optimal currency analysis that focused on current account–trade balance–factors, but his own thinking emphasizes the importance of capital flows (see Mundell 1973a, b, from the proceedings of a 1970 conference in Madrid). He believes that uncertainty about exchange rates can cause capital flows to be excessive and even destabilizing. Friedman's thinking on this point is very linear: speculators cannot systematically make profits unless they buy low and sell high; hence, capital movements must reduce exchange rate volatility, not the reverse. Mundell thinks differently. Repeatedly, he argues that today's short-term capital flows–"hot money" flows whose daily gross volumes greatly exceed their net volumes–are largely a response to exchange rate uncertainty, not necessarily a response to market-driven flexible rates, per se, but to uncertainty about monetary policy, or perhaps uncertainty about whether "pegged" rates might become unpegged. He believes that this wasteful churning of money would largely cease were exchange rates firmly stabilized, as it has within "Euroland" since the European Monetary System locked in exchange rates during the 1990s. In his words, "There are no bad capital flows; there are only bad exchange rate systems."

In short, Mundell believes that under credibly fixed exchange rates, policymakers have less room to make mistakes. Under the Bretton Woods arrangements of fixed exchange rates, inflation was kept under control. But after that system broke down in the early 1970s, major countries, including the United States, went on an inflation binge that created large swings in exchange rates, swings that were exacerbated by speculative capital movements. Gradually, central banks and governments learned some lessons and by the 1990s, most of the Organization for Economic Cooperation and Development (OECD)countries had brought inflation under control. Mundell thinks that because inflation targets are now similar in the dollar, euro, and yen areas, a three-currency monetary union would work and could become a platform for a new international monetary system with a world currency.

Perhaps the appropriate distinction between Mundell's 1961 analytical framework and his advocacy of common currencies–and now a world currency–is a distinction between Mundell the pure theorist and Mundell the visionary. In fact, the word "distinction" may put too fine a point on it: "marriage" might be better. For if anything characterizes the span of his work over a lifetime, it is an inextricable marriage between theory and policy. Few theorists dare draw out clear policy implications. Fewer still dare to predict. Mundell has been living dangerously in both respects for at least thirty years. Remarkably, both his policy advocacy and his crystal ball have served to enhance rather than diminish his professional reputation, particularly beyond academia. For his advocacy of a European common currency, he is often called "Father of the Euro," and for his advocacy of tax cuts, "Godfather of Supply-Side Economics."

THE MUNDELL-FLEMING MODEL, INSTRUMENT ASSIGNMENT AND SUPPLY SIDE ECONOMICS

In 1952, Jan Tinbergen, who in 1969, along with Ragnar Frisch, was the first Nobel prize winner for economics, formulated the rudiments of what is now the theory of economic policy. Tinbergen's core principle was that to realize X targets, a policymaker must deploy at least X instruments. Eight years later, Mundell substantially extended this principle and ultimately launched a revolution in real-world economic policy with ramifications that are hard to exaggerate. Mundell (1960) addressed the appropriate assignment of instruments to targets. His specific application was that under flexible exchange rates, interest rates should be assigned to achieving external balance and price level adjustments, to achieving internal balance. His methodological innovation was to introduce dynamic considerations and take into account capital movements, asking which instrument assignment was likelier to produce stable macroeconomic equilibrium. He called this the "principle of effective market classification."

Two years later, he applied this principle to fixed exchange rates. In four related articles, Mundell (1961b, 1961c, 1962, 1963) laid out the most seminal of all his theoretical work, the Mundell-Fleming model, which clearly distinguishes between the effects of monetary and fiscal policies under fixed and flexible exchange rates. Then in the early 1970s, Mundell utterly confounded conventional wisdom by advocating the assignment of monetary policy to inflation and fiscal policy to real growth. This sowed the seeds for the American "supply-side revolution" that took root a decade later and has borne fruit ever since.

In the early 1970s, the United States was suffering from incipient inflation and slow growth. After the oil price hikes of 1973-1974, the United States, along with most rich countries, sank into a quagmire of persistent inflation and recession–so-called "stagflation." One possible instrument assignment, advocated by liberal Keynesians like James Tobin, was government spending (to stimulate aggregate demand), funded and reinforced by easy money. A second, advocated by fiscal conservatives, was balanced budgets and tight money (to fight inflation). But Mundell advocated a policy mix that was decried by liberals and conservatives alike: tax reduction to target real supply, and tight money to target nominal demand.

The novel part of the Mundellian policy mix was not targeting inflation with tight money, since this had already been advocated for decades, notably by Milton Friedman. Moreover, the Phillips tradeoff between inflation and output was already in disrepute due to the new Phelps/Friedman theory of a Phillips curve that is vertical in the long run. Nevertheless, it is probably fair to claim that Mundell's advocacy of tight money provided moral succor to Paul Volcker, a close friend of Mundell's, who as governor of the Federal Reserve System, doggedly wrung inflation out of the United States economy between 1980 and 1982.

The novel part of the Mundellian mix was targeting real output via tax reduction and, by extension, via deregulation. The behavioral link ran through incentives to save and work, and improved factor allocation. A fabled cabal–Mundell, Jack Kemp (congressman from upstate New York and former star quarterback of the Buffalo Bills), Jude Wanniski (editorial writer for the Wall Street Journal), and Arthur Laffer (Mundell's ex-student from Chicago)–met frequently during the mid-1970s in New York, usually at a Wall Street watering hole called Michael One. According to legend, the famous Laffer Curve (whereby a reduction in tax rates, above a certain level, actually increases tax revenue) was invented on cocktail napkins.

Serendipitously, Mundell's influence outside academia, not least among readers of the Wall Street Journal, had been enhanced in the early 1970s by a series of spectacular forecasts that built him the reputation of a gifted, almost magical, economic seer. Mundell predicted, in the order that they occurred, the collapse of the Bretton Woods system, a spiraling gold price, a sharp hike in oil prices, and the inflation and output stagnation that ensued. Wall Street respected Mundell, and the macroeconomic merits of tax reduction soon found their way onto the editorial page of the Wall Street Journal. Jude Wanniski was inspired to write a best-selling book, The Way the World Works (Basic Books, 1978).

Ultimately, the supply-side message rationalized Reagan's tax cuts and industrial deregulation during the 1980s. And as predicted by the Mundell-Fleming model, tax cuts and tight money led, in the short run, to higher budget deficits, higher interest rates, capital inflows, a rising dollar, and a deteriorating current account. But the deficits have turned into surpluses, interest rates have plummeted, and capital inflows now feed the private sector, not the U.S. government. And except for a brief dip in 1990–1991, the U.S. economy has seen a sustained boom from 1982 through to the turn of the century, the longest in industrialized history. Such is the legacy of a Canadian economist to America, and indeed to the world at large.

CONCLUSION

The Royal Swedish Academy of Sciences justified its 1999 choice for the Bank of Sweden Prize in Economic Sciences in Memory of Alfred Nobel as follows:

Robert Mundell has established the foundation for the theory which still dominates in practical considerations of monetary and fiscal policy in open economies. His work on monetary dynamics and optimum currency areas has inspired generations of researchers. Although dating back several decades, Mundell's contributions remain outstanding and constitute the core of teaching in international macroeconomics. Mundell's research has had such far-reaching and lasting impact because it combines formal–but still accessible–analysis, intuitive interpretations, and results with immediate policy implications. Above all, Mundell chose his problems with uncommon–almost prophetic–accuracy in terms of predicting the future development of international monetary arrangements and capital markets. Mundell's contributions serve as a superb reminder of the significance of basic research. At a given point in time, academic achievements might appear rather esoteric; not long afterwards, they may take on great practical importance. (Press release, October 13, 1999)

NOTE

I have referred to a very small subset of Robert Mundell's publications, focusing on some of the contributions that won him the Nobel Prize. A full listing, running from 1957 to the present, can be *found at* <**www.columbia.edu/~ram15**>.

RECOMMENDED READINGS

Bubic, Mate. (2000). "Robert Alexander Mundell–Nobel Prize Laureate 1999," *Zagreb Journal of Economics*, Vol. 4, No. 6, pp. 91-130.

Mundell, Robert. (1960, May). "The Monetary Dynamics of International Adjustment Under Fixed and Flexible Exchange Rates," *Quarterly Journal of Economics*, Vol. 84, No. 2, pp. 227-257.

——. (1961a, November). "A Theory of Optimum Currency Areas," *American Economic Review*, Vol. 51, No. 4, pp. 509- 17. Reprinted in Mundell (1968).

——. (1961b, November). "Flexible Exchange Rates and Employment Policy," *Canadian Journal of Economics and Political Science*, Vol. 27, No. 4, pp. 509-17. Reprinted in Mundell (1968).

——. (1961c). "The International Disequilibrium System," *Kyklos*, Vol. 14, No. 2, pp. 154-72. Reprinted in Mundell (1968).

——. (1962, March). "The Appropriate Use of Monetary and Fiscal Policy for Internal and External Stability," *IMF Staff Papers*, 70-9. Reprinted in Mundell (1968).

——. (1963, November). "Capital Mobility and Stabilization Policy Under Fixed and Flexible Exchange Rates," *Canadian Journal of Economics and Political Science*, Vol. 29, No. 4, pp. 475-85.

——. (1968). *International Economics*. New York: Macmillan.

——. (1971). *Monetary Theory: Interest, Inflation and Growth in the World Economy.* Pacific Palisades, CA: Goodyear.

——. (1973a). "Uncommon Arguments for Common Currencies," in *The Economics of Common Currencies*, (H. Johnson and A. Swoboda, (eds.)). London: George Allen & Unwin Ltd., pp.114-32.

——. (1973b). "A Plan for a European Currency," In *The Economics of Common Currencies,* (H. Johnson and A. Swoboda, (eds.)). London: George Allen & Unwin Ltd., pp.143-73.

Prasch, Robert E. (2001). "The Economic Contributions of Robert A. Mundell," *Review of Political Economy*, Vol. 13, No. 1, pp. 41-58.

Salvatore, Dominick. (2000, May). "Robert Mundell–Three Brilliant Ideas, One Nobel," *Journal of Policy Modeling*, Vol. 22, No. 3, pp. 305-309.

Index

Page references in boldface refer to the actual entries of the Nobel laureates.